ICONITES
AIR FRYER
OVEN COOKBOOK

500 Easy and Crispy Air Fryer Oven Recipes on a Budget to Watch Your Health and Save Your Money and Time

Anna J. Reyes

Copyright © 2020 By Jessie J. Leonard

All rights are reserved.

No portion of this book may be reproduced or duplicated using any form whether mechanical, electronic, or otherwise. No portion of this book may be transmitted, stored in a retrieval database, or otherwise made available in any manner whether public or private unless specific permission is granted by the publisher.

This book does not offer advice, but merely provides information. The author offers no advice whether medical, financial, legal, or otherwise, nor does the author encourage any person to pursue any specific course of action discussed in this book. This book is not a substitute for professional advice. The reader accepts complete and sole responsibility for the manner in which this book and its contents are used. The publisher and the author will not be held liable for any damages caused.

Table of Content

Appetizers and Snacks ········· 1

    Air Fried Lemon-Pepper Wings ········· 1
    Avocado Chips ········· 1
    Broiled Prosciutto-Wrapped Pears ········· 1
    Browned Ricotta with Capers and Lemon ········· 1
    Bruschetta with Tomato and Basil ········· 2
    Baked Sardines with Tomato Sauce ········· 2
    Carrot Chips ········· 2
    Air Fried Chicken Wings ········· 2
    Cheese and Ham Stuffed Baby Bella ········· 3
    Caramelized Peaches ········· 3
    Cheesy Baked Potatoes ········· 3
    Crispy Cinnamon Apple Chips ········· 3
    Cheesy Roasted Jalapeño Poppers ········· 4
    Cheesy Zucchini Tots ········· 4
    Corn and Black Bean Salsa ········· 4
    Easy Muffuletta Sliders with Olives ········· 4
    Crispy Artichoke Bites ········· 5
    Crispy Cod Fingers ········· 5
    Cheesy Crab Toasts ········· 5
    Mozzarella Pepperoni Pizza Bites ········· 5
    Crispy Green Tomatoes with Horseradish ········· 6
    Crunchy Chickpeas ········· 6
    Mushroom and Spinach Calzones ········· 6
    Crunchy Parmesan Snack Mix ········· 7
    Sausage and Mushroom Empanadas ········· 7
    Cuban Sandwiches ········· 7
    Green Chiles Nachos ········· 7
    Cinnamon Apple Wedges ········· 8
    Hush Puppies ········· 8
    Paprika Deviled Eggs ········· 8
    Garlic Edamame ········· 8
    Garlicky Roasted Mushrooms ········· 9

    Polenta Fries with Chili-Lime Mayo ········· 9
    Homemade BBQ Chicken Pizza ········· 9
    Tuna Melts with Scallions ········· 9
    Italian Rice Balls ········· 10
    Cheese-Stuffed Mushrooms with Pimientos ········· 10
    Parmesan Cauliflower ········· 10
    Kale Chips with Sesame ········· 11
    Deluxe Cheese Sandwiches ········· 11
    Old Bay Chicken Wings ········· 11
    Paprika Potato Chips ········· 11
    Roasted Grapes with Yogurt ········· 11
    Roasted Mixed Nuts ········· 12
    Shrimp Toasts with Sesame Seeds ········· 12
    Salty Baked Almonds ········· 12
    Sausage and Onion Rolls ········· 12
    Sausage Balls with Cheese ········· 13
    Sweet and Salty Snack Mix ········· 13
    Tangy Fried Pickle Spears ········· 13
    Spicy Tortilla Chips ········· 13
    Spiced Apple Chips ········· 14
    Spicy and Sweet Roasted Nuts ········· 14
    Sweet Cinnamon Peaches ········· 14
    Turkey Bacon-Wrapped Dates ········· 14

Breakfasts ········· 15

    Air Fryer Baked Eggs ········· 15
    Bacon and Egg Bread Cups ········· 15
    Baked Avocado with Eggs ········· 15
    Blueberry Cake ········· 15
    Banana and Oat Bread Pudding ········· 16
    Carrot Banana Muffin ········· 16
    Bourbon Vanilla French Toast ········· 16
    Breakfast Blueberry Cobbler ········· 16

Breakfast Cheese Sandwiches	17
Cheesy Breakfast Casserole	17
Breakfast Tater Tot Casserole	17
Canadian Bacon Muffin Sandwiches	17
Cheesy Artichoke-Mushroom Frittata	18
Cinnamon Sweet Potato Chips	18
Cheesy Hash Brown Casserole	18
Chicken Breakfast Sausages	18
Asparagus and Cheese Strata	19
Cashew Granola with Cranberries	19
Cheesy Hash Brown Cups	19
Chocolate Banana Bread	19
Coconut Brown Rice Porridge with Dates	20
Corned Beef Hash with Eggs	20
Cornmeal Pancake	20
Creamy Quesadillas with Blueberries	20
Crustless Broccoli Quiche	21
Easy Buttermilk Biscuits	21
Egg in a Hole	21
Egg and Avocado Burrito	21
Egg Florentine with Spinach	22
Easy French Toast Casserole	22
Eggs in Bell Pepper Rings	22
French Toast Sticks	22
Fried Cheese Grits	23
Maple Walnut Pancake	23
Ham and Cheese Toast	23
Mini Brown Rice Quiches	23
Mixed Berry Dutch Baby Pancake	24
Olives, Kale, and Pecorino Baked Eggs	24
Glazed Strawberry Toast	24
Mini Cinnamon Rolls	24
Peanut Butter-Pumpkin Muffins	25
Peppered Maple Bacon Knots	25
Rice, Shrimp, and Spinach Frittata	25
Spinach and Bacon English Muffins	25
Sausage and Cheese Quiche	26
Spinach, Leek and Cheese Frittata	26
Simple Monkey Bread	26
Spinach and Bacon Roll-ups	26
Sweet Banana Bread Pudding	27
Fried Potatoes with Peppers and Onions	27
Vanilla Granola	27
Veggie Frittata	27
Tomato-Corn Frittata with Avocado Dressing	28
Spicy Apple Turnovers	28
Turkey Breakfast Sausage Patties	28
Western Omelet	29
Whole-Wheat Blueberry Scones	29
Whole-Wheat Muffins with Blueberries	29

Casseroles, Frittata, and Quiche ···································· 30

Broccoli, Carrot, and Tomato Quiche	30
Burgundy Beef and Mushroom Casserole	30
Cauliflower and Pumpkin Casserole	30
Cheesy Green Bean Casserole	31
Chicken Divan	31
Chicken Ham Casserole	31
Chicken Sausage and Broccoli Casserole	31
Chorizo, Corn, and Potato Frittata	32
Easy Corn and Bell Pepper Casserole	32
Goat Cheese and Asparagus Frittata	32
Greek Frittata	32
Grits and Asparagus Casserole	33
Herbed Cheddar Frittata	33
Hillbilly Broccoli Cheese Casserole	33
Creamy Pork Gratin	33
Kale Frittata	34
Keto Cheese Quiche	34
Ritzy Chicken and Vegetable Casserole	34
Lush Seafood Casserole	35
Pastrami Casserole	35
Riced Cauliflower Casserole	35
Sumptuous Vegetable Frittata	35
Sausage and Colorful Peppers Casserole	36
Shrimp Spinach Frittata	36
Smoked Trout and Crème Fraiche Frittata	36
Mediterranean Quiche	36
Spinach and Chickpea Casserole	37
Sumptuous Beef and Bean Chili Casserole	37
Ritzy Pimento and Almond Turkey Casserole	37
Taco Beef and Chile Casserole	38

Desserts ··· 38

Almond Flour Blackberry Muffins	38
Blackberry and Peach Cobbler	38
Apple Fritters	39
Coconut Pineapple Sticks	39
Apple-Peach Crisp with Oatmeal	39
Apple-Peach Crumble with Honey	39

Baked Peaches and Blueberries ············ 40
Berry Crumble ············ 40
Black and White Brownies ············ 40
Apple Wedges with Apricots ············ 40
Blackberry Chocolate Cake ············ 41
Breaded Bananas with Chocolate Sauce ····· 41
Caramelized Fruit Kebabs ············ 41
Chocolate and Coconut Cake ············ 41
Caramelized Pear Tart ············ 42
Blueberry and Peach Galette ············ 42
Chocolate Cheesecake ············ 42
Chia Pudding ············ 43
Chocolate Cupcakes with Blueberries ········ 43
Chocolate Pecan Pie ············ 43
Easy Blackberry Cobbler ············ 43
Cinnamon S'mores ············ 44
Classic Pound Cake ············ 44
Coconut Chip Mixed Berry Crisp ············ 44
Coconut Cookies with Pecans ············ 44
Coffee Chocolate Cake ············ 45
Cinnamon Candied Apples ············ 45
Crispy Pineapple Rings ············ 45
Fudge Pie ············ 45
Fudgy Chocolate Brownies ············ 46
Gooey White Chocolate Cookies ············ 46
Honey Walnut Baklava ············ 46
Lemon Ricotta Cake ············ 47
Lemon-Raspberry Muffins ············ 47
Lemon-Butter Shortbread ············ 47
Mixed Berries with Pecan Streusel Topping ·· 47
Oaty Chocolate Chip Cookies ············ 48
Orange and Anise Cake ············ 48
Peach-Blueberry Tart ············ 48
Orange Coconut Cake ············ 49
Vanilla Walnuts Tart ············ 49
Peanut Butter-Chocolate Bread Pudding ····· 49
Ultimate Coconut Chocolate Cake ············ 49
Pumpkin Pudding and Vanilla Wafers ············ 50
Strawberry and Rhubarb Crumble ············ 50
Summer Berry Crisp ············ 50
Vanilla Chocolate Chip Cookies ············ 50

Fast and Easy Everyday Favorites ········ 51

Air Fried Bacon Pinwheels ············ 51
Air Fried Crispy Brussels Sprouts ············ 51
Apple Fritters with Sugary Glaze ············ 51
Buttery Knots with Parsley ············ 52
Bartlett Pears with Lemony Ricotta ············ 52
Butternut Squash with Hazelnuts ············ 52
Baked Cherry Tomatoes with Basil ············ 52
Cheddar Jalapeño Cornbread ············ 53
Citrus Avocado Wedge Fries ············ 53
Classic Worcestershire Poutine ············ 53
Corn on the Cob with Mayonnaise ············ 54
Yogurt Dip ············ 54
Golden Salmon and Carrot Croquettes ······· 54
Crispy Cheese Wafer ············ 54
Crispy Zucchini Sticks ············ 55
Crunchy Green Tomatoes Slices ············ 55
Crunchy and Beery Onion Rings ············ 55
Kale Chips with Soy Sauce ············ 55
Fast Cinnamon Toast ············ 56
Garlicky Spiralized Zucchini and Squash ····· 56
Hot Wings ············ 56
Spanakopita ············ 56
Lemony and Garlicky Asparagus ············ 57
Simple Cheesy Shrimps ············ 57
Lemony Shishito Peppers ············ 57
Parsnip Fries with Garlic-Potato Chips with Lemony Cream Dip ············ 57
Parmesan Cauliflower Fritters ············ 58
Southwest Corn and Bell Pepper Roast ······· 58
Salty Tortilla Chips ············ 58
Simple Air Fried Edamame ············ 58
Simple Air Fried Okra Chips ············ 58
Simple Baked Green Beans ············ 59
South Carolina Shrimp and Corn Bake ······· 59
Roasted Carrot Chips ············ 59
Spicy Air Fried Old Bay Shrimp ············ 59
Sweet Air Fried Pecans ············ 60
Sweet and Sour Peanuts ············ 60
Sweet Cinnamon Chickpeas ············ 60
Traditional French Fries ············ 60
Traditional Latkes ············ 60

Fish and Seafood ············ 61

Air Fried Cod Fillets ············ 61
Chili Prawns ············ 61
Air-Fried Scallops ············ 61
Lemon Tilapia ············ 61

Asian-Inspired Swordfish Steaks	62
Teriyaki Salmon	62
Bacon-Wrapped Scallops	62
Basil Salmon with Tomatoes	62
Baked Flounder Fillets	63
Easy Scallops	63
Baked Salmon Spring Rolls	63
Crispy Fish Sticks	63
Baked Tilapia with Garlic Aioli	64
Lemony Shrimp	64
Breaded Calamari with Lemon	64
Breaded Scallops	64
Browned Shrimp Patties	65
Fish Tacos	65
Butter-Wine Baked Salmon	65
Cajun and Lemon Pepper Cod	65
Breaded Fish Fillets	66
Caesar Shrimp Salad	66
Cajun Catfish Cakes with Cheese	66
Cheesy Tuna Patties	67
Chili Tuna Casserole	67
Roasted Nicoise Salad	67
Coconut Chili Fish Curry	68
Easy Salmon Patties	68
Crab Cakes with Bell Peppers	68
Crab Ratatouille with Eggplant and Tomatoes	68
Crispy Crab and Fish Cakes	69
Garlic-Butter Shrimp with Vegetables	69
Coconut-Crusted Prawns	69
Easy Shrimp and Vegetable Paella	70
Fired Shrimp with Mayonnaise Sauce	70
Garlic Butter Shrimp Scampi	70
Garlic Shrimp with Parsley	70
Garlicky Cod Fillets	71
Glazed Tuna and Fruit Kebabs	71
Seafood Spring Rolls	71
Goat Cheese Shrimp	72
Golden Beer-Battered Cod	72
Roasted Salmon with Asparagus	72
Herbed Scallops with Vegetables	72
Herbed Salmon with Roasted Asparagus	73
Mustard-Crusted Sole Fillets	73
Lemon-Honey Snapper with Fruit	73
Panko Catfish Nuggets	73
Panko Crab Sticks with Mayo Sauce	74
Homemade Fish Sticks	74
Paprika Shrimp	74
Parmesan-Crusted Hake with Garlic Sauce	74
Parmesan Fish Fillets	75
Pecan-Crusted Catfish Fillets	75
Parmesan-Crusted Halibut Fillets	75
Roasted Halibut Steaks with Parsley	75
Roasted Scallops with Snow Peas	76
Piri-Piri King Prawns	76
Parmesan-Crusted Salmon Patties	76
Spiced Red Snapper	76
Shrimp and Cherry Tomato Kebabs	77
Snapper with Tomatoes and Olives	77
Sole and Cauliflower Fritters	77
Tuna Lettuce Wraps	78
Sticky Hoisin Tuna	78
Tex-Mex Salmon Bowl	78
Tilapia Meunière with Vegetables	78
Spicy Orange Shrimp	79

Meats 79

Apple-Glazed Pork	79
Air Fried Beef Satay with Peanut Dipping Sauce	79
Air Fried Crispy Venison	80
Air Fried Golden Wasabi Spam	80
Air Fried London Broil	80
Apple and Pork Bake	80
Asparagus and Prosciutto Tart	81
Bacon-Wrapped Sausage with Tomato Relish	81
Beef and Spinach Meatloaves	81
Beef and Tomato Sauce Meatloaf	82
Beef Meatballs with Zesty Marinara Sauce	82
Air Fried Beef and Mushroom Stroganoff	82
Bacon-Wrapped Hot Dogs with Mayo-Ketchup Sauce	82
Bo Luc Lac	83
Calf's Liver Golden Strips	83
Caraway Crusted Beef Steaks	83
Carne Asada	84
Easy Lamb Chops with Asparagus	84
Crispy Pork Tenderloin	84
Dijon Pork Tenderloin	84

Cinnamon-Beef Kofta	85
Chuck and Sausage Subs	85
Citrus Carnitas	85
Char Siu	86
Classic Walliser Schnitzel	86
Gold Cutlets with Aloha Salsa	86
Golden Lamb Chops	87
Hearty Mushroom and Sausage Calzones	87
Lahmacun (Turkish Pizza)	87
Homemade Teriyaki Pork Ribs	88
Lamb Kofta	88
Italian Sausages and Red Grapes	88
Kielbasa Sausage with Pineapple and Bell Peppers	88
Italian Steak and Spinach Rolls	89
Lamb Loin Chops with Horseradish Cream Sauce	89
Lamb Rack with Pistachio	89
Lechon Kawali	90
Lemony Pork Loin Chop Schnitzel	90
Lush Salisbury Steak with Mushroom Gravy	90
Macadamia Nuts Crusted Pork Rack	91
Meat and Rice Stuffed Bell Peppers	91
Mushroom in Bacon-Wrapped Filets Mignons	91
New York Strip with Honey-Mustard Butter	92
Panko Crusted Calf's Liver Strips	92
Pork, Bell Pepper, and Pineapple Skewers	92
Ravioli with Beef-Marinara Sauce	92
Easy Pork Chop Roast	93
Pork and Tricolor Vegetables Kebabs	93
Pork Butt with Garlicky Coriander-Parsley Sauce	93
Pork Fried Rice with Scrambled Egg	94
Pork Leg Roast with Candy Onions	94
Sausage Ratatouille	94
Thai Curry Beef Meatballs	95
Pork Schnitzels with Sour Cream and Dill Sauce	95
Pork with Butternut Squash and Apples	95
Pork Sausage with Cauliflower Mash	96
Reuben Beef Rolls with Thousand Island Sauce	96
Spicy Pork Chops with Carrots and Mushrooms	96
Sriracha Beef and Broccoli	97
Roasted Lamb Chops with Potatoes	97
Salsa Beef Meatballs	97
Simple Pork Meatballs with Red Chili	98
Sirloin Steak and Pepper Fajitas	98
Smoky Paprika Pork and Vegetable Kabobs	98
Simple Ground Beef with Zucchini	99
Spice-Coated Steaks with Cucumber and Snap Pea Salad	99
Spicy Pork Lettuce Wraps	99
Stuffed Beef Tenderloin with Feta Cheese	100
Worcestershire Ribeye Steaks	100
Sumptuous Beef and Pork Sausage Meatloaf	100
Tonkatsu	100
Teriyaki Rump Steak with Broccoli and Capsicum	101
Tuscan Air Fried Veal Loin	101

Poultry ········ 101

Apricot-Glazed Chicken Drumsticks	101
Air Fried Chicken Potatoes with Sun-Dried Tomato	102
Air Fried Chicken Wings with Buffalo Sauce	102
Bacon-Wrapped Chicken Breasts Rolls	102
Bacon-Wrapped and Cheese-Stuffed Chicken	103
Bacon-Wrapped Turkey with Carrots	103
Barbecue Chicken and Coleslaw Tostadas	103
Bell Pepper Stuffed Chicken Roll-Ups	104
Braised Chicken with Hot Peppers	104
Bruschetta Chicken	104
Cheese-Encrusted Chicken Tenderloins with Peanuts	105
Cheesy Marinara Chicken Breasts	105
Balsamic Chicken Breast Roast	105
Cheesy Pepperoni and Chicken Pizza	106
Cheesy Turkey Burgers	106
Chicken and Ham Meatballs with Dijon Sauce	106
Chicken and Sweet Potato Curry	107
Duck Breasts with Marmalade Balsamic Glaze	107
Chicken Ciabatta Sandwiches	107
Chicken Rochambeau with Mushroom Sauce	108

Chicken Schnitzel ··· 108
Deep Fried Duck Leg Quarters ··············· 108
Chicken Shawarma ·· 109
Chicken Thighs in Waffles ························· 109
Easy Cajun Chicken Drumsticks ············· 110
Chicken Skewers with Corn Salad············ 110
Chicken Thighs with Radish Slaw ·········· 110
Crispy Chicken Skin ···································· 111
Chicken with Asparagus, Beans, and Arugula
··· 111
Chicken with Potatoes and Corn ············· 111
China Spicy Turkey Thighs ······················· 112
Creole Hens ·· 112
Drumsticks with Barbecue-Honey Sauce ···· 112
Easy Chicken Fingers·································· 112
Golden Chicken Cutlets ····························· 113
Glazed Duck with Cherry Sauce ············· 113
Gnocchi with Chicken and Spinach ········ 113
Golden Chicken Fries ································· 114
Hawaiian Chicken Bites ····························· 114
Herbed Turkey Breast with Simple Dijon Sauce
··· 114
Honey Glazed Chicken Breasts ··············· 115
Italian Chicken Breasts with Tomatoes ········ 115
Korean Flavor Glazed Chicken Wings········ 115
Lettuce Chicken Tacos with Peanut Sauce · 116
Lettuce-Wrapped Turkey and Mushroom Meatballs··· 116
Wings ··· 116
Gold Livers··· 117
Lime Chicken with Cilantro ······················ 117
Nice Goulash ··· 117
Peach and Cherry Chicken ························ 117
Pineapple Chicken ······································· 118
Pomegranate Chicken with Couscous Salad 118
Ritzy Chicken Roast···································· 118
Rosemary Turkey Breast····························· 119
Rosemary Turkey Scotch Eggs·················· 119
Spicy Chicken Skewers with Satay Sauce ·· 119
Simple Air Fried Chicken Simple Chicken Nuggets ··· 120
Thai Drumsticks with Green Beans········· 120
Simple Herbed Hens ··································· 120
Simple Whole Chicken Bake ···················· 120
Spicy Tandoori Chicken Drumsticks ······ 121

Strawberry-Glazed Turkey ························ 121
Turkey and Carrot Meatloaves················· 121
Sweet-and-Sour Chicken Nuggets ·········· 121
Spanish Chicken and Pepper Baguette ······ 122
Teriyaki Chicken Thighs with Lemony Snow Peas··· 122
Yakitori ·· 122
Super Lemon Chicken ································ 123
Turkey and Bean Stuffed Peppers ··········· 123
Turkey and Cauliflower Meatloaf············ 123
Thai Game Hens with Cucumber and Chile Salad ··· 124

Rotisserie Recipes·································· 124

Whole Rotisserie Chicken ························· 124
Air Fried Beef Roast···································· 125
Marinated Medium Rare Rotisserie Beef ···· 125
Easy Rotisserie Chicken ····························· 125
Sriracha Honey Pork Tenderloin ············· 125
Bourbon Rotisserie Pork Shoulder ········· 126
Greek Rotisserie Lamb Leg ······················· 126
Honey Glazed Rotisserie Ham ················· 126
Apple and Carrot Stuffed Rotisserie Turkey · 127
Red Wine Rotisserie Lamb Leg ··············· 127
Rotisserie Chicken with Lemon··············· 127

Staples ·· 128

Air Fryer Oven Grits ··································· 128
Roasted Mushrooms ··································· 128
Asian Dipping Sauce ··································· 128
Classic Marinara Sauce ······························ 128
Caesar Salad Dressing ································ 129
Enchilada Sauce ··· 129
Shawarma Spice Mix··································· 129
Simple Teriyaki Sauce ································ 129
Southwest Seasoning ·································· 129
Air Fryer Oven Baked Rice ······················· 129

Vegan and Vegetarian ···························· 130

Asian-Inspired Broccoli ····························· 130
Caramelized Eggplant with Yogurt Sauce ···· 130
Air Fried Winter Vegetables ····················· 130
Bean, Salsa, and Cheese Tacos ················ 130
Balsamic Asparagus····································· 131
Crispy Eggplant Slices with Parsley ······· 131

Cinnamon Celery Roots	131
Cashew Cauliflower with Yogurt Sauce	131
Baked Turnip and Zucchini	132
Cheesy Asparagus and Potato Platter	132
Cheesy Broccoli Tots	132
Crispy Fried Okra with Chili	132
Crispy Tofu Sticks	133
Cheesy Rice and Olives Stuffed Peppers	133
Cream Cheese Stuffed Bell Peppers	133
Fried Root Vegetable Medley with Thyme	133
Cayenne Tahini Kale	134
Cheese-Walnut Stuffed Mushrooms	134
Hearty Roasted Veggie Salad	134
Lemony Wax Beans	134
Easy Cheesy Vegetable Quesadilla	135
Rosemary Beets with Balsamic Glaze	135
Cheesy Cabbage Wedges	135
Spicy Thai-Style Vegetables	135
Crispy Veggies with Halloumi	136
Sweet and Spicy Broccoli	136
Herbed Broccoli with Cheese	136
Sesame-Thyme Whole Maitake Mushrooms	136
Garlicky Sesame Carrots	137
Honey-Glazed Roasted Veggies	137
Roasted Bell Peppers with Garlic	137
Italian Baked Tofu	138
Vegetable and Cheese Stuffed Tomatoes	138
Honey-Glazed Baby Carrots	138
Roasted Asparagus with Eggs and Tomatoes	138
Garlic Stuffed Mushrooms	139
Ratatouille	139
Stuffed Squash with Tomatoes and Poblano	139
Lemony Brussels Sprouts and Tomatoes	140
Tofu, Carrot and Cauliflower Rice	140
Maple and Pecan Granola	140
Mediterranean Baked Eggs with Spinach	140
Paprika Cauliflower	141
Stuffed Portobellos with Peppers and Cheese	141
Stuffed Peppers with Beans and Rice	141
Panko Green Beans	142
Parmesan Zucchini Chips	142
Roasted Vegetables with Basil	142
Roasted Vegetable Mélange with Herbs	142
Roasted Vegetables with Rice	143
Stuffed Portobello Mushrooms with Vegetables	143
Rosemary Roasted Squash with Cheese	143
Roasted Brussels Sprouts with Parmesan	143
Spicy Kung Pao Tofu	144
Sweet-and-Sour Brussels Sprouts	144
Simple Ratatouille	144
Teriyaki Cauliflower	144
Tortellini with Veggies and Parmesan	145
Vegetarian Meatballs	145

Vegetable Sides · · · 146

Blistered Shishito Peppers with Lime Juice	146
Scalloped Potatoes	146
Baked Potatoes with Yogurt and Chives	146
Butternut Squash Croquettes	146
Balsamic-Glazed Carrots	147
Chili Corn on the Cob	147
Buttered Broccoli with Parmesan	147
Sweet Brussels Sprouts	147
Creamy Corn Casserole	148
Crispy Zucchini Sticks	148
Charred Green Beans with Sesame Seeds	148
Crusted Brussels Sprouts with Sage	148
Cheesy Broccoli Gratin	149
Parmesan Asparagus Fries	149
Rosemary Roasted Potatoes	149
Spicy Broccoli with Hot Sauce	149
Spicy Cabbage	150
Cinnamon-Spiced Acorn Squash	150
Garlic Roasted Asparagus	150
Simple Zucchini Crisps	150
Tamarind Sweet Potatoes	150

Wraps and Sandwiches · · · 151

Air Fried Cream Cheese Wontons	151
Air Fried Crispy Spring Rolls	151
Beef and Bell Pepper Fajitas	151
Air Fried Philly Cheesesteaks	152
Avocado and Slaw Tacos	152
Avocado and Tomato Egg Rolls	152
Baja Fish Tacos	153
Bulgogi Burgers	153
Turkey, Leek, and Pepper Hamburger	153

Cheesy Bacon and Egg Wraps············· 154
Cheesy Spring Chicken Wraps············ 154
Cabbage and Mushroom Spring Rolls········ 154
Cabbage and Pork Gyoza ··············· 155
Cheesy Potato Taquitos ················ 155
Mexican Flavor Chicken Burgers ············ 155
Cheesy Veggie Wraps ·················· 156
Chicken and Yogurt Taquitos ············· 156
Prawn and Cabbage Egg Rolls Wraps ······· 156
Crispy Chicken Egg Rolls ················ 157
Crispy Crab and Cream Cheese Wontons ·· 157
Crispy Tilapia Tacos ··················· 157
Eggplant Hoagies ····················· 158
Golden Cod Tacos with Salsa ············· 158
Empanadas ························· 158
Korean Flavor Beef and Onion Tacos········ 159
Lamb and Feta Hamburgers ············· 159
Montreal Steak and Seeds Burgers ········· 159
Pea and Potato Samosas with Chutney······ 160
Salsa Verde Golden Chicken Shrimp and Zucchini Curry Potstickers ················ 160
Pork Momos ························ 161
Spinach and Ricotta Pockets ············· 161
Sweet Potato and Black Bean Burritos ······ 161
Turkey Sliders with Chive Mayo ··········· 162
Thai Pork Sliders ····················· 162

Holiday Specials··························· 162
Chocolate Buttermilk Cake ·············· 162
Air Fried Blistered Tomatoes ············· 163
Arancini ···························· 163
Kale Salad Sushi Rolls with Sriracha Mayonnaise
································· 163
Banana Cake························ 164
Chinese Pork and Mushroom Egg Rolls ····· 164
Chocolate and Coconut Macaroons ·········· 165
Cinnamon Rolls with Cream Glaze ·········· 165
Classic Churros······················ 165
Custard Donut Holes with Chocolate Glaze ·· 166
Fried Dill Pickles with Buttermilk Dressing··· 166
Garlicky Olive Stromboli ················ 167
Golden Nuggets ····················· 167
Jewish Blintzes ······················ 167
Milky Pecan Tart······················ 168
Pão de Queijo······················· 168
Shrimp with Sriracha and Worcestershire Sauce ····························· 168
Simple Butter Cake ··················· 169
Supplì al Telefono (Risotto Croquettes) ······ 169
Teriyaki Shrimp Skewers ················ 170
Pigs in a Blanket ···················· 170

Appetizers and Snacks

Air Fried Lemon-Pepper Wings

Prep time: 5 minutes | Cook time: 24 minutes | Serves 10

2 pounds (907 g) chicken wings
4½ teaspoons salt-free lemon pepper seasoning
1½ teaspoons baking powder
1½ teaspoons kosher salt

1. In a large bowl, toss together all the ingredients until well coated. Place the wings on a sheet pan, making sure they don't crowd each other too much.
2. Slide the pan into the air fryer oven. Cook at 375°F (190°C) for 24 minutes.
3. After 12 minutes, remove from the air fryer oven. Use a tong to turn the wings over. Return the pan to the air fryer oven to continue cooking.
4. When cooking is complete, the wings should be dark golden brown and charred. Remove the pan from the air fryer oven and let rest for 5 minutes before serving.

Avocado Chips

Prep time: 15 minutes | Cook time: 10 minutes | Serves 4

1 egg
1 tablespoon lime juice
⅛ teaspoon hot sauce
2 tablespoons flour
¾ cup panko bread crumbs
¼ cup cornmeal
¼ teaspoon salt
1 large avocado, pitted, peeled, and cut into ½-inch slices
Cooking spray

1. Whisk together the egg, lime juice, and hot sauce in a small bowl.
2. On a sheet of wax paper, place the flour. In a separate sheet of wax paper, combine the bread crumbs, cornmeal, and salt.
3. Dredge the avocado slices one at a time in the flour, then in the egg mixture, finally roll them in the bread crumb mixture to coat well.
4. Place the breaded avocado slices in an air fryer basket and mist them with cooking spray.
5. Slide the basket into the air fryer oven. Cook at 390°F (199°C) for 10 minutes.
6. When cooking is complete, the slices should be nicely browned and crispy. Transfer the avocado slices to a plate and serve.

Broiled Prosciutto-Wrapped Pears

Prep time: 12 minutes | Cook time: 6 minutes | Serves 8

2 large, ripe Anjou pears
4 thin slices Parma prosciutto
2 teaspoons aged balsamic vinegar

1. Peel the pears. Slice into 8 wedges and cut out the core from each wedge.
2. Cut the prosciutto into 8 long strips. Wrap each pear wedge with a strip of prosciutto. Place the wrapped pears in a sheet pan.
3. Slide the pan into the air fryer oven. Cook for 6 minutes.
4. After 2 or 3 minutes, check the pears. The pears should be turned over if the prosciutto is beginning to crisp up and brown. Return to the air fryer oven and continue cooking.
5. When cooking is complete, remove from the air fryer oven. Drizzle the pears with the balsamic vinegar and serve warm.

Browned Ricotta with Capers and Lemon

Prep time: 10 minutes | Cook time: 8 minutes | Serves 4 to 6

1½ cups whole milk ricotta cheese
2 tablespoons extra-virgin olive oil
2 tablespoons capers, rinsed
Zest of 1 lemon, plus more for garnish
1 teaspoon finely chopped fresh rosemary
Pinch crushed red pepper flakes
Salt and freshly ground black pepper, to taste
1 tablespoon grated Parmesan cheese

1. In a mixing bowl, stir together the ricotta cheese, olive oil, capers, lemon zest, rosemary, red pepper flakes, salt, and pepper until well combined.
2. Spread the mixture evenly in a baking dish.
3. Slide the baking dish into the air fryer oven. Cook at 380°F (193°C) for 8 minutes.
4. When cooking is complete, the top should be nicely browned. Remove from the air fryer oven and top with a sprinkle of grated Parmesan cheese. Garnish with the lemon zest and serve warm.

Bruschetta with Tomato and Basil

Prep time: 5 minutes | Cook time: 3 minutes | Serves 6

4 tomatoes, diced
⅓ cup shredded fresh basil
¼ cup shredded Parmesan cheese
1 tablespoon balsamic vinegar
1 tablespoon minced garlic
1 teaspoon olive oil
1 teaspoon salt
1 teaspoon freshly ground black pepper
1 loaf French bread, cut into 1-inch-thick slices
Cooking spray

1. Mix the tomatoes and basil in a medium bowl. Add the cheese, vinegar, garlic, olive oil, salt, and pepper and stir until well incorporated. Set aside.
2. Spritz an air fryer basket with cooking spray and lay the bread slices in the basket. Spray the slices with cooking spray.
3. Slide the basket into the air fryer oven. Cook at 250°F (121°C) for 3 minutes.
4. When cooking is complete, remove from the air fryer oven to a plate. Top each slice with a generous spoonful of the tomato mixture and serve.

Baked Sardines with Tomato Sauce

Prep time: 10 minutes | Cook time: 20 minutes | Serves 4

2 pounds (907 g) fresh sardines
3 tablespoons olive oil, divided
4 Roma tomatoes, peeled and chopped
1 small onion, sliced thinly
Zest of 1 orange
Sea salt and freshly ground pepper, to taste
2 tablespoons whole-wheat bread crumbs
½ cup white wine

1. Brush a sheet pan with a little olive oil. Set aside.
2. Rinse the sardines under running water. Slit the belly, remove the spine and butterfly the fish. Set aside.
3. Heat the remaining olive oil in a large skillet. Add the tomatoes, onion, orange zest, salt and pepper to the skillet and simmer for 20 minutes, or until the mixture thickens and softens.
4. Place half the sauce in the bottom of the sheet pan. Arrange the sardines on top and spread the remaining half the sauce over the fish. Sprinkle with the bread crumbs and drizzle with the white wine.
5. Slide the pan into the air fryer oven. Cook at 425°F (220°C) for 20 minutes.
6. When cooking is complete, remove from the air fryer oven. Serve immediately.

Carrot Chips

Prep time: 15 minutes | Cook time: 10 minutes | Serves 4

4 to 5 medium carrots, trimmed and thinly sliced
1 tablespoon olive oil, plus more for greasing
1 teaspoon seasoned salt

1. Toss the carrot slices with 1 tablespoon of olive oil and salt in a medium bowl until thoroughly coated.
2. Grease an air fryer basket with the olive oil. Place the carrot slices in the greased basket.
3. Slide the basket into the air fryer oven. Cook at 390°F (199°C) for 10 minutes.
4. Stir the carrot slices halfway through the cooking time.
5. When cooking is complete, the chips should be crisp-tender. Remove the basket from the air fryer oven and allow to cool for 5 minutes before serving.

Air Fried Chicken Wings

Prep time: 1 hour 20 minutes | Cook time: 18 minutes | Serves 4

2 pounds (907 g) chicken wings
Cooking spray
Marinade:
1 cup buttermilk
½ teaspoon salt
½ teaspoon black pepper
Coating:
1 cup flour
1 cup panko bread crumbs
2 tablespoons poultry seasoning
2 teaspoons salt

1. Whisk together all the ingredients for the marinade in a large bowl.
2. Add the chicken wings to the marinade and toss well. Transfer to the refrigerator to marinate for at least an hour.
3. Spritz an air fryer basket with cooking spray. Set aside.
4. Thoroughly combine all the ingredients for the coating in a shallow bowl.
5. Remove the chicken wings from the marinade and shake off any excess. Roll them in the coating mixture.
6. Place the chicken wings in the air fryer basket. Mist the wings with cooking spray.
7. Slide the basket into the air fryer oven. Cook at 360°F (182°C) for 18 minutes.
8. Flip the wings halfway through the cooking time.
9. When cooking is complete, the wings should be crisp and golden brown on the outside. Remove from the air fryer oven to a plate and serve hot.

Cheese and Ham Stuffed Baby Bella

Prep time: 15 minutes | Cook time: 12 minutes | Serves 8

4 ounces (113 g) Mozzarella cheese, cut into pieces
½ cup diced ham
2 green onions, chopped
2 tablespoons bread crumbs
½ teaspoon garlic powder
¼ teaspoon ground oregano
¼ teaspoon ground black pepper
1 to 2 teaspoons olive oil
16 fresh Baby Bella mushrooms, stemmed removed

1. Process the cheese, ham, green onions, bread crumbs, garlic powder, oregano, and pepper in a food processor until finely chopped.
2. With the food processor running, slowly drizzle in 1 to 2 teaspoons olive oil until a thick paste has formed. Transfer the mixture to a bowl.
3. Evenly divide the mixture into the mushroom caps and lightly press down the mixture.
4. Lay the mushrooms in an air fryer basket.
5. Slide the basket into the air fryer oven. Cook at 390°F (199°C) for 12 minutes.
6. When cooking is complete, the mushrooms should be lightly browned and tender. Remove from the air fryer oven to a plate. Let the mushrooms cool for 5 minutes and serve warm.

Caramelized Peaches

Prep time: 10 minutes | Cook time: 10 to 13 minutes | Serves 4

2 tablespoons sugar
¼ teaspoon ground cinnamon
4 peaches, cut into wedges
Cooking spray

1. Toss the peaches with the sugar and cinnamon in a medium bowl until evenly coated.
2. Lightly spray an air fryer basket with cooking spray. Place the peaches in the air fryer basket. Lightly mist the peaches with cooking spray.
3. Slide the basket into the air fryer oven. Cook at 350°F (180°C) for 10 minutes.
4. After 5 minutes, remove from the air fryer oven and flip the peaches. Return to the air fryer oven and continue cooking for 5 minutes.
5. When cooking is complete, the peaches should be caramelized. If necessary, continue cooking for 3 minutes. Remove from the air fryer oven. Let the peaches cool for 5 minutes and serve warm.

Cheesy Baked Potatoes

Prep time: 5 minutes | Cook time: 20 minutes | Serves 6

12 small red potatoes
1 teaspoon kosher salt, divided
1 tablespoon extra-virgin olive oil
¼ cup grated sharp Cheddar cheese
¼ cup sour cream
2 tablespoons chopped chives
2 tablespoons grated Parmesan cheese

1. Add the potatoes to a large bowl. Sprinkle with the ½ teaspoon of the salt and drizzle with the olive oil. Toss to coat. Place the potatoes in a sheet pan.
2. Slide the pan into the air fryer oven. Cook at 375°F (190°C) for 15 minutes.
3. After 10 minutes, rotate the pan and continue cooking.
4. When cooking is complete, remove the pan and let the potatoes rest for 5 minutes. Halve the potatoes lengthwise. Using a spoon, scoop the flesh into a bowl, leaving a thin shell of skin. Arrange the potato halves on the sheet pan.
5. Mash the potato flesh until smooth. Stir in the remaining ½ teaspoon of the salt, Cheddar cheese, sour cream and chives. Transfer the filling into a pastry bag with one corner snipped off. Pipe the filling into the potato shells, mounding up slightly. Sprinkle with the Parmesan cheese.
6. Slide the pan into the air fryer oven. Cook at 375°F (190°C) for 5 minutes.
7. When cooking is complete, the tops should be browned slightly. Remove the pan from the air fryer oven and let the potatoes cool slightly before serving.

Crispy Cinnamon Apple Chips

Prep time: 10 minutes | Cook time: 10 minutes | Serves 4

2 apples, cored and cut into thin slices
2 heaped teaspoons ground cinnamon
Cooking spray

1. Spritz an air fryer basket with cooking spray.
2. In a medium bowl, sprinkle the apple slices with the cinnamon. Toss until evenly coated. Spread the coated apple slices in the basket.
3. Slide the basket into the air fryer oven. Cook at 350°F (180°C) for 10 minutes.
4. After 5 minutes, remove from the air fryer oven. Stir the apple slices and return the basket back to the air fryer oven to continue cooking.
5. When cooking is complete, the slices should be until crispy Remove the basket from the air fryer oven and let rest for 5 minutes before serving.

Cheesy Roasted Jalapeño Poppers

Prep time: 10 minutes | Cook time: 15 minutes | Serves 8

6 ounces (170 g) cream cheese, at room temperature
4 ounces (113 g) shredded Cheddar cheese
1 teaspoon chili powder
12 large jalapeño peppers, deseeded and sliced in half lengthwise
2 slices cooked bacon, chopped
¼ cup panko bread crumbs
1 tablespoon butter, melted

1. In a medium bowl, whisk together the cream cheese, Cheddar cheese and chili powder. Spoon the cheese mixture into the jalapeño halves and arrange them on a sheet pan.
2. In a small bowl, stir together the bacon, bread crumbs and butter. Sprinkle the mixture over the jalapeño halves.
3. Slide the pan into the air fryer oven. Cook at 375°F (190°C) for 15 minutes.
4. After 7 or 8 minutes, rotate the pan and continue cooking until the peppers are softened, the filling is bubbling and the bread crumbs are browned.
5. When cooking is complete, remove from the air fryer oven. Let the poppers cool for 5 minutes before serving.

Cheesy Zucchini Tots

Prep time: 15 minutes | Cook time: 6 minutes | Serves 8

2 medium zucchini (about 12 ounces / 340 g), shredded
1 large egg, whisked
½ cup grated pecorino romano cheese
½ cup panko bread crumbs
¼ teaspoon black pepper
1 clove garlic, minced
Cooking spray

1. Using your hands, squeeze out as much liquid from the zucchini as possible. In a large bowl, mix the zucchini with the remaining ingredients except the oil until well incorporated.
2. Make the zucchini tots: Use a spoon or cookie scoop to place tablespoonfuls of the zucchini mixture onto a lightly floured cutting board and form into 1-inch logs.
3. Spritz an air fryer basket with cooking spray. Place the zucchini tots in the basket.
4. Slide the basket into the air fryer oven. Cook at 375°F (190°C) for 6 minutes.
5. When cooking is complete, the tots should be golden brown. Remove from the air fryer oven to a serving plate and serve warm.

Corn and Black Bean Salsa

Prep time: 10 minutes | Cook time: 10 minutes | Serves 4

½ (15-ounce / 425-g) can corn, drained and rinsed
½ (15-ounce / 425-g) can black beans, drained and rinsed
¼ cup chunky salsa
2 ounces (57 g) reduced-fat cream cheese, softened
¼ cup shredded reduced-fat Cheddar cheese
½ teaspoon paprika
½ teaspoon ground cumin
Salt and freshly ground black pepper, to taste

1. Combine the corn, black beans, salsa, cream cheese, Cheddar cheese, paprika, and cumin in a medium bowl. Sprinkle with salt and pepper and stir until well blended.
2. Pour the mixture into a baking dish.
3. Slide the baking dish into the air fryer oven. Cook at 325°F (163°C) for 10 minutes.
4. When cooking is complete, the mixture should be heated through. Rest for 5 minutes and serve warm.

Easy Muffuletta Sliders with Olives

Prep time: 10 minutes | Cook time: 6 minutes | Makes 8 sliders

¼ pound (113 g) thinly sliced deli ham
¼ pound (113 g) thinly sliced pastrami
4 ounces (113 g) low-fat Mozzarella cheese, grated
8 slider buns, split in half
Cooking spray
1 tablespoon sesame seeds
Olive Mix:
½ cup sliced green olives with pimentos
¼ cup sliced black olives
¼ cup chopped kalamata olives
1 teaspoon red wine vinegar
¼ teaspoon basil
⅛ teaspoon garlic powder

1. Combine all the ingredients for the olive mix in a small bowl and stir well.
2. Stir together the ham, pastrami, and cheese in a medium bowl and divide the mixture into 8 equal portions.
3. Assemble the sliders: Top each bottom bun with 1 portion of meat and cheese, 2 tablespoons of olive mix, finished by the remaining buns. Lightly spritz the tops with cooking spray. Scatter the sesame seeds on top.
4. Arrange the sliders in an air fryer basket.
5. Slide the basket into the air fryer oven. Cook at 360°F (182°C) for 6 minutes.
6. When cooking is complete, the cheese should be melted. Remove the basket from the air fryer oven and serve.

Crispy Artichoke Bites

Prep time: 10 minutes | Cook time: 8 minutes | Serves 4

14 whole artichoke hearts packed in water
½ cup all-purpose flour
1 egg
⅓ cup panko bread crumbs
1 teaspoon Italian seasoning
Cooking spray

1. Drain the artichoke hearts and dry thoroughly with paper towels.
2. Place the flour on a plate. Beat the egg in a shallow bowl until frothy. Thoroughly combine the bread crumbs and Italian seasoning in a separate shallow bowl.
3. Dredge the artichoke hearts in the flour, then in the beaten egg, and finally roll in the bread crumb mixture until evenly coated.
4. Place the artichoke hearts in an air fryer basket and mist them with cooking spray.
5. Slide the basket into the air fryer oven. Cook at 375°F (190°C) for 8 minutes.
6. Flip the artichoke hearts halfway through the cooking time.
7. When cooking is complete, the artichoke hearts should be browned and the edges should be crispy. Remove from the air fryer oven. Let the artichoke hearts sit for 5 minutes before serving.

Crispy Cod Fingers

Prep time: 5 minutes | Cook time: 12 minutes | Serves 4

2 eggs
2 tablespoons milk
2 cups flour
1 cup cornmeal
1 teaspoon seafood seasoning
Salt and black pepper, to taste
1 cup bread crumbs
1 pound (454 g) cod fillets, cut into 1-inch strips

1. Beat the eggs with the milk in a shallow bowl. In another shallow bowl, combine the flour, cornmeal, seafood seasoning, salt, and pepper. On a plate, place the bread crumbs.
2. Dredge the cod strips, one at a time, in the flour mixture, then in the egg mixture, finally roll in the bread crumb to coat evenly.
3. Transfer the cod strips to an air fryer basket.
4. Slide the basket into the air fryer oven. Cook at 400°F (205°C) for 12 minutes.
5. When cooking is complete, the cod strips should be crispy. Remove from the air fryer oven to a paper towel-lined plate and serve warm.

Cheesy Crab Toasts

Prep time: 10 minutes | Cook time: 5 minutes | Makes 15 to 18 toasts

1 (6-ounce / 170-g) can flaked crabmeat, well drained
3 tablespoons light mayonnaise
¼ cup shredded Parmesan cheese
¼ cup shredded Cheddar cheese
1 teaspoon Worcestershire sauce
½ teaspoon lemon juice
1 loaf artisan bread, French bread, or baguette, cut into ⅜-inch-thick slices

1. In a large bowl, stir together all the ingredients except the bread slices.
2. On a clean work surface, lay the bread slices. Spread ½ tablespoon of crab mixture onto each slice of bread.
3. Arrange the bread slices in an air fryer basket.
4. Slide the basket into the air fryer oven. Cook at 360°F (182°C) for 5 minutes.
5. When cooking is complete, the tops should be lightly browned. Remove from the air fryer oven. Serve warm.

Mozzarella Pepperoni Pizza Bites

Prep time: 5 minutes | Cook time: 12 minutes | Serves 8

1 cup finely shredded Mozzarella cheese
½ cup chopped pepperoni
¼ cup Marinara sauce
1 (8-ounce / 227-g) can crescent roll dough
All-purpose flour, for dusting

1. In a small bowl, stir together the cheese, pepperoni and Marinara sauce.
2. Lay the dough on a lightly floured work surface. Separate it into 4 rectangles. Firmly pinch the perforations together and pat the dough pieces flat.
3. Divide the cheese mixture evenly between the rectangles and spread it out over the dough, leaving a ¼-inch border. Roll a rectangle up tightly, starting with the short end. Pinch the edge down to seal the roll. Repeat with the remaining rolls.
4. Slice the rolls into 4 or 5 even slices. Place the slices on a sheet pan, leaving a few inches between each slice.
5. Slide the pan into the air fryer oven. Cook at 350°F (180°C) for 12 minutes.
6. After 6 minutes, rotate the pan and continue cooking.
7. When cooking is complete, the rolls will be golden brown with crisp edges. Remove from the air fryer oven. Serve hot.

Crispy Green Tomatoes with Horseradish

Prep time: 18 minutes | Cook time: 13 minutes | Serves 4

2 eggs
¼ cup buttermilk
½ cup bread crumbs
½ cup cornmeal
¼ teaspoon salt
1½ pounds (680 g) firm green tomatoes, cut into ¼-inch slices
Cooking spray
Horseradish Sauce:
¼ cup sour cream
¼ cup mayonnaise
2 teaspoons prepared horseradish
½ teaspoon lemon juice
½ teaspoon Worcestershire sauce
⅛ teaspoon black pepper

1. Spritz an air fryer basket with cooking spray. Set aside.
2. In a small bowl, whisk together all the ingredients for the horseradish sauce until smooth. Set aside.
3. In a shallow dish, beat the eggs and buttermilk.
4. In a separate shallow dish, thoroughly combine the bread crumbs, cornmeal, and salt.
5. Dredge the tomato slices, one at a time, in the egg mixture, then roll in the bread crumb mixture until evenly coated.
6. Place the tomato slices in the air fryer basket. Spray them with cooking spray.
7. Slide the basket into the air fryer oven. Cook at 390°F (199°C) for 13 minutes.
8. Flip the tomato slices halfway through the cooking time.
9. When cooking is complete, the tomato slices should be nicely browned and crisp. Remove from the air fryer oven to a platter and serve drizzled with the prepared horseradish sauce.

Crunchy Chickpeas

Prep time: 5 minutes | Cook time: 18 minutes | Serves 4

½ teaspoon chili powder
½ teaspoon ground cumin
¼ teaspoon cayenne pepper
¼ teaspoon salt
1 (19-ounce / 539-g) can chickpeas, drained and rinsed
Cooking spray

1. Lina an air fryer basket with parchment paper and lightly spritz with cooking spray.
2. Mix the chili powder, cumin, cayenne pepper, and salt in a small bowl.
3. Place the chickpeas in a medium bowl and lightly mist with cooking spray.
4. Add the spice mixture to the chickpeas and toss until evenly coated. Transfer the chickpeas to the parchment.
5. Slide the basket into the air fryer oven. Cook at 390°F (199°C) for 18 minutes.
6. Stir the chickpeas twice during cooking.
7. When cooking is complete, the chickpeas should be crunchy. Remove from the air fryer oven. Let the chickpeas cool for 5 minutes before serving.

Mushroom and Spinach Calzones

Prep time: 15 minutes | Cook time: 26 to 27 minutes | Serves 4

2 tablespoons olive oil
1 onion, chopped
2 garlic cloves, minced
¼ cup chopped mushrooms
1 pound (454 g) spinach, chopped
1 tablespoon Italian seasoning
½ teaspoon oregano
Salt and black pepper, to taste
1½ cups marinara sauce
1 cup ricotta cheese, crumbled
1 (13-ounce / 369-g) pizza crust
Cooking spray

Make the Filling:
1. Heat the olive oil in a pan over medium heat until shimmering.
2. Add the onion, garlic, and mushrooms and sauté for 4 minutes, or until softened.
3. Stir in the spinach and sauté for 2 to 3 minutes, or until the spinach is wilted. Sprinkle with the Italian seasoning, oregano, salt, and pepper and mix well.
4. Add the marinara sauce and cook for about 5 minutes, stirring occasionally, or until the sauce is thickened.
5. Remove the pan from the heat and stir in the ricotta cheese. Set aside.
Make the Calzones:
6. Spritz an air fryer basket with cooking spray. Set aside.
7. Roll the pizza crust out with a rolling pin on a lightly floured work surface, then cut it into 4 rectangles.
8. Spoon ¼ of the filling into each rectangle and fold in half. Crimp the edges with a fork to seal. Mist them with cooking spray. Transfer the calzones to the air fryer basket.
9. Slide the basket into the air fryer oven. Cook at 375°F (190°C) for 15 minutes.
10. Flip the calzones halfway through the cooking time.
11. When cooking is complete, the calzones should be golden brown and crisp. Transfer the calzones to a paper towel-lined plate and serve.

Crunchy Parmesan Snack Mix

Prep time: 5 minutes | Cook time: 6 minutes | Makes 6 cups

2 cups oyster crackers
2 cups Chex rice
1 cup sesame sticks
⅔ cup finely grated Parmesan cheese
8 tablespoons unsalted butter, melted
1½ teaspoons granulated garlic
½ teaspoon kosher salt

1. Toss together all the ingredients in a large bowl until well coated. Spread the mixture on a sheet pan.
2. Slide the pan into the air fryer oven. Cook at 350°F (180°C) for 6 minutes.
3. After 3 minutes, remove the pan and stir the mixture. Return to the air fryer oven and continue cooking.
4. When cooking is complete, the mixture should be lightly browned and fragrant. Let cool before serving.

Sausage and Mushroom Empanadas

Prep time: 5 minutes | Cook time: 12 minutes | Serves 4

½ pound (227 g) Kielbasa smoked sausage, chopped
4 chopped canned mushrooms
2 tablespoons chopped onion
½ teaspoon ground cumin
¼ teaspoon paprika
Salt and black pepper, to taste
½ package puff pastry dough, at room temperature
1 egg, beaten
Cooking spray

1. Combine the sausage, mushrooms, onion, cumin, paprika, salt, and pepper in a bowl and stir to mix well.
2. Make the empanadas: Place the puff pastry dough on a lightly floured surface. Cut circles into the dough with a glass. Place 1 tablespoon of the sausage mixture into the center of each pastry circle. Fold each in half and pinch the edges to seal. Using a fork, crimp the edges. Brush them with the beaten egg and mist with cooking spray.
3. Spritz an air fryer basket with cooking spray. Place the empanadas in the air fryer basket.
4. Slide the basket into the air fryer oven. Cook at 360°F (182°C) for 12 minutes.
5. Flip the empanadas halfway through the cooking time.
6. When cooking is complete, the empanadas should be golden brown. Remove from the air fryer oven. Allow them to cool for 5 minutes and serve hot.

Cuban Sandwiches

Prep time: 20 minutes | Cook time: 8 minutes | Makes 4 sandwiches

8 slices ciabatta bread, about ¼-inch thick
Cooking spray
1 tablespoon brown mustard
Toppings:
6 to 8 ounces (170 to 227 g) thinly sliced leftover roast pork
4 ounces (113 g) thinly sliced deli turkey
⅓ cup bread and butter pickle slices
2 to 3 ounces (57 to 85 g) Pepper Jack cheese slices

1. On a clean work surface, spray one side of each slice of bread with cooking spray. Spread the other side of each slice of bread evenly with brown mustard.
2. Top 4 of the bread slices with the roast pork, turkey, pickle slices, cheese, and finish with remaining bread slices. Transfer to an air fryer basket.
3. Slide the basket into the air fryer oven. Cook at 390°F (199°C) for 8 minutes.
4. When cooking is complete, remove from the air fryer oven. Cool for 5 minutes and serve warm.

Green Chiles Nachos

Prep time: 10 minutes | Cook time: 10 minutes | Serves 6

8 ounces (227 g) tortilla chips
3 cups shredded Monterey Jack cheese, divided
2 (7-ounce / 198-g) cans chopped green chiles, drained
1 (8-ounce / 227-g) can tomato sauce
¼ teaspoon dried oregano
¼ teaspoon granulated garlic
¼ teaspoon freshly ground black pepper
Pinch cinnamon
Pinch cayenne pepper

1. Arrange the tortilla chips close together in a single layer on a sheet pan. Sprinkle 1½ cups of the cheese over the chips. Arrange the green chiles over the cheese as evenly as possible. Top with the remaining 1½ cups of the cheese.
2. Slide the pan into the air fryer oven. Cook at 375°F (190°C) for 10 minutes.
3. After 5 minutes, rotate the pan and continue cooking.
4. Meanwhile, stir together the remaining ingredients in a bowl.
5. When cooking is complete, the cheese will be melted and starting to crisp around the edges of the pan. Remove from the air fryer oven. Drizzle the sauce over the nachos and serve warm.

Appetizers and Snacks

Cinnamon Apple Wedges

Prep time: 10 minutes | Cook time: 12 minutes | Serves 4

2 medium apples, cored and sliced into ¼-inch wedges
1 teaspoon canola oil
2 teaspoons peeled and grated fresh ginger
½ teaspoon ground cinnamon
½ cup low-fat Greek vanilla yogurt, for serving

1. In a large bowl, toss the apple wedges with the canola oil, ginger, and cinnamon until evenly coated. Put the apple wedges in an air fryer basket.
2. Slide the basket into the air fryer oven. Cook at 360°F (182°C) for 12 minutes.
3. When cooking is complete, the apple wedges should be crisp-tender. Remove the apple wedges from the air fryer oven and serve drizzled with the yogurt.

Hush Puppies

Prep time: 45 minutes | Cook time: 10 minutes | Serves 12

1 cup self-rising yellow cornmeal
½ cup all-purpose flour
1 teaspoon sugar
1 teaspoon salt
1 teaspoon freshly ground black pepper
1 large egg
⅓ cup canned creamed corn
1 cup minced onion
2 teaspoons minced jalapeño pepper
2 tablespoons olive oil, divided

1. Thoroughly combine the cornmeal, flour, sugar, salt, and pepper in a large bowl.
2. Whisk together the egg and corn in a small bowl. Pour the egg mixture into the bowl of cornmeal mixture and stir to combine. Stir in the minced onion and jalapeño. Cover the bowl with plastic wrap and place in the refrigerator for 30 minutes.
3. Line an air fryer basket with parchment paper and lightly brush it with 1 tablespoon of olive oil.
4. Scoop out the cornmeal mixture and form into 24 balls, about 1 inch.
5. Arrange the balls on the parchment, leaving space between each ball.
6. Slide the basket into the air fryer oven. Cook at 375°F (190°C) for 10 minutes.
7. After 5 minutes, remove from the air fryer oven. Flip the balls and brush them with the remaining 1 tablespoon of olive oil. Return to the air fryer oven and continue cooking for 5 minutes until golden brown.
8. When cooking is complete, remove the balls (hush puppies) from the air fryer oven and serve on a plate.

Paprika Deviled Eggs

Prep time: 20 minutes | Cook time: 16 minutes | Serves 12

3 cups ice
12 large eggs
½ cup mayonnaise
10 hamburger dill pickle chips, diced
¼ cup diced onion
2 teaspoons salt
2 teaspoons yellow mustard
1 teaspoon freshly ground black pepper
½ teaspoon paprika

1. Put the ice in a large bowl and set aside. Carefully place the eggs in an air fryer basket.
2. Slide the basket into the air fryer oven. Cook at 250°F (121°C) for 16 minutes.
3. When cooking is complete, transfer the eggs to the large bowl of ice to cool.
4. When cool enough to handle, peel the eggs. Slice them in half lengthwise and scoop out yolks into a small bowl. Stir in the mayonnaise, pickles, onion, salt, mustard, and pepper. Mash the mixture with a fork until well combined.
5. Fill each egg white half with 1 to 2 teaspoons of the egg yolk mixture.
6. Sprinkle the paprika on top and serve immediately.

Garlic Edamame

Prep time: 5 minutes | Cook time: 9 minutes | Serves 4

1 (16-ounce / 454-g) bag frozen edamame in pods
2 tablespoon olive oil, divided
½ teaspoon garlic salt
½ teaspoon salt
¼ teaspoon freshly ground black pepper
½ teaspoon red pepper flakes (optional)

1. Place the edamame in a medium bowl and drizzle with 1 tablespoon of olive oil. Toss to coat well.
2. Stir together the garlic salt, salt, pepper, and red pepper flakes (if desired) in a small bowl. Pour the mixture into the bowl of edamame and toss until the edamame is fully coated.
3. Grease an air fryer basket with the remaining 1 tablespoon of olive oil.
4. Place the edamame in the greased air fryer basket.
5. Slide the basket into the air fryer oven. Cook at 375°F (190°C) for 9 minutes.
6. Stir the edamame once halfway through the cooking time.
7. When cooking is complete, the edamame should be crisp. Remove from the air fryer oven to a plate and serve warm.

Garlicky Roasted Mushrooms

Prep time: 5 minutes | Cook time: 27 minutes | Serves 4

16 garlic cloves, peeled
2 teaspoons olive oil, divided
16 button mushrooms
½ teaspoon dried marjoram
⅛ teaspoon freshly ground black pepper
1 tablespoon white wine

1. Place the garlic cloves on a sheet pan and drizzle with 1 teaspoon of the olive oil. Toss to coat well.
2. Slide the pan into the air fryer oven. Cook at 350°F (180°C) for 12 minutes.
3. When cooking is complete, remove from the air fryer oven. Stir in the mushrooms, marjoram and pepper. Drizzle with the remaining 1 teaspoon of the olive oil and the white wine. Toss to coat well. Return the pan back to the air fryer oven.
4. Cook at 350°F (180°C) for 15 minutes.
5. Once done, the mushrooms and garlic cloves will be softened. Remove from the air fryer oven.
6. Serve warm.

Polenta Fries with Chili-Lime Mayo

Prep time: 10 minutes | Cook time: 28 minutes | Serves 4

Polenta Fries:
2 teaspoons vegetable or olive oil
¼ teaspoon paprika
1 pound (454 g) prepared polenta, cut into 3-inch × ½-inch strips
Salt and freshly ground black pepper, to taste
Chili-Lime Mayo:
½ cup mayonnaise
1 teaspoon chili powder
1 teaspoon chopped fresh cilantro
¼ teaspoon ground cumin
Juice of ½ lime
Salt and freshly ground black pepper, to taste

1. Mix the oil and paprika in a bowl. Add the polenta strips and toss until evenly coated. Transfer the polenta strips to an air fryer basket.
2. Slide the basket into the air fryer oven. Cook at 400°F (205°C) for 28 minutes.
3. Stir the polenta strips halfway through the cooking time.
4. Meanwhile, whisk together all the ingredients for the chili-lime mayo in a small bowl.
5. When cooking is complete, remove the polenta fries from the air fryer oven to a plate. Season as desired with salt and pepper. Serve alongside the chili-lime mayo as a dipping sauce.

Homemade BBQ Chicken Pizza

Prep time: 5 minutes | Cook time: 8 minutes | Serves 1

1 piece naan bread
¼ cup Barbecue sauce
¼ cup shredded Monterrey Jack cheese
¼ cup shredded Mozzarella cheese
½ chicken herby sausage, sliced
2 tablespoons red onion, thinly sliced
Chopped cilantro or parsley, for garnish
Cooking spray

1. Spritz the bottom of naan bread with cooking spray, then transfer to an air fryer basket.
2. Brush with the Barbecue sauce. Top with the cheeses, sausage, and finish with the red onion.
3. Slide the basket into the air fryer oven. Cook at 400°F (205°C) for 8 minutes.
4. When cooking is complete, the cheese should be melted. Remove from the air fryer oven. Garnish with the chopped cilantro or parsley before slicing to serve.

Tuna Melts with Scallions

Prep time: 10 minutes | Cook time: 6 minutes | Serves 6

2 (5- to 6-ounce / 142- to 170-g) cans oil-packed tuna, drained
1 large scallion, chopped
1 small stalk celery, chopped
⅓ cup mayonnaise
1 tablespoon chopped fresh dill
1 tablespoon capers, drained
¼ teaspoon celery salt
12 slices cocktail rye bread
2 tablespoons butter, melted
6 slices sharp Cheddar cheese

1. In a medium bowl, stir together the tuna, scallion, celery, mayonnaise, dill, capers and celery salt.
2. Brush one side of the bread slices with the butter. Arrange the bread slices on a sheet pan, buttered-side down. Scoop a heaping tablespoon of the tuna mixture on each slice of bread, spreading it out even to the edges.
3. Cut the cheese slices to fit the dimensions of the bread and place a cheese slice on each piece.
4. Slide the pan into the air fryer oven. Cook at 375°F (190°C) for 6 minutes.
5. After 4 minutes, remove from the air fryer oven and check the tuna melts. The tuna melts are done when the cheese has melted and the tuna is heated through. If needed, continue cooking.
6. When cooking is complete, remove from the air fryer oven. Use a spatula to transfer the tuna melts to a clean work surface and slice each one in half diagonally. Serve warm.

Italian Rice Balls

Prep time: 20 minutes | Cook time: 10 minutes | Makes 8 rice balls

1½ cups cooked sticky rice
½ teaspoon Italian seasoning blend
¾ teaspoon salt, divided
8 black olives, pitted
1 ounce (28 g) Mozzarella cheese, cut into tiny pieces (small enough to stuff into olives)
2 eggs
⅓ cup Italian bread crumbs
¾ cup panko bread crumbs
Cooking spray

1. Stuff each black olive with a piece of Mozzarella cheese.
2. In a bowl, combine the cooked sticky rice, Italian seasoning blend, and ½ teaspoon of salt and stir to mix well. Form the rice mixture into a log with your hands and divide it into 8 equal portions. Mold each portion around a black olive and roll into a ball.
3. Transfer to the freezer to chill for 10 to 15 minutes until firm.
4. In a shallow dish, place the Italian bread crumbs. In a separate shallow dish, whisk the eggs. In a third shallow dish, combine the panko bread crumbs and remaining salt.
5. One by one, roll the rice balls in the Italian bread crumbs, then dip in the whisked eggs, finally coat them with the panko bread crumbs.
6. Arrange the rice balls in an air fryer basket and spritz both sides with cooking spray.
7. Slide the basket into the air fryer oven. Cook at 390°F (199°C) for 10 minutes.
8. Flip the balls halfway through the cooking time.
9. When cooking is complete, the rice balls should be golden brown. Remove from the air fryer oven and serve warm.

Cheese-Stuffed Mushrooms with Pimientos

Prep time: 10 minutes | Cook time: 18 minutes | Serves 12

24 medium raw white button mushrooms, rinsed and drained
4 ounces (113 g) shredded extra-sharp Cheddar cheese
2 ounces (57 g) cream cheese, at room temperature
1 ounce (28 g) chopped jarred pimientos
2 tablespoons grated onion
⅛ teaspoon smoked paprika
⅛ teaspoon hot sauce
2 tablespoons butter, melted, divided
⅓ cup panko bread crumbs
2 tablespoons grated Parmesan cheese

1. Gently pull out the stems of the mushrooms and discard. Set aside.
2. In a medium bowl, stir together the Cheddar cheese, cream cheese, pimientos, onion, paprika and hot sauce.
3. Brush a sheet pan with 1 tablespoon of the melted butter. Arrange the mushrooms evenly on the pan, hollow-side up.
4. Place the cheese mixture into a large heavy plastic bag and cut off the end. Fill the mushrooms with the cheese mixture.
5. In a small bowl, whisk together the remaining 1 tablespoon of the melted butter, bread crumbs and Parmesan cheese. Sprinkle the panko mixture over each mushroom.
6. Slide the pan into the air fryer oven. Cook at 350°F (180°C) for 18 minutes.
7. After about 9 minutes, rotate the pan and continue cooking.
8. When cooking is complete, let the stuffed mushrooms rest for 2 minutes before serving.

Parmesan Cauliflower

Prep time: 15 minutes | Cook time: 15 minutes | Makes 5 cups

8 cups small cauliflower florets (about 1¼ pounds / 567 g)
3 tablespoons olive oil
1 teaspoon garlic powder
½ teaspoon salt
½ teaspoon turmeric
¼ cup shredded Parmesan cheese

1. In a bowl, combine the cauliflower florets, olive oil, garlic powder, salt, and turmeric and toss to coat. Transfer to an air fryer basket.
2. Slide the basket into the air fryer oven. Cook at 390°F (199°C) for 15 minutes.
3. After 5 minutes, remove from the air fryer oven and stir the cauliflower florets. Return to the air fryer oven and continue cooking.
4. After 6 minutes, remove from the air fryer oven and stir the cauliflower. Return to the air fryer oven and continue cooking for 4 minutes. The cauliflower florets should be crisp-tender.
5. When cooking is complete, remove from the air fryer oven to a plate. Sprinkle with the shredded Parmesan cheese and toss well. Serve warm.

Kale Chips with Sesame

Prep time: 15 minutes | Cook time: 8 minutes | Serves 5

8 cups deribbed kale leaves, torn into 2-inch pieces
1½ tablespoons olive oil
¾ teaspoon chili powder
¼ teaspoon garlic powder
½ teaspoon paprika
2 teaspoons sesame seeds

1. In a large bowl, toss the kale with the olive oil, chili powder, garlic powder, paprika, and sesame seeds until well coated.
2. Transfer the kale to an air fryer basket.
3. Slide the basket into the air fryer oven. Cook at 350°F (180°C) for 8 minutes.
4. Flip the kale twice during cooking.
5. When cooking is complete, the kale should be crispy. Remove from the air fryer oven and serve warm.

Deluxe Cheese Sandwiches

Prep time: 10 minutes | Cook time: 6 minutes | Serves 4 to 8

8 ounces (227 g) Brie
8 slices oat nut bread
1 large ripe pear, cored and cut into ½-inch-thick slices
2 tablespoons butter, melted

1. Make the sandwiches: Spread each of 4 slices of bread with ¼ of the Brie. Top the Brie with the pear slices and remaining 4 bread slices.
2. Brush the melted butter lightly on both sides of each sandwich.
3. Arrange the sandwiches in an air fryer basket.
4. Slide the basket into the air fryer oven. Cook at 360°F (182°C) for 6 minutes.
5. When cooking is complete, the cheese should be melted. Remove the basket from the air fryer oven and serve warm.

Old Bay Chicken Wings

Prep time: 10 minutes | Cook time: 13 minutes | Serves 4

2 tablespoons Old Bay seasoning
2 teaspoons baking powder
2 teaspoons salt
2 pounds (907 g) chicken wings, patted dry
Cooking spray

1. Combine the Old Bay seasoning, baking powder, and salt in a large zip-top plastic bag. Add the chicken wings, seal, and shake until the wings are thoroughly coated in the seasoning mixture.
2. Lightly spray an air fryer basket with cooking spray. Lay the chicken wings in the air fryer basket and lightly mist them with cooking spray.
3. Slide the basket into the air fryer oven. Cook at 400°F (205°C) for 13 minutes.
4. Flip the wings halfway through the cooking time.
5. When cooking is complete, the wings should reach an internal temperature of 165°F (74°C) on a meat thermometer. Remove from the air fryer oven to a plate and serve hot.

Paprika Potato Chips

Prep time: 5 minutes | Cook time: 22 minutes | Serves 3

2 medium potatoes, preferably Yukon Gold, scrubbed
Cooking spray
2 teaspoons olive oil
½ teaspoon garlic granules
¼ teaspoon paprika
¼ teaspoon plus ⅛ teaspoon sea salt
¼ teaspoon freshly ground black pepper
Ketchup or hot sauce, for serving

1. Spritz an air fryer basket with cooking spray.
2. On a flat work surface, cut the potatoes into ¼-inch-thick slices. Transfer the potato slices to a medium bowl, along with the olive oil, garlic granules, paprika, salt, and pepper and toss to coat well. Transfer the potato slices to the air fryer basket.
3. Slide the basket into the air fryer oven. Cook at 392°F (200°C) for 22 minutes.
4. Stir the potato slices twice during the cooking process.
5. When cooking is complete, the potato chips should be tender and nicely browned. Remove from the air fryer oven and serve alongside the ketchup for dipping.

Roasted Grapes with Yogurt

Prep time: 5 minutes | Cook time: 10 minutes | Serves 6

2 cups seedless red grapes, rinsed and patted dry
1 tablespoon apple cider vinegar
1 tablespoon honey
1 cup low-fat Greek yogurt
2 tablespoons 2 percent milk
2 tablespoons minced fresh basil

1. Spread the red grapes in an air fryer basket and drizzle with the cider vinegar and honey. Lightly toss to coat.
2. Slide the basket into the air fryer oven. Cook at 380°F (193°C) for 10 minutes.
3. When cooking is complete, the grapes will be wilted but still soft. Remove from the air fryer oven.
4. In a medium bowl, whisk together the yogurt and milk. Gently fold in the grapes and basil.
5. Serve immediately.

Roasted Mixed Nuts

Prep time: 5 minutes | Cook time: 20 minutes | Serves 6

2 cups mixed nuts (walnuts, pecans, and almonds)
2 tablespoons egg white
2 tablespoons sugar
1 teaspoon paprika
1 teaspoon ground cinnamon
Cooking spray

1. Line an air fryer basket with parchment paper and spray with cooking spray.
2. Stir together the mixed nuts, egg white, sugar, paprika, and cinnamon in a small bowl until the nuts are fully coated. Place the nuts in the air fryer basket.
3. Slide the basket into the air fryer oven. Cook at 300ºF (150ºC) for 20 minutes.
4. Stir the nuts halfway through the cooking time.
5. When cooking is complete, remove from the air fryer oven. Transfer the nuts to a bowl and serve warm.

Salty Baked Almonds

Prep time: 5 minutes | Cook time: 25 minutes | Serves 4

1 cup raw almonds
1 egg white, beaten
½ teaspoon coarse sea salt

1. Spread the almonds on the sheet pan in an even layer.
2. Slide the pan into the air fryer oven. Cook at 350ºF (180ºC) for 20 minutes.
3. When cooking is complete, the almonds should be lightly browned and fragrant. Remove from the air fryer oven.
4. Coat the almonds with the egg white and sprinkle with the salt. Return the pan back to the air fryer oven.
5. Cook at 350ºF (180ºC) for 5 minutes.
6. When cooking is complete, the almonds should be dried. Cool completely before serving.

Shrimp Toasts with Sesame Seeds

Prep time: 15 minutes | Cook time: 8 minutes | Serves 4 to 6

½ pound (227 g) raw shrimp, peeled and deveined
1 egg, beaten
2 scallions, chopped, plus more for garnish
2 tablespoons chopped fresh cilantro
2 teaspoons grated fresh ginger
1 to 2 teaspoons sriracha sauce
1 teaspoon soy sauce
½ teaspoon toasted sesame oil
6 slices thinly sliced white sandwich bread
½ cup sesame seeds
Cooking spray
Thai chili sauce, for serving

1. In a food processor, add the shrimp, egg, scallions, cilantro, ginger, sriracha sauce, soy sauce and sesame oil, and pulse until chopped finely. Stop the food processor occasionally to scrape down the sides. Transfer the shrimp mixture to a bowl.
2. On a clean work surface, cut the crusts off the sandwich bread. Using a brush, generously brush one side of each slice of bread with shrimp mixture.
3. Place the sesame seeds on a plate. Press bread slices, shrimp-side down, into sesame seeds to coat evenly. Cut each slice diagonally into quarters.
4. Spritz an air fryer basket with cooking spray. Spread the coated slices in a single layer in the air fryer basket.
5. Slide the basket into the air fryer oven. Cook at 400ºF (205ºC) for 8 minutes.
6. Flip the bread slices halfway through.
7. When cooking is complete, they should be golden and crispy. Remove from the air fryer oven to a plate and let cool for 5 minutes. Top with the chopped scallions and serve warm with Thai chili sauce.

Sausage and Onion Rolls

Prep time: 15 minutes | Cook time: 15 minutes | Serves 12

1 pound (454 g) bulk breakfast sausage
½ cup finely chopped onion
½ cup fresh bread crumbs
½ teaspoon dried mustard
½ teaspoon dried sage
¼ teaspoon cayenne pepper
1 large egg, beaten
1 garlic clove, minced
2 sheets (1 package) frozen puff pastry, thawed
All-purpose flour, for dusting

1. In a medium bowl, break up the sausage. Stir in the onion, bread crumbs, mustard, sage, cayenne pepper, egg and garlic. Divide the sausage mixture in half and tightly wrap each half in plastic wrap. Refrigerate for 5 to 10 minutes.
2. Lay the pastry sheets on a lightly floured work surface. Using a rolling pin, lightly roll out the pastry to smooth out the dough. Take out one of the sausage packages and form the sausage into a long roll. Remove the plastic wrap and place the sausage on top of the puff pastry about 1 inch from one of the long edges. Roll the pastry around the sausage and pinch the edges of the dough together to seal. Repeat with the other pastry sheet and sausage.
3. Slice the logs into lengths about 1½ inches long. Place the sausage rolls on a sheet pan, cut-side down.
4. Slide the pan into the air fryer oven. Cook at 350ºF (180ºC) for 15 minutes.
5. After 7 or 8 minutes, rotate the pan and continue cooking.
6. When cooking is complete, the rolls will be golden brown and sizzling. Remove the pan from the air fryer oven and let cool for 5 minutes.

Sausage Balls with Cheese

Prep time: 10 minutes | Cook time: 10 minutes | Serves 8

12 ounces (340 g) mild ground sausage
1½ cups baking mix
1 cup shredded mild Cheddar cheese
3 ounces (85 g) cream cheese, at room temperature
1 to 2 tablespoons olive oil

1. Line an air fryer basket with parchment paper. Set aside.
2. Mix the ground sausage, baking mix, Cheddar cheese, and cream cheese in a large bowl and stir to incorporate.
3. Divide the sausage mixture into 16 equal portions and roll them into 1-inch balls with your hands. Arrange the sausage balls on the parchment, leaving space between each ball. Brush the sausage balls with the olive oil.
4. Slide the basket into the air fryer oven. Cook at 325°F (163°C) for 10 minutes.
5. Flip the balls halfway through the cooking time.
6. When cooking is complete, the balls should be firm and lightly browned on both sides. Remove from the air fryer oven to a plate and serve warm.

Sweet and Salty Snack Mix

Prep time: 5 minutes | Cook time: 10 minutes | Makes about 10 cups

3 tablespoons butter, melted
½ cup honey
1 teaspoon salt
2 cups granola
2 cups sesame sticks
2 cups crispy corn puff cereal
2 cups mini pretzel crisps
1 cup cashews
1 cup pepitas
1 cup dried cherries

1. In a small mixing bowl, mix the butter, honey, and salt until well incorporated.
2. In a large bowl, combine the granola, sesame sticks, corn puff cereal and pretzel crisps, cashews, and pepitas. Drizzle with the butter mixture and toss until evenly coated. Transfer the snack mix to a sheet pan.
3. Slide the pan into the air fryer oven. Cook at 370°F (188°C) for 10 minutes.
4. Stir the snack mix halfway through the cooking time.
5. When cooking is complete, they should be lightly toasted. Remove from the air fryer oven and allow to cool completely. Scatter with the dried cherries and mix well. Serve immediately.

Tangy Fried Pickle Spears

Prep time: 5 minutes | Cook time: 15 minutes | Serves 6

2 jars sweet and sour pickle spears, patted dry
2 medium-sized eggs
⅓ cup milk
1 teaspoon garlic powder
1 teaspoon sea salt
½ teaspoon shallot powder
⅓ teaspoon chili powder
⅓ cup all-purpose flour
Cooking spray

1. Spritz an air fryer basket with cooking spray.
2. In a bowl, beat together the eggs with milk. In another bowl, combine garlic powder, sea salt, shallot powder, chili powder and all-purpose flour until well blended.
3. One by one, roll the pickle spears in the powder mixture, then dredge them in the egg mixture. Dip them in the powder mixture a second time for additional coating.
4. Place the coated pickles in the air fryer basket.
5. Slide the basket into the air fryer oven. Cook at 385°F (196°C) for 15 minutes.
6. Stir the pickles halfway through the cooking time.
7. When cooking is complete, they should be golden and crispy. Transfer to a plate and let cool for 5 minutes before serving.

Spicy Tortilla Chips

Prep time: 5 minutes | Cook time: 5 minutes | Serves 4

½ teaspoon ground cumin
½ teaspoon paprika
½ teaspoon chili powder
½ teaspoon salt
Pinch cayenne pepper
8 (6-inch) corn tortillas, each cut into 6 wedges
Cooking spray

1. Lightly spritz an air fryer basket with cooking spray.
2. Stir together the cumin, paprika, chili powder, salt, and pepper in a small bowl.
3. Place the tortilla wedges in the air fryer basket. Lightly mist them with cooking spray. Sprinkle the seasoning mixture on top of the tortilla wedges.
4. Slide the basket into the air fryer oven. Cook at 375°F (190°C) for 5 minutes.
5. Stir the tortilla wedges halfway through the cooking time.
6. When cooking is complete, the chips should be lightly browned and crunchy. Remove from the air fryer oven. Let the tortilla chips cool for 5 minutes and serve.

Spiced Apple Chips

Prep time: 10 minutes | Cook time: 10 minutes | Serves 4

4 medium apples (any type will work), cored and thinly sliced
¼ teaspoon nutmeg
¼ teaspoon cinnamon
Cooking spray

1. Place the apple slices in a large bowl and sprinkle the spices on top. Toss to coat.
2. Put the apple slices in an air fryer basket and spray them with cooking spray.
3. Slide the basket into the air fryer oven. Cook at 360°F (182°C) for 10 minutes.
4. Stir the apple slices halfway through.
5. When cooking is complete, the apple chips should be crispy. Transfer the apple chips to a paper towel-lined plate and rest for 5 minutes before serving.

Spicy and Sweet Roasted Nuts

Prep time: 5 minutes | Cook time: 15 minutes | Makes 4 cups

1 pound (454 g) walnut halves and pieces
½ cup granulated sugar
3 tablespoons vegetable oil
1 teaspoon cayenne pepper
½ teaspoon fine salt

1. Soak the walnuts in a large bowl with boiling water for a minute or two. Drain the walnuts. Stir in the sugar, oil and cayenne pepper to coat well. Spread the walnuts in a single layer on a sheet pan.
2. Slide the pan into the air fryer oven. Cook at 325°F (163°C) for 15 minutes.
3. After 7 or 8 minutes, remove from the air fryer oven. Stir the nuts. Return to the air fryer oven and continue cooking, check frequently.
4. When cooking is complete, the walnuts should be dark golden brown. Remove from the air fryer oven. Sprinkle the nuts with the salt and let cool. Serve.

Sweet Cinnamon Peaches

Prep time: 5 minutes | Cook time: 10 minutes | Serves 4

2 tablespoons sugar
¼ teaspoon ground cinnamon
4 peaches, cut into wedges
Cooking spray

1. Spritz an air fryer basket with cooking spray.
2. In a large bowl, stir together the sugar and cinnamon. Add the peaches to the bowl and toss to coat evenly.
3. Spread the coated peaches in a single layer on the air fryer basket.
4. Slide the basket into the air fryer oven. Cook at 350°F (180°C) for 10 minutes.
5. After 5 minutes, remove from the air fryer oven. Use a tong to turn the peaches skin side down. Lightly mist them with cooking spray. Return the pan back to the air fryer oven to continue cooking.
6. When cooking is complete, the peaches will be lightly browned and caramelized. Remove the pan from the air fryer oven and let rest for 5 minutes before serving.

Turkey Bacon-Wrapped Dates

Prep time: 10 minutes | Cook time: 6 minutes | Makes 16 appetizers

16 whole dates, pitted
16 whole almonds
6 to 8 strips turkey bacon, cut in half

Special Equipment:
16 toothpicks, soaked in water for at least 30 minutes

1. On a flat work surface, stuff each pitted date with a whole almond.
2. Wrap half slice of bacon around each date and secure it with a toothpick.
3. Place the bacon-wrapped dates in an air fryer basket.
4. Slide the basket into the air fryer oven. Cook at 390°F (199°C) for 6 minutes.
5. When cooking is complete, transfer the dates to a paper towel-lined plate to drain. Serve hot.

Breakfasts

Air Fryer Baked Eggs

Prep time: 5 minutes | Cook time: 6 to 7 minutes | Serves 2

2 large eggs
2 tablespoons half-and-half
2 teaspoons shredded Cheddar cheese
Salt and freshly ground black pepper, to taste
Cooking spray

1. Spritz 2 ramekins lightly with cooking spray. Crack an egg into each ramekin.
2. Top each egg with 1 tablespoon of half-and-half and 1 teaspoon of Cheddar cheese. Sprinkle with salt and black pepper. Stir the egg mixture with a fork until well combined.
3. Place the ramekins in the air fryer oven. Cook at 330°F (166°C) for 6 minutes.
4. When cooking is complete, the eggs should be set. Check for doneness and continue cooking for 1 minute more as needed. Allow to cool for 5 minutes before removing and serving.

Bacon and Egg Bread Cups

Prep time: 10 minutes | Cook time: 10 minutes | Serves 4

4 (3-by-4-inch) crusty rolls
4 thin slices Gouda or Swiss cheese mini wedges
5 eggs
2 tablespoons heavy cream
3 strips precooked bacon, chopped
½ teaspoon dried thyme
Pinch salt
Freshly ground black pepper, to taste

1. On a clean work surface, cut the tops off the rolls. Using your fingers, remove the insides of the rolls to make bread cups, leaving a ½-inch shell. Place a slice of cheese onto each roll bottom.
2. Whisk together the eggs and heavy cream in a medium bowl until well combined. Fold in the bacon, thyme, salt, and pepper and stir well.
3. Scrape the egg mixture into the prepared bread cups.
4. Place the bread cups into the air fryer oven. Cook at 330°F (166°C) for 10 minutes.
5. When cooked, the eggs should be cooked to your preference.
6. Serve warm.

Baked Avocado with Eggs

Prep time: 5 minutes | Cook time: 9 minutes | Serves 2

1 large avocado, halved and pitted
2 large eggs
2 tomato slices, divided
½ cup nonfat Cottage cheese, divided
½ teaspoon fresh cilantro, for garnish

1. Line the sheet pan with the aluminium foil.
2. Slice a thin piece from the bottom of each avocado half so they sit flat. Remove a small amount from each avocado half to make a bigger hole to hold the egg.
3. Arrange the avocado halves on the pan, hollow-side up. Break 1 egg into each half. Top each half with 1 tomato slice and ¼ cup of the Cottage cheese.
4. Slide the pan into the air fryer oven. Cook at 425°F (220°C) for 9 minutes.
5. When cooking is complete, remove from the air fryer oven. Garnish with the fresh cilantro and serve.

Blueberry Cake

Prep time: 5 minutes | Cook time: 10 minutes | Serves 8

1½ cups Bisquick
¼ cup granulated sugar
2 large eggs, beaten
¾ cup whole milk
1 teaspoon vanilla extract
½ teaspoon lemon zest
Cooking spray
2 cups blueberries

1. Stir together the Bisquick and sugar in a medium bowl. Stir together the eggs, milk, vanilla and lemon zest. Add the wet ingredients to the dry ingredients and stir until well combined.
2. Spritz the sheet pan with cooking spray and line with the parchment paper, pressing it into place. Spray the parchment paper with cooking spray. Pour the batter on the pan and spread it out evenly. Sprinkle the blueberries evenly over the top.
3. Slide the pan into the air fryer oven. Cook at 375°F (190°C) for 10 minutes.
4. When cooking is complete, the cake should be pulled away from the edges of the pan and the top should be just starting to turn golden brown.
5. Let the cake rest for a minute before cutting into 16 squares. Serve immediately.

Banana and Oat Bread Pudding

Prep time: 10 minutes | Cook time: 16 minutes | Serves 4

2 medium ripe bananas, mashed
½ cup low-fat milk
2 tablespoons maple syrup
2 tablespoons peanut butter
1 teaspoon vanilla extract
1 teaspoon ground cinnamon
2 slices whole-grain bread, cut into bite-sized cubes
¼ cup quick oats
Cooking spray

1. Spritz a baking dish lightly with cooking spray.
2. Mix the bananas, milk, maple syrup, peanut butter, vanilla, and cinnamon in a large mixing bowl and stir until well incorporated.
3. Add the bread cubes to the banana mixture and stir until thoroughly coated. Fold in the oats and stir to combine.
4. Transfer the mixture to the baking dish. Wrap the baking dish in aluminum foil.
5. Slide the baking dish into the air fryer oven. Cook at 350°F (180°C) for 16 minutes.
6. After 10 minutes, remove from the air fryer oven. Remove the foil. Return to the air fryer oven and continue to cook another 6 minutes.
7. When done, the pudding should be set.
8. Let the pudding cool for 5 minutes before serving.

Carrot Banana Muffin

Prep time: 10 minutes | Cook time: 20 minutes | Serves 12

1½ cups whole-wheat flour
1 cup grated carrot
1 cup mashed banana
½ cup bran
½ cup low-fat buttermilk
2 tablespoons agave nectar
2 teaspoons baking powder
1 teaspoon vanilla
1 teaspoon baking soda
½ teaspoon nutmeg
Pinch cloves
2 egg whites

1. Line a muffin pan with 12 paper liners.
2. In a large bowl, stir together all the ingredients. Mix well, but do not over beat.
3. Scoop the mixture into the muffin cups.
4. Slide the pan into the air fryer oven. Cook at 400°F (205°C) for 20 minutes.
5. When cooking is complete, remove the pan and let rest for 5 minutes.
6. Serve warm or at room temperature.

Bourbon Vanilla French Toast

Prep time: 15 minutes | Cook time: 6 minutes | Serves 4

2 large eggs
2 tablespoons water
⅔ cup whole or 2% milk
1 tablespoon butter, melted
2 tablespoons bourbon
1 teaspoon vanilla extract
8 (1-inch-thick) French bread slices
Cooking spray

1. Line an air fryer basket with parchment paper and spray it with cooking spray.
2. Beat the eggs with the water in a shallow bowl until combined. Add the milk, melted butter, bourbon, and vanilla and stir to mix well.
3. Dredge 4 slices of bread in the batter, turning to coat both sides evenly. Transfer the bread slices onto the parchment paper.
4. Slide the basket into the air fryer oven. Cook at 320°F (160°C) for 6 minutes.
5. Flip the slices halfway through the cooking time.
6. When cooking is complete, the bread slices should be nicely browned.
7. Remove from the air fryer oven to a plate and serve warm.

Breakfast Blueberry Cobbler

Prep time: 5 minutes | Cook time: 15 minutes | Serves 4

¾ teaspoon baking powder
⅓ cup whole-wheat pastry flour
Dash sea salt
⅓ cup unsweetened nondairy milk
2 tablespoons maple syrup
½ teaspoon vanilla
Cooking spray
½ cup blueberries
¼ cup granola
Nondairy yogurt, for topping (optional)

1. Spritz a baking pan with cooking spray.
2. Mix the baking powder, flour, and salt in a medium bowl. Add the milk, maple syrup, and vanilla and whisk to combine.
3. Scrape the mixture into the prepared pan. Scatter the blueberries and granola on top.
4. Slide the pan into the air fryer oven. Cook at 347°F (175°C) for 15 minutes.
5. When done, the top should be browned and a knife inserted in the center should come out clean.
6. Let the cobbler cool for 5 minutes and serve with a drizzle of nondairy yogurt.

Breakfast Cheese Sandwiches

Prep time: 5 minutes | Cook time: 8 minutes | Serves 2

1 teaspoon butter, softened
4 slices bread
4 slices smoked country ham
4 slices Cheddar cheese
4 thick slices tomato

1. Spoon ½ teaspoon of butter onto one side of 2 slices of bread and spread it all over.
2. Assemble the sandwiches: Top each of 2 slices of unbuttered bread with 2 slices of ham, 2 slices of cheese, and 2 slices of tomato. Place the remaining 2 slices of bread on top, butter-side up.
3. Lay the sandwiches in an air fryer basket, buttered side down.
4. Slide the basket into the air fryer oven. Cook at 370°F (188°C) for 8 minutes.
5. Flip the sandwiches halfway through the cooking time.
6. When cooking is complete, the sandwiches should be golden brown on both sides and the cheese should be melted. Remove from the air fryer oven. Allow to cool for 5 minutes before slicing to serve.

Cheesy Breakfast Casserole

Prep time: 10 minutes | Cook time: 16 minutes | Serves 4

6 slices bacon
6 eggs
Salt and pepper, to taste
Cooking spray
½ cup chopped green bell pepper
½ cup chopped onion
¾ cup shredded Cheddar cheese

1. Place the bacon in a skillet over medium-high heat and cook each side for about 4 minutes until evenly crisp. Remove from the heat to a paper towel-lined plate to drain. Crumble it into small pieces and set aside.
2. Whisk the eggs with the salt and pepper in a medium bowl.
3. Spritz a baking pan with cooking spray.
4. Place the whisked eggs, crumbled bacon, green bell pepper, and onion in the prepared pan.
5. Place the pan into the air fryer oven. Cook at 400°F (205°C) for 8 minutes.
6. After 6 minutes, remove from the air fryer oven. Scatter the Cheddar cheese all over. Return to the air fryer oven and continue to cook another 2 minutes.
7. When cooking is complete, let sit for 5 minutes and serve on plates.

Breakfast Tater Tot Casserole

Prep time: 5 minutes | Cook time: 17 to 18 minutes | Serves 4

4 eggs
1 cup milk
Salt and pepper, to taste
12 ounces (340 g) ground chicken sausage
1 pound (454 g) frozen tater tots, thawed
¾ cup grated Cheddar cheese
Cooking spray

1. Whisk together the eggs and milk in a medium bowl. Season with salt and pepper to taste and stir until mixed. Set aside.
2. Place a skillet over medium-high heat and spritz with cooking spray. Place the ground sausage in the skillet and break it into smaller pieces with a spatula or spoon. Cook for 3 to 4 minutes until the sausage browns, stirring occasionally. Remove from heat and set aside.
3. Coat a baking pan with cooking spray. Arrange the tater tots in the baking pan.
4. Slide the pan into the air fryer oven. Cook at 400°F (205°C) for 14 minutes.
5. After 6 minutes, remove from the air fryer oven. Stir the tater tots and add the egg mixture and cooked sausage. Return to the air fryer oven and continue cooking.
6. After 6 minutes, remove from the air fryer oven. Scatter the cheese on top of the tater tots. Return to the air fryer oven and continue to cook another 2 minutes.
7. When done, the cheese should be bubbly and melted.
8. Let the mixture cool for 5 minutes and serve warm.

Canadian Bacon Muffin Sandwiches

Prep time: 5 minutes | Cook time: 8 minutes | Serves 4

4 English muffins, split
8 slices Canadian bacon
4 slices cheese
Cooking spray

1. Make the sandwiches: Top each of 4 muffin halves with 2 slices of Canadian bacon, 1 slice of cheese, and finish with the remaining muffin half.
2. Put the sandwiches in an air fryer basket and spritz the tops with cooking spray.
3. Slide the basket into the air fryer oven. Cook at 370°F (188°C) for 8 minutes.
4. Flip the sandwiches halfway through the cooking time.
5. When cooking is complete, remove the basket from the air fryer oven. Divide the sandwiches among four plates and serve warm.

Breakfasts 17

Cheesy Artichoke-Mushroom Frittata

Prep time: 10 minutes | Cook time: 15 minutes | Serves 6

8 eggs
½ teaspoon kosher salt
¼ cup whole milk
¾ cup shredded Mozzarella cheese, divided
2 tablespoons unsalted butter, melted
1 cup coarsely chopped artichoke hearts
¼ cup chopped onion
½ cup mushrooms
¼ cup grated Parmesan cheese
¼ teaspoon freshly ground black pepper

1. In a medium bowl, whisk together the eggs and salt. Let rest for a minute or two, then pour in the milk and whisk again. Stir in ½ cup of the Mozzarella cheese.
2. Grease a sheet pan with the butter. Stir in the artichoke hearts and onion and toss to coat with the butter.
3. Slide the pan into the air fryer oven. Cook at 375°F (190°C) for 12 minutes.
4. After 5 minutes, remove the pan. Spread the mushrooms over the vegetables. Pour the egg mixture on top. Stir gently just to distribute the vegetables evenly. Return to the air fryer oven and continue cooking for 10 minutes, or until the edges are set. The center will still be liquid.
5. After 1 minute, remove the pan and sprinkle the remaining ¼ cup of the Mozzarella and Parmesan cheese over the frittata. Return to the air fryer oven and continue cooking.
6. When cooking is complete, the cheese should be melted with the top completely set but not browned. Sprinkle the black pepper on top and serve.

Cinnamon Sweet Potato Chips

Prep time: 5 minutes | Cook time: 8 minutes | Makes 6 to 8 slices

1 small sweet potato, cut into ⅜ inch-thick slices
2 tablespoons olive oil
1 to 2 teaspoon ground cinnamon

1. Add the sweet potato slices and olive oil in a bowl and toss to coat. Fold in the cinnamon and stir to combine.
2. Lay the sweet potato slices in a single layer in an air fryer basket.
3. Slide the basket into the air fryer oven. Cook at 390°F (199°C) for 8 minutes.
4. Stir the potato slices halfway through the cooking time.
5. When cooking is complete, the chips should be crisp. Remove the basket from the air fryer oven. Allow to cool for 5 minutes before serving.

Cheesy Hash Brown Casserole

Prep time: 15 minutes | Cook time: 30 minutes | Serves 4

3½ cups frozen hash browns, thawed
1 teaspoon salt
1 teaspoon freshly ground black pepper
3 tablespoons butter, melted
1 (10.5-ounce / 298-g) can cream of chicken soup
½ cup sour cream
1 cup minced onion
½ cup shredded sharp Cheddar cheese
Cooking spray

1. Put the hash browns in a large bowl and season with salt and black pepper. Add the melted butter, cream of chicken soup, and sour cream and stir until well incorporated. Mix in the minced onion and cheese and stir well.
2. Spray a baking pan with cooking spray.
3. Spread the hash brown mixture evenly into the baking pan.
4. Place the pan into the air fryer oven. Cook at 325°F (163°C) for 30 minutes.
5. When cooked, the hash brown mixture will be browned.
6. Cool for 5 minutes before serving.

Chicken Breakfast Sausages

Prep time: 15 minutes | Cook time: 10 minutes | Makes 8 patties

1 Granny Smith apple, peeled and finely chopped
2 tablespoons apple juice
2 garlic cloves, minced
1 egg white
⅓ cup minced onion
3 tablespoons ground almonds
⅛ teaspoon freshly ground black pepper
1 pound (454 g) ground chicken breast

1. Combine all the ingredients except the chicken in a medium mixing bowl and stir well.
2. Add the chicken breast to the apple mixture and mix with your hands until well incorporated.
3. Divide the mixture into 8 equal portions and shape into patties. Arrange the patties in an air fryer basket.
4. Slide the basket into the air fryer oven. Cook at 330°F (166°C) for 10 minutes.
5. When done, a meat thermometer inserted in the center of the chicken should reach at least 165°F (74°C).
6. Remove from the air fryer oven to a plate. Let the chicken cool for 5 minutes and serve warm.

Asparagus and Cheese Strata

Prep time: 10 minutes | Cook time: 17 minutes | Serves 4

6 asparagus spears, cut into 2-inch pieces
1 tablespoon water
2 slices whole-wheat bread, cut into ½-inch cubes
4 eggs
3 tablespoons whole milk
2 tablespoons chopped flat-leaf parsley
½ cup grated Havarti or Swiss cheese
Pinch salt
Freshly ground black pepper, to taste
Cooking spray

1. Add the asparagus spears and 1 tablespoon of water in a baking pan.
2. Slide the pan into the air fryer oven. Cook at 330°F (166°C) for 4 minutes.
3. When cooking is complete, the asparagus spears will be crisp-tender.
4. Remove the asparagus from the pan and drain on paper towels.
5. Spritz the pan with cooking spray. Place the bread and asparagus in the pan.
6. Whisk together the eggs and milk in a medium mixing bowl until creamy. Fold in the parsley, cheese, salt, and pepper and stir to combine. Pour this mixture into the baking pan.
7. Place the basket back to the air fryer oven. Bake for 13 minutes. When done, the eggs will be set and the top will be lightly browned.
8. Let cool for 5 minutes before slicing and serving.

Cashew Granola with Cranberries

Prep time: 5 minutes | Cook time: 12 minutes | Serves 6

3 cups old-fashioned rolled oats
2 cups raw cashews
1 cup unsweetened coconut chips
½ cup honey
¼ cup vegetable oil
⅓ cup packed light brown sugar
¼ teaspoon kosher salt
1 cup dried cranberries

1. In a large bowl, stir together all the ingredients, except for the cranberries. Spread the mixture on a sheet pan.
2. Slide the pan into the air fryer oven. Cook at 325°F (163°C) for 12 minutes.
3. After 5 to 6 minutes, remove the pan and stir the granola. Return to the air fryer oven and continue cooking.
4. When cooking is complete, remove the pan. Let the granola cool to room temperature. Stir in the cranberries before serving.

Cheesy Hash Brown Cups

Prep time: 10 minutes | Cook time: 9 minutes | Serves 6

4 eggs, beaten
2¼ cups frozen hash browns, thawed
1 cup diced ham
½ cup shredded Cheddar cheese
½ teaspoon Cajun seasoning
Cooking spray

1. Lightly spritz a 12-cup muffin tin with cooking spray.
2. Combine the beaten eggs, hash browns, diced ham, cheese, and Cajun seasoning in a medium bowl and stir until well blended.
3. Spoon a heaping 1½ tablespoons of egg mixture into each muffin cup.
4. Place the muffin tin into the air fryer oven. Cook at 350°F (180°C) for 9 minutes.
5. When cooked, the muffins will be golden brown.
6. Allow to cool for 5 to 10 minutes on a wire rack and serve warm.

Chocolate Banana Bread

Prep time: 10 minutes | Cook time: 30 minutes | Serves 4

¼ cup cocoa powder
6 tablespoons plus 2 teaspoons all-purpose flour, divided
½ teaspoon kosher salt
¼ teaspoon baking soda
1½ ripe bananas
1 large egg, whisked
¼ cup vegetable oil
½ cup sugar
3 tablespoons buttermilk or plain yogurt (not Greek)
½ teaspoon vanilla extract
6 tablespoons chopped white chocolate
6 tablespoons chopped walnuts

1. Mix the cocoa powder, 6 tablespoons of the flour, salt, and baking soda in a medium bowl.
2. Mash the bananas with a fork in another medium bowl until smooth. Fold in the egg, oil, sugar, buttermilk, and vanilla, and whisk until thoroughly combined. Add the wet mixture to the dry mixture and stir until well incorporated.
3. Combine the white chocolate, walnuts, and the remaining 2 tablespoons of flour in a third bowl and toss to coat. Add this mixture to the batter and stir until well incorporated. Pour the batter into a baking pan and smooth the top with a spatula.
4. Slide the pan into the air fryer oven. Cook at 310°F (154°C) for 30 minutes.
5. When done, a toothpick inserted into the center of the bread should come out clean.
6. Remove from the air fryer oven and allow to cool on a wire rack for 10 minutes before serving.

Coconut Brown Rice Porridge with Dates

Prep time: 5 minutes | Cook time: 23 minutes | Serves 1 or 2

½ cup cooked brown rice
1 cup canned coconut milk
¼ cup unsweetened shredded coconut
¼ cup packed dark brown sugar
4 large Medjool dates, pitted and roughly chopped
½ teaspoon kosher salt
¼ teaspoon ground cardamom
Heavy cream, for serving (optional)

1. Place all the ingredients except the heavy cream in a baking pan and stir until blended.
2. Slide the pan into the air fryer oven. Cook at 375°F (190°C) for 23 minutes.
3. Stir the porridge halfway through the cooking time.
4. When cooked, the porridge will be thick and creamy.
5. Remove from the air fryer oven and ladle the porridge into bowls.
6. Serve hot with a drizzle of the cream, if desired.

Corned Beef Hash with Eggs

Prep time: 10 minutes | Cook time: 25 minutes | Serves 4

2 medium Yukon Gold potatoes, peeled and cut into ¼-inch cubes
1 medium onion, chopped
⅓ cup diced red bell pepper
3 tablespoons vegetable oil
½ teaspoon dried thyme
½ teaspoon kosher salt, divided
½ teaspoon freshly ground black pepper, divided
¾ pound (340 g) corned beef, cut into ¼-inch pieces
4 large eggs

1. In a large bowl, stir together the potatoes, onion, red pepper, vegetable oil, thyme, ¼ teaspoon of the salt and ¼ teaspoon of the pepper. Spread the vegetable mixture on the sheet pan in an even layer.
2. Slide the pan into the air fryer oven. Cook at 375°F (190°C) for 25 minutes.
3. After 15 minutes, remove from the air fryer oven and add the corned beef. Stir the mixture to incorporate the corned beef. Return to the air fryer oven and continue cooking.
4. After 5 minutes, remove from the air fryer oven. Using a large spoon, create 4 circles in the hash to hold the eggs. Gently crack an egg into each circle. Season the eggs with the remaining ¼ teaspoon of the salt and ¼ teaspoon of the pepper. Return the pan to the air fryer oven. Continue cooking for 3 to 5 minutes, depending on how you like your eggs.
5. When cooking is complete, remove from the air fryer oven. Serve immediately.

Cornmeal Pancake

Prep time: 10 minutes | Cook time: 6 minutes | Serves 4

1½ cups yellow cornmeal
½ cup all-purpose flour
2 tablespoons sugar
1 teaspoon salt
1 teaspoon baking powder
1 cup whole or 2% milk
1 large egg, lightly beaten
1 tablespoon butter, melted
Cooking spray

1. Line an air fryer basket with parchment paper.
2. Stir together the cornmeal, flour, sugar, salt, and baking powder in a large bowl. Mix in the milk, egg, and melted butter and whisk to combine.
3. Drop tablespoonfuls of the batter onto the parchment paper for each pancake. Spray the pancakes with cooking spray. Arrange the pancakes on the air fryer basket.
4. Slide the basket into the air fryer oven. Cook at 350°F (180°C) for 6 minutes.
5. Flip the pancakes and spray with cooking spray again halfway through the cooking time.
6. When cooking is complete, remove the pancakes from the air fryer oven to a plate.
7. Cool for 5 minutes and serve immediately.

Creamy Quesadillas with Blueberries

Prep time: 5 minutes | Cook time: 4 minutes | Serves 2

¼ cup nonfat Ricotta cheese
¼ cup plain nonfat Greek yogurt
2 tablespoons finely ground flaxseeds
1 tablespoon granulated stevia
½ teaspoon cinnamon
¼ teaspoon vanilla extract
2 (8-inch) low-carb whole-wheat tortillas
½ cup fresh blueberries, divided

1. Line the sheet pan with the aluminum foil.
2. In a small bowl, whisk together the Ricotta cheese, yogurt, flaxseeds, stevia, cinnamon and vanilla.
3. Place the tortillas on the sheet pan. Spread half of the yogurt mixture on each tortilla, almost to the edges. Top each tortilla with ¼ cup of blueberries. Fold the tortillas in half.
4. Slide the pan into the air fryer oven. Cook at 400°F (205°C) for 4 minutes.
5. When cooking is complete, remove from the air fryer oven. Serve immediately.

Crustless Broccoli Quiche

Prep time: 5 minutes | Cook time: 10 minutes | Serves 4

1 cup broccoli florets
¾ cup chopped roasted red peppers
1¼ cups grated Fontina cheese
6 eggs
¾ cup heavy cream
½ teaspoon salt
Freshly ground black pepper, to taste
Cooking spray

1. Spritz a baking pan with cooking spray
2. Add the broccoli florets and roasted red peppers to the pan and scatter the grated Fontina cheese on top.
3. In a bowl, beat together the eggs and heavy cream. Sprinkle with salt and pepper. Pour the egg mixture over the top of the cheese. Wrap the pan in foil.
4. Slide the pan into the air fryer oven. Cook at 325°F (163°C) for 10 minutes.
5. After 8 minutes, remove from the air fryer oven. Remove the foil. Return to the air fryer oven and continue to cook another 2 minutes.
6. When cooked, the quiche should be golden brown.
7. Rest for 5 minutes before cutting into wedges and serve warm.

Easy Buttermilk Biscuits

Prep time: 5 minutes | Cook time: 18 minutes | Makes 16 biscuits

2½ cups all-purpose flour
1 tablespoon baking powder
1 teaspoon kosher salt
1 teaspoon sugar
½ teaspoon baking soda
8 tablespoons (1 stick) unsalted butter, at room temperature
1 cup buttermilk, chilled

1. Stir together the flour, baking powder, salt, sugar, and baking powder in a large bowl.
2. Add the butter and stir to mix well. Pour in the buttermilk and stir with a rubber spatula just until incorporated.
3. Place the dough onto a lightly floured surface and roll the dough out to a disk, ½ inch thick. Cut out the biscuits with a 2-inch round cutter and re-roll any scraps until you have 16 biscuits.
4. Arrange the biscuits in an air fryer basket.
5. Place the basket into the air fryer oven. Cook at 325°F (163°C) for 18 minutes.
6. When cooked, the biscuits will be golden brown.
7. Remove from the air fryer oven to a plate and serve hot.

Egg in a Hole

Prep time: 5 minutes | Cook time: 5 minutes | Serves 1

1 slice bread
1 teaspoon butter, softened
1 egg
Salt and pepper, to taste
1 tablespoon shredded Cheddar cheese
2 teaspoons diced ham

1. On a flat work surface, cut a hole in the center of the bread slice with a 2½-inch-diameter biscuit cutter.
2. Spread the butter evenly on each side of the bread slice and transfer to a baking dish.
3. Crack the egg into the hole and season as desired with salt and pepper. Scatter the shredded cheese and diced ham on top.
4. Place the baking dish in the air fryer oven. Cook at 330°F (166°C) for 5 minutes.
5. When cooking is complete, the bread should be lightly browned and the egg should be set. Remove from the air fryer oven and serve hot.

Egg and Avocado Burrito

Prep time: 10 minutes | Cook time: 4 minutes | Serves 4

4 low-sodium whole-wheat flour tortillas
Filling:
1 hard-boiled egg, chopped
2 hard-boiled egg whites, chopped
1 ripe avocado, peeled, pitted, and chopped
1 red bell pepper, chopped
1 (1.2-ounce / 34-g) slice low-sodium, low-fat American cheese, torn into pieces
3 tablespoons low-sodium salsa, plus additional for serving (optional)

Special Equipment:
4 toothpicks (optional), soaked in water for at least 30 minutes

1. Make the filling: Combine the egg, egg whites, avocado, red bell pepper, cheese, and salsa in a medium bowl and stir until blended.
2. Assemble the burritos: Arrange the tortillas on a clean work surface and place ¼ of the prepared filling in the middle of each tortilla, leaving about 1½-inch on each end unfilled. Fold in the opposite sides of each tortilla and roll up. Secure with toothpicks through the center, if needed.
3. Transfer the burritos to an air fryer basket.
4. Slide the basket into the air fryer oven. Cook at 390°F (199°C) for 4 minutes.
5. When cooking is complete, the burritos should be crisp and golden brown.
6. Allow to cool for 5 minutes and serve with salsa, if desired.

Breakfasts 21

Egg Florentine with Spinach

Prep time: 10 minutes | Cook time: 15 minutes | Serves 4

3 cups frozen spinach, thawed and drained
2 tablespoons heavy cream
¼ teaspoon kosher salt
⅛ teaspoon freshly ground black pepper
4 ounces (113 g) Ricotta cheese
2 garlic cloves, minced
½ cup panko bread crumbs
3 tablespoons grated Parmesan cheese
2 teaspoons unsalted butter, melted
4 large eggs

1. In a medium bowl, whisk together the spinach, heavy cream, salt, pepper, Ricotta cheese and garlic.
2. In a small bowl, whisk together the bread crumbs, Parmesan cheese and butter. Set aside.
3. Spoon the spinach mixture on the sheet pan and form four even circles.
4. Slide the pan into the air fryer oven. Cook at 375°F (190°C) for 15 minutes.
5. After 8 minutes, press Cancel and remove the pan. The spinach should be bubbling. With the back of a large spoon, make indentations in the spinach for the eggs. Crack the eggs into the indentations and sprinkle the panko mixture over the surface of the eggs.
6. Return to the air fryer oven and press Start to continue cooking.
7. When cooking is complete, remove from the air fryer oven. Serve hot.

Easy French Toast Casserole

Prep time: 5 minutes | Cook time: 12 minutes | Serves 6

3 large eggs, beaten
1 cup whole milk
1 tablespoon pure maple syrup
1 teaspoon vanilla extract
¼ teaspoon cinnamon
¼ teaspoon kosher salt
3 cups stale bread cubes
1 tablespoon unsalted butter, at room temperature

1. In a medium bowl, whisk together the eggs, milk, maple syrup, vanilla extract, cinnamon and salt. Stir in the bread cubes to coat well.
2. Grease the bottom of a sheet pan with the butter. Spread the bread mixture into the pan in an even layer.
3. Slide the pan into the air fryer oven. Cook at 350°F (180°C) for 12 minutes.
4. After about 10 minutes, remove the pan and check the casserole. The top should be browned and the middle of the casserole just set. If more time is needed, return the pan to the air fryer oven and continue cooking.
5. When cooking is complete, serve warm.

Eggs in Bell Pepper Rings

Prep time: 5 minutes | Cook time: 7 minutes | Serves 4

1 large red, yellow, or orange bell pepper, cut into four ¾-inch rings
4 eggs
Salt and freshly ground black pepper, to taste
2 teaspoons salsa
Cooking spray

1. Coat a baking pan lightly with cooking spray.
2. Put 4 bell pepper rings in the prepared baking pan. Crack one egg into each bell pepper ring and sprinkle with salt and pepper. Top each egg with ½ teaspoon of salsa.
3. Place the pan into the air fryer oven. Cook at 350°F (180°C) for 7 minutes.
4. When done, the eggs should be cooked to your desired doneness.
5. Remove the rings from the pan to a plate and serve warm.

French Toast Sticks

Prep time: 5 minutes | Cook time: 12 minutes | Serves 4

3 slices low-sodium whole-wheat bread, each cut into 4 strips
1 tablespoon unsalted butter, melted
1 tablespoon 2 percent milk
1 tablespoon sugar
1 egg, beaten
1 egg white
1 cup sliced fresh strawberries
1 tablespoon freshly squeezed lemon juice

1. Arrange the bread strips on a plate and drizzle with the melted butter.
2. In a bowl, whisk together the milk, sugar, egg and egg white.
3. Dredge the bread strips into the egg mixture and place on a wire rack to let the batter drip off. Arrange half the coated bread strips on the sheet pan.
4. Slide the pan into the air fryer oven. Cook at 380°F (193°C) for 6 minutes.
5. After 3 minutes, remove from the air fryer oven. Use a tong to turn the strips over. Rotate the pan and return the pan to the air fryer oven to continue cooking.
6. When cooking is complete, the strips should be golden brown. Repeat with the remaining strips.
7. In a small bowl, mash the strawberries with a fork and stir in the lemon juice. Serve the French toast sticks with the strawberry sauce.

Fried Cheese Grits

Prep time: 10 minutes | Cook time: 11 minutes | Serves 4

⅔ cup instant grits
1 teaspoon salt
1 teaspoon freshly ground black pepper
¾ cup whole or 2% milk
3 ounces (85 g) cream cheese, at room temperature
1 large egg, beaten
1 tablespoon butter, melted
1 cup shredded mild Cheddar cheese
Cooking spray

1. Mix the grits, salt, and black pepper in a large bowl. Add the milk, cream cheese, beaten egg, and melted butter and whisk to combine. Fold in the Cheddar cheese and stir well.
2. Spray a baking pan with cooking spray. Spread the grits mixture into the baking pan.
3. Place the pan into the air fryer oven. Cook at 400°F (205°C) for 11 minutes.
4. Stir the mixture halfway through the cooking time.
5. When done, a knife inserted in the center should come out clean.
6. Rest for 5 minutes and serve warm.

Maple Walnut Pancake

Prep time: 10 minutes | Cook time: 20 minutes | Serves 4

3 tablespoons melted butter, divided
1 cup flour
2 tablespoons sugar
1½ teaspoons baking powder
¼ teaspoon salt
1 egg, beaten
¾ cup milk
1 teaspoon pure vanilla extract
½ cup roughly chopped walnuts
Maple syrup or fresh sliced fruit, for serving

1. Grease a baking pan with 1 tablespoon of melted butter.
2. Mix the flour, sugar, baking powder, and salt in a medium bowl. Add the beaten egg, milk, the remaining 2 tablespoons of melted butter, and vanilla and stir until the batter is sticky but slightly lumpy.
3. Slowly pour the batter into the greased baking pan and scatter with the walnuts.
4. Place the pan into the air fryer oven. Cook at 330°F (166°C) for 20 minutes.
5. When cooked, the pancake should be golden brown and cooked through.
6. Let the pancake rest for 5 minutes and serve topped with the maple syrup or fresh fruit, if desired.

Ham and Cheese Toast

Prep time: 5 minutes | Cook time: 6 minutes | Serves: 1

1 slice bread
1 teaspoon butter, at room temperature
1 egg
Salt and freshly ground black pepper, to taste
2 teaspoons diced ham
1 tablespoon grated Cheddar cheese

1. On a clean work surface, use a 2½-inch biscuit cutter to make a hole in the center of the bread slice with about ½-inch of bread remaining.
2. Spread the butter on both sides of the bread slice. Crack the egg into the hole and season with salt and pepper to taste. Transfer the bread to an air fryer basket.
3. Slide the basket into the air fryer oven. Cook at 325°F (163°C) for 6 minutes.
4. After 5 minutes, remove from the air fryer oven. Scatter the cheese and diced ham on top and continue cooking for an additional 1 minute.
5. When cooking is complete, the egg should be set and the cheese should be melted. Remove the toast from the air fryer oven to a plate and let cool for 5 minutes before serving.

Mini Brown Rice Quiches

Prep time: 10 minutes | Cook time: 14 minutes | Serves 6

4 ounces (113 g) diced green chilies
3 cups cooked brown rice
1 cup shredded reduced-fat Cheddar cheese, divided
½ cup egg whites
⅓ cup fat-free milk
¼ cup diced pimiento
½ teaspoon cumin
1 small eggplant, cubed
1 bunch fresh cilantro, finely chopped
Cooking spray

1. Spritz a 12-cup muffin pan with cooking spray.
2. In a large bowl, stir together all the ingredients, except for ½ cup of the cheese.
3. Scoop the mixture evenly into the muffin cups and sprinkle the remaining ½ cup of the cheese on top.
4. Slide the pan into the air fryer oven. Cook at 400°F (205°C) for 14 minutes.
5. When cooking is complete, remove the pan and check the quiches. They should be set.
6. Carefully transfer the quiches to a platter and serve immediately.

Mixed Berry Dutch Baby Pancake

Prep time: 10 minutes | Cook time: 14 minutes | Serves 4

1 tablespoon unsalted butter, at room temperature
1 egg
2 egg whites
½ cup 2% milk
½ cup whole-wheat pastry flour
1 teaspoon pure vanilla extract
1 cup sliced fresh strawberries
½ cup fresh raspberries
½ cup fresh blueberries

1. Grease a baking pan with the butter.
2. Using a hand mixer, beat together the egg, egg whites, milk, pastry flour, and vanilla in a medium mixing bowl until well incorporated.
3. Pour the batter into the pan.
4. Slide the pan into the air fryer oven. Cook at 330°F (166°C) for 14 minutes.
5. When cooked, the pancake should puff up in the center and the edges should be golden brown
6. Allow the pancake to cool for 5 minutes and serve topped with the berries.

Olives, Kale, and Pecorino Baked Eggs

Prep time: 5 minutes | Cook time: 11 minutes | Serves 2

1 cup roughly chopped kale leaves, stems and center ribs removed
¼ cup grated pecorino cheese
¼ cup olive oil
1 garlic clove, peeled
3 tablespoons whole almonds
Kosher salt and freshly ground black pepper, to taste
4 large eggs
2 tablespoons heavy cream
3 tablespoons chopped pitted mixed olives

1. Place the kale, pecorino, olive oil, garlic, almonds, salt, and pepper in a small blender and blitz until well incorporated.
2. One at a time, crack the eggs in a baking pan. Drizzle the kale pesto on top of the egg whites. Top the yolks with the cream and swirl together the yolks and the pesto.
3. Slide the pan into the air fryer oven. Cook at 300°F (150°C) for 11 minutes.
4. When cooked, the top should be browned and the eggs should be set.
5. Allow the eggs to cool for 5 minutes. Scatter the olives on top and serve warm.

Glazed Strawberry Toast

Prep time: 5 minutes | Cook time: 8 minutes | Makes 4 toasts

4 slices bread, ½-inch thick
1 cup sliced strawberries
1 teaspoon sugar
Cooking spray

1. On a clean work surface, lay the bread slices and spritz one side of each slice of bread with cooking spray.
2. Place the bread slices in an air fryer basket, sprayed side down. Top with the strawberries and a sprinkle of sugar.
3. Slide the basket into the air fryer oven. Cook at 375°F (190°C) for 8 minutes.
4. When cooking is complete, the toast should be well browned on each side. Remove from the air fryer oven to a plate and serve.

Mini Cinnamon Rolls

Prep time: 5 minutes | Cook time: 25 minutes | Makes 18 rolls

⅓ cup light brown sugar
2 teaspoons cinnamon
1 (9-by-9-inch) frozen puff pastry sheet, thawed
All-purpose flour, for dusting
6 teaspoons unsalted butter, melted, divided

1. In a small bowl, stir together the brown sugar and cinnamon.
2. On a clean work surface, lightly dust with the flour and lay the puff pastry sheet. Using a rolling pin, press the folds together and roll the dough out in one direction so it measures about 9 by 11 inches. Cut it in half to form two squat rectangles of about 5½ by 9 inches.
3. Brush 2 teaspoons of the butter over each pastry half. Sprinkle with 2 tablespoons of the cinnamon sugar. Pat it down lightly with the palm of your hand to help it adhere to the butter.
4. Starting with the 9-inch side of one rectangle. Using your hands, carefully roll the dough into a cylinder. Repeat with the other rectangle. To make slicing easier, refrigerate the rolls for 10 to 20 minutes.
5. Using a sharp knife, slice each roll into nine 1-inch pieces. Transfer the rolls to the center of the sheet pan. They should be very close to each other, but not quite touching. Drizzle the remaining 2 teaspoons of the butter over the rolls and sprinkle with the remaining cinnamon sugar.
6. Slide the pan into the air fryer oven. Cook at 350°F (180°C) for 25 minutes.
7. When cooking is complete, remove the pan and check the rolls. They should be puffed up and golden brown.
8. Let the rolls rest for 5 minutes and transfer them to a wire rack to cool completely. Serve.

Peanut Butter-Pumpkin Muffins

Prep time: 10 minutes | Cook time: 25 minutes | Serves 2

2 tablespoons powdered peanut butter
2 tablespoons finely ground flaxseeds
2 tablespoons coconut flour
1 tablespoon dried cranberries
1 teaspoon pumpkin pie spice
½ teaspoon baking powder
½ cup water
1 cup canned pumpkin
2 large eggs
½ teaspoon vanilla extract
Cooking spray

1. In a bowl, stir together the powdered peanut butter, flaxseeds, coconut flour, dried cranberries, pumpkin pie spice, baking powder and water.
2. In another bowl, stir together the pumpkin and eggs until smooth.
3. Add the pumpkin mixture to the peanut butter mixture. Stir to combine. Add the vanilla extract to the bowl. Mix well.
4. Spritz 2 ramekins with cooking spray. Spoon half of the batter into each ramekin. Place the ramekins on a sheet pan.
5. Slide the pan into the air fryer oven. Cook at 350°F (180°C) for 25 minutes.
6. When cooking is complete, a toothpick inserted in the center should come out clean. Serve immediately.

Peppered Maple Bacon Knots

Prep time: 5 minutes | Cook time: 7 to 8 minutes | Serves 6

1 pound (454 g) maple smoked center-cut bacon
¼ cup maple syrup
¼ cup brown sugar
Coarsely cracked black peppercorns, to taste

1. On a clean work surface, tie each bacon strip in a loose knot.
2. Stir together the maple syrup and brown sugar in a bowl. Generously brush this mixture over the bacon knots.
3. Place the bacon knots in an air fryer basket and sprinkle with the coarsely cracked black peppercorns.
4. Slide the basket into the air fryer oven. Cook at 390°F (199°C) for 8 minutes.
5. After 5 minutes, remove the basket from the air fryer oven and flip the bacon knots. Return the basket to the air fryer oven and continue cooking for 2 to 3 minutes more.
6. When cooking is complete, the bacon should be crisp. Remove from the air fryer oven to a paper towel-lined plate. Let the bacon knots cool for a few minutes and serve warm.

Rice, Shrimp, and Spinach Frittata

Prep time: 15 minutes | Cook time: 16 minutes | Serves 4

4 eggs
Pinch salt
½ cup cooked rice
½ cup chopped cooked shrimp
½ cup baby spinach
½ cup grated Monterey Jack cheese
Nonstick cooking spray

1. Spritz a baking pan with nonstick cooking spray.
2. Whisk the eggs and salt in a small bowl until frothy.
3. Place the cooked rice, shrimp, and baby spinach in the baking pan. Pour in the whisked eggs and scatter the cheese on top.
4. Slide the pan into the air fryer oven. Cook at 320°F (160°C) for 16 minutes.
5. When cooking is complete, the frittata should be golden and puffy.
6. Let the frittata cool for 5 minutes before slicing to serve.

Spinach and Bacon English Muffins

Prep time: 5 minutes | Cook time: 10 minutes | Serves 4

2 strips turkey bacon, cut in half crosswise
2 whole-grain English muffins, split
1 cup fresh baby spinach, long stems removed
¼ ripe pear, peeled and thinly sliced
4 slices Provolone cheese

1. Put the turkey bacon strips in an air fryer basket.
2. Slide the basket into the air fryer oven. Cook at 390°F (199°C) for 6 minutes.
3. Flip the strips halfway through the cooking time.
4. When cooking is complete, the bacon should be crisp.
5. Remove from the air fryer oven and drain on paper towels. Set aside.
6. Put the muffin halves in the air fryer basket.
7. Cook for 2 minutes. Place the basket back to the air fryer oven. When done, the muffin halves will be lightly browned.
8. Remove from the air fryer oven. Top each muffin half with ¼ of the baby spinach, several pear slices, a strip of turkey bacon, followed by a slice of cheese.
9. Cook at 360°F (182°C) for 2 minutes. Place the basket back to the air fryer oven. When done, the cheese will be melted.
10. Serve warm.

Sausage and Cheese Quiche

Prep time: 5 minutes | Cook time: 25 minutes | Serves 4

12 large eggs
1 cup heavy cream
Salt and black pepper, to taste
12 ounces (340 g) sugar-free breakfast sausage
2 cups shredded Cheddar cheese
Cooking spray

1. Coat a casserole dish with cooking spray.
2. Beat together the eggs, heavy cream, salt and pepper in a large bowl until creamy. Stir in the breakfast sausage and Cheddar cheese.
3. Pour the sausage mixture into the prepared casserole dish.
4. Slide the dish into the air fryer oven. Cook at 375°F (190°C) for 25 minutes.
5. When done, the top of the quiche should be golden brown and the eggs will be set.
6. Remove from the air fryer oven and let sit for 5 to 10 minutes before serving.

Spinach, Leek and Cheese Frittata

Prep time: 10 minutes | Cook time: 22 minutes | Serves 2

4 large eggs
4 ounces (113 g) baby bella mushrooms, chopped
1 cup (1 ounce / 28-g) baby spinach, chopped
½ cup (2 ounces / 57-g) shredded Cheddar cheese
⅓ cup (from 1 large) chopped leek, white part only
¼ cup halved grape tomatoes
1 tablespoon 2% milk
¼ teaspoon dried oregano
¼ teaspoon garlic powder
½ teaspoon kosher salt
Freshly ground black pepper, to taste
Cooking spray

1. Lightly spritz a baking dish with cooking spray.
2. Whisk the eggs in a large bowl until frothy. Add the mushrooms, baby spinach, cheese, leek, tomatoes, milk, oregano, garlic powder, salt, and pepper and stir until well blended. Pour the mixture into the prepared baking dish.
3. Slide the baking dish into the air fryer oven. Cook at 300°F (150°C) for 22 minutes.
4. When cooked, the center will be puffed up and the top will be golden brown.
5. Let the frittata cool for 5 minutes before slicing to serve.

Simple Monkey Bread

Prep time: 5 minutes | Cook time: 8 minutes | Serves 4

1 (8-ounce / 227-g) can refrigerated biscuits
3 tablespoons melted unsalted butter
¼ cup white sugar
3 tablespoons brown sugar
½ teaspoon cinnamon
⅛ teaspoon nutmeg

1. On a clean work surface, cut each biscuit into 4 pieces.
2. In a shallow bowl, place the melted butter. In another shallow bowl, stir together the white sugar, brown sugar, cinnamon, and nutmeg until combined.
3. Dredge the biscuits, one at a time, in the melted butter, then roll them in the sugar mixture to coat well. Spread the biscuits evenly in a baking pan.
4. Slide the baking pan into the air fryer oven. Cook at 350°F (180°C) for 8 minutes.
5. When cooked, the biscuits should be golden brown.
6. Cool for 5 minutes before serving.

Spinach and Bacon Roll-ups

Prep time: 5 minutes | Cook time: 8 to 9 minutes | Serves 4

4 flour tortillas (6- or 7-inch size)
4 slices Swiss cheese
1 cup baby spinach leaves
4 slices turkey bacon

Special Equipment:
4 toothpicks, soak in water for at least 30 minutes

1. On a clean work surface, top each tortilla with one slice of cheese and ¼ cup of spinach, then tightly roll them up.
2. Wrap each tortilla with a strip of turkey bacon and secure with a toothpick.
3. Arrange the roll-ups in an air fryer basket, leaving space between each roll-up.
4. Slider the basket in the air fryer oven. Cook at 390°F (199°C) for 8 minutes.
5. After 4 minutes, remove from the air fryer oven. Flip the roll-ups with tongs and rearrange them for more even cooking. Return to the air fryer oven and continue cooking for another 4 minutes.
6. When cooking is complete, the bacon should be crisp. If necessary, continue cooking for 1 minute more. Remove from the air fryer oven. Rest for 5 minutes and remove the toothpicks before serving.

Sweet Banana Bread Pudding

Prep time: 10 minutes | Cook time: 18 minutes | Serves 4

2 medium ripe bananas, mashed
½ cup low-fat milk
2 tablespoons maple syrup
2 tablespoons peanut butter
1 teaspoon vanilla extract
1 teaspoon ground cinnamon
2 slices whole-grain bread, torn into bite-sized pieces
¼ cup quick oats
Cooking spray

1. Spritz the sheet pan with cooking spray.
2. In a large bowl, combine the bananas, milk, maple syrup, peanut butter, vanilla extract and cinnamon. Use an immersion blender to mix until well combined.
3. Stir in the bread pieces to coat well. Add the oats and stir until everything is combined.
4. Transfer the mixture to the sheet pan. Cover with the aluminum foil.
5. Slide the pan into the air fryer oven. Cook at 375°F (190°C) for 18 minutes.
6. After 10 minutes, remove the foil and continue to cook for 8 minutes.
7. Serve immediately.

Fried Potatoes with Peppers and Onions

Prep time: 10 minutes | Cook time: 35 minutes | Serves 4

1 pound (454 g) red potatoes, cut into ½-inch dices
1 large red bell pepper, cut into ½-inch dices
1 large green bell pepper, cut into ½-inch dices
1 medium onion, cut into ½-inch dices
1½ tablespoons extra-virgin olive oil
1¼ teaspoons kosher salt
¾ teaspoon sweet paprika
¾ teaspoon garlic powder
Freshly ground black pepper, to taste

1. Mix the potatoes, bell peppers, onion, oil, salt, paprika, garlic powder, and black pepper in a large mixing and toss to coat.
2. Transfer the potato mixture to an air fryer basket.
3. Slide the basket into the air fryer oven. Cook at 350°F (180°C) for 35 minutes.
4. Stir the potato mixture three times during cooking.
5. When done, the potatoes should be nicely browned.
6. Remove from the air fryer oven to a plate and serve warm.

Vanilla Granola

Prep time: 5 minutes | Cook time: 40 minutes | Serves 4

1 cup rolled oats
3 tablespoons maple syrup
1 tablespoon sunflower oil
1 tablespoon coconut sugar
¼ teaspoon vanilla
¼ teaspoon cinnamon
¼ teaspoon sea salt

1. Mix the oats, maple syrup, sunflower oil, coconut sugar, vanilla, cinnamon, and sea salt in a medium bowl and stir to combine. Transfer the mixture to a baking pan.
2. Slide the pan into the air fryer oven. Cook at 248°F (120°C) for 40 minutes.
3. Stir the granola four times during cooking.
4. When cooking is complete, the granola will be mostly dry and lightly browned.
5. Let the granola stand for 5 to 10 minutes before serving.

Veggie Frittata

Prep time: 10 minutes | Cook time: 12 minutes | Serves 4

½ cup chopped red bell pepper
⅓ cup grated carrot
⅓ cup minced onion
1 teaspoon olive oil
1 egg
6 egg whites
⅓ cup 2% milk
1 tablespoon shredded Parmesan cheese

1. Mix the red bell pepper, carrot, onion, and olive oil in a baking pan and stir to combine.
2. Place the pan into the air fryer oven. Cook at 350°F (180°C) for 12 minutes.
3. After 3 minutes, remove from the air fryer oven. Stir the vegetables. Return to the air fryer oven and continue cooking.
4. Meantime, whisk together the egg, egg whites, and milk in a medium bowl until creamy.
5. After 3 minutes, remove from the air fryer oven. Pour the egg mixture over the top and scatter with the Parmesan cheese. Return to the air fryer oven and continue cooking for additional 6 minutes.
6. When cooking is complete, the eggs will be set and the top will be golden around the edges.
7. Allow the frittata to cool for 5 minutes before slicing and serving.

Tomato-Corn Frittata with Avocado Dressing

Prep time: 10 minutes | Cook time: 20 minutes | Serves 2 or 3

½ cup cherry tomatoes, halved
Kosher salt and freshly ground black pepper, to taste
6 large eggs, lightly beaten
½ cup fresh corn kernels
¼ cup milk
1 tablespoon finely chopped fresh dill
½ cup shredded Monterey Jack cheese
Avocado Dressing:
1 ripe avocado, pitted and peeled
2 tablespoons fresh lime juice
¼ cup olive oil
1 scallion, finely chopped
8 fresh basil leaves, finely chopped

1. Put the tomato halves in a colander and lightly season with salt. Set aside for 10 minutes to drain well. Pour the tomatoes into a large bowl and fold in the eggs, corn, milk, and dill. Sprinkle with salt and pepper and stir until mixed.
2. Pour the egg mixture into a baking pan.
3. Slide the pan into the air fryer oven. Cook at 300°F (150°C) for 15 minutes.
4. When done, remove from the air fryer oven. Scatter the cheese on top.
5. Cook at 315°F (157°C) for 5 minutes. Return the pan back to the air fryer oven.
6. When cooking is complete, the frittata will be puffy and set.
7. Meanwhile, make the avocado dressing: Mash the avocado with the lime juice in a medium bowl until smooth. Mix in the olive oil, scallion, and basil and stir until well incorporated.
8. Let the frittata cool for 5 minutes and serve alongside the avocado dressing.

Spicy Apple Turnovers

Prep time: 10 minutes | Cook time: 20 minutes | Serves 4

1 cup diced apple
1 tablespoon brown sugar
1 teaspoon freshly squeezed lemon juice
1 teaspoon all-purpose flour, plus more for dusting
¼ teaspoon cinnamon
⅛ teaspoon allspice
½ package frozen puff pastry, thawed
1 large egg, beaten
2 teaspoons granulated sugar

1. Whisk together the apple, brown sugar, lemon juice, flour, cinnamon and allspice in a medium bowl.
2. On a clean work surface, lightly dust with the flour and lay the puff pastry sheet. Using a rolling pin, gently roll the dough to smooth out the folds, seal any tears and form it into a square. Cut the dough into four squares.
3. Spoon a quarter of the apple mixture into the center of each puff pastry square and spread it evenly in a triangle shape over half the pastry, leaving a border of about ½ inch around the edges of the pastry. Fold the pastry diagonally over the filling to form triangles. With a fork, crimp the edges to seal them. Place the turnovers on the sheet pan, spacing them evenly.
4. Cut two or three small slits in the top of each turnover. Brush with the egg. Sprinkle evenly with the granulated sugar.
5. Slide the pan into the air fryer oven. Cook at 350°F (180°C) for 20 minutes.
6. After 10 to 12 minutes, remove from the air fryer oven. Check the pastries. If they are browned unevenly, rotate the pan. Return to the air fryer oven and continue cooking.
7. When cooking is complete, remove from the air fryer oven. The turnovers should be golden brown and the filling bubbling. Let cool for about 10 minutes before serving.

Turkey Breakfast Sausage Patties

Prep time: 5 minutes | Cook time: 10 minutes | Serves 4

1 tablespoon chopped fresh thyme
1 tablespoon chopped fresh sage
1¼ teaspoons kosher salt
1 teaspoon chopped fennel seeds
¾ teaspoon smoked paprika
½ teaspoon onion powder
½ teaspoon garlic powder
⅛ teaspoon crushed red pepper flakes
⅛ teaspoon freshly ground black pepper
1 pound (454 g) 93% lean ground turkey
½ cup finely minced sweet apple (peeled)

1. Thoroughly combine the thyme, sage, salt, fennel seeds, paprika, onion powder, garlic powder, red pepper flakes, and black pepper in a medium bowl.
2. Add the ground turkey and apple and stir until well incorporated. Divide the mixture into 8 equal portions and shape into patties with your hands, each about ¼ inch thick and 3 inches in diameter.
3. Place the patties in an air fryer basket.
4. Slide the basket into the air fryer oven. Cook at 400°F (205°C) for 10 minutes.
5. Flip the patties halfway through the cooking time.
6. When cooking is complete, the patties should be nicely browned and cooked through. Remove from the air fryer oven to a plate and serve warm.

Western Omelet

Prep time: 5 minutes | Cook time: 20 minutes | Serves 2

¼ cup chopped bell pepper, green or red
¼ cup chopped onion
¼ cup diced ham
1 teaspoon butter
4 large eggs
2 tablespoons milk
⅛ teaspoon salt
¾ cup shredded sharp Cheddar cheese

1. Put the bell pepper, onion, ham, and butter in a baking pan and mix well.
2. Slide the pan into the air fryer oven. Cook at 390°F (199°C) for 5 minutes.
3. After 1 minute, remove from the air fryer oven. Stir the mixture. Return to the air fryer oven and continue to cook another 4 minutes.
4. When done, the veggies should be softened.
5. Whisk together the eggs, milk, and salt in a bowl. Pour the egg mixture over the veggie mixture.
6. Place the pan in the air fryer oven. Cook at 360°F (182°C) for 15 minutes.
7. After 14 minutes, remove from the air fryer oven. Scatter the omelet with the shredded cheese. Return to the air fryer oven and continue to cook another 1 minute.
8. When cooking is complete, the top will be lightly golden browned, the eggs will be set and the cheese will be melted.
9. Let the omelet cool for 5 minutes before serving.

Whole-Wheat Blueberry Scones

Prep time: 5 minutes | Cook time: 20 minutes | Serves 14

½ cup low-fat buttermilk
¾ cup orange juice
Zest of 1 orange
2¼ cups whole-wheat pastry flour
⅓ cup agave nectar
¼ cup canola oil
1 teaspoon baking soda
1 teaspoon cream of tartar
1 cup fresh blueberries

1. In a small bowl, stir together the buttermilk, orange juice and orange zest.
2. In a large bowl, whisk together the flour, agave nectar, canola oil, baking soda and cream of tartar.
3. Add the buttermilk mixture and blueberries to the bowl with the flour mixture. Mix gently by hand until well combined.
4. Transfer the batter onto a lightly floured baking sheet. Pat into a circle about ¾ inch thick and 8 inches across. Use a knife to cut the circle into 14 wedges, cutting almost all the way through.
5. Slide the baking sheet into the air fryer oven. Cook at 375°F (190°C) for 20 minutes.
6. When cooking is complete, remove the baking sheet and check the scones. They should be lightly browned.
7. Let rest for 5 minutes and cut through the wedges before serving.

Whole-Wheat Muffins with Blueberries

Prep time: 5 minutes | Cook time: 25 minutes | Makes 8 muffins

½ cup unsweetened applesauce
½ cup plant-based milk
½ cup maple syrup
1 teaspoon vanilla extract
2 cups whole-wheat flour
½ teaspoon baking soda
1 cup blueberries
Cooking spray

1. Spritz a 8-cup muffin pan with cooking spray.
2. In a large bowl, stir together the applesauce, milk, maple syrup and vanilla extract. Whisk in the flour and baking soda until no dry flour is left and the batter is smooth. Gently mix in the blueberries until they are evenly distributed throughout the batter.
3. Spoon the batter into the muffin cups, three-quarters full.
4. Slide the pan into the air fryer oven. Cook at 375°F (190°C) for 25 minutes.
5. When cooking is complete, remove the pan and check the muffins. You can stick a knife into the center of a muffin and it should come out clean.
6. Let rest for 5 minutes before serving.

Casseroles, Frittata, and Quiche

Broccoli, Carrot, and Tomato Quiche

Prep time: 6 minutes | Cook time: 14 minutes | Serves 4

4 eggs
1 teaspoon dried thyme
1 cup whole milk
1 steamed carrots, diced
2 cups steamed broccoli florets
2 medium tomatoes, diced
¼ cup crumbled feta cheese
1 cup grated Cheddar cheese
1 teaspoon chopped parsley
Salt and ground black pepper, to taste
Cooking spray

1. Spritz a baking pan with cooking spray.
2. Whisk together the eggs, thyme, salt, and ground black pepper in a bowl and fold in the milk while mixing.
3. Put the carrots, broccoli, and tomatoes in the prepared baking pan, then spread with feta cheese and ½ cup Cheddar cheese. Pour the egg mixture over, then scatter with remaining Cheddar on top.
4. Slide the pan into the air fryer oven. Cook at 350°F (180°C) for 14 minutes.
5. When cooking is complete, the egg should be set and the quiche should be puffed.
6. Remove the quiche from the air fryer oven and top with chopped parsley, then slice to serve.

Burgundy Beef and Mushroom Casserole

Prep time: 10 minutes | Cook time: 25 minutes | Serves 4

1½ pounds (680 g) beef steak
1 ounce (28 g) dry onion soup mix
2 cups sliced mushrooms
1 (14.5-ounce / 411-g) can cream of mushroom soup
½ cup beef broth
¼ cup red wine
3 garlic cloves, minced
1 whole onion, chopped

1. Put the beef steak in a large bowl, then sprinkle with dry onion soup mix. Toss to coat well.
2. Combine the mushrooms with mushroom soup, beef broth, red wine, garlic, and onion in a large bowl. Stir to mix well.
3. Transfer the beef steak in a baking pan, then pour in the mushroom mixture.
4. Slide the pan into the air fryer oven. Cook at 360°F (182°C) for 25 minutes.
5. When cooking is complete, the mushrooms should be soft and the beef should be well browned.
6. Remove the baking pan from the air fryer oven and serve immediately.

Cauliflower and Pumpkin Casserole

Prep time: 15 minutes | Cook time: 50 minutes | Serves 6

1 cup chicken broth
2 cups cauliflower florets
1 cup canned pumpkin purée
¼ cup heavy cream
1 teaspoon vanilla extract
2 large eggs, beaten
⅓ cup unsalted butter, melted, plus more for greasing the pan
¼ cup sugar
1 teaspoon fine sea salt
Chopped fresh parsley leaves, for garnish
TOPPING:
½ cup blanched almond flour
1 cup chopped pecans
⅓ cup unsalted butter, melted
½ cup sugar

1. Pour the chicken broth in a baking pan, then add the cauliflower.
2. Slide the pan into the air fryer oven. Cook at 350°F (180°C) for 20 minutes.
3. When cooking is complete, the cauliflower should be soft.
4. Meanwhile, combine the ingredients for the topping in a large bowl. Stir to mix well.
5. Pat the cauliflower dry with paper towels, then place in a food processor and pulse with pumpkin purée, heavy cream, vanilla extract, eggs, butter, sugar, and salt until smooth.
6. Clean the baking pan and grease with more butter, then pour the purée mixture in the pan. Spread the topping over the mixture.
7. Place the baking pan back to the air fryer oven. Bake for 30 minutes.
8. When baking is complete, the topping of the casserole should be lightly browned.
9. Remove the casserole from the air fryer oven and serve with fresh parsley on top.

Cheesy Green Bean Casserole

Prep time: 4 minutes | Cook time: 6 minutes | Serves 4

1 tablespoon melted butter
1 cup green beans
6 ounces (170 g) Cheddar cheese, shredded
7 ounces (198 g) Parmesan cheese, shredded
¼ cup heavy cream
Sea salt, to taste

1. Grease a baking pan with the melted butter.
2. Add the green beans, Cheddar, salt, and black pepper to the prepared baking pan. Stir to mix well, then spread the Parmesan and cream on top.
3. Slide the pan into the air fryer oven. Cook at 400°F (205°C) for 6 minutes.
4. When cooking is complete, the beans should be tender and the cheese should be melted.
5. Serve immediately.

Chicken Divan

Prep time: 5 minutes | Cook time: 24 minutes | Serves 4

4 chicken breasts
Salt and ground black pepper, to taste
1 head broccoli, cut into florets
½ cup cream of mushroom soup
1 cup shredded Cheddar cheese
½ cup croutons
Cooking spray

1. Spritz an air fryer basket with cooking spray.
2. Put the chicken breasts in the air fryer basket and sprinkle with salt and ground black pepper.
3. Slide the basket into the air fryer oven. Cook at 390°F (199°C) for 14 minutes.
4. Flip the breasts halfway through the cooking time.
5. When cooking is complete, the breasts should be well browned and tender.
6. Remove the breasts from the air fryer oven and allow to cool for a few minutes on a plate, then cut the breasts into bite-size pieces.
7. Combine the chicken, broccoli, mushroom soup, and Cheddar cheese in a large bowl. Stir to mix well.
8. Spritz a baking pan with cooking spray. Pour the chicken mixture into the pan. Spread the croutons over the mixture.
9. Set time to 10 minutes. Place the pan into the air fryer oven.
10. When cooking is complete, the croutons should be lightly browned and the mixture should be set.
11. Remove the baking pan from the air fryer oven and serve immediately.

Chicken Ham Casserole

Prep time: 15 minutes | Cook time: 15 minutes | Serves 4 to 6

2 cups diced cooked chicken
1 cup diced ham
¼ teaspoon ground nutmeg
½ cup half-and-half
½ teaspoon ground black pepper
6 slices Swiss cheese
Cooking spray

1. Spritz a baking pan with cooking spray.
2. Combine the chicken, ham, nutmeg, half-and-half, and ground black pepper in a large bowl. Stir to mix well.
3. Pour half of the mixture into the baking pan, then top the mixture with 3 slices of Swiss cheese, then pour in the remaining mixture and top with remaining cheese slices.
4. Slide the pan into the air fryer oven. Cook at 350°F (180°C) for 15 minutes.
5. When cooking is complete, the egg should be set and the cheese should be melted.
6. Serve immediately.

Chicken Sausage and Broccoli Casserole

Prep time: 10 minutes | Cook time: 20 minutes | Serves 8

10 eggs
1 cup Cheddar cheese, shredded and divided
¾ cup heavy whipping cream
1 (12-ounce / 340-g) package cooked chicken sausage
1 cup broccoli, chopped
2 cloves garlic, minced
½ tablespoon salt
¼ tablespoon ground black pepper
Cooking spray

1. Spritz a baking pan with cooking spray.
2. Whisk the eggs with Cheddar and cream in a large bowl to mix well.
3. Combine the cooked sausage, broccoli, garlic, salt, and ground black pepper in a separate bowl. Stir to mix well.
4. Pour the sausage mixture into the baking pan, then spread the egg mixture over to cover.
5. Slide the pan into the air fryer oven. Cook at 400°F (205°C) for 20 minutes.
6. When cooking is complete, the egg should be set and a toothpick inserted in the center should come out clean.
7. Serve immediately.

Chorizo, Corn, and Potato Frittata

Prep time: 8 minutes | Cook time: 12 minutes | Serves 4

2 tablespoons olive oil
1 chorizo, sliced
4 eggs
½ cup corn
1 large potato, boiled and cubed
1 tablespoon chopped parsley
½ cup feta cheese, crumbled
Salt and ground black pepper, to taste

1. Heat the olive oil in a nonstick skillet over medium heat until shimmering.
2. Add the chorizo and cook for 4 minutes or until golden brown.
3. Whisk the eggs in a bowl, then sprinkle with salt and ground black pepper.
4. Mix the remaining ingredients in the egg mixture, then pour the chorizo and its fat into a baking pan. Pour in the egg mixture.
5. Slide the pan into the air fryer oven. Cook at 330°F (166°C) for 8 minutes.
6. Stir the mixture halfway through.
7. When cooking is complete, the eggs should be set.
8. Serve immediately.

Easy Corn and Bell Pepper Casserole

Prep time: 10 minutes | Cook time: 20 minutes | Serves 4

1 cup corn kernels
¼ cup bell pepper, finely chopped
½ cup low-fat milk
1 large egg, beaten
½ cup yellow cornmeal
½ cup all-purpose flour
½ teaspoon baking powder
2 tablespoons melted unsalted butter
1 tablespoon granulated sugar
Pinch of cayenne pepper
¼ teaspoon kosher salt
Cooking spray

1. Spritz a baking pan with cooking spray.
2. Combine all the ingredients in a large bowl. Stir to mix well. Pour the mixture into the baking pan.
3. Slide the pan into the air fryer oven. Cook at 330°F (166°C) for 20 minutes.
4. When cooking is complete, the casserole should be lightly browned and set.
5. Remove the baking pan from the air fryer oven and serve immediately.

Goat Cheese and Asparagus Frittata

Prep time: 5 minutes | Cook time: 25 minutes | Serves 2 to 4

1 cup asparagus spears, cut into 1-inch pieces
1 teaspoon vegetable oil
1 tablespoon milk
6 eggs, beaten
2 ounces (57 g) goat cheese, crumbled
1 tablespoon minced chives, optional
Kosher salt and pepper, to taste

1. Add the asparagus spears to a small bowl and drizzle with the vegetable oil. Toss until well coated and transfer to an air fryer basket.
2. Slide the basket into the air fryer oven. Cook at 400°F (205°C) for 5 minutes.
3. Flip the asparagus halfway through.
4. When cooking is complete, the asparagus should be tender and slightly wilted.
5. Remove the basket from the air fryer oven. Transfer the asparagus in a baking pan.
6. Stir together the milk and eggs in a medium bowl. Pour the mixture over the asparagus in the pan. Sprinkle with the goat cheese and the chives (if using) over the eggs. Season with salt and pepper.
7. Slide the pan into the air fryer oven. Cook at 320°F (160°C) for 20 minutes. Press Start.
8. When cooking is complete, the top should be golden and the eggs should be set.
9. Transfer to a serving dish. Slice and serve.

Greek Frittata

Prep time: 7 minutes | Cook time: 8 minutes | Serves 2

1 cup chopped mushrooms
2 cups spinach, chopped
4 eggs, lightly beaten
3 ounces (85 g) feta cheese, crumbled
2 tablespoons heavy cream
A handful of fresh parsley, chopped
Salt and ground black pepper, to taste
Cooking spray

1. Spritz a baking pan with cooking spray.
2. Whisk together all the ingredients in a large bowl. Stir to mix well.
3. Pour the mixture in the prepared baking pan.
4. Slide the pan into the air fryer oven. Cook at 350°F (180°C) for 8 minutes.
5. Stir the mixture halfway through.
6. When cooking is complete, the eggs should be set.
7. Serve immediately.

Casseroles, Frittata, and Quiche

Grits and Asparagus Casserole

Prep time: 5 minutes | Cook time: 30 minutes | Serves 4

10 fresh asparagus spears, cut into 1-inch pieces
2 cups cooked grits, cooled to room temperature
2 teaspoons Worcestershire sauce
1 egg, beaten
½ teaspoon garlic powder
¼ teaspoon salt
2 slices provolone cheese, crushed
Cooking spray

1. Spritz a baking pan with cooking spray.
2. Set the asparagus in the air fryer basket. Spritz the asparagus with cooking spray.
3. Slide the pan into the air fryer oven. Cook at 390°F (199°C) for 5 minutes.
4. Flip the asparagus halfway through.
5. When cooking is complete, the asparagus should be lightly browned and crispy.
6. Meanwhile, combine the grits, Worcestershire sauce, egg, garlic powder, and salt in a bowl. Stir to mix well.
7. Pour half of the grits mixture in the prepared baking pan, then spread with fried asparagus.
8. Spread the cheese over the asparagus and pour the remaining grits over.
9. Set time to 25 minutes. Place the pan into the air fryer oven.
10. When cooking is complete, the egg should be set.
11. Serve immediately.

Herbed Cheddar Frittata

Prep time: 10 minutes | Cook time: 20 minutes | Serves 4

½ cup shredded Cheddar cheese
½ cup half-and-half
4 large eggs
2 tablespoons chopped scallion greens
2 tablespoons chopped fresh parsley
½ teaspoon kosher salt
½ teaspoon ground black pepper
Cooking spray

1. Spritz a baking pan with cooking spray.
2. Whisk together all the ingredients in a large bowl, then pour the mixture into the prepared baking pan.
3. Slide the pan into the air fryer oven. Cook at 300°F (150°C) for 20 minutes.
4. Stir the mixture halfway through.
5. When cooking is complete, the eggs should be set.
6. Serve immediately.

Hillbilly Broccoli Cheese Casserole

Prep time: 5 minutes | Cook time: 30 minutes | Serves 6

4 cups broccoli florets
¼ cup heavy whipping cream
½ cup sharp Cheddar cheese, shredded
¼ cup ranch dressing
Kosher salt and ground black pepper, to taste

1. Combine all the ingredients in a large bowl. Toss to coat well broccoli well.
2. Pour the mixture into a baking pan.
3. Slide the pan into the air fryer oven. Cook at 375°F (190°C) for 30 minutes.
4. When cooking is complete, the broccoli should be tender.
5. Remove the baking pan from the air fryer oven and serve immediately.

Creamy Pork Gratin

Prep time: 15 minutes | Cook time: 21 minutes | Serves 4

2 tablespoons olive oil
2 pounds (907 g) pork tenderloin, cut into serving-size pieces
1 teaspoon dried marjoram
¼ teaspoon chili powder
1 teaspoon coarse sea salt
½ teaspoon freshly ground black pepper
1 cup Ricotta cheese
1½ cups chicken broth
1 tablespoon mustard
Cooking spray

1. Spritz a baking pan with cooking spray.
2. Heat the olive oil in a nonstick skillet over medium-high heat until shimmering.
3. Add the pork and sauté for 6 minutes or until lightly browned.
4. Transfer the pork to the prepared baking pan and sprinkle with marjoram, chili powder, salt, and ground black pepper.
5. Combine the remaining ingredients in a large bowl. Stir to mix well. Pour the mixture over the pork in the pan.
6. Slide the pan into the air fryer oven. Cook at 350°F (180°C) for 15 minutes.
7. Stir the mixture halfway through.
8. When cooking is complete, the mixture should be frothy and the cheese should be melted.
9. Serve immediately.

Kale Frittata

Prep time: 5 minutes | Cook time: 11 minutes | Serves 2

1 cup kale, chopped
1 teaspoon olive oil
4 large eggs, beaten
Kosher salt, to taste
2 tablespoons water
3 tablespoons crumbled feta
Cooking spray

1. Spritz a baking pan with cooking spray.
2. Add the kale to the baking pan and drizzle with olive oil.
3. Slide the pan into the air fryer oven. Cook at 360°F (182°C) for 3 minutes.
4. Stir the kale halfway through.
5. When cooking is complete, the kale should be wilted.
6. Meanwhile, combine the eggs with salt and water in a large bowl. Stir to mix well.
7. Make the frittata: When broiling is complete, pour the eggs into the baking pan and spread with feta cheese.
8. Slide the pan into the air fryer oven. Cook at 300°F (150°C) for 8 minutes. Press Start.
9. When cooking is complete, the eggs should be set and the cheese should be melted.
10. Remove the baking pan from the air fryer oven and serve the frittata immediately.

Keto Cheese Quiche

Prep time: 20 minutes | Cook time: 1 hour | Serves 8

Crust:
1¼ cups blanched almond flour
1 large egg, beaten
1¼ cups grated Parmesan cheese
¼ teaspoon fine sea salt
Filling:
4 ounces (113 g) cream cheese
1 cup shredded Swiss cheese
⅓ cup minced leeks
4 large eggs, beaten
½ cup chicken broth
⅛ teaspoon cayenne pepper
¾ teaspoon fine sea salt
1 tablespoon unsalted butter, melted
Chopped green onions, for garnish
Cooking spray

1. Spritz a pie pan with cooking spray.
2. Combine the flour, egg, Parmesan, and salt in a large bowl. Stir to mix until a satiny and firm dough forms.
3. Arrange the dough between two grease parchment papers, then roll the dough into a ¹⁄₁₆-inch thick circle.
4. Make the crust: Transfer the dough into the prepared pie pan and press to coat the bottom.
5. Slide the pan into the air fryer oven. Cook at 325°F (163°C) for 12 minutes.
6. When cooking is complete, the edges of the crust should be lightly browned.
7. Meanwhile, combine the ingredient for the filling, except for the green onions in a large bowl.
8. Pour the filling over the cooked crust and cover the edges of the crust with aluminum foil.
9. Set time to 15 minutes. Press Start.
10. When cooking is complete, reduce the heat to 300°F (150°C) for 30 minutes.
11. When cooking is complete, a toothpick inserted in the center should come out clean.
12. Remove the pie pan from the air fryer oven and allow to cool for 10 minutes before serving.

Ritzy Chicken and Vegetable Casserole

Prep time: 15 minutes | Cook time: 15 minutes | Serves 4

4 boneless and skinless chicken breasts, cut into cubes
2 carrots, sliced
1 yellow bell pepper, cut into strips
1 red bell pepper, cut into strips
15 ounces (425 g) broccoli florets
1 cup snow peas
1 scallion, sliced
Cooking spray
Sauce:
1 teaspoon Sriracha
3 tablespoons soy sauce
2 tablespoons oyster sauce
1 tablespoon rice wine vinegar
1 teaspoon cornstarch
1 tablespoon grated ginger
2 garlic cloves, minced
1 teaspoon sesame oil
1 tablespoon brown sugar

1. Spritz a baking pan with cooking spray.
2. Combine the chicken, carrot, and bell peppers in a large bowl. Stir to mix well.
3. Combine the ingredients for the sauce in a separate bowl. Stir to mix well.
4. Pour the chicken mixture into the baking pan, then pour the sauce over. Stir to coat well.
5. Slide the pan into the air fryer oven. Cook at 370°F (188°C) for 13 minutes.
6. Add the broccoli and snow peas to the pan halfway through.
7. When cooking is complete, the vegetables should be tender.
8. Remove the pan from the air fryer oven and sprinkle with sliced scallion before serving.

Lush Seafood Casserole

Prep time: 8 minutes | Cook time: 22 minutes | Serves 2

1 tablespoon olive oil
1 small yellow onion, chopped
2 garlic cloves, minced
4 ounces (113 g) tilapia pieces
4 ounces (113 g) rockfish pieces
½ teaspoon dried basil
Salt and ground white pepper, to taste
4 eggs, lightly beaten
1 tablespoon dry sherry
4 tablespoons cheese, shredded

1. Heat the olive oil in a nonstick skillet over medium-high heat until shimmering.
2. Add the onion and garlic and sauté for 2 minutes or until fragrant.
3. Add the tilapia, rockfish, basil, salt, and white pepper to the skillet. Sauté to combine well and transfer them on a baking pan.
4. Combine the eggs, sherry and cheese in a large bowl. Stir to mix well. Pour the mixture in the baking pan over the fish mixture.
5. Slide the pan into the air fryer oven. Cook at 360°F (182°C) for 20 minutes.
6. When cooking is complete, the eggs should be set and the casserole edges should be lightly browned.
7. Serve immediately.

Pastrami Casserole

Prep time: 10 minutes | Cook time: 8 minutes | Serves 2

1 cup pastrami, sliced
1 bell pepper, chopped
¼ cup Greek yogurt
2 spring onions, chopped
½ cup Cheddar cheese, grated
4 eggs
¼ teaspoon ground black pepper
Sea salt, to taste
Cooking spray

1. Spritz a baking pan with cooking spray.
2. Whisk together all the ingredients in a large bowl. Stir to mix well. Pour the mixture into the baking pan.
3. Slide the pan into the air fryer oven. Cook at 330°F (166°C) for 8 minutes.
4. When cooking is complete, the eggs should be set and the casserole edges should be lightly browned.
5. Remove the baking pan from the air fryer oven and allow to cool for 10 minutes before serving.

Riced Cauliflower Casserole

Prep time: 8 minutes | Cook time: 12 minutes | Serves 4

1 head cauliflower, cut into florets
1 cup okra, chopped
1 yellow bell pepper, chopped
2 eggs, beaten
½ cup chopped onion
1 tablespoon soy sauce
2 tablespoons olive oil
Salt and ground black pepper, to taste

1. Spritz a baking pan with cooking spray.
2. Put the cauliflower in a food processor and pulse to rice the cauliflower.
3. Pour the cauliflower rice in the baking pan and add the remaining ingredients. Stir to mix well.
4. Slide the pan into the air fryer oven. Cook at 380°F (193°C) for 12 minutes.
5. When cooking is complete, the eggs should be set.
6. Remove the baking pan from the air fryer oven and serve immediately.

Sumptuous Vegetable Frittata

Prep time: 15 minutes | Cook time: 20 minutes | Serves 2

4 eggs
⅓ cup milk
2 teaspoons olive oil
1 large zucchini, sliced
2 asparagus, sliced thinly
⅓ cup sliced mushrooms
1 cup baby spinach
1 small red onion, sliced
⅓ cup crumbled feta cheese
⅓ cup grated Cheddar cheese
¼ cup chopped chives
Salt and ground black pepper, to taste

1. Line a baking pan with parchment paper.
2. Whisk together the eggs, milk, salt, and ground black pepper in a large bowl. Set aside.
3. Heat the olive oil in a nonstick skillet over medium heat until shimmering.
4. Add the zucchini, asparagus, mushrooms, spinach, and onion to the skillet and sauté for 5 minutes or until tender.
5. Pour the sautéed vegetables into the prepared baking pan, then spread the egg mixture over and scatter with cheeses.
6. Slide the pan into the air fryer oven. Cook at 380°F (193°C) for 15 minutes.
7. Stir the mixture halfway through.
8. When cooking is complete, the egg should be set and the edges should be lightly browned.
9. Remove the frittata from the air fryer oven and sprinkle with chives before serving.

Sausage and Colorful Peppers Casserole

Prep time: 15 minutes | Cook time: 25 minutes | Serves 6

1 pound (454 g) minced breakfast sausage
1 yellow pepper, diced
1 red pepper, diced
1 green pepper, diced
1 sweet onion, diced
2 cups Cheddar cheese, shredded
6 eggs
Salt and freshly ground black pepper, to taste
Fresh parsley, for garnish

1. Cook the sausage in a nonstick skillet over medium heat for 10 minutes or until well browned. Stir constantly.
2. When the cooking is finished, transfer the cooked sausage to a baking pan and add the peppers and onion. Scatter with Cheddar cheese.
3. Whisk the eggs with salt and ground black pepper in a large bowl, then pour the mixture into the baking pan.
4. Slide the pan into the air fryer oven. Cook at 360°F (182°C) for 15 minutes.
5. When cooking is complete, the egg should be set and the edges of the casserole should be lightly browned.
6. Remove the baking pan from the air fryer oven and top with fresh parsley before serving.

Shrimp Spinach Frittata

Prep time: 6 minutes | Cook time: 14 minutes | Serves 4

4 whole eggs
1 teaspoon dried basil
½ cup shrimp, cooked and chopped
½ cup baby spinach
½ cup rice, cooked
½ cup Monterey Jack cheese, grated
Salt, to taste
Cooking spray

1. Spritz a baking pan with cooking spray.
2. Whisk the eggs with basil and salt in a large bowl until bubbly, then mix in the shrimp, spinach, rice, and cheese.
3. Pour the mixture into the baking pan.
4. Slide the pan into the air fryer oven. Cook at 360°F (182°C) for 14 minutes.
5. Stir the mixture halfway through.
6. When cooking is complete, the eggs should be set and the frittata should be golden brown.
7. Slice to serve.

Smoked Trout and Crème Fraiche Frittata

Prep time: 8 minutes | Cook time: 17 minutes | Serves 4

2 tablespoons olive oil
1 onion, sliced
1 egg, beaten
½ tablespoon horseradish sauce
6 tablespoons crème fraiche
1 cup diced smoked trout
2 tablespoons chopped fresh dill
Cooking spray

1. Spritz a baking pan with cooking spray.
2. Heat the olive oil in a nonstick skillet over medium heat until shimmering.
3. Add the onion and sauté for 3 minutes or until translucent.
4. Combine the egg, horseradish sauce, and crème fraiche in a large bowl. Stir to mix well, then mix in the sautéed onion, smoked trout, and dill.
5. Pour the mixture in the prepared baking pan.
6. Slide the pan into the air fryer oven. Cook at 350°F (180°C) for 14 minutes.
7. Stir the mixture halfway through.
8. When cooking is complete, the egg should be set and the edges should be lightly browned.
9. Serve immediately.

Mediterranean Quiche

Prep time: 10 minutes | Cook time: 30 minutes | Serves 4

4 eggs
¼ cup chopped Kalamata olives
½ cup chopped tomatoes
¼ cup chopped onion
½ cup milk
1 cup crumbled feta cheese
½ tablespoon chopped oregano
½ tablespoon chopped basil
Salt and ground black pepper, to taste
Cooking spray

1. Spritz a baking pan with cooking spray.
2. Whisk the eggs with remaining ingredients in a large bowl. Stir to mix well.
3. Pour the mixture into the prepared baking pan.
4. Slide the pan into the air fryer oven. Cook at 340°F (171°C) for 30 minutes.
5. When cooking is complete, the eggs should be set and a toothpick inserted in the center should come out clean.
6. Serve immediately.

Spinach and Chickpea Casserole

Prep time: 10 minutes | Cook time: 21 to 22 minutes | Serves 4

2 tablespoons olive oil
2 garlic cloves, minced
1 tablespoon ginger, minced
1 onion, chopped
1 chili pepper, minced
Salt and ground black pepper, to taste
1 pound (454 g) spinach
1 can coconut milk
½ cup dried tomatoes, chopped
1 (14-ounce / 397-g) can chickpeas, drained

1. Heat the olive oil in a saucepan over medium heat. Sauté the garlic and ginger in the olive oil for 1 minute, or until fragrant.
2. Add the onion, chili pepper, salt and pepper to the saucepan. Sauté for 3 minutes.
3. Mix in the spinach and sauté for 3 to 4 minutes or until the vegetables become soft. Remove from heat.
4. Pour the vegetable mixture into a baking pan. Stir in coconut milk, dried tomatoes and chickpeas until well blended.
5. Slide the pan into the air fryer oven. Cook at 370°F (188°C) for 15 minutes.
6. When cooking is complete, transfer the casserole to a serving dish. Let cool for 5 minutes before serving.

Sumptuous Beef and Bean Chili Casserole

Prep time: 15 minutes | Cook time: 31 minutes | Serves 4

1 tablespoon olive oil
½ cup finely chopped bell pepper
½ cup chopped celery
1 onion, chopped
2 garlic cloves, minced
1 pound (454 g) ground beef
1 can diced tomatoes
½ teaspoon parsley
½ tablespoon chili powder
1 teaspoon chopped cilantro
1½ cups vegetable broth
1 (8-ounce / 227-g) can cannellini beans
Salt and ground black pepper, to taste

1. Heat the olive oil in a nonstick skillet over medium heat until shimmering.
2. Add the bell pepper, celery, onion, and garlic to the skillet and sauté for 5 minutes or until the onion is translucent.
3. Add the ground beef and sauté for an additional 6 minutes or until lightly browned.
4. Mix in the tomatoes, parsley, chili powder, cilantro and vegetable broth, then cook for 10 more minutes. Stir constantly.
5. Pour them in a baking pan, then mix in the beans and sprinkle with salt and ground black pepper.
6. Slide the pan into the air fryer oven. Cook at 350°F (180°C) for 10 minutes.
7. When cooking is complete, the vegetables should be tender and the beef should be well browned.
8. Remove the baking pan from the air fryer oven and serve immediately.

Ritzy Pimento and Almond Turkey Casserole

Prep time: 5 minutes | Cook time: 32 minutes | Serves 4

1 pound (454 g) turkey breasts
1 tablespoon olive oil
2 boiled eggs, chopped
2 tablespoons chopped pimentos
¼ cup slivered almonds, chopped
¼ cup mayonnaise
½ cup diced celery
2 tablespoons chopped green onion
¼ cup cream of chicken soup
¼ cup breadcrumbs
Salt and ground black pepper, to taste

1. Put the turkey breasts in a large bowl. Sprinkle with salt and ground black pepper and drizzle with olive oil. Toss to coat well.
2. Transfer the turkey in an air fryer basket.
3. Slide the basket into the air fryer oven. Cook at 390°F (199°C) for 12 minutes.
4. Flip the turkey halfway through.
5. When cooking is complete, the turkey should be well browned.
6. Remove the turkey breasts from the air fryer oven and cut into cubes, then combine the chicken cubes with eggs, pimentos, almonds, mayo, celery, green onions, and chicken soup in a large bowl. Stir to mix.
7. Pour the mixture into a baking pan, then spread with breadcrumbs.
8. Set time to 20 minutes. Place the pan into the air fryer oven.
9. When cooking is complete, the eggs should be set.
10. Remove the baking pan from the air fryer oven and serve immediately.

Taco Beef and Chile Casserole

Prep time: 10 minutes | Cook time: 15 minutes | Serves 4

1 pound (454 g) 85% lean ground beef
1 tablespoon taco seasoning
1 (7-ounce / 198-g) can diced mild green chiles
½ cup milk
2 large eggs
1 cup shredded Mexican cheese blend
2 tablespoons all-purpose flour
½ teaspoon kosher salt
Cooking spray

1. Spritz a baking pan with cooking spray.
2. Toss the ground beef with taco seasoning in a large bowl to mix well. Pour the seasoned ground beef in the prepared baking pan.
3. Combing the remaining ingredients in a medium bowl. Whisk to mix well, then pour the mixture over the ground beef.
4. Slide the pan into the air fryer oven. Cook at 350°F (180°C) for 15 minutes.
5. When cooking is complete, a toothpick inserted in the center should come out clean.
6. Remove the casserole from the air fryer oven and allow to cool for 5 minutes, then slice to serve.

Desserts

Almond Flour Blackberry Muffins

Prep time: 5 minutes | Cook time: 12 minutes | Serves 8

½ cup fresh blackberries
Dry Ingredients:
1½ cups almond flour
1 teaspoon baking powder
½ teaspoon baking soda
½ cup Swerve
¼ teaspoon kosher salt
Wet Ingredients:
2 eggs
¼ cup coconut oil, melted
½ cup milk
½ teaspoon vanilla paste

1. Line an 8-cup muffin tin with paper liners.
2. Thoroughly combine the almond flour, baking powder, baking soda, Swerve, and salt in a mixing bowl.
3. Whisk together the eggs, coconut oil, milk, and vanilla in a separate mixing bowl until smooth.
4. Add the wet mixture to the dry and fold in the blackberries. Stir with a spatula just until well incorporated.
5. Spoon the batter into the prepared muffin cups, filling each about three-quarters full.
6. Slide the muffin tin into the air fryer oven. Cook at 350°F (180°C) for 12 minutes.
7. When done, the tops should be golden and a toothpick inserted in the middle should come out clean.
8. Allow the muffins to cool in the muffin tin for 10 minutes before removing and serving

Blackberry and Peach Cobbler

Prep time: 10 minutes | Cook time: 20 minutes | Serves 4
Filling:
1 (6-ounce / 170-g) package blackberries
1½ cups chopped peaches, cut into ½-inch thick slices
2 teaspoons arrowroot or cornstarch
2 tablespoons coconut sugar
1 teaspoon lemon juice
Topping:
2 tablespoons sunflower oil
1 tablespoon maple syrup
1 teaspoon vanilla
3 tablespoons coconut sugar
½ cup rolled oats
⅓ cup whole-wheat pastry flour
1 teaspoon cinnamon
¼ teaspoon nutmeg
⅛ teaspoon sea salt

Make the Filling:
1. Combine the blackberries, peaches, arrowroot, coconut sugar, and lemon juice in a baking pan.
2. Using a rubber spatula, stir until well incorporated. Set aside.
Make the Topping:
1. Combine the oil, maple syrup, and vanilla in a mixing bowl and stir well. Whisk in the remaining ingredients. Spread this mixture evenly over the filling.
2. Slide the pan into the air fryer oven. Cook at 320°F (160°C) for 20 minutes.
3. When cooked, the topping should be crispy and golden brown. Serve warm

Apple Fritters

Prep time: 30 minutes | Cook time: 7 minutes | Serves 6

1 cup chopped, peeled Granny Smith apple
½ cup granulated sugar
1 teaspoon ground cinnamon
1 cup all-purpose flour
1 teaspoon baking powder
1 teaspoon salt
2 tablespoons milk
2 tablespoons butter, melted
1 large egg, beaten
Cooking spray
¼ cup confectioners' sugar (optional)

1. Mix the apple, granulated sugar, and cinnamon in a small bowl. Allow to sit for 30 minutes.
2. Combine the flour, baking powder, and salt in a medium bowl. Add the milk, butter, and egg and stir to incorporate.
3. Pour the apple mixture into the bowl of flour mixture and stir with a spatula until a dough forms.
4. Make the fritters: On a clean work surface, divide the dough into 12 equal portions and shape into 1-inch balls. Flatten them into patties with your hands.
5. Line an air fryer basket with parchment paper and spray it with cooking spray.
6. Transfer the apple fritters onto the parchment paper, evenly spaced but not too close together. Spray the fritters with cooking spray.
7. Slide the basket into the air fryer oven. Cook at 350°F (180°C) for 7 minutes.
8. Flip the fritters halfway through the cooking time.
9. When cooking is complete, the fritters should be lightly browned.
10. Remove from the air fryer oven to a plate and serve with the confectioners' sugar sprinkled on top, if desired.

Coconut Pineapple Sticks

Prep time: 10 minutes | Cook time: 10 minutes | Serves 4

½ fresh pineapple, cut into sticks
¼ cup desiccated coconut

1. Place the desiccated coconut on a plate and roll the pineapple sticks in the coconut until well coated.
2. Lay the pineapple sticks in an air fryer basket.
3. Slide the basket into the air fryer oven. Cook at 400°F (205°C) for 10 minutes.
4. When cooking is complete, the pineapple sticks should be crisp-tender.
5. Serve warm.

Apple-Peach Crisp with Oatmeal

Prep time: 10 minutes | Cook time: 10 to 12 minutes | Serves 4

2 peaches, peeled, pitted, and chopped
1 apple, peeled and chopped
2 tablespoons honey
3 tablespoons packed brown sugar
2 tablespoons unsalted butter, at room temperature
½ cup quick-cooking oatmeal
⅓ cup whole-wheat pastry flour
½ teaspoon ground cinnamon

1. Place the peaches, apple, and honey in a baking pan and toss until thoroughly combined.
2. Mix the brown sugar, butter, oatmeal, pastry flour, and cinnamon in a medium bowl and stir until crumbly. Sprinkle this mixture generously on top of the peaches and apples.
3. Slide the pan into the air fryer oven. Cook at 380°F (193°C) for 10 minutes.
4. Bake until the fruit is bubbling and the topping is golden brown.
5. Once cooking is complete, remove from the air fryer oven and allow to cool for 5 minutes before serving.

Apple-Peach Crumble with Honey

Prep time: 10 minutes | Cook time: 11 minutes | Serves 4

1 apple, peeled and chopped
2 peaches, peeled, pitted, and chopped
2 tablespoons honey
½ cup quick-cooking oatmeal
⅓ cup whole-wheat pastry flour
2 tablespoons unsalted butter, at room temperature
3 tablespoons packed brown sugar
½ teaspoon ground cinnamon

1. Mix the apple, peaches, and honey in a baking pan until well incorporated.
2. In a bowl, combine the oatmeal, pastry flour, butter, brown sugar, and cinnamon and stir to mix well. Spread this mixture evenly over the fruit.
3. Slide the pan into the air fryer oven. Cook at 380°F (193°C) for 11 minutes.
4. When cooking is complete, the fruit should be bubbling around the edges and the topping should be golden brown.
5. Remove from the air fryer oven and serve warm.

Baked Peaches and Blueberries

Prep time: 10 minutes | Cook time: 10 minutes | Serves 6

3 peaches, peeled, halved, and pitted
2 tablespoons packed brown sugar
1 cup plain Greek yogurt
¼ teaspoon ground cinnamon
1 teaspoon pure vanilla extract
1 cup fresh blueberries

1. Arrange the peaches in an air fryer basket, cut-side up. Top with a generous sprinkle of brown sugar.
2. Slide the basket into the air fryer oven. Cook at 380°F (193°C) for 10 minutes.
3. Meanwhile, whisk together the yogurt, cinnamon, and vanilla in a small bowl until smooth.
4. When cooking is complete, the peaches should be lightly browned and caramelized.
5. Remove the peaches from the air fryer oven to a plate. Serve topped with the yogurt mixture and fresh blueberries.

Berry Crumble

Prep time: 5 minutes | Cook time: 35 minutes | Serves 6

2 ounces (57 g) unsweetened mixed berries
½ cup granulated Swerve
2 tablespoons golden flaxseed meal
1 teaspoon xanthan gum
½ teaspoon ground cinnamon
¼ teaspoon ground star anise
Topping:
½ stick butter, cut into small pieces
1 cup powdered Swerve
⅔ cup almond flour
⅓ cup unsweetened coconut, finely shredded
½ teaspoon baking powder
Cooking spray

1. Coat 6 ramekins with cooking spray.
2. In a mixing dish, stir together the mixed berries, granulated Swerve, flaxseed meal, xanthan gum, cinnamon, star anise. Divide the berry mixture evenly among the prepared ramekins.
3. Combine the remaining ingredients in a separate mixing dish and stir well. Scatter the topping over the berry mixture.
4. Slide the ramekins into the air fryer oven. Cook at 330°F (166°C) for 35 minutes.
5. When done, the topping should be golden brown.
6. Serve warm.

Black and White Brownies

Prep time: 10 minutes | Cook time: 20 minutes | Makes 1 dozen brownies

1 egg
¼ cup brown sugar
2 tablespoons white sugar
2 tablespoons safflower oil
1 teaspoon vanilla
⅓ cup all-purpose flour
¼ cup cocoa powder
¼ cup white chocolate chips
Nonstick cooking spray

1. Spritz a baking pan with nonstick cooking spray.
2. Whisk together the egg, brown sugar, and white sugar in a medium bowl. Mix in the safflower oil and vanilla and stir to combine.
3. Add the flour and cocoa powder and stir just until incorporated. Fold in the white chocolate chips.
4. Scrape the batter into the prepared baking pan.
5. Slide the pan into the air fryer oven. Cook at 340°F (171°C) for 20 minutes.
6. When done, the brownie should spring back when touched lightly with your fingers.
7. Transfer to a wire rack and let cool for 30 minutes before slicing to serve.

Apple Wedges with Apricots

Prep time: 5 minutes | Cook time: 15 to 18 minutes | Serves 4

4 large apples, peeled and sliced into 8 wedges
2 tablespoons olive oil
½ cup dried apricots, chopped
1 to 2 tablespoons sugar
½ teaspoon ground cinnamon

1. Toss the apple wedges with the olive oil in a mixing bowl until well coated.
2. Place the apple wedges in an air fryer basket.
3. Slide the basket into the air fryer oven. Cook at 350°F (180°C) for 15 minutes.
4. After about 12 minutes, remove from the air fryer oven. Sprinkle with the dried apricots and air fry for another 3 minutes.
5. Meanwhile, thoroughly combine the sugar and cinnamon in a small bowl.
6. Remove the apple wedges from the air fryer oven to a plate. Serve sprinkled with the sugar mixture.

Blackberry Chocolate Cake

Prep time: 10 minutes | Cook time: 22 minutes | Serves 8

½ cup butter, at room temperature
2 ounces (57 g) Swerve
4 eggs
1 cup almond flour
1 teaspoon baking soda
⅓ teaspoon baking powder
½ cup cocoa powder
1 teaspoon orange zest
⅓ cup fresh blackberries

1. With an electric mixer or hand mixer, beat the butter and Swerve until creamy.
2. One at a time, mix in the eggs and beat again until fluffy.
3. Add the almond flour, baking soda, baking powder, cocoa powder, orange zest and mix well. Add the butter mixture to the almond flour mixture and stir until well blended. Fold in the blackberries.
4. Scrape the batter into a baking pan.
5. Slide the pan into the air fryer oven. Cook at 335°F (168°C) for 22 minutes.
6. When cooking is complete, a toothpick inserted into the center of the cake should come out clean.
7. Allow the cake cool on a wire rack to room temperature. Serve immediately.

Breaded Bananas with Chocolate Sauce

Prep time: 10 minutes | Cook time: 7 minutes | Serves 6

¼ cup cornstarch
¼ cup plain bread crumbs
1 large egg, beaten
3 bananas, halved crosswise
Cooking spray
Chocolate sauce, for serving

1. Place the cornstarch, bread crumbs, and egg in three separate bowls.
2. Roll the bananas in the cornstarch, then in the beaten egg, and finally in the bread crumbs to coat well.
3. Spritz an air fryer basket with cooking spray.
4. Arrange the banana halves in the air fryer basket and mist them with cooking spray.
5. Slide the basket into the air fryer oven. Cook at 350°F (180°C) for 7 minutes.
6. After about 5 minutes, flip the bananas and continue to air fry for another 2 minutes.
7. When cooking is complete, remove the bananas from the air fryer oven to a serving plate. Serve with the chocolate sauce drizzled over the top.

Caramelized Fruit Kebabs

Prep time: 10 minutes | Cook time: 4 minutes | Serves 4

2 peaches, peeled, pitted, and thickly sliced
3 plums, halved and pitted
3 nectarines, halved and pitted
1 tablespoon honey
½ teaspoon ground cinnamon
¼ teaspoon ground allspice
Pinch cayenne pepper

Special Equipment:
8 metal skewers

1. Thread, alternating peaches, plums, and nectarines onto the metal skewers that fit into the air fryer oven.
2. Thoroughly combine the honey, cinnamon, allspice, and cayenne in a small bowl. Brush generously the glaze over the fruit skewers.
3. Transfer the fruit skewers to an air fryer basket.
4. Slide the basket into the air fryer oven. Cook at 400°F (205°C) for 4 minutes.
5. When cooking is complete, the fruit should be caramelized.
6. Remove the fruit skewers from the air fryer oven and let rest for 5 minutes before serving.

Chocolate and Coconut Cake

Prep time: 5 minutes | Cook time: 15 minutes | Serves 6

½ cup unsweetened chocolate, chopped
½ stick butter, at room temperature
1 tablespoon liquid stevia
1½ cups coconut flour
2 eggs, whisked
½ teaspoon vanilla extract
A pinch of fine sea salt
Cooking spray

1. Place the chocolate, butter, and stevia in a microwave-safe bowl. Microwave for about 30 seconds until melted.
2. Let the chocolate mixture cool for 5 to 10 minutes.
3. Add the remaining ingredients to the bowl of chocolate mixture and whisk to incorporate.
4. Lightly spray a baking pan with cooking spray.
5. Scrape the chocolate mixture into the prepared baking pan.
6. Slide the pan into the air fryer oven. Cook at 330°F (166°C) for 15 minutes.
7. When cooking is complete, the top should spring back lightly when gently pressed with your fingers.
8. Let the cake cool for 5 minutes and serve.

Caramelized Pear Tart

Prep time: 15 minutes | Cook time: 25 minutes | Serves 8

Juice of 1 lemon
4 cups water
3 medium or 2 large ripe or almost ripe pears (preferably Bosc or Anjou), peeled, stemmed, and halved lengthwise
1 sheet (½ package) frozen puff pastry, thawed
All-purpose flour, for dusting
4 tablespoons caramel sauce such as Smucker's Salted Caramel, divided

1. Combine the lemon juice and water in a large bowl.
2. Remove the seeds from the pears with a melon baller and cut out the blossom end. Remove any tough fibers between the stem end and the center. As you work, place the pear halves in the acidulated water.
3. On a lightly floured cutting board, unwrap and unfold the puff pastry, roll it lightly with a rolling pin to press the folds together. Place it on a sheet pan.
4. Roll about ½ inch of the pastry edges up to form a ridge around the perimeter. Crimp the corners together to create a solid rim around the pastry to hold in the liquid as the tart cooks.
5. Brush 2 tablespoons of caramel sauce over the bottom of the pastry.
6. Remove the pear halves from the water and blot off any remaining water with paper towels.
7. Place one of the halves on the board cut-side down and cut ¼-inch-thick slices radially. Repeat with the remaining halves. Arrange the pear slices over the pastry. Drizzle the remaining 2 tablespoons of caramel sauce over the top.
8. Slide the pan into the air fryer oven. Cook at 350°F (180°C) for 25 minutes.
9. After 15 minutes, check the tart, rotating the pan if the crust is not browning evenly. Continue cooking for another 10 minutes, or until the pastry is golden brown, the pears are soft, and the caramel is bubbling.
10. When done, remove from the air fryer oven and allow to cool for about 10 minutes.
11. Served warm.

Blueberry and Peach Galette

Prep time: 10 minutes | Cook time: 20 minutes | Serves 6

1 pint blueberries, rinsed and picked through (about 2 cups)
2 large peaches or nectarines, peeled and cut into ½-inch slices (about 2 cups)
⅓ cup plus 2 tablespoons granulated sugar, divided
2 tablespoons unbleached all-purpose flour
½ teaspoon grated lemon zest (optional)
¼ teaspoon ground allspice or cinnamon
Pinch kosher or fine salt
1 (9-inch) refrigerated piecrust (or use homemade)
2 teaspoons unsalted butter, cut into pea-size pieces
1 large egg, beaten

1. Mix the blueberries, peaches, ⅓ cup of sugar, flour, lemon zest (if desired), allspice, and salt in a medium bowl.
2. Unroll the crust on a sheet pan, patching any tears if needed. Place the fruit in the center of the crust, leaving about 1½ inches of space around the edges. Scatter the butter pieces over the fruit. Fold the outside edge of the crust over the outer circle of the fruit, making pleats as needed.
3. Brush the egg over the crust. Sprinkle the crust and fruit with the remaining 2 tablespoons of sugar.
4. Slide the pan into the air fryer oven. Cook at 350°F (180°C) for 20 minutes.
5. After about 15 minutes, check the galette, rotating the pan if the crust is not browning evenly. Continue cooking until the crust is deep golden brown and the fruit is bubbling.
6. When cooking is complete, remove from the air fryer oven and allow to cool for 10 minutes before slicing and serving.

Chocolate Cheesecake

Prep time: 5 minutes | Cook time: 18 minutes | Serves 6

Crust:
½ cup butter, melted
½ cup coconut flour
2 tablespoons stevia
Cooking spray
Topping:
4 ounces (113 g) unsweetened baker's chocolate
1 cup mascarpone cheese, at room temperature
1 teaspoon vanilla extract
2 drops peppermint extract

1. Lightly coat a baking pan with cooking spray.
2. In a mixing bowl, whisk together the butter, flour, and stevia until well combined. Transfer the mixture to the prepared baking pan.
3. Slide the pan into the air fryer oven. Cook at 350°F (180°C) for 18 minutes.
4. When done, a toothpick inserted in the center should come out clean.
5. Remove the crust from the air fryer oven to a wire rack to cool.
6. Once cooled completely, place it in the freezer for 20 minutes.
7. When ready, combine all the ingredients for the topping in a small bowl and stir to incorporate.
8. Spread this topping over the crust and let it sit for another 15 minutes in the freezer.
9. Serve chilled.

Chia Pudding

Prep time: 5 minutes | Cook time: 4 minutes | Serves 2

1 cup chia seeds
1 cup unsweetened coconut milk
1 teaspoon liquid stevia
1 tablespoon coconut oil
1 teaspoon butter, melted

1. Mix the chia seeds, coconut milk, and stevia in a large bowl. Add the coconut oil and melted butter and stir until well blended.
2. Divide the mixture evenly between the ramekins, filling only about ⅔ of the way.
3. Slide the ramekins into the air fryer oven. Cook at 360°F (182°C) for 4 minutes.
4. When cooking is complete, allow to cool for 5 minutes and serve warm.

Chocolate Cupcakes with Blueberries

Prep time: 5 minutes | Cook time: 15 minutes | Serves 6

¾ cup granulated erythritol
1¼ cups almond flour
1 teaspoon unsweetened baking powder
3 teaspoons cocoa powder
½ teaspoon baking soda
½ teaspoon ground cinnamon
¼ teaspoon grated nutmeg
⅛ teaspoon salt
½ cup milk
1 stick butter, at room temperature
3 eggs, whisked
1 teaspoon pure rum extract
½ cup blueberries
Cooking spray

1. Spray a 6-cup muffin tin with cooking spray.
2. In a mixing bowl, combine the erythritol, almond flour, baking powder, cocoa powder, baking soda, cinnamon, nutmeg, and salt and stir until well blended.
3. In another mixing bowl, mix the milk, butter, egg, and rum extract until thoroughly combined. Slowly and carefully pour this mixture into the bowl of dry mixture. Stir in the blueberries.
1. Spoon the batter into the greased muffin cups, filling each about three-quarters full.
4. Slide the muffin tin into the air fryer oven. Cook at 345°F (174°C) for 15 minutes.
5. When done, the center should be springy and a toothpick inserted in the middle should come out clean.
6. Remove from the air fryer oven and place on a wire rack to cool. Serve immediately.

Chocolate Pecan Pie

Prep time: 20 minutes | Cook time: 25 minutes | Serves 8

1 (9-inch) unbaked pie crust
Filling:
2 large eggs
⅓ cup butter, melted
1 cup sugar
½ cup all-purpose flour
1 cup milk chocolate chips
1½ cups coarsely chopped pecans
2 tablespoons bourbon

1. Whisk the eggs and melted butter in a large bowl until creamy.
2. Add the sugar and flour and stir to incorporate. Mix in the milk chocolate chips, pecans, and bourbon and stir until well combined.
3. Use a fork to prick holes in the bottom and sides of the pie crust. Pour the prepared filling into the pie crust. Place the pie crust in an air fryer basket.
4. Slide the basket into the air fryer oven. Cook at 350°F (180°C) for 25 minutes.
5. When cooking is complete, a toothpick inserted in the center should come out clean.
6. Allow the pie cool for 10 minutes in the basket before serving.

Easy Blackberry Cobbler

Prep time: 15 minutes | Cook time: 20 to 25 minutes | Serves 6

3 cups fresh or frozen blackberries
1¾ cups sugar, divided
1 teaspoon vanilla extract
8 tablespoons (1 stick) butter, melted
1 cup self-rising flour
Cooking spray

1. Spritz a baking pan with cooking spray.
2. Mix the blackberries, 1 cup of sugar, and vanilla in a medium bowl and stir to combine.
3. Stir together the melted butter, remaining sugar, and flour in a separate medium bowl.
4. Spread the blackberry mixture evenly in the prepared pan and top with the butter mixture.
5. Slide the pan into the air fryer oven. Cook at 350°F (180°C) for 25 minutes.
6. After about 20 minutes, check if the cobbler has a golden crust and you can't see any batter bubbling while it cooks. If needed, bake for another 5 minutes.
7. Remove from the air fryer oven and place on a wire rack to cool to room temperature. Serve immediately.

Desserts 43

Cinnamon S'mores

Prep time: 5 minutes | Cook time: 3 minutes | Makes 12 s'mores

12 whole cinnamon graham crackers, halved
2 (1.55-ounce / 44-g) chocolate bars, cut into 12 pieces
12 marshmallows

1. Arrange 12 graham cracker squares in an air fryer basket.
2. Top each square with a piece of chocolate.
3. Slide the basket into the air fryer oven. Cook at 350°F (180°C) for 3 minutes.
4. Bake for 2 minutes. Remove the basket and place a marshmallow on each piece of melted chocolate. Bake for another 1 minute.
5. Remove from the air fryer oven to a serving plate.
6. Serve topped with the remaining graham cracker squares

Classic Pound Cake

Prep time: 5 minutes | Cook time: 30 minutes | Serves 8

1 stick butter, at room temperature
1 cup Swerve
4 eggs
1½ cups coconut flour
½ cup buttermilk
½ teaspoon baking soda
½ teaspoon baking powder
¼ teaspoon salt
1 teaspoon vanilla essence
A pinch of ground star anise
A pinch of freshly grated nutmeg
Cooking spray

1. Spray a baking pan with cooking spray.
2. With an electric mixer or hand mixer, beat the butter and Swerve until creamy. One at a time, mix in the eggs and whisk until fluffy. Add the remaining ingredients and stir to combine.
3. Transfer the batter to the prepared baking pan.
4. Slide the pan into the air fryer oven. Cook at 320°F (160°C) for 30 minutes.
5. Rotate the pan halfway through the cooking time.
6. When cooking is complete, the center of the cake should be springy.
7. Allow the cake to cool in the pan for 10 minutes before removing and serving.

Coconut Chip Mixed Berry Crisp

Prep time: 5 minutes | Cook time: 20 minutes | Serves 6

1 tablespoon butter, melted
12 ounces (340 g) mixed berries
⅓ cup granulated Swerve
1 teaspoon pure vanilla extract
½ teaspoon ground cinnamon
¼ teaspoon ground cloves
¼ teaspoon grated nutmeg
½ cup coconut chips, for garnish

1. Coat a baking pan with melted butter.
2. Put the remaining ingredients except the coconut chips in the prepared baking pan.
3. Slide the pan into the air fryer oven. Cook at 330°F (166°C) for 20 minutes.
4. When cooking is complete, remove from the air fryer oven. Serve garnished with the coconut chips.

Coconut Cookies with Pecans

Prep time: 10 minutes | Cook time: 25 minutes | Serves 10

1½ cups coconut flour
1½ cups extra-fine almond flour
½ teaspoon baking powder
⅓ teaspoon baking soda
3 eggs plus an egg yolk, beaten
¾ cup coconut oil, at room temperature
1 cup unsalted pecan nuts, roughly chopped
¾ cup monk fruit
¼ teaspoon freshly grated nutmeg
⅓ teaspoon ground cloves
½ teaspoon pure vanilla extract
½ teaspoon pure coconut extract
⅛ teaspoon fine sea salt

1. Line an air fryer basket with parchment paper.
2. Mix the coconut flour, almond flour, baking powder, and baking soda in a large mixing bowl.
3. In another mixing bowl, stir together the eggs and coconut oil. Add the wet mixture to the dry mixture.
4. Mix in the remaining ingredients and stir until a soft dough forms.
5. Drop about 2 tablespoons of dough on the parchment paper for each cookie and flatten each biscuit until it's 1 inch thick.
6. Slide the basket into the air fryer oven. Cook at 370°F (188°C) for 25 minutes.
7. When cooking is complete, the cookies should be golden and firm to the touch.
8. Remove from the air fryer oven to a plate. Let the cookies cool to room temperature and serve.

Coffee Chocolate Cake

Prep time: 5 minutes | Cook time: 30 minutes | Serves 8

Dry Ingredients:
1½ cups almond flour
½ cup coconut meal
⅔ cup Swerve
1 teaspoon baking powder
¼ teaspoon salt
Wet Ingredients:
1 egg
1 stick butter, melted
½ cup hot strongly brewed coffee
Topping:
½ cup confectioner's Swerve
¼ cup coconut flour
3 tablespoons coconut oil
1 teaspoon ground cinnamon
½ teaspoon ground cardamom

1. In a medium bowl, combine the almond flour, coconut meal, Swerve, baking powder, and salt.
2. In a large bowl, whisk the egg, melted butter, and coffee until smooth.
3. Add the dry mixture to the wet and stir until well incorporated. Transfer the batter to a greased baking pan.
4. Stir together all the ingredients for the topping in a small bowl. Spread the topping over the batter and smooth the top with a spatula.
5. Slide the pan into the air fryer oven. Cook at 330°F (166°C) for 30 minutes.
6. When cooking is complete, the cake should spring back when gently pressed with your fingers.
7. Rest for 10 minutes before serving.

Cinnamon Candied Apples

Prep time: 15 minutes | Cook time: 12 minutes | Serves 4

1 cup packed light brown sugar
2 teaspoons ground cinnamon
2 medium Granny Smith apples, peeled and diced

1. Thoroughly combine the brown sugar and cinnamon in a medium bowl.
2. Add the apples to the bowl and stir until well coated. Transfer the apples to a baking pan.
3. Slide the pan into the air fryer oven. Cook at 350°F (180°C) for 12 minutes.
4. After about 9 minutes, stir the apples and bake for an additional 3 minutes. When cooking is complete, the apples should be softened.
5. Serve warm.

Crispy Pineapple Rings

Prep time: 5 minutes | Cook time: 7 minutes | Serves 6

1 cup rice milk
⅔ cup flour
½ cup water
¼ cup unsweetened flaked coconut
4 tablespoons sugar
½ teaspoon baking soda
½ teaspoon baking powder
½ teaspoon vanilla essence
½ teaspoon ground cinnamon
¼ teaspoon ground anise star
Pinch of kosher salt
1 medium pineapple, peeled and sliced

1. In a large bowl, stir together all the ingredients except the pineapple.
2. Dip each pineapple slice into the batter until evenly coated.
3. Arrange the pineapple slices in an air fryer basket.
4. Slide the basket into the air fryer oven. Cook at 380°F (193°C) for 7 minutes.
5. When cooking is complete, the pineapple rings should be golden brown.
6. Remove from the air fryer oven to a plate and cool for 5 minutes before serving.

Fudge Pie

Prep time: 15 minutes | Cook time: 26 minutes | Serves 8

1½ cups sugar
½ cup self-rising flour
⅓ cup unsweetened cocoa powder
3 large eggs, beaten
12 tablespoons (1½ sticks) butter, melted
1½ teaspoons vanilla extract
1 (9-inch) unbaked pie crust
¼ cup confectioners' sugar (optional)

1. Thoroughly combine the sugar, flour, and cocoa powder in a medium bowl. Add the beaten eggs and butter and whisk to combine. Stir in the vanilla.
2. Pour the prepared filling into the pie crust and transfer to an air fryer basket.
3. Slide the basket into the air fryer oven. Cook at 350°F (180°C) for 26 minutes.
4. When cooking is complete, the pie should be set.
5. Allow the pie to cool for 5 minutes. Sprinkle with the confectioners' sugar, if desired. Serve warm.

Fudgy Chocolate Brownies

Prep time: 5 minutes | Cook time: 21 minutes | Serves 8

1 stick butter, melted
1 cup Swerve
2 eggs
1 cup coconut flour
½ cup unsweetened cocoa powder
2 tablespoons flaxseed meal
1 teaspoon baking powder
1 teaspoon vanilla essence
A pinch of salt
A pinch of ground cardamom
Cooking spray

1. Spray a baking pan with cooking spray.
2. Beat together the melted butter and Swerve in a large mixing dish until fluffy. Whisk in the eggs.
3. Add the coconut flour, cocoa powder, flaxseed meal, baking powder, vanilla essence, salt, and cardamom and stir with a spatula until well incorporated. Spread the mixture evenly into the prepared baking pan.
4. Slide the pan into the air fryer oven. Cook at 350°F (180°C) for 21 minutes.
5. When cooking is complete, a toothpick inserted in the center should come out clean.
6. Remove from the air fryer oven and place on a wire rack to cool completely. Cut into squares and serve immediately.

Gooey White Chocolate Cookies

Prep time: 5 minutes | Cook time: 11 minutes | Serves 10

8 ounces (227 g) unsweetened white chocolate
2 eggs, well beaten
¾ cup butter, at room temperature
1⅔ cups almond flour
½ cup coconut flour
¾ cup granulated Swerve
2 tablespoons coconut oil
⅓ teaspoon grated nutmeg
⅓ teaspoon ground allspice
⅓ teaspoon ground anise star
¼ teaspoon fine sea salt

1. Line a baking sheet with parchment paper.
2. Combine all the ingredients in a mixing bowl and knead for about 3 to 4 minutes, or until a soft dough forms. Transfer to the refrigerator to chill for 20 minutes.
3. Make the cookies: Roll the dough into 1-inch balls and transfer to the parchment-lined baking sheet, spacing 2 inches apart. Flatten each with the back of a spoon.
4. Slide the baking sheet into the air fryer oven. Cook at 350°F (180°C) for 11 minutes.
5. When cooking is complete, the cookies should be golden and firm to the touch.
6. Transfer to a wire rack and let the cookies cool completely. Serve immediately.

Honey Walnut Baklava

Prep time: 10 minutes | Cook time: 16 minutes | Serves 10

1 cup walnut pieces
1 cup shelled raw pistachios
½ cup unsalted butter, melted
¼ cup plus 2 tablespoons honey, divided
3 tablespoons granulated sugar
1 teaspoon ground cinnamon
2 (1.9-ounce / 54-g) packages frozen miniature phyllo tart shells

1. Place the walnuts and pistachios in an air fryer basket in an even layer.
2. Slide the basket into the air fryer oven. Cook at 350°F (180°C) for 4 minutes.
3. After 2 minutes, remove the basket and stir the nuts. Transfer the basket back to the air fryer oven and cook for another 1 to 2 minutes until the nuts are golden brown and fragrant.
4. Meanwhile, stir together the butter, ¼ cup of honey, sugar, and cinnamon in a medium bowl.
5. When done, remove from the air fryer oven and place the nuts on a cutting board and allow to cool for 5 minutes. Finely chop the nuts. Add the chopped nuts and all the "nut dust" to the butter mixture and stir well.
6. Arrange the phyllo cups on a sheet pan. Evenly fill the phyllo cups with the nut mixture, mounding it up. As you work, stir the nuts in the bowl frequently so that the syrup is evenly distributed throughout the filling.
7. Slide the pan into the air fryer oven. Cook at 350°F (180°C) for 12 minutes.
8. After about 8 minutes, check the cups, and rotate the pan if they are not browning evenly. Continue cooking until the cups are golden brown and the syrup is bubbling.
9. When cooking is complete, remove the baklava from the air fryer oven, drizzle each cup with about ⅛ teaspoon of the remaining honey over the top.
10. Allow to cool for 5 minutes before serving.

Lemon Ricotta Cake

Prep time: 5 minutes | Cook time: 25 minutes | Serves 6

17.5 ounces (496 g) ricotta cheese
5.4 ounces (153 g) sugar
3 eggs, beaten
3 tablespoons flour
1 lemon, juiced and zested
2 teaspoons vanilla extract

1. In a large mixing bowl, stir together all the ingredients until the mixture reaches a creamy consistency.
2. Pour the mixture into a baking pan and place in the air fryer oven.
3. Slide the pan into the air fryer oven. Cook at 320°F (160°C) for 25 minutes.
4. When cooking is complete, a toothpick inserted in the center should come out clean.
5. Allow to cool for 10 minutes on a wire rack before serving.

Lemon-Raspberry Muffins

Prep time: 5 minutes | Cook time: 15 minutes | Serves 6

2 cups almond flour
¾ cup Swerve
1¼ teaspoons baking powder
⅓ teaspoon ground allspice
⅓ teaspoon ground anise star
½ teaspoon grated lemon zest
¼ teaspoon salt
2 eggs
1 cup sour cream
½ cup coconut oil
½ cup raspberries

1. Line a muffin pan with 6 paper liners.
2. In a mixing bowl, mix the almond flour, Swerve, baking powder, allspice, anise, lemon zest, and salt.
3. In another mixing bowl, beat the eggs, sour cream, and coconut oil until well mixed. Add the egg mixture to the flour mixture and stir to combine. Mix in the raspberries.
4. Scrape the batter into the prepared muffin cups, filling each about three-quarters full.
5. Slide the pan into the air fryer oven. Cook at 345°F (174°C) for 15 minutes.
6. When cooking is complete, the tops should be golden and a toothpick inserted in the middle should come out clean.
7. Allow the muffins to cool for 10 minutes in the muffin pan before removing and serving.

Lemon-Butter Shortbread

Prep time: 10 minutes | Cook time: 36 to 40 minutes | Makes 4 dozen cookies

1 tablespoon grated lemon zest
1 cup granulated sugar
1 pound (454 g) unsalted butter, at room temperature
¼ teaspoon fine salt
4 cups all-purpose flour
⅓ cup cornstarch
Cooking spray

1. Add the lemon zest and sugar to a stand mixer fitted with the paddle attachment and beat on medium speed for 1 to 2 minute. Let stand for about 5 minutes. Fold in the butter and salt and blend until fluffy.
2. Mix the flour and cornstarch in a large bowl. Add to the butter mixture and mix to combine.
3. Spritz a sheet pan with cooking spray and spread a piece of parchment paper onto the pan. Scrape the dough into the pan until even and smooth.
4. Slide the pan into the air fryer oven. Cook at 325°F (160°C) for 36 minutes.
5. After 20 minutes, check the shortbread, rotating the pan if it is not browning evenly. Continue cooking for another 16 minutes until lightly browned.
6. When done, remove from the air fryer oven. Slice and allow to cool for 5 minutes before serving.

Mixed Berries with Pecan Streusel Topping

Prep time: 5 minutes | Cook time: 17 minutes | Serves 3

½ cup mixed berries
Cooking spray
Topping:
1 egg, beaten
3 tablespoons almonds, slivered
3 tablespoons chopped pecans
2 tablespoons chopped walnuts
3 tablespoons granulated Swerve
2 tablespoons cold salted butter, cut into pieces
½ teaspoon ground cinnamon

1. Lightly spray a baking dish with cooking spray.
2. Make the topping: In a medium bowl, stir together the beaten egg, nuts, Swerve, butter, and cinnamon until well blended.
3. Put the mixed berries in the bottom of the baking dish and spread the topping over the top.
4. Slide the baking dish into the air fryer oven. Cook at 340°F (171°C) for 17 minutes.
5. When cooking is complete, the fruit should be bubbly and topping should be golden brown.
6. Allow to cool for 5 to 10 minutes before serving.

Desserts 47

Oaty Chocolate Chip Cookies

Prep time: 10 minutes | Cook time: 20 minutes | Makes 4 dozen (1-by-1½-inch) bars

1 cup unsalted butter, at room temperature
1 cup dark brown sugar
½ cup granulated sugar
2 large eggs
1 tablespoon vanilla extract
Pinch salt
2 cups old-fashioned rolled oats
1½ cups all-purpose flour
1 teaspoon baking powder
1 teaspoon baking soda
2 cups chocolate chips

1. Stir together the butter, brown sugar, and granulated sugar in a large mixing bowl until smooth and light in color.
2. Crack the eggs into the bowl, one at a time, mixing after each addition. Stir in the vanilla and salt.
3. Mix the oats, flour, baking powder, and baking soda in a separate bowl. Add the mixture to the butter mixture and stir until mixed. Stir in the chocolate chips.
4. Spread the dough into a sheet pan.
5. Slide the pan into the air fryer oven. Cook at 350°F (180°C) for 20 minutes.
6. After 15 minutes, check the cookie, rotating the pan if the crust is not browning evenly. Continue cooking for 18 to 20 minutes or until golden brown.
7. When cooking is complete, remove from the air fryer oven and allow to cool completely before slicing and serving.

Orange and Anise Cake

Prep time: 5 minutes | Cook time: 20 minutes | Serves 6

1 stick butter, at room temperature
5 tablespoons liquid monk fruit
2 eggs plus 1 egg yolk, beaten
⅓ cup hazelnuts, roughly chopped
3 tablespoons sugar-free orange marmalade
6 ounces (170 g) unbleached almond flour
1 teaspoon baking soda
½ teaspoon baking powder
½ teaspoon ground cinnamon
½ teaspoon ground allspice
½ ground anise seed
Cooking spray

1. Lightly spritz a baking pan with cooking spray.
2. In a mixing bowl, whisk the butter and liquid monk fruit until the mixture is pale and smooth. Mix in the beaten eggs, hazelnuts, and marmalade and whisk again until well incorporated.
3. Add the almond flour, baking soda, baking powder, cinnamon, allspice, anise seed and stir to mix well.
4. Scrape the batter into the prepared baking pan.
5. Slide the pan into the air fryer oven. Cook at 310°F (154°C) for 20 minutes.
6. When cooking is complete, the top of the cake should spring back when gently pressed with your fingers.
7. Transfer to a wire rack and let the cake cool to room temperature. Serve immediately.

Peach-Blueberry Tart

Prep time: 10 minutes | Cook time: 30 minutes | Serves 6 to 8

4 peaches, pitted and sliced
1 cup fresh blueberries
2 tablespoons cornstarch
3 tablespoons sugar
1 tablespoon freshly squeezed lemon juice
Cooking spray
1 sheet frozen puff pastry, thawed
1 tablespoon nonfat or low-fat milk
Confectioners' sugar, for dusting

1. Add the peaches, blueberries, cornstarch, sugar, and lemon juice to a large bowl and toss to coat.
2. Spritz a round baking pan with cooking spray.
3. Unfold the pastry and put on the prepared baking pan.
4. Lay the peach slices on the pan, slightly overlapping them. Scatter the blueberries over the peach.
5. Drape the pastry over the outside of the fruit and press pleats firmly together. Brush the milk over the pastry.
6. Slide the pan into the air fryer oven. Cook at 400°F (205°C) for 30 minutes.
7. Bake until the crust is golden brown and the fruit is bubbling.
8. When cooking is complete, remove from the air fryer oven and allow to cool for 10 minutes.
9. Serve the tart with the confectioners' sugar sprinkled on top.

Orange Coconut Cake

Prep time: 5 minutes | Cook time: 17 minutes | Serves 6

1 stick butter, melted
¾ cup granulated Swerve
2 eggs, beaten
¾ cup coconut flour
¼ teaspoon salt
⅓ teaspoon grated nutmeg
⅓ cup coconut milk
1¼ cups almond flour
½ teaspoon baking powder
2 tablespoons unsweetened orange jam
Cooking spray

1. Coat a baking pan with cooking spray. Set aside.
2. In a large mixing bowl, whisk together the melted butter and granulated Swerve until fluffy.
3. Mix in the beaten eggs and whisk again until smooth. Stir in the coconut flour, salt, and nutmeg and gradually pour in the coconut milk. Add the remaining ingredients and stir until well incorporated.
4. Scrape the batter into the baking pan.
5. Slide the pan into the air fryer oven. Cook at 355°F (179°C) for 17 minutes.
6. When cooking is complete, the top of the cake should spring back when gently pressed with your fingers.
7. Remove from the air fryer oven to a wire rack to cool. Serve chilled.

Vanilla Walnuts Tart

Prep time: 5 minutes | Cook time: 13 minutes | Serves 6

1 cup coconut milk
½ cup walnuts, ground
½ cup Swerve
½ cup almond flour
½ stick butter, at room temperature
2 eggs
1 teaspoon vanilla essence
¼ teaspoon ground cardamom
¼ teaspoon ground cloves
Cooking spray

1. Coat a baking pan with cooking spray.
2. Combine all the ingredients except the oil in a large bowl and stir until well blended. Spoon the batter mixture into the baking pan.
3. Slide the pan into the air fryer oven. Cook at 360°F (182°C) for 13 minutes.
4. When cooking is complete, a toothpick inserted into the center of the tart should come out clean.
5. Remove from the air fryer oven and place on a wire rack to cool. Serve immediately.

Peanut Butter-Chocolate Bread Pudding

Prep time: 10 minutes | Cook time: 10 minutes | Serves 8

1 egg
1 egg yolk
¾ cup chocolate milk
3 tablespoons brown sugar
3 tablespoons peanut butter
2 tablespoons cocoa powder
1 teaspoon vanilla
5 slices firm white bread, cubed
Nonstick cooking spray

1. Spritz a baking pan with nonstick cooking spray.
2. Whisk together the egg, egg yolk, chocolate milk, brown sugar, peanut butter, cocoa powder, and vanilla until well combined.
3. Fold in the bread cubes and stir to mix well. Allow the bread soak for 10 minutes.
4. When ready, transfer the egg mixture to the prepared baking pan.
5. Slide the pan into the air fryer oven. Cook at 330°F (166°C) for 10 minutes.
6. When done, the pudding should be just firm to the touch.
7. Serve at room temperature.

Ultimate Coconut Chocolate Cake

Prep time: 5 minutes | Cook time: 15 minutes | Serves 10

1¼ cups unsweetened bakers' chocolate
1 stick butter
1 teaspoon liquid stevia
⅓ cup shredded coconut
2 tablespoons coconut milk
2 eggs, beaten
Cooking spray

1. Lightly spritz a baking pan with cooking spray.
2. Place the chocolate, butter, and stevia in a microwave-safe bowl. Microwave for about 30 seconds until melted. Let the chocolate mixture cool to room temperature.
3. Add the remaining ingredients to the chocolate mixture and stir until well incorporated. Pour the batter into the prepared baking pan.
4. Slide the pan into the air fryer oven. Cook at 330°F (166°C) for 15 minutes.
5. When cooking is complete, a toothpick inserted in the center should come out clean.
6. Remove from the air fryer oven and allow to cool for about 10 minutes before serving.

Pumpkin Pudding and Vanilla Wafers

Prep time: 10 minutes | Cook time: 15 minutes | Serves 4

1 cup canned no-salt-added pumpkin purée (not pumpkin pie filling)
¼ cup packed brown sugar
3 tablespoons all-purpose flour
1 egg, whisked
2 tablespoons milk
1 tablespoon unsalted butter, melted
1 teaspoon pure vanilla extract
4 low-fat vanilla wafers, crumbled
Cooking spray

1. Coat a baking pan with cooking spray. Set aside.
2. Mix the pumpkin purée, brown sugar, flour, whisked egg, milk, melted butter, and vanilla in a medium bowl and whisk to combine. Transfer the mixture to the baking pan.
3. Slide the pan into the air fryer oven. Cook at 350°F (180°C) for 15 minutes.
4. When cooking is complete, the pudding should be set.
5. Remove the pudding from the air fryer oven to a wire rack to cool.
6. Divide the pudding into four bowls and serve with the vanilla wafers sprinkled on top.

Strawberry and Rhubarb Crumble

Prep time: 10 minutes | Cook time: 12 to 17 minutes | Serves 6

1½ cups sliced fresh strawberries
⅓ cup sugar
¾ cup sliced rhubarb
⅔ cup quick-cooking oatmeal
¼ cup packed brown sugar
½ cup whole-wheat pastry flour
½ teaspoon ground cinnamon
3 tablespoons unsalted butter, melted

2. Place the strawberries, sugar, and rhubarb in a baking pan and toss to coat.
3. Combine the oatmeal, brown sugar, pastry flour, and cinnamon in a medium bowl.
4. Add the melted butter to the oatmeal mixture and stir until crumbly. Sprinkle this generously on top of the strawberries and rhubarb.
5. Slide the pan into the air fryer oven. Cook at 370°F (188°C) for 12 minutes.
6. Bake until the fruit is bubbly and the topping is golden brown. Continue cooking for an additional 2 to 5 minutes if needed.
7. When cooking is complete, remove from the air fryer oven and serve warm.

Summer Berry Crisp

Prep time: 10 minutes | Cook time: 12 minutes | Serves 4

½ cup fresh blueberries
½ cup chopped fresh strawberries
⅓ cup frozen raspberries, thawed
1 tablespoon honey
1 tablespoon freshly squeezed lemon juice
⅔ cup whole-wheat pastry flour
3 tablespoons packed brown sugar
2 tablespoons unsalted butter, melted

1. Place the blueberries, strawberries, and raspberries in a baking pan and drizzle the honey and lemon juice over the top.
2. Combine the pastry flour and brown sugar in a small mixing bowl.
3. Add the butter and whisk until the mixture is crumbly. Scatter the flour mixture on top of the fruit.
4. Slide the pan into the air fryer oven. Cook at 380°F (193°C) for 12 minutes.
5. When cooking is complete, the fruit should be bubbly and the topping should be golden brown.
6. Remove from the air fryer oven and serve on a plate.

Vanilla Chocolate Chip Cookies

Prep time: 10 minutes | Cook time: 22 minutes | Makes 30 cookies

⅓ cup (80g) organic brown sugar
⅓ cup (80g) organic cane sugar
4 ounces (112g) cashew-based vegan butter
½ cup coconut cream
1 teaspoon vanilla extract
2 tablespoons ground flaxseed
1 teaspoon baking powder
1 teaspoon baking soda
Pinch of salt
2¼ cups (220g) almond flour
½ cup (90g) dairy-free dark chocolate chips

1. Line a baking sheet with parchment paper.
2. Mix the brown sugar, cane sugar, and butter in a medium bowl or the bowl of a stand mixer. Cream together with a mixer.
3. Fold in the coconut cream, vanilla, flaxseed, baking powder, baking soda, and salt. Stir well.
4. Add the almond flour, a little at a time, mixing after each addition until fully incorporated. Stir in the chocolate chips with a spatula.
5. Scoop the dough onto the prepared baking sheet.
6. Slide the baking sheet into the air fryer oven. Cook at 325°F (160°C) for 22 minutes.
7. Bake until the cookies are golden brown.
8. When cooking is complete, transfer the baking sheet onto a wire rack to cool completely before serving.

Fast and Easy Everyday Favorites

Air Fried Bacon Pinwheels

Prep time: 5 minutes | Cook time: 10 minutes | Makes 8 pinwheels

1 sheet puff pastry
2 tablespoons maple syrup
¼ cup brown sugar
8 slices bacon
Ground black pepper, to taste
Cooking spray

1. Spritz an air fryer basket with cooking spray.
2. Roll the puff pastry into a 10-inch square with a rolling pin on a clean work surface, then cut the pastry into 8 strips.
3. Brush the strips with maple syrup and sprinkle with sugar, leaving a 1-inch far end uncovered.
4. Arrange each slice of bacon on each strip, leaving a ⅛-inch length of bacon hang over the end close to you. Sprinkle with black pepper.
5. From the end close to you, roll the strips into pinwheels, then dab the uncovered end with water and seal the rolls.
6. Arrange the pinwheels in the air fryer basket and spritz with cooking spray.
7. Slide the basket into the air fryer oven. Cook at 360°F (182°C) for 10 minutes.
8. Flip the pinwheels halfway through.
9. When cooking is complete, the pinwheels should be golden brown. Remove from the air fryer oven.
10. Serve immediately.

Air Fried Crispy Brussels Sprouts

Prep time: 5 minutes | Cook time: 20 minutes | Serves 4

¼ teaspoon salt
⅛ teaspoon ground black pepper
1 tablespoon extra-virgin olive oil
1 pound (454 g) Brussels sprouts, trimmed and halved
Lemon wedges, for garnish

1. Combine the salt, black pepper, and olive oil in a large bowl. Stir to mix well.
2. Add the Brussels sprouts to the bowl of mixture and toss to coat well. Arrange the Brussels sprouts in an air fryer basket.
3. Slide the basket into the air fryer oven. Cook at 350°F (180°C) for 20 minutes.
4. Stir the Brussels sprouts two times during cooking.
5. When cooked, the Brussels sprouts will be lightly browned and wilted. Remove from the air fryer oven.
6. Transfer the cooked Brussels sprouts to a large plate and squeeze the lemon wedges on top to serve.

Apple Fritters with Sugary Glaze

Prep time: 10 minutes | Cook time: 8 minutes | Makes 15 fritters

Apple Fritters:
2 firm apples, peeled, cored, and diced
½ teaspoon cinnamon
Juice of 1 lemon
1 cup all-purpose flour
1½ teaspoons baking powder
½ teaspoon kosher salt
2 eggs
¼ cup milk
2 tablespoons unsalted butter, melted
2 tablespoons granulated sugar
Cooking spray
Glaze:
½ teaspoon vanilla extract
1¼ cups powdered sugar, sifted
¼ cup water

1. Line an air fryer basket with parchment paper.
2. Combine the apples with cinnamon and lemon juice in a small bowl. Toss to coat well.
3. Combine the flour, baking powder, and salt in a large bowl. Stir to mix well.
4. Whisk the egg, milk, butter, and sugar in a medium bowl. Stir to mix well.
5. Make a well in the center of the flour mixture, then pour the egg mixture into the well and stir to mix well. Mix in the apple until a dough forms.
6. Use an ice cream scoop to scoop 15 balls from the dough into the basket. Spritz with cooking spray.
7. Slide the basket into the air fryer oven. Cook at 360°F (182°C) for 8 minutes.
8. Flip the apple fritters halfway through the cooking time.
9. Meanwhile, combine the ingredients for the glaze in a separate small bowl. Stir to mix well.
10. When cooking is complete, the apple fritters will be golden brown. Serve the fritters with the glaze on top or use the glaze for dipping.

Buttery Knots with Parsley

Prep time: 5 minutes | Cook time: 5 minutes | Makes 8 knots

1 teaspoon dried parsley
¼ cup melted butter
2 teaspoons garlic powder
1 (11-ounce / 312-g) tube refrigerated French bread dough, cut into 8 slices

1. Combine the parsley, butter, and garlic powder in a bowl. Stir to mix well.
2. Place the French bread dough slices on a clean work surface, then roll each slice into a 6-inch long rope. Tie the ropes into knots and arrange them on a plate.
3. Transfer the knots into a baking pan. Brush the knots with butter mixture.
4. Slide the pan into the air fryer oven. Cook at 350°F (180°C) for 5 minutes.
5. Flip the knots halfway through the cooking time.
6. When done, the knots should be golden brown. Remove from the air fryer oven.
7. Serve immediately.

Bartlett Pears with Lemony Ricotta

Prep time: 10 minutes | Cook time: 8 minutes | Serves 4

2 large Bartlett pears, peeled, cut in half, cored
3 tablespoons melted butter
½ teaspoon ground ginger
¼ teaspoon ground cardamom
3 tablespoons brown sugar
½ cup whole-milk ricotta cheese
1 teaspoon pure lemon extract
1 teaspoon pure almond extract
1 tablespoon honey, plus additional for drizzling

1. Toss the pears with butter, ginger, cardamom, and sugar in a large bowl. Toss to coat well. Arrange the pears in a baking pan, cut side down.
2. Slide the pan into the air fryer oven. Cook at 375°F (190°C) for 8 minutes.
3. After 5 minutes, remove the pan and flip the pears. Return to the air fryer oven and continue cooking.
4. When cooking is complete, the pears should be soft and browned. Remove from the air fryer oven.
5. In the meantime, combine the remaining ingredients in a separate bowl. Whip for 1 minute with a hand mixer until the mixture is puffed.
6. Divide the mixture into four bowls, then put the pears over the mixture and drizzle with more honey to serve.

Butternut Squash with Hazelnuts

Prep time: 10 minutes | Cook time: 23 minutes | Makes 3 cups

2 tablespoons whole hazelnuts
3 cups butternut squash, peeled, deseeded and cubed
¼ teaspoon kosher salt
¼ teaspoon freshly ground black pepper
2 teaspoons olive oil
Cooking spray

1. Spritz an air fryer basket with cooking spray. Spread the hazelnuts in the basket.
2. Slide the basket into the air fryer oven. Cook at 300°F (150°C) for 3 minutes.
3. When done, the hazelnuts should be soft. Remove from the air fryer oven. Chopped the hazelnuts roughly and transfer to a small bowl. Set aside.
4. Put the butternut squash in a large bowl, then sprinkle with salt and pepper and drizzle with olive oil. Toss to coat well. Transfer the squash to the lightly greased air fryer basket.
5. Slide the basket into the air fryer oven. Cook at 360°F (182°C) for 20 minutes.
6. Slide the basket into the air fryer oven. Flip the squash halfway through the cooking time.
7. When cooking is complete, the squash will be soft. Transfer the squash to a plate and sprinkle with the chopped hazelnuts before serving.

Baked Cherry Tomatoes with Basil

Prep time: 5 minutes | Cook time: 5 minutes | Serves 2

2 cups cherry tomatoes
1 clove garlic, thinly sliced
1 teaspoon olive oil
⅛ teaspoon kosher salt
1 tablespoon freshly chopped basil, for topping
Cooking spray

1. Spritz a baking pan with cooking spray and set aside.
2. In a large bowl, toss together the cherry tomatoes, sliced garlic, olive oil, and kosher salt. Spread the mixture in an even layer in the prepared pan.
3. Slide the pan into the air fryer oven. Cook at 360°F (182°C) for 5 minutes.
4. When cooking is complete, the tomatoes should be the soft and wilted.
5. Transfer to a bowl and rest for 5 minutes. Top with the chopped basil and serve warm.

Cheddar Jalapeño Cornbread

Prep time: 10 minutes | Cook time: 20 minutes | Serves 8

⅔ cup cornmeal
⅓ cup all-purpose flour
¾ teaspoon baking powder
2 tablespoons buttery spread, melted
½ teaspoon kosher salt
1 tablespoon granulated sugar
¾ cup whole milk
1 large egg, beaten
1 jalapeño pepper, thinly sliced
⅓ cup shredded sharp Cheddar cheese
Cooking spray

1. Spritz a baking pan with cooking spray.
2. Combine all the ingredients in a large bowl. Stir to mix well. Pour the mixture in the baking pan.
3. Slide the pan into the air fryer oven. Cook at 300°F (150°C) for 20 minutes.
4. When the cooking is complete, a toothpick inserted in the center of the bread should come out clean.
5. Remove the baking pan from the air fryer oven and allow the bread to cool for 5 minutes before slicing to serve.

Citrus Avocado Wedge Fries

Prep time: 10 minutes | Cook time: 8 minutes | Makes 12 fries

1 cup all-purpose flour
3 tablespoons lime juice
¾ cup orange juice
1¼ cups plain dried bread crumbs
1 cup yellow cornmeal
1½ tablespoons chile powder
2 large Hass avocados, peeled, pitted, and cut into wedges
Coarse sea salt, to taste
Cooking spray

1. Spritz an air fryer basket with cooking spray.
2. Pour the flour in a bowl. Mix the lime juice with orange juice in a second bowl. Combine the bread crumbs, cornmeal, and chile powder in a third bowl.
3. Dip the avocado wedges in the bowl of flour to coat well, then dredge the wedges into the bowl of juice mixture, and then dunk the wedges in the bread crumbs mixture. Shake the excess off.
4. Arrange the coated avocado wedges in a single layer in the air fryer basket. Spritz with cooking spray.
5. Slide the basket into the air fryer oven. Cook at 400°F (205°C) for 8 minutes.
6. Stir the avocado wedges and sprinkle with salt halfway through the cooking time.
7. When cooking is complete, the avocado wedges should be tender and crispy.
8. Serve immediately.

Classic Worcestershire Poutine

Prep time: 15 minutes | Cook time: 33 minutes | Serves 2

2 russet potatoes, scrubbed and cut into ½-inch sticks
2 teaspoons vegetable oil
2 tablespoons butter
¼ onion, minced
¼ teaspoon dried thyme
1 clove garlic, smashed
3 tablespoons all-purpose flour
1 teaspoon tomato paste
1½ cups beef stock
2 teaspoons Worcestershire sauce
Salt and freshly ground black pepper, to taste
⅔ cup chopped string cheese

1. Bring a pot of water to a boil, then put in the potato sticks and blanch for 4 minutes.
2. Drain the potato sticks and rinse under running cold water, then pat dry with paper towels.
3. Transfer the sticks in a large bowl and drizzle with vegetable oil. Toss to coat well. Place the potato sticks in an air fryer basket.
4. Slide the basket into the air fryer oven. Cook at 400°F (205°C) for 25 minutes.
5. Stir the potato sticks at least three times during cooking.
6. Meanwhile, make the gravy: Heat the butter in a saucepan over medium heat until melted.
7. Add the onion, thyme, and garlic and sauté for 5 minutes or until the onion is translucent.
8. Add the flour and sauté for an additional 2 minutes. Pour in the tomato paste and beef stock and cook for 1 more minute or until lightly thickened.
9. Drizzle the gravy with Worcestershire sauce and sprinkle with salt and ground black pepper. Reduce the heat to low to keep the gravy warm until ready to serve.
10. When done, the sticks should be golden brown. Remove from the air fryer oven. Transfer the fried potato sticks onto a plate, then sprinkle with salt and ground black pepper. Scatter with string cheese and pour the gravy over. Serve warm.

Corn on the Cob with Mayonnaise

Prep time: 10 minutes | Cook time: 10 minutes | Serves 4

2 tablespoons mayonnaise
2 teaspoons minced garlic
½ teaspoon sea salt
1 cup panko bread crumbs
4 (4-inch length) ears corn on the cob, husk and silk removed
Cooking spray

1. Spritz an air fryer basket with cooking spray.
2. Combine the mayonnaise, garlic, and salt in a bowl. Stir to mix well. Pour the panko on a plate.
3. Brush the corn on the cob with mayonnaise mixture, then roll the cob in the bread crumbs and press to coat well.
4. Transfer the corn on the cob in the air fryer basket and spritz with cooking spray.
5. Slide the basket into the air fryer oven. Cook at 400°F (205°C) for 10 minutes.
6. Flip the corn on the cob at least three times during the cooking.
7. When cooked, the corn kernels on the cob should be almost browned. Remove from the air fryer oven.
8. Serve immediately.

Yogurt Dip

Prep time: 10 minutes | Cook time: 10 minutes | Serves 4

3 medium parsnips, peeled, cut into sticks
¼ teaspoon kosher salt
1 teaspoon olive oil
1 garlic clove, unpeeled
Cooking spray
Dip:
¼ cup plain Greek yogurt
⅛ teaspoon garlic powder
1 tablespoon sour cream
¼ teaspoon kosher salt
Freshly ground black pepper, to taste

1. Spritz an air fryer basket with cooking spray.
2. Put the parsnip sticks in a large bowl, then sprinkle with salt and drizzle with olive oil.
3. Transfer the parsnip into the air fryer basket and add the garlic.
4. Slide the basket into the air fryer oven. Cook at 360°F (182°C) for 10 minutes.
5. Stir the parsnip halfway through the cooking time.
6. Meanwhile, peel the garlic and crush it. Combine the crushed garlic with the ingredients for the dip. Stir to mix well.
7. When cooked, the parsnip sticks should be crisp. Remove the parsnip fries from the air fryer oven and serve with the dipping sauce.

Golden Salmon and Carrot Croquettes

Prep time: 15 minutes | Cook time: 10 minutes | Serves 6

2 egg whites
1 cup almond flour
1 cup panko bread crumbs
1 pound (454 g) chopped salmon fillet
⅔ cup grated carrots
2 tablespoons minced garlic cloves
½ cup chopped onion
2 tablespoons chopped chives
Cooking spray

1. Spritz an air fryer basket with cooking spray.
2. Whisk the egg whites in a bowl. Put the flour in a second bowl. Pour the bread crumbs in a third bowl. Set aside.
3. Combine the salmon, carrots, garlic, onion, and chives in a large bowl. Stir to mix well.
4. Form the mixture into balls with your hands. Dredge the balls into the flour, then egg, and then bread crumbs to coat well.
5. Arrange the salmon balls in the air fryer basket and spritz with cooking spray.
6. Slide the basket into the air fryer oven. Cook at 350°F (180°C) for 10 minutes.
7. Flip the salmon balls halfway through cooking.
8. When cooking is complete, the salmon balls will be crispy and browned. Remove from the air fryer oven.
9. Serve immediately.

Crispy Cheese Wafer

Prep time: 5 minutes | Cook time: 5 minutes | Serves 2

1 cup shredded aged Manchego cheese
1 teaspoon all-purpose flour
½ teaspoon cumin seeds
¼ teaspoon cracked black pepper

1. Line an air fryer basket with parchment paper.
2. Combine the cheese and flour in a bowl. Stir to mix well. Spread the mixture in the basket into a 4-inch round.
3. Combine the cumin and black pepper in a small bowl. Stir to mix well. Sprinkle the cumin mixture over the cheese round.
4. Slide the basket into the air fryer oven. Cook at 375°F (190°C) for 5 minutes.
5. When cooked, the cheese will be lightly browned and frothy.
6. Use tongs to transfer the cheese wafer onto a plate and slice to serve.

Crispy Zucchini Sticks

Prep time: 5 minutes | Cook time: 10 minutes | Serves 4

1 medium zucchini, cut into 48 sticks
¼ cup seasoned bread crumbs
1 tablespoon melted buttery spread
Cooking spray

1. Spritz an air fryer basket with cooking spray and set aside.
2. In 2 different shallow bowls, add the seasoned bread crumbs and the buttery spread.
3. One by one, dredge the zucchini sticks into the buttery spread, then roll in the bread crumbs to coat evenly. Arrange the crusted sticks in the air fryer basket.
4. Slide the basket into the air fryer oven. Cook at 360°F (182°C) for 10 minutes.
5. Stir the sticks halfway through the cooking time.
6. When done, the sticks should be golden brown and crispy. Transfer the fries to a plate. Rest for 5 minutes and serve warm.

Crunchy Green Tomatoes Slices

Prep time: 10 minutes | Cook time: 8 minutes | Makes 12 slices

½ cup all-purpose flour
1 egg
½ cup buttermilk
1 cup cornmeal
1 cup panko
2 green tomatoes, cut into ¼-inch-thick slices, patted dry
½ teaspoon salt
½ teaspoon ground black pepper
Cooking spray

1. Spritz a baking sheet with cooking spray.
2. Pour the flour in a bowl. Whisk the egg and buttermilk in a second bowl. Combine the cornmeal and panko in a third bowl.
3. Dredge the tomato slices in the bowl of flour first, then into the egg mixture, and then dunk the slices into the cornmeal mixture. Shake the excess off.
4. Transfer the well-coated tomato slices in the baking sheet and sprinkle with salt and ground black pepper. Spritz the tomato slices with cooking spray.
5. Slide the baking sheet into the air fryer oven. Cook at 400°F (205°C) for 8 minutes.
6. Flip the slices halfway through the cooking time.
7. When cooking is complete, the tomato slices should be crispy and lightly browned. Remove the baking sheet from the air fryer oven.
8. Serve immediately.

Crunchy and Beery Onion Rings

Prep time: 10 minutes | Cook time: 16 minutes | Serves 2 to 4

⅔ cup all-purpose flour
1 teaspoon paprika
½ teaspoon baking soda
1 teaspoon salt
½ teaspoon freshly ground black pepper
1 egg, beaten
¾ cup beer
1½ cups bread crumbs
1 tablespoons olive oil
1 large Vidalia onion, peeled and sliced into ½-inch rings
Cooking spray

1. Spritz an air fryer basket with cooking spray.
2. Combine the flour, paprika, baking soda, salt, and ground black pepper in a bowl. Stir to mix well.
3. Combine the egg and beer in a separate bowl. Stir to mix well.
4. Make a well in the center of the flour mixture, then pour the egg mixture in the well. Stir to mix everything well.
5. Pour the bread crumbs and olive oil in a shallow plate. Stir to mix well.
6. Dredge the onion rings gently into the flour and egg mixture, then shake the excess off and put into the plate of bread crumbs. Flip to coat the both sides well. Arrange the onion rings in the air fryer basket.
7. Slide the basket into the air fryer oven. Cook at 360°F (182°C) for 16 minutes.
8. Flip the rings and put the bottom rings to the top halfway through.
9. When cooked, the rings will be golden brown and crunchy. Remove from the air fryer oven.
10. Serve immediately.

Kale Chips with Soy Sauce

Prep time: 5 minutes | Cook time: 5 minutes | Serves 2

4 medium kale leaves, about 1 ounce (28 g) each, stems removed, tear the leaves in thirds
2 teaspoons soy sauce
2 teaspoons olive oil

1. Toss the kale leaves with soy sauce and olive oil in a large bowl to coat well. Place the leaves in a baking pan.
2. Slide the pan into the air fryer oven. Cook at 400°F (205°C) for 5 minutes.
3. Flip the leaves with tongs gently halfway through.
4. When cooked, the kale leaves should be crispy. Remove from the air fryer oven.
5. Serve immediately.

Fast Cinnamon Toast

Prep time: 5 minutes | Cook time: 5 minutes | Serves 6

1½ teaspoons cinnamon
1½ teaspoons vanilla extract
½ cup sugar
2 teaspoons ground black pepper
2 tablespoons melted coconut oil
12 slices whole wheat bread

1. Combine all the ingredients, except for the bread, in a large bowl. Stir to mix well.
2. Dunk the bread in the bowl of mixture gently to coat and infuse well. Shake the excess off. Arrange the bread slices in an air fryer basket.
3. Slide the basket into the air fryer oven. Cook at 400°F (205°C) for 5 minutes.
4. Flip the bread halfway through.
5. When cooking is complete, the bread should be golden brown.
6. Remove the bread slices from the air fryer oven and slice to serve.

Garlicky Spiralized Zucchini and Squash

Prep time: 10 minutes | Cook time: 10 minutes | Serves 4

2 large zucchini, peeled and spiralized
2 large yellow summer squash, peeled and spiralized
1 tablespoon olive oil, divided
½ teaspoon kosher salt
1 garlic clove, whole
2 tablespoons fresh basil, chopped
Cooking spray

1. Spritz an air fryer basket with cooking spray.
2. Combine the zucchini and summer squash with 1 teaspoon of the olive oil and salt in a large bowl. Toss to coat well.
3. Transfer the zucchini and summer squash to the air fryer basket and add the garlic.
4. Slide the basket into the air fryer oven. Cook at 360°F (182°C) for 10 minutes.
5. Stir the zucchini and summer squash halfway through the cooking time.
6. When cooked, the zucchini and summer squash will be tender and fragrant. Transfer the cooked zucchini and summer squash onto a plate and set aside.
7. Remove the garlic from the air fryer oven and allow to cool for 5 minutes. Mince the garlic and combine with remaining olive oil in a small bowl. Stir to mix well.
8. Drizzle the spiralized zucchini and summer squash with garlic oil and sprinkle with basil. Toss to serve.

Hot Wings

Prep time: 5 minutes | Cook time: 15 minutes | Makes 16 wings

16 chicken wings
3 tablespoons hot sauce
Cooking spray

1. Spritz an air fryer basket with cooking spray.
2. Arrange the chicken wings in the air fryer basket.
3. Slide the basket into the air fryer oven. Cook at 360°F (182°C) for 15 minutes.
4. Flip the wings at lease three times during cooking.
5. When cooking is complete, the chicken wings will be well browned. Remove from the air fryer oven.
6. Transfer the air fried wings to a plate and serve with hot sauce.

Spanakopita

Prep time: 10 minutes | Cook time: 8 minutes | Serves 6

½ (10-ounce / 284-g) package frozen spinach, thawed and squeezed dry
1 egg, lightly beaten
¼ cup pine nuts, toasted
¼ cup grated Parmesan cheese
¾ cup crumbled feta cheese
⅛ teaspoon ground nutmeg
½ teaspoon salt
Freshly ground black pepper, to taste
6 sheets phyllo dough
½ cup butter, melted

1. Combine all the ingredients, except for the phyllo dough and butter, in a large bowl. Whisk to combine well. Set aside.
2. Place a sheet of phyllo dough on a clean work surface. Brush with butter then top with another layer sheet of phyllo. Brush with butter, then cut the layered sheets into six 3-inch-wide strips.
3. Top each strip with 1 tablespoon of the spinach mixture, then fold the bottom left corner over the mixture towards the right strip edge to make a triangle. Keep folding triangles until each strip is folded over.
4. Brush the triangles with butter and repeat with remaining strips and phyllo dough.
5. Place the triangles in a baking pan.
6. Slide the pan into the air fryer oven. Cook at 350°F (180°C) for 8 minutes.
7. Flip the triangles halfway through the cooking time.
8. When cooking is complete, the triangles should be golden brown. Remove from the air fryer oven.
9. Serve immediately.

Lemony and Garlicky Asparagus

Prep time: 5 minutes | Cook time: 10 minutes | Makes 10 spears

10 spears asparagus (about ½ pound / 227 g in total), snap the ends off
1 tablespoon lemon juice
2 teaspoons minced garlic
½ teaspoon salt
¼ teaspoon ground black pepper
Cooking spray

1. Line an air fryer basket with parchment paper.
2. Put the asparagus spears in a large bowl. Drizzle with lemon juice and sprinkle with minced garlic, salt, and ground black pepper. Toss to coat well.
3. Transfer the asparagus to the air fryer basket and spritz with cooking spray.
4. Slide the basket into the air fryer oven. Cook at 400°F (205°C) for 10 minutes.
5. Flip the asparagus halfway through cooking.
6. When cooked, the asparagus should be wilted and soft. Remove from the air fryer oven.
7. Serve immediately.

Simple Cheesy Shrimps

Prep time: 10 minutes | Cook time: 8 minutes | Serves 4 to 6

⅔ cup grated Parmesan cheese
4 minced garlic cloves
1 teaspoon onion powder
½ teaspoon oregano
1 teaspoon basil
1 teaspoon ground black pepper
2 tablespoons olive oil
2 pounds (907 g) cooked large shrimps, peeled and deveined
Lemon wedges, for topping
Cooking spray

1. Spritz an air fryer basket with cooking spray.
2. Combine all the ingredients, except for the shrimps, in a large bowl. Stir to mix well.
3. Dunk the shrimps in the mixture and toss to coat well. Shake the excess off. Arrange the shrimps in the air fryer basket.
4. Slide the basket into the air fryer oven. Cook at 350°F (180°C) for 8 minutes.
5. Flip the shrimps halfway through the cooking time.
6. When cooking is complete, the shrimps should be opaque. Remove from the air fryer oven.
7. Transfer the cooked shrimps on a large plate and squeeze the lemon wedges over before serving.

Lemony Shishito Peppers

Prep time: 5 minutes | Cook time: 5 minutes | Serves 4

½ pound (227 g) shishito peppers (about 24)
1 tablespoon olive oil
Coarse sea salt, to taste
Lemon wedges, for serving
Cooking spray

1. Spritz an air fryer basket with cooking spray.
2. Toss the peppers with olive oil in a large bowl to coat well.
3. Arrange the peppers in the air fryer basket.
4. Slide the basket into the air fryer oven. Cook at 400°F (205°C) for 5 minutes.
5. Flip the peppers and sprinkle the peppers with salt halfway through the cooking time.
6. When cooked, the peppers should be blistered and lightly charred. Transfer the peppers onto a plate and squeeze the lemon wedges on top before serving.

Parsnip Fries with Garlic-Potato Chips with Lemony Cream Dip

Prep time: 20 minutes | Cook time: 15 minutes | Serves 2 to 4

2 large russet potatoes, sliced into ⅛-inch slices, rinsed
Sea salt and freshly ground black pepper, to taste
Cooking spray
Lemony Cream Dip:
½ cup sour cream
¼ teaspoon lemon juice
2 scallions, white part only, minced
1 tablespoon olive oil
¼ teaspoon salt
Freshly ground black pepper, to taste

1. Soak the potato slices in water for 10 minutes, then pat dry with paper towels.
2. Transfer the potato slices in an air fryer basket. Spritz the slices with cooking spray.
3. Slide the basket into the air fryer oven. Cook at 300°F (150°C) for 15 minutes.
4. Stir the potato slices three times during cooking. Sprinkle with salt and ground black pepper in the last minute.
5. Meanwhile, combine the ingredients for the dip in a small bowl. Stir to mix well.
6. When cooking is complete, the potato slices will be crispy and golden brown. Remove from the air fryer oven.
7. Serve the potato chips immediately with the dip.

Fast and Easy Everyday Favorites

Parmesan Cauliflower Fritters

Prep time: 5 minutes | Cook time: 8 minutes | Serves 6

2 cups cooked cauliflower
1 cup panko bread crumbs
1 large egg, beaten
½ cup grated Parmesan cheese
1 tablespoon chopped fresh chives
Cooking spray

1. Spritz an air fryer basket with cooking spray.
2. Put the cauliflower, panko bread crumbs, egg, Parmesan, and chives in a food processor, then pulse to lightly mash and combine the mixture until chunky and thick.
3. Shape the mixture into 6 flat patties, then arrange them in the air fryer basket and spritz with cooking spray.
4. Slide the basket into the air fryer oven. Cook at 390°F (199°C) for 8 minutes.
5. Flip the patties halfway through the cooking time.
6. When done, the patties should be crispy and golden brown. Remove from the air fryer oven.
7. Serve immediately.

Southwest Corn and Bell Pepper Roast

Prep time: 10 minutes | Cook time: 10 minutes | Serves 4

Corn:
1½ cups thawed frozen corn kernels
1 cup mixed diced bell peppers
1 jalapeño, diced
1 cup diced yellow onion
½ teaspoon ancho chile powder
1 tablespoon fresh lemon juice
1 teaspoon ground cumin
½ teaspoon kosher salt
Cooking spray
For Serving:
¼ cup feta cheese
¼ cup chopped fresh cilantro
1 tablespoon fresh lemon juice

1. Spritz an air fryer basket with cooking spray.
2. Combine the ingredients for the corn in a large bowl. Stir to mix well.
3. Pour the mixture into the air fryer basket.
4. Slide the basket into the air fryer oven. Cook at 375°F (190°C) for 10 minutes.
5. Stir the mixture halfway through the cooking time.
6. When done, the corn and bell peppers should be soft.
7. Transfer them onto a large plate, then spread with feta cheese and cilantro. Drizzle with lemon juice and serve.

Salty Tortilla Chips

Prep time: 5 minutes | Cook time: 10 minutes | Serves 4

4 six-inch corn tortillas, cut in half and slice into thirds
1 tablespoon canola oil
¼ teaspoon kosher salt
Cooking spray

1. Spritz an air fryer basket with cooking spray.
2. On a clean work surface, brush the tortilla chips with canola oil, then transfer the chips to the air fryer basket.
3. Slide the basket into the air fryer oven. Cook at 360°F (182°C) for 10 minutes.
4. Flip the chips and sprinkle with salt halfway through the cooking time.
5. When cooked, the chips will be crunchy and lightly browned. Transfer the chips to a plate lined with paper towels. Serve immediately.

Simple Air Fried Edamame

Prep time: 5 minutes | Cook time: 7 minutes | Serves 6

1½ pounds (680 g) unshelled edamame
2 tablespoons olive oil
1 teaspoon sea salt

1. Place the edamame in a large bowl, then drizzle with olive oil. Toss to coat well. Transfer the edamame to an air fryer basket.
2. Slide the basket into the air fryer oven. Cook at 400°F (205°C) for 7 minutes.
3. Stir the edamame at least three times during cooking.
4. When done, the edamame will be tender and warmed through.
5. Transfer the cooked edamame onto a plate and sprinkle with salt. Toss to combine well and set aside for 3 minutes to infuse before serving.

Simple Air Fried Okra Chips

Prep time: 5 minutes | Cook time: 16 minutes | Serves 6

2 pounds (907 g) fresh okra pods, cut into 1-inch pieces
2 tablespoons canola oil
1 teaspoon coarse sea salt

1. Stir the oil and salt in a bowl to mix well. Add the okra and toss to coat well. Place the okra in an air fryer basket.
2. Slide the basket into the air fryer oven. Cook at 400°F (205°C) for 16 minutes.
3. Flip the okra at least three times during cooking.
4. When cooked, the okra should be lightly browned. Remove from the air fryer oven.
5. Serve immediately.

Simple Baked Green Beans

Prep time: 5 minutes | Cook time: 10 minutes | Makes 2 cups

½ teaspoon lemon pepper
2 teaspoons granulated garlic
½ teaspoon salt
1 tablespoon olive oil
2 cups fresh green beans, trimmed and snapped in half

1. Combine the lemon pepper, garlic, salt, and olive oil in a bowl. Stir to mix well.
2. Add the green beans to the bowl of mixture and toss to coat well.
3. Arrange the green beans in an air fryer basket.
4. Slide the basket into the air fryer oven. Cook at 370°F (188°C) for 10 minutes.
5. Stir the green beans halfway through the cooking time.
6. When cooking is complete, the green beans will be tender and crispy. Remove from the air fryer oven.
7. Serve immediately.

South Carolina Shrimp and Corn Bake

Prep time: 10 minutes | Cook time: 18 minutes | Serves 2

1 ear corn, husk and silk removed, cut into 2-inch rounds
8 ounces (227 g) red potatoes, unpeeled, cut into 1-inch pieces
2 teaspoons Old Bay Seasoning, divided
2 teaspoons vegetable oil, divided
¼ teaspoon ground black pepper
8 ounces (227 g) large shrimps (about 12 shrimps), deveined
6 ounces (170 g) andouille or chorizo sausage, cut into 1-inch pieces
2 garlic cloves, minced
1 tablespoon chopped fresh parsley

1. Put the corn rounds and potatoes in a large bowl. Sprinkle with 1 teaspoon of Old Bay seasoning and drizzle with vegetable oil. Toss to coat well.
2. Transfer the corn rounds and potatoes into a baking pan.
3. Slide the pan into the air fryer oven. Cook at 400°F (205°C) for 18 minutes.
4. After 6 minutes, remove from the air fryer oven. Stir the corn rounds and potatoes. Return to the air fryer oven and continue cooking.
5. Meanwhile, cut slits into the shrimps but be careful not to cut them through. Combine the shrimps, sausage, remaining Old Bay seasoning, and remaining vegetable oil in the large bowl. Toss to coat well.
6. After 6 minutes, remove from the air fryer oven. Add the shrimps and sausage to the pan. Return the pan back to the air fryer oven and continue cooking for 6 minutes. Stir the shrimp mixture halfway through the cooking time.
7. When done, the shrimps should be opaque. Remove from the air fryer oven.
8. Transfer the dish to a plate and spread with parsley before serving.

Roasted Carrot Chips

Prep time: 5 minutes | Cook time: 15 minutes | Makes 3 cups

3 large carrots, peeled and sliced into long and thick chips diagonally
1 tablespoon granulated garlic
1 teaspoon salt
¼ teaspoon ground black pepper
1 tablespoon olive oil
1 tablespoon finely chopped fresh parsley

1. Toss the carrots with garlic, salt, ground black pepper, and olive oil in a large bowl to coat well. Place the carrots in an air fryer basket.
2. Slide the basket into the air fryer oven. Cook at 360°F (182°C) for 15 minutes.
3. Stir the carrots halfway through the cooking time.
4. When cooking is complete, the carrot chips should be soft. Remove from the air fryer oven.
5. Serve the carrot chips with parsley on top.

Spicy Air Fried Old Bay Shrimp

Prep time: 10 minutes | Cook time: 10 minutes | Makes 2 cups

½ teaspoon Old Bay Seasoning
1 teaspoon ground cayenne pepper
½ teaspoon paprika
1 tablespoon olive oil
⅛ teaspoon salt
½ pound (227 g) shrimps, peeled and deveined
Juice of half a lemon

1. Combine the Old Bay Seasoning, cayenne pepper, paprika, olive oil, and salt in a large bowl, then add the shrimps and toss to coat well.
2. Put the shrimps in an air fryer basket.
3. Slide the basket into the air fryer oven. Cook at 390°F (199°C) for 10 minutes.
4. Flip the shrimps halfway through the cooking time.
5. When cooking is complete, the shrimps should be opaque. Remove from the air fryer oven.
6. Serve the shrimps with lemon juice on top.

Fast and Easy Everyday Favorites

Sweet Air Fried Pecans

Prep time: 5 minutes | Cook time: 10 minutes | Makes 4 cups

2 egg whites
1 tablespoon cumin
2 teaspoons smoked paprika
½ cup brown sugar
2 teaspoons kosher salt
1 pound (454 g) pecan halves
Cooking spray

1. Spritz an air fryer basket with cooking spray.
2. Combine the egg whites, cumin, paprika, sugar, and salt in a large bowl. Stir to mix well. Add the pecans to the bowl and toss to coat well.
3. Transfer the pecans to the air fryer basket.
4. Slide the basket into the air fryer oven. Cook at 300°F (150°C) for 10 minutes.
5. Stir the pecans at least two times during the cooking.
6. When cooking is complete, the pecans should be lightly caramelized. Remove from the air fryer oven.
7. Serve immediately.

Sweet and Sour Peanuts

Prep time: 5 minutes | Cook time: 5 minutes | Serves 9

3 cups shelled raw peanuts
1 tablespoon hot red pepper sauce
3 tablespoons granulated white sugar

1. Put the peanuts in a large bowl, then drizzle with hot red pepper sauce and sprinkle with sugar. Toss to coat well.
2. Pour the peanuts in an air fryer basket.
3. Slide the basket into the air fryer oven. Cook at 400°F (205°C) for 5 minutes.
4. Stir the peanuts halfway through the cooking time.
5. When cooking is complete, the peanuts will be crispy and browned. Remove from the air fryer oven.
6. Serve immediately.

Sweet Cinnamon Chickpeas

Prep time: 10 minutes | Cook time: 10 minutes | Serves 2

1 tablespoon cinnamon
1 tablespoon sugar
1 cup chickpeas, soaked in water overnight, rinsed and drained

1. Combine the cinnamon and sugar in a bowl. Stir to mix well.
2. Add the chickpeas to the bowl, then toss to coat well.
3. Pour the chickpeas in an air fryer basket.
4. Slide the basket into the air fryer oven. Cook at 390°F (199°C) for 10 minutes.
5. Stir the chickpeas three times during cooking.
6. When cooked, the chickpeas should be golden brown and crispy. Remove from the air fryer oven.
7. Serve immediately.

Traditional French Fries

Prep time: 5 minutes | Cook time: 25 minutes | Serves 2

2 russet potatoes, peeled and cut into ½-inch sticks
2 teaspoons olive oil
Salt, to taste
¼ cup ketchup, for serving

1. Bring a pot of salted water to a boil. Put the potato sticks into the pot and blanch for 4 minutes.
2. Rinse the potatoes under running cold water and pat dry with paper towels.
3. Put the potato sticks in a large bowl and drizzle with olive oil. Toss to coat well.
4. Transfer the potato sticks to an air fryer basket.
5. Slide the basket into the air fryer oven. Cook at 400°F (205°C) for 25 minutes.
6. Stir the potato sticks and sprinkle with salt halfway through.
7. When cooked, the potato sticks will be crispy and golden brown. Remove the French fries from the air fryer oven and serve with ketchup.

Traditional Latkes

Prep time: 15 minutes | Cook time: 10 minutes | Makes 4 latkes

1 egg
2 tablespoons all-purpose flour
2 medium potatoes, peeled and shredded, rinsed and drained
¼ teaspoon granulated garlic
½ teaspoon salt
Cooking spray

1. Spritz an air fryer basket with cooking spray.
2. Whisk together the egg, flour, potatoes, garlic, and salt in a large bowl. Stir to mix well.
3. Divide the mixture into four parts, then flatten them into four circles. Arrange the circles into the air fryer basket and spritz with cooking spray.
4. Slide the basket into the air fryer oven. Cook at 380°F (193°C) for 10 minutes.
5. Flip the latkes halfway through.
6. When cooked, the latkes will be golden brown and crispy. Remove from the air fryer oven.
7. Serve immediately.

Fish and Seafood

Air Fried Cod Fillets

Prep time: 15 minutes | Cook time: 12 minutes | Serves 4

4 cod fillets
¼ teaspoon fine sea salt
1 teaspoon cayenne pepper
¼ teaspoon ground black pepper, or more to taste
½ cup fresh Italian parsley, coarsely chopped
½ cup non-dairy milk
4 garlic cloves, minced
1 Italian pepper, chopped
1 teaspoon dried basil
½ teaspoon dried oregano
Cooking spray

1. Lightly spritz a baking dish with cooking spray.
2. Season the fillets with salt, cayenne pepper, and black pepper.
3. Pulse the remaining ingredients in a food processor, then transfer the mixture to a shallow bowl. Coat the fillets with the mixture.
4. Slide the baking dish into the air fryer oven. Cook at 375°F (190°C) for 12 minutes.
5. When cooking is complete, the fish will be flaky. Remove from the air fryer oven and serve on a plate.

Chili Prawns

Prep time: 10 minutes | Cook time: 8 minutes | Serves 2

8 prawns, cleaned
Salt and black pepper, to taste
½ teaspoon ground cayenne pepper
½ teaspoon garlic powder
½ teaspoon ground cumin
½ teaspoon red chili flakes
Cooking spray

1. Spritz an air fryer basket with cooking spray.
2. Toss the remaining ingredients in a large bowl until the prawns are well coated.
3. Spread the coated prawns evenly in the air fryer basket and spray them with cooking spray.
4. Slide the basket into the air fryer oven. Cook at 340°F (171°C) for 8 minutes.
5. Flip the prawns halfway through the cooking time.
6. When cooking is complete, the prawns should be pink. Remove the prawns from the air fryer oven to a plate.

Air-Fried Scallops

Prep time: 10 minutes | Cook time: 12 minutes | Serves 2

⅓ cup shallots, chopped
1½ tablespoons olive oil
1½ tablespoons coconut aminos
1 tablespoon Mediterranean seasoning mix
½ tablespoon balsamic vinegar
½ teaspoon ginger, grated
1 clove garlic, chopped
1 pound (454 g) scallops, cleaned Cooking spray
Belgian endive, for garnish

1. Place all the ingredients except the scallops and Belgian endive in a small skillet over medium heat and stir to combine. Let this mixture simmer for about 2 minutes.
2. Remove the mixture from the skillet to a large bowl and set aside to cool.
3. Add the scallops, coating them all over, then transfer to the refrigerator to marinate for at least 2 hours.
4. When ready, place the scallops in an air fryer basket and spray with cooking spray.
5. Slide the basket into the air fryer oven. Cook at 345°F (174°C) for 10 minutes.
6. Flip the scallops halfway through the cooking time.
7. When cooking is complete, the scallops should be tender and opaque. Remove from the air fryer oven and serve garnished with the Belgian endive.

Lemon Tilapia

Prep time: 10 minutes | Cook time: 12 minutes | Serves 4

1 tablespoon olive oil
1 tablespoon lemon juice
1 teaspoon minced garlic
½ teaspoon chili powder
4 tilapia fillets

1. Line a baking pan with parchment paper.
2. In a shallow bowl, stir together the olive oil, lemon juice, garlic, and chili powder to make a marinade. Put the tilapia fillets in the bowl, turning to coat evenly.
3. Place the fillets in the baking pan in a single layer.
4. Slide the pan into the air fryer oven. Cook at 375°F (190°C) for 12 minutes.
5. When cooked, the fish will flake apart with a fork. Remove from the air fryer oven to a plate and serve hot.

Asian-Inspired Swordfish Steaks

Prep time: 10 minutes | Cook time: 8 minutes | Serves 4

4 (4-ounce / 113-g) swordfish steaks
½ teaspoon toasted sesame oil
1 jalapeño pepper, finely minced
2 garlic cloves, grated
2 tablespoons freshly squeezed lemon juice
1 tablespoon grated fresh ginger
½ teaspoon Chinese five-spice powder
⅛ teaspoon freshly ground black pepper

1. On a clean work surface, place the swordfish steaks and brush both sides of the fish with the sesame oil.
2. Combine the jalapeño, garlic, lemon juice, ginger, five-spice powder, and black pepper in a small bowl and stir to mix well. Rub the mixture all over the fish until coated. Allow to sit for 10 minutes.
3. When ready, arrange the swordfish steaks in an air fryer basket.
4. Slide the basket into the air fryer oven. Cook at 380°F (193°C) for 8 minutes.
5. Flip the steaks halfway through.
6. When cooking is complete, remove from the air fryer oven and cool for 5 minutes before serving.

Teriyaki Salmon

Prep time: 15 minutes | Cook time: 15 minutes | Serves 4

¾ cup Teriyaki sauce, divided
4 (6-ounce / 170-g) skinless salmon fillets
4 heads baby bok choy, root ends trimmed off and cut in half lengthwise through the root
1 teaspoon sesame oil
1 tablespoon vegetable oil
1 tablespoon toasted sesame seeds

1. Set aside ¼ cup of Teriyaki sauce and pour the remaining sauce into a resealable plastic bag. Put the salmon into the bag and seal, squeezing as much air out as possible. Allow the salmon to marinate for at least 10 minutes.
2. Arrange the bok choy halves on a sheet pan. Drizzle the oils over the vegetables, tossing to coat. Drizzle about 1 tablespoon of the reserved Teriyaki sauce over the bok choy, then push them to the sides of the sheet pan.
3. Put the salmon fillets in the middle of the sheet pan.
4. Slide the pan into the air fryer oven. Cook at 375°F (190°C) for 15 minutes.
5. When done, remove the pan and brush the salmon with the remaining Teriyaki sauce. Serve garnished with the sesame seeds.

Bacon-Wrapped Scallops

Prep time: 5 minutes | Cook time: 10 minutes | Serves 4

8 slices bacon, cut in half
16 sea scallops, patted dry
Cooking spray
Salt and freshly ground black pepper, to taste
16 toothpicks, soaked in water for at least 30 minutes

1. On a clean work surface, wrap half of a slice of bacon around each scallop and secure with a toothpick.
2. Lay the bacon-wrapped scallops in an air fryer basket.
3. Spritz the scallops with cooking spray and sprinkle the salt and pepper to season.
4. Slide the basket into the air fryer oven. Cook at 370°F (188°C) for 10 minutes.
5. Flip the scallops halfway through the cooking time.
6. When cooking is complete, the bacon should be cooked through and the scallops should be firm. Remove the scallops from the air fryer oven to a plate Serve warm.

Basil Salmon with Tomatoes

Prep time: 10 minutes | Cook time: 15 minutes | Serves 4

4 (6-ounce / 170-g) salmon fillets, patted dry
1 teaspoon kosher salt, divided
2 pints cherry or grape tomatoes, halved if large, divided
3 tablespoons extra-virgin olive oil, divided
2 garlic cloves, minced
1 small red bell pepper, deseeded and chopped
2 tablespoons chopped fresh basil, divided

1. Season both sides of the salmon with ½ teaspoon of kosher salt.
2. Put about half of the tomatoes in a large bowl, along with the remaining ½ teaspoon of kosher salt, 2 tablespoons of olive oil, garlic, bell pepper, and 1 tablespoon of basil. Toss to coat and then transfer to the sheet pan.
3. Arrange the salmon fillets on the sheet pan, skin-side down. Brush them with the remaining 1 tablespoon of olive oil.
4. Slide the pan into the air fryer oven. Cook at 375°F (190°C) for 15 minutes.
5. After 7 minutes, remove the pan and fold in the remaining tomatoes. Return to the air fryer oven and continue cooking.
6. When cooked, remove from the air fryer oven. Serve sprinkled with the remaining 1 tablespoon of basil.

Baked Flounder Fillets

Prep time: 8 minutes | Cook time: 12 minutes | Serves 2

2 flounder fillets, patted dry
1 egg
½ teaspoon Worcestershire sauce
¼ cup almond flour
¼ cup coconut flour
½ teaspoon coarse sea salt
½ teaspoon lemon pepper
¼ teaspoon chili powder
Cooking spray

1. In a shallow bowl, beat together the egg with Worcestershire sauce until well incorporated.
2. In another bowl, thoroughly combine the almond flour, coconut flour, sea salt, lemon pepper, and chili powder.
3. Dredge the fillets in the egg mixture, shaking off any excess, then roll in the flour mixture to coat well.
4. Spritz an air fryer basket with cooking spray. Place the fillets in the basket.
5. Slide the basket into the air fryer oven. Cook at 390°F (199°C) for 12 minutes.
6. After 7 minutes, remove from the air fryer oven and flip the fillets and spray with cooking spray. Return to the air fryer oven and continue cooking for 5 minutes, or until the fish is flaky.
7. When cooking is complete, remove from the air fryer oven and serve warm.

Easy Scallops

Prep time: 5 minutes | Cook time: 4 minutes | Serves 2

12 medium sea scallops, rinsed and patted dry
1 teaspoon fine sea salt
¾ teaspoon ground black pepper, plus more for garnish
Fresh thyme leaves, for garnish (optional)
Avocado oil spray

1. Coat an air fryer basket with avocado oil spray.
2. Place the scallops in a medium bowl and spritz with avocado oil spray. Sprinkle the salt and pepper to season.
3. Transfer the seasoned scallops to the air fryer basket, spacing them apart.
4. Slide the basket into the air fryer oven. Cook at 390°F (199°C) for 4 minutes.
5. Flip the scallops halfway through the cooking time.
6. When cooking is complete, the scallops should reach an internal temperature of just 145°F (63°C) on a meat thermometer. Remove from the air fryer oven. Sprinkle the pepper and thyme leaves on top for garnish, if desired. Serve immediately.

Baked Salmon Spring Rolls

Prep time: 20 minutes | Cook time: 18 minutes | Serves 4

½ pound (227 g) salmon fillet
1 teaspoon toasted sesame oil
1 onion, sliced
1 carrot, shredded
1 yellow bell pepper, thinly sliced
⅓ cup chopped fresh flat-leaf parsley
¼ cup chopped fresh basil
8 rice paper wrappers

1. Arrange the salmon in an air fryer basket. Drizzle the sesame oil all over the salmon and scatter the onion on top.
2. Slide the basket into the air fryer oven. Cook at 370°F (188°C) for 10 minutes.
3. Meanwhile, fill a small shallow bowl with warm water. One by one, dip the rice paper wrappers into the water for a few seconds or just until moistened, then put them on a work surface.
4. When cooking is complete, the fish should flake apart with a fork. Remove from the air fryer oven to a plate.
5. Make the spring rolls: Place ⅛ of the salmon and onion mixture, carrot, bell pepper, parsley, and basil into the center of the rice wrapper and fold the sides over the filling. Roll up the wrapper carefully and tightly. Repeat with the remaining wrappers and filling.
6. Transfer the rolls to the air fryer basket.
7. Slide the basket into the air fryer oven. Cook at 380°F (193°C) for 8 minutes.
8. When cooking is complete, the rolls should be crispy and lightly browned. Remove from the air fryer oven and cut each roll in half and serve warm.

Crispy Fish Sticks

Prep time: 10 minutes | Cook time: 6 minutes | Serves 8

8 ounces (227 g) fish fillets (pollock or cod), cut into ½ × 3 inches strips
Salt, to taste (optional)
½ cup plain bread crumbs
Cooking spray

1. Season the fish strips with salt to taste, if desired.
2. Place the bread crumbs on a plate, then roll the fish in the bread crumbs until well coated. Spray all sides of the fish with cooking spray. Transfer to an air fryer basket.
3. Slide the basket into the air fryer oven. Cook at 400°F (205°C) for 6 minutes.
4. When cooked, the fish sticks should be golden brown and crispy. Remove from the air fryer oven to a plate and serve hot.

Baked Tilapia with Garlic Aioli

Prep time: 5 minutes | Cook time: 15 minutes | Serves 4

Tilapia:
4 tilapia fillets
1 tablespoon extra-virgin olive oil
1 teaspoon garlic powder
1 teaspoon paprika
1 teaspoon dried basil
A pinch of lemon-pepper seasoning
Garlic Aioli:
2 garlic cloves, minced
1 tablespoon mayonnaise
Juice of ½ lemon
1 teaspoon extra-virgin olive oil
Salt and pepper, to taste

1. On a clean work surface, brush both sides of each fillet with the olive oil. Sprinkle with the garlic powder, paprika, basil, and lemon-pepper seasoning. Place the fillets in an air fryer basket.
2. Slide the basket into the air fryer oven. Cook at 400ºF (205ºC) for 15 minutes.
3. Flip the fillets halfway through.
4. Meanwhile, make the garlic aioli: Whisk together the garlic, mayo, lemon juice, olive oil, salt, and pepper in a small bowl until smooth.
5. When cooking is complete, the fish should flake apart with a fork and no longer translucent in the center. Remove the fish from the air fryer oven and serve with the garlic aioli on the side.

Lemony Shrimp

Prep time: 10 minutes | Cook time: 8 minutes | Serves 4

1 pound (454 g) shrimp, deveined
4 tablespoons olive oil
1½ tablespoons lemon juice
1½ tablespoons fresh parsley, roughly chopped
2 cloves garlic, finely minced
1 teaspoon crushed red pepper flakes, or more to taste
Garlic pepper, to taste
Sea salt flakes, to taste

1. Toss all the ingredients in a large bowl until the shrimp are coated on all sides.
2. Arrange the shrimp in an air fryer basket.
3. Slide the basket into the air fryer oven. Cook at 385ºF (196ºC) for 8 minutes.
4. When cooking is complete, the shrimp should be pink and cooked through. Remove from the air fryer oven and serve warm.

Breaded Calamari with Lemon

Prep time: 5 minutes | Cook time: 12 minutes | Serves 4

2 large eggs
2 garlic cloves, minced
½ cup cornstarch
1 cup bread crumbs
1 pound (454 g) calamari rings
Cooking spray
1 lemon, sliced

1. In a small bowl, whisk the eggs with minced garlic. Place the cornstarch and bread crumbs into separate shallow dishes.
2. Dredge the calamari rings in the cornstarch, then dip in the egg mixture, shaking off any excess, finally roll them in the bread crumbs to coat well. Let the calamari rings sit for 10 minutes in the refrigerator.
3. Spritz an air fryer basket with cooking spray. Transfer the calamari rings to the pan.
4. Slide the basket into the air fryer oven. Cook at 390ºF (199ºC) for 12 minutes.
5. Stir the calamari rings once halfway through the cooking time.
6. When cooking is complete, remove from the air fryer oven. Serve the calamari rings with the lemon slices sprinkled on top.

Breaded Scallops

Prep time: 5 minutes | Cook time: 7 minutes | Serves 4

1 egg
3 tablespoons flour
1 cup bread crumbs
1 pound (454 g) fresh scallops
2 tablespoons olive oil
Salt and black pepper, to taste

1. In a bowl, lightly beat the egg. Place the flour and bread crumbs into separate shallow dishes.
2. Dredge the scallops in the flour and shake off any excess. Dip the flour-coated scallops in the beaten egg and roll in the bread crumbs.
3. Brush the scallops generously with olive oil and season with salt and pepper, to taste. Transfer the scallops to an air fryer basket.
4. Slide the basket into the air fryer oven. Cook at 360ºF (182ºC) for 7 minutes.
5. Flip the scallops halfway through the cooking time.
6. When cooking is complete, the scallops should reach an internal temperature of just 145ºF (63ºC) on a meat thermometer. Remove from the air fryer oven. Let the scallops cool for 5 minutes and serve.

Browned Shrimp Patties

Prep time: 15 minutes | Cook time: 12 minutes | Serves 4

½ pound (227 g) raw shrimp, shelled, deveined, and chopped finely
2 cups cooked sushi rice
¼ cup chopped red bell pepper
¼ cup chopped celery
¼ cup chopped green onion
2 teaspoons Worcestershire sauce
½ teaspoon salt
½ teaspoon garlic powder
½ teaspoon Old Bay seasoning
½ cup plain bread crumbs
Cooking spray

1. Put all the ingredients except the bread crumbs and oil in a large bowl and stir to incorporate.
2. Scoop out the shrimp mixture and shape into 8 equal-sized patties with your hands, no more than ½-inch thick. Roll the patties in the bread crumbs on a plate and spray both sides with cooking spray. Place the patties in an air fryer basket.
3. Slide the basket into the air fryer oven. Cook at 390°F (199°C) for 12 minutes.
4. Flip the patties halfway through the cooking time.
5. When cooking is complete, the outside should be crispy brown. Remove from the air fryer oven. Divide the patties among four plates and serve warm.

Fish Tacos

Prep time: 10 minutes | Cook time: 10 to 15 minutes | Serves 6

1 tablespoon avocado oil
1 tablespoon Cajun seasoning
4 (5 to 6 ounce / 142 to 170 g) tilapia fillets
1 (14-ounce / 397-g) package coleslaw mix
12 corn tortillas
2 limes, cut into wedges

1. Line a baking pan with parchment paper.
2. In a shallow bowl, stir together the avocado oil and Cajun seasoning to make a marinade. Place the tilapia fillets into the bowl, turning to coat evenly.
3. Put the fillets in the baking pan in a single layer.
4. Slide the pan into the air fryer oven. Cook at 375°F (190°C) for 10 minutes.
5. When cooked, the fish should be flaky. If necessary, continue cooking for 5 minutes more. Remove the fish from the air fryer oven to a plate.
6. Assemble the tacos: Spoon some coleslaw mix into each tortilla and top each with ⅓ of a tilapia fillet. Squeeze some lime juice over the top of each taco and serve immediately.

Butter-Wine Baked Salmon

Prep time: 5 minutes | Cook time: 10 minutes | Serves 4

4 tablespoons butter, melted
2 cloves garlic, minced
Sea salt and ground black pepper, to taste
¼ cup dry white wine
1 tablespoon lime juice
1 teaspoon smoked paprika
½ teaspoon onion powder
4 salmon steaks
Cooking spray

1. Place all the ingredients except the salmon and oil in a shallow dish and stir to mix well.
2. Add the salmon steaks, turning to coat well on both sides. Transfer the salmon to the refrigerator to marinate for 30 minutes.
3. When ready, put the salmon steaks in an air fryer basket, discarding any excess marinade. Spray the salmon steaks with cooking spray.
4. Slide the basket into the air fryer oven. Cook at 360°F (182°C) for 10 minutes.
5. Flip the salmon steaks halfway through.
6. When cooking is complete, remove from the air fryer oven and divide the salmon steaks among four plates. Serve warm.

Cajun and Lemon Pepper Cod

Prep time: 5 minutes | Cook time: 12 minutes | Makes 2 cod fillets

1 tablespoon Cajun seasoning
1 teaspoon salt
½ teaspoon lemon pepper
½ teaspoon freshly ground black pepper
2 (8-ounce / 227-g) cod fillets, cut to fit into an air fryer basket
Cooking spray
2 tablespoons unsalted butter, melted
1 lemon, cut into 4 wedges

1. Spritz an air fryer basket with cooking spray.
2. Thoroughly combine the Cajun seasoning, salt, lemon pepper, and black pepper in a small bowl. Rub this mixture all over the cod fillets until coated.
3. Put the fillets in an air fryer basket and brush the melted butter over both sides of each fillet.
4. Slide the basket into the air fryer oven. Cook at 360°F (182°C) for 12 minutes.
5. Flip the fillets halfway through the cooking time.
6. When cooking is complete, the fish should flake apart with a fork. Remove the fillets from the air fryer oven and serve with fresh lemon wedges.

Breaded Fish Fillets

Prep time: 20 minutes | Cook time: 7 minutes | Serves 4

1 pound (454 g) fish fillets
1 tablespoon coarse brown mustard
1 teaspoon Worcestershire sauce
½ teaspoon hot sauce
Salt, to taste
Cooking spray
Crumb Coating:
¾ cup panko bread crumbs
¼ cup stone-ground cornmeal
¼ teaspoon salt

1. On your cutting board, cut the fish fillets crosswise into slices, about 1 inch wide.
2. In a small bowl, stir together the mustard, Worcestershire sauce, and hot sauce to make a paste and rub this paste on all sides of the fillets. Season with salt to taste.
3. In a shallow bowl, thoroughly combine all the ingredients for the crumb coating and spread them on a sheet of wax paper.
4. Roll the fish fillets in the crumb mixture until thickly coated. Spritz all sides of the fish with cooking spray, then arrange them in an air fryer basket.
5. Slide the basket into the air fryer oven. Cook at 400°F (205°C) for 7 minutes.
6. When cooking is complete, the fish should flake apart with a fork. Remove from the air fryer oven and serve warm.

Caesar Shrimp Salad

Prep time: 10 minutes | Cook time: 15 minutes | Serves 4

½ baguette, cut into 1-inch cubes (about 2½ cups)
4 tablespoons extra-virgin olive oil, divided
¼ teaspoon granulated garlic
¼ teaspoon kosher salt
¾ cup Caesar dressing, divided
2 romaine lettuce hearts, cut in half lengthwise and ends trimmed
1 pound (454 g) medium shrimp, peeled and deveined
2 ounces (57 g) Parmesan cheese, coarsely grated

1. Make the croutons: Put the bread cubes in a medium bowl and drizzle 3 tablespoons of olive oil over top. Season with granulated garlic and salt and toss to coat. Transfer to an air fryer basket.
2. Slide the basket into the air fryer oven. Cook at 400°F (205°C) for 4 minutes.
3. Toss the croutons halfway through the cooking time.
4. When done, remove the air fryer basket from the air fryer oven and set aside.
5. Brush 2 tablespoons of Caesar dressing on the cut side of the lettuce. Set aside.
6. Toss the shrimp with the ¼ cup of Caesar dressing in a large bowl until well coated. Set aside.
7. Coat a sheet pan with the remaining 1 tablespoon of olive oil. Arrange the romaine halves on the coated pan, cut side down. Brush the tops with the remaining 2 tablespoons of Caesar dressing.
8. Slide the pan into the air fryer oven. Cook at 375°F (190°C) for 10 minutes.
9. After 5 minutes, remove from the air fryer oven and flip the romaine halves. Spoon the shrimp around the lettuce. Return to the air fryer oven and continue cooking.
10. When done, remove the sheet pan from the air fryer oven. If they are not quite cooked through, roast for another 1 minute.
11. On each of four plates, put a romaine half. Divide the shrimp among the plates and top with croutons and grated Parmesan cheese. Serve immediately.

Cajun Catfish Cakes with Cheese

Prep time: 5 minutes | Cook time: 15 minutes | Serves 4

2 catfish fillets
3 ounces (85 g) butter
1 cup shredded Parmesan cheese
1 cup shredded Swiss cheese
½ cup buttermilk
1 teaspoon baking powder
1 teaspoon baking soda
1 teaspoon Cajun seasoning

1. Bring a pot of salted water to a boil. Add the catfish fillets to the boiling water and let them boil for 5 minutes until they become opaque.
2. Remove the fillets from the pot to a mixing bowl and flake them into small pieces with a fork.
3. Add the remaining ingredients to the bowl of fish and stir until well incorporated.
4. Divide the fish mixture into 12 equal portions and shape each portion into a patty. Place the patties in an air fryer basket.
5. Slide the basket into the air fryer oven. Cook at 380°F (193°C) for 15 minutes.
6. Flip the patties halfway through the cooking time.
7. When cooking is complete, the patties should be golden brown and cooked through. Remove from the air fryer oven. Let the patties sit for 5 minutes and serve.

Cheesy Tuna Patties

Prep time: 5 minutes | Cook time: 17 to 18 minutes | Serves 4

Tuna Patties:
1 pound (454 g) canned tuna, drained
1 egg, whisked
2 tablespoons shallots, minced
1 garlic clove, minced
1 cup grated Romano cheese
Sea salt and ground black pepper, to taste
1 tablespoon sesame oil
Cheese Sauce:
1 tablespoon butter
1 cup beer
2 tablespoons grated Colby cheese

1. Mix the canned tuna, whisked egg, shallots, garlic, cheese, salt, and pepper in a large bowl and stir to incorporate.
2. Divide the tuna mixture into four equal portions and form each portion into a patty with your hands. Refrigerate the patties for 2 hours.
3. When ready, brush both sides of each patty with sesame oil, then place in an air fryer basket.
4. Slide the basket into the air fryer oven. Cook at 360°F (182°C) for 14 minutes.
5. Flip the patties halfway through the cooking time.
6. Meanwhile, melt the butter in a saucepan over medium heat.
7. Pour in the beer and whisk constantly, or until it begins to bubble. Add the grated Colby cheese and mix well. Continue cooking for 3 to 4 minutes, or until the cheese melts. Remove from the heat.
8. When cooking is complete, the patties should be lightly browned and cooked through. Remove the patties from the air fryer oven to a plate. Drizzle them with the cheese sauce and serve immediately.

Chili Tuna Casserole

Prep time: 10 minutes | Cook time: 16 minutes | Serves 4

½ tablespoon sesame oil
⅓ cup yellow onions, chopped
½ bell pepper, deveined and chopped
2 cups canned tuna, chopped
Cooking spray
5 eggs, beaten
½ chili pepper, deveined and finely minced
1½ tablespoons sour cream
⅓ teaspoon dried basil
⅓ teaspoon dried oregano
Fine sea salt and ground black pepper, to taste

1. Heat the sesame oil in a nonstick skillet over medium heat until it shimmers.
2. Add the onions and bell pepper and sauté for 4 minutes, stirring occasionally, or until tender.
3. Add the canned tuna and keep stirring until the tuna is heated through.
4. Meanwhile, coat a baking dish lightly with cooking spray.
5. Transfer the tuna mixture to the baking dish, along with the beaten eggs, chili pepper, sour cream, basil, and oregano. Stir to combine well. Season with sea salt and black pepper.
6. Slide the baking dish into the air fryer oven. Cook at 325°F (160°C) for 12 minutes.
7. When cooking is complete, the eggs should be completely set and the top lightly browned. Remove from the air fryer oven and serve on a plate.

Roasted Nicoise Salad

Prep time: 10 minutes | Cook time: 15 minutes | Serves 4

10 ounces (283 g) small red potatoes, quartered
8 tablespoons extra-virgin olive oil, divided
1 teaspoon kosher salt, divided
½ pound (227 g) green beans, trimmed
1 pint cherry tomatoes
1 teaspoon Dijon mustard
3 tablespoons red wine vinegar
Freshly ground black pepper, to taste
1 (9-ounce / 255-g) bag spring greens, washed and dried if needed
2 (5-ounce / 142-g) cans oil-packed tuna, drained
2 hard-cooked eggs, peeled and quartered
⅓ cup kalamata olives, pitted

1. In a large bowl, drizzle the potatoes with 1 tablespoon of olive oil and season with ¼ teaspoon of kosher salt. Transfer to a sheet pan.
2. Slide the pan into the air fryer oven. Cook at 375°F (190°C) for 15 minutes.
3. Meanwhile, in a mixing bowl, toss the green beans and cherry tomatoes with 1 tablespoon of olive oil and ¼ teaspoon of kosher salt until evenly coated.
4. After 10 minutes, remove the pan and fold in the green beans and cherry tomatoes. Return to the air fryer oven and continue cooking.
5. Meanwhile, make the vinaigrette by whisking together the remaining 6 tablespoons of olive oil, mustard, vinegar, the remaining ½ teaspoon of kosher salt, and black pepper in a small bowl. Set aside.
6. When done, remove from the air fryer oven. Allow the vegetables to cool for 5 minutes.
7. Spread out the spring greens on a plate and spoon the tuna into the center of the greens. Arrange the potatoes, green beans, cheery tomatoes, and eggs around the tuna. Serve drizzled with the vinaigrette and scattered with the olives.

Coconut Chili Fish Curry

Prep time: 10 minutes | Cook time: 22 minutes | Serves 4

2 tablespoons sunflower oil, divided
1 pound (454 g) fish, chopped
1 ripe tomato, pureéd
2 red chilies, chopped
1 shallot, minced
1 garlic clove, minced
1 cup coconut milk
1 tablespoon coriander powder
1 teaspoon red curry paste
½ teaspoon fenugreek seeds
Salt and white pepper, to taste

1. Coat an air fryer basket with 1 tablespoon of sunflower oil. Place the fish in the air fryer basket.
2. Slide the basket into the air fryer oven. Cook at 380°F (193°C) for 10 minutes.
3. Flip the fish halfway through the cooking time.
4. When cooking is complete, transfer the cooked fish to a baking pan greased with the remaining 1 tablespoon of sunflower oil. Stir in the remaining ingredients.
5. Slide the pan into the air fryer oven. Cook at 350°F (180°C) for 12 minutes.
6. When cooking is complete, they should be heated through. Cool for 5 to 8 minutes before serving.

Easy Salmon Patties

Prep time: 5 minutes | Cook time: 11 minutes | Makes 6 patties

1 (14.75-ounce / 418-g) can Alaskan pink salmon, drained and bones removed
½ cup bread crumbs
1 egg, whisked
2 scallions, diced
1 teaspoon garlic powder
Salt and pepper, to taste
Cooking spray

1. Stir together the salmon, bread crumbs, whisked egg, scallions, garlic powder, salt, and pepper in a large bowl until well incorporated.
2. Divide the salmon mixture into six equal portions and form each into a patty with your hands.
3. Arrange the salmon patties in an air fryer basket and spritz them with cooking spray.
4. Slide the basket into the air fryer oven. Cook at 400°F (205°C) for 10 minutes.
5. Flip the patties once halfway through.
6. When cooking is complete, the patties should be golden brown and cooked through. Remove the patties from the air fryer oven and serve on a plate.

Crab Cakes with Bell Peppers

Prep time: 5 minutes | Cook time: 10 minutes | Serves 4

8 ounces (227 g) jumbo lump crab meat
1 egg, beaten
Juice of ½ lemon
⅓ cup bread crumbs
¼ cup diced green bell pepper
¼ cup diced red bell pepper
¼ cup mayonnaise
1 tablespoon Old Bay seasoning
1 teaspoon flour
Cooking spray

1. Make the crab cakes: Place all the ingredients except the flour and oil in a large bowl and stir until well incorporated.
2. Divide the crab mixture into four equal portions and shape each portion into a patty with your hands. Top each patty with a sprinkle of ¼ teaspoon of flour.
3. Arrange the crab cakes in an air fryer basket and spritz them with cooking spray.
4. Slide the basket into the air fryer oven. Cook at 375°F (190°C) for 10 minutes.
5. Flip the crab cakes halfway through.
6. When cooking is complete, the cakes should be cooked through. Remove from the air fryer oven. Divide the crab cakes among four plates and serve.

Crab Ratatouille with Eggplant and Tomatoes

Prep time: 15 minutes | Cook time: 13 minutes | Serves 4

1½ cups peeled and cubed eggplant
2 large tomatoes, chopped
1 red bell pepper, chopped
1 onion, chopped
1 tablespoon olive oil
½ teaspoon dried basil
½ teaspoon dried thyme
Pinch salt
Freshly ground black pepper, to taste
1½ cups cooked crab meat

1. In a metal bowl, stir together the eggplant, tomatoes, bell pepper, onion, olive oil, basil and thyme. Season with salt and pepper.
2. Place the metal bowl into the air fryer oven. Cook at 400°F (205°C) for 13 minutes.
3. After 9 minutes, remove the bowl from the air fryer oven. Add the crabmeat and stir well and continue roasting for another 4 minutes, or until the vegetables are softened and the ratatouille is bubbling.
4. When cooking is complete, remove from the air fryer oven and serve warm.

Crispy Crab and Fish Cakes

Prep time: 20 minutes | Cook time: 12 minutes | Serves 4

8 ounces (227 g) imitation crab meat
4 ounces (113 g) leftover cooked fish (such as cod, pollock, or haddock)
2 tablespoons minced celery
2 tablespoons minced green onion
2 tablespoons light mayonnaise
1 tablespoon plus 2 teaspoons Worcestershire sauce
¾ cup crushed saltine cracker crumbs
2 teaspoons dried parsley flakes
1 teaspoon prepared yellow mustard
½ teaspoon garlic powder
½ teaspoon dried dill weed, crushed
½ teaspoon Old Bay seasoning
½ cup panko bread crumbs
Cooking spray

1. Pulse the crab meat and fish in a food processor until finely chopped.
2. Transfer the meat mixture to a large bowl, along with the celery, green onion, mayo, Worcestershire sauce, cracker crumbs, parsley flakes, mustard, garlic powder, dill weed, and Old Bay seasoning. Stir to mix well.
3. Scoop out the meat mixture and form into 8 equal-sized patties with your hands.
4. Place the panko bread crumbs on a plate. Roll the patties in the bread crumbs until they are evenly coated on both sides. Put the patties in an air fryer basket and spritz them with cooking spray.
5. Slide the basket into the air fryer oven. Cook at 390ºF (199ºC) for 12 minutes.
6. Flip the patties halfway through the cooking time.
7. When cooking is complete, they should be golden brown and cooked through. Remove from the air fryer oven. Divide the patties among four plates and serve.

Garlic-Butter Shrimp with Vegetables

Prep time: 10 minutes | Cook time: 15 minutes | Serves 4

1 pound (454 g) small red potatoes, halved
2 ears corn, shucked and cut into rounds, 1 to 1½ inches thick
2 tablespoons Old Bay or similar seasoning
½ cup unsalted butter, melted
1 (12- to 13-ounce / 340- to 369-g) package kielbasa or other smoked sausages
3 garlic cloves, minced
1 pound (454 g) medium shrimp, peeled and deveined

1. Place the potatoes and corn in a large bowl.
2. Stir together the butter and Old Bay seasoning in a small bowl. Drizzle half the butter mixture over the potatoes and corn, tossing to coat. Spread out the vegetables on a sheet pan.
3. Slide the pan into the air fryer oven. Cook at 350ºF (180ºC) for 15 minutes.
4. Meanwhile, cut the sausages into 2-inch lengths, then cut each piece in half lengthwise. Put the sausages and shrimp in a medium bowl and set aside.
5. Add the garlic to the bowl of remaining butter mixture and stir well.
6. After 10 minutes, remove the sheet pan and pour the vegetables into the large bowl. Drizzle with the garlic butter and toss until well coated. Arrange the vegetables, sausages, and shrimp on the sheet pan.
7. Return to the air fryer oven and continue cooking. After 5 minutes, check the shrimp for doneness. The shrimp should be pink and opaque. If they are not quite cooked through, roast for an additional 1 minute.
8. When done, remove from the air fryer oven and serve on a plate.

Coconut-Crusted Prawns

Prep time: 15 minutes | Cook time: 8 minutes | Serves 4

12 prawns, cleaned and deveined
1 teaspoon fresh lemon juice
½ teaspoon cumin powder
Salt and ground black pepper, to taste
1 medium egg
⅓ cup beer
½ cup flour, divided
1 tablespoon curry powder
1 teaspoon baking powder
½ teaspoon grated fresh ginger
1 cup flaked coconut

1. In a large bowl, toss the prawns with the lemon juice, cumin powder, salt, and pepper until well coated. Set aside.
2. In a shallow bowl, whisk together the egg, beer, ¼ cup of flour, curry powder, baking powder, and ginger until combined.
3. In a separate shallow bowl, put the remaining ¼ cup of flour, and on a plate, place the flaked coconut.
4. Dip the prawns in the flour, then in the egg mixture, finally roll in the flaked coconut to coat well. Transfer the prawns to a baking sheet.
5. Slide the baking sheet into the air fryer oven. Cook at 350ºF (180ºC) for 8 minutes.
6. After 5 minutes, remove from the air fryer oven and flip the prawns. Return to the air fryer oven and continue cooking for 3 minutes more.
7. When cooking is complete, remove from the air fryer oven and serve warm.

Fish and Seafood

Easy Shrimp and Vegetable Paella

Prep time: 5 minutes | Cook time: 16 minutes | Serves 4

1 (10-ounce / 284-g) package frozen cooked rice, thawed
1 (6-ounce / 170-g) jar artichoke hearts, drained and chopped
¼ cup vegetable broth
½ teaspoon dried thyme
½ teaspoon turmeric
1 cup frozen cooked small shrimp
½ cup frozen baby peas
1 tomato, diced

1. Mix the cooked rice, chopped artichoke hearts, vegetable broth, thyme, and turmeric in a baking pan and stir to combine.
2. Slide the pan into the air fryer oven. Cook at 340°F (171°C) for 16 minutes.
3. After 9 minutes, remove from the air fryer oven and add the shrimp, baby peas, and diced tomato to the baking pan. Mix well. Return to the air fryer oven and continue cooking for 7 minutes more, or until the shrimp are done and the paella is bubbling.
4. When cooking is complete, remove from the air fryer oven. Cool for 5 minutes before serving.

Fired Shrimp with Mayonnaise Sauce

Prep time: 5 minutes | Cook time: 7 minutes | Serves 4

Shrimp
12 jumbo shrimp
½ teaspoon garlic salt
¼ teaspoon freshly cracked mixed peppercorns
Sauce:
4 tablespoons mayonnaise
1 teaspoon grated lemon rind
1 teaspoon Dijon mustard
1 teaspoon chipotle powder
½ teaspoon cumin powder

1. In a medium bowl, season the shrimp with garlic salt and cracked mixed peppercorns.
2. Place the shrimp in an air fryer basket.
3. Slide the basket into the air fryer oven. Cook at 395°F (202°C) for 7 minutes.
4. After 5 minutes, remove from the air fryer oven and flip the shrimp. Return to the air fryer oven and continue cooking for 2 minutes more, or until they are pink and no longer opaque.
5. Meanwhile, stir together all the ingredients for the sauce in a small bowl until well mixed.
6. When cooking is complete, remove the shrimp from the air fryer oven and serve alongside the sauce.

Garlic Butter Shrimp Scampi

Prep time: 5 minutes | Cook time: 8 minutes | Serves 4

Sauce:
¼ cup unsalted butter
2 tablespoons fish stock or chicken broth
2 cloves garlic, minced
2 tablespoons chopped fresh basil leaves
1 tablespoon lemon juice
1 tablespoon chopped fresh parsley, plus more for garnish
1 teaspoon red pepper flakes
Shrimp:
1 pound (454 g) large shrimp, peeled and deveined, tails removed
Fresh basil sprigs, for garnish

1. Put all the ingredients for the sauce in a baking pan and stir to incorporate.
2. Slide the pan into the air fryer oven. Cook at 350°F (180°C) for 8 minutes.
3. After 3 minutes, remove from the air fryer oven and add the shrimp to the baking pan, flipping to coat in the sauce. Return to the air fryer oven and continue cooking for 5 minutes until the shrimp are pink and opaque. Stir the shrimp twice during cooking.
4. When cooking is complete, remove from the air fryer oven. Serve garnished with the parsley and basil sprigs.

Garlic Shrimp with Parsley

Prep time: 10 minutes | Cook time: 5 minutes | Serves 4

18 shrimp, shelled and deveined
2 garlic cloves, peeled and minced
2 tablespoons extra-virgin olive oil
2 tablespoons freshly squeezed lemon juice
½ cup fresh parsley, coarsely chopped
1 teaspoon onion powder
1 teaspoon lemon-pepper seasoning
½ teaspoon hot paprika
½ teaspoon salt
¼ teaspoon cumin powder

1. Toss all the ingredients in a mixing bowl until the shrimp are well coated.
2. Cover and allow to marinate in the refrigerator for 30 minutes.
3. When ready, transfer the shrimp to an air fryer basket.
4. Slide the basket into the air fryer oven. Cook at 400°F (205°C) for 5 minutes.
5. When cooking is complete, the shrimp should be pink on the outside and opaque in the center. Remove from the air fryer oven and serve warm.

Fish and Seafood

Garlicky Cod Fillets

Prep time: 10 minutes | Cook time: 12 minutes | Serves 4

1 teaspoon olive oil
4 cod fillets
¼ teaspoon fine sea salt
¼ teaspoon ground black pepper, or more to taste
1 teaspoon cayenne pepper
½ cup fresh Italian parsley, coarsely chopped
½ cup nondairy milk
1 Italian pepper, chopped
4 garlic cloves, minced
1 teaspoon dried basil
½ teaspoon dried oregano

1. Lightly coat the sides and bottom of a baking dish with the olive oil. Set aside.
2. In a large bowl, sprinkle the fillets with salt, black pepper, and cayenne pepper.
3. In a food processor, pulse the remaining ingredients until smoothly puréed.
4. Add the purée to the bowl of fillets and toss to coat, then transfer to the prepared baking dish.
5. Slide the baking dish into the air fryer oven. Cook at 380°F (193°C) for 12 minutes.
6. When cooking is complete, the fish should flake when pressed lightly with a fork. Remove from the air fryer oven and serve warm.

Glazed Tuna and Fruit Kebabs

Prep time: 15 minutes | Cook time: 10 minutes | Serves 4

Kebabs:
1 pound (454 g) tuna steaks, cut into 1-inch cubes
½ cup canned pineapple chunks, drained, juice reserved
½ cup large red grapes
Marinade:
1 tablespoon honey
1 teaspoon olive oil
2 teaspoons grated fresh ginger
Pinch cayenne pepper

Special Equipment:
4 metal skewers

1. Make the kebabs: Thread, alternating tuna cubes, pineapple chunks, and red grapes, onto the metal skewers.
2. Make the marinade: Whisk together the honey, olive oil, ginger, and cayenne pepper in a small bowl. Brush generously the marinade over the kebabs and allow to sit for 10 minutes.
3. When ready, transfer the kebabs to an air fryer basket.
4. Slide the basket into the air fryer oven. Cook at 370°F (188°C) for 10 minutes.
5. After 5 minutes, remove from the air fryer oven and flip the kebabs and brush with the remaining marinade. Return to the air fryer oven and continue cooking for an additional 5 minutes.
6. When cooking is complete, the kebabs should reach an internal temperature of 145°F (63°C) on a meat thermometer. Remove from the air fryer oven and discard any remaining marinade. Serve hot.

Seafood Spring Rolls

Prep time: 10 minutes | Cook time: 20 minutes | Serves 4

1 tablespoon olive oil
2 teaspoons minced garlic
1 cup matchstick cut carrots
2 cups finely sliced cabbage
2 (4-ounce / 113-g) cans tiny shrimp, drained
4 teaspoons soy sauce
Salt and freshly ground black pepper, to taste
16 square spring roll wrappers
Cooking spray

1. Spray an air fryer basket with cooking spray. Set aside.
2. Heat the olive oil in a medium skillet over medium heat until it shimmers.
3. Add the garlic to the skillet and cook for 30 seconds. Stir in the cabbage and carrots and sauté for about 5 minutes, stirring occasionally, or until the vegetables are lightly tender.
4. Fold in the shrimp and soy sauce and sprinkle with salt and pepper, then stir to combine. Sauté for another 2 minutes, or until the moisture is evaporated. Remove from the heat and set aside to cool.
5. Put a spring roll wrapper on a work surface and spoon 1 tablespoon of the shrimp mixture onto the lower end of the wrapper.
6. Roll the wrapper away from you halfway, and then fold in the right and left sides, like an envelope. Continue to roll to the very end, using a little water to seal the edge. Repeat with the remaining wrappers and filling.
7. Place the spring rolls in an air fryer basket, leaving space between each spring roll. Mist them lightly with cooking spray.
8. Slide the basket into the air fryer oven. Cook at 375°F (190°C) for 10 minutes.
9. Flip the rolls halfway through the cooking time.
10. When cooking is complete, the spring rolls will be heated through and browned. If necessary, continue cooking for 5 minutes more. Remove from the air fryer oven and cool for a few minutes before serving.

Goat Cheese Shrimp

Prep time: 15 minutes | Cook time: 8 minutes | Serves 2

1 pound (454 g) shrimp, deveined
1½ tablespoons olive oil
1½ tablespoons balsamic vinegar
1 tablespoon coconut aminos
½ tablespoon fresh parsley, roughly chopped
Sea salt flakes, to taste
1 teaspoon Dijon mustard
½ teaspoon smoked cayenne pepper
½ teaspoon garlic powder
Salt and ground black peppercorns, to taste
1 cup shredded goat cheese

1. Except for the cheese, stir together all the ingredients in a large bowl until the shrimp are evenly coated.
2. Place the shrimp in an air fryer basket.
3. Slide the basket into the air fryer oven. Cook at 385°F (196°C) for 8 minutes.
4. When cooking is complete, the shrimp should be pink and cooked through. Remove from the air fryer oven and serve with the shredded goat cheese sprinkled on top.

Golden Beer-Battered Cod

Prep time: 5 minutes | Cook time: 15 minutes | Serves 4

2 eggs
1 cup malty beer
1 cup all-purpose flour
½ cup cornstarch
1 teaspoon garlic powder
Salt and pepper, to taste
4 (4-ounce / 113-g) cod fillets
Cooking spray

1. In a shallow bowl, beat together the eggs with the beer. In another shallow bowl, thoroughly combine the flour and cornstarch. Sprinkle with the garlic powder, salt, and pepper.
2. Dredge each cod fillet in the flour mixture, then in the egg mixture. Dip each piece of fish in the flour mixture a second time.
3. Spritz an air fryer basket with cooking spray. Arrange the cod fillets in the basket.
4. Slide the basket into the air fryer oven. Cook at 400°F (205°C) for 15 minutes.
5. Flip the fillets halfway through the cooking time.
6. When cooking is complete, the cod should reach an internal temperature of 145°F (63°C) on a meat thermometer and the outside should be crispy. Let the fish cool for 5 minutes and serve.

Roasted Salmon with Asparagus

Prep time: 10 minutes | Cook time: 15 minutes | Serves 4

4 (6-ounce / 170 g) salmon fillets, patted dry
1 teaspoon kosher salt, divided
1 tablespoon honey
2 tablespoons unsalted butter, melted
2 teaspoons Dijon mustard
2 pounds (907 g) asparagus, trimmed
Lemon wedges, for serving

1. Season both sides of the salmon fillets with ½ teaspoon of kosher salt.
2. Whisk together the honey, 1 tablespoon of butter, and mustard in a small bowl. Set aside.
3. Arrange the asparagus on a sheet pan. Drizzle the remaining 1 tablespoon of butter all over and season with the remaining ½ teaspoon of salt, tossing to coat. Move the asparagus to the outside of the sheet pan.
4. Put the salmon fillets on the sheet pan, skin-side down. Brush the fillets generously with the honey mixture.
5. Slide the pan into the air fryer oven. Cook at 375°F (190°C) for 15 minutes.
6. Toss the asparagus once halfway through the cooking time.
7. When done, transfer the salmon fillets and asparagus to a plate. Serve warm with a squeeze of lemon juice.

Herbed Scallops with Vegetables

Prep time: 15 minutes | Cook time: 9 minutes | Serves 4

1 cup frozen peas
1 cup green beans
1 cup frozen chopped broccoli
2 teaspoons olive oil
½ teaspoon dried oregano
½ teaspoon dried basil
12 ounces (340 g) sea scallops, rinsed and patted dry

1. Put the peas, green beans, and broccoli in a large bowl. Drizzle with the olive oil and toss to coat well. Transfer the vegetables to an air fryer basket.
2. Slide the basket into the air fryer oven. Cook at 400°F (205°C) for 5 minutes.
3. When cooking is complete, the vegetables should be fork-tender. Transfer the vegetables to a serving bowl. Scatter with the oregano and basil and set aside.
4. Place the scallops in the air fryer basket.
5. Slide the basket into the air fryer oven. Cook at 400°F (205°C) for 4 minutes.
6. When cooking is complete, the scallops should be firm and just opaque in the center. Remove from the air fryer oven to the bowl of vegetables and toss well. Serve warm.

Herbed Salmon with Roasted Asparagus

Prep time: 5 minutes | Cook time: 12 minutes | Serves 2

2 teaspoons olive oil, plus additional for drizzling
2 (5-ounce / 142-g) salmon fillets, with skin
Salt and freshly ground black pepper, to taste
1 bunch asparagus, trimmed
1 teaspoon dried tarragon
1 teaspoon dried chives
Fresh lemon wedges, for serving

1. Rub the olive oil all over the salmon fillets. Sprinkle with salt and pepper to taste.
2. Put the asparagus on a foil-lined baking sheet and place the salmon fillets on top, skin-side down.
3. Slide the baking sheet into the air fryer oven. Cook at 425°F (220°C) for 12 minutes.
4. When cooked, the fillets should register 145°F (63°C) on an instant-read thermometer. Remove from the air fryer oven and cut the salmon fillets in half crosswise, then use a metal spatula to lift flesh from skin and transfer to a serving plate. Discard the skin and drizzle the salmon fillets with additional olive oil. Scatter with the herbs.
5. Serve the salmon fillets with roasted asparagus spears and lemon wedges on the side.

Mustard-Crusted Sole Fillets

Prep time: 5 minutes | Cook time: 10 minutes | Serves 4

5 teaspoons low-sodium yellow mustard
1 tablespoon freshly squeezed lemon juice
4 (3.5-ounce / 99-g) sole fillets
2 teaspoons olive oil
½ teaspoon dried marjoram
½ teaspoon dried thyme
⅛ teaspoon freshly ground black pepper
1 slice low-sodium whole-wheat bread, crumbled

1. Whisk together the mustard and lemon juice in a small bowl until thoroughly mixed and smooth. Spread the mixture evenly over the sole fillets, then transfer the fillets to an air fryer basket.
2. In a separate bowl, combine the olive oil, marjoram, thyme, black pepper, and bread crumbs and stir to mix well. Gently but firmly press the mixture onto the top of fillets, coating them completely.
3. Slide the basket into the air fryer oven. Cook at 320°F (160°C) for 10 minutes.
4. When cooking is complete, the fish should reach an internal temperature of 145°F (63°C) on a meat thermometer. Remove the basket from the air fryer oven and serve on a plate.

Lemon-Honey Snapper with Fruit

Prep time: 15 minutes | Cook time: 12 minutes | Serves 4

4 (4-ounce / 113-g) red snapper fillets
2 teaspoons olive oil
3 plums, halved and pitted
3 nectarines, halved and pitted
1 cup red grapes
1 tablespoon freshly squeezed lemon juice
1 tablespoon honey
½ teaspoon dried thyme

1. Arrange the red snapper fillets in an air fryer basket and drizzle the olive oil over the top.
2. Slide the basket into the air fryer oven. Cook at 390°F (199°C) for 12 minutes.
3. After 4 minutes, remove from the air fryer oven. Top the fillets with the plums and nectarines. Scatter the red grapes all over the fillets. Drizzle with the lemon juice and honey and sprinkle the thyme on top. Return to the air fryer oven and continue cooking for 8 minutes, or until the fish is flaky.
4. When cooking is complete, remove from the air fryer oven and serve warm.

Panko Catfish Nuggets

Prep time: 10 minutes | Cook time: 7 to 8 minutes | Serves 4

2 medium catfish fillets, cut into chunks (approximately 1 × 2 inch)
Salt and pepper, to taste
2 eggs
2 tablespoons skim milk
½ cup cornstarch
1 cup panko bread crumbs
Cooking spray

1. In a medium bowl, season the fish chunks with salt and pepper to taste.
2. In a small bowl, beat together the eggs with milk until well combined.
3. Place the cornstarch and bread crumbs into separate shallow dishes.
4. Dredge the fish chunks one at a time in the cornstarch, coating well on both sides, then dip in the egg mixture, shaking off any excess, finally press well into the bread crumbs. Spritz the fish chunks with cooking spray.
5. Arrange the fish chunks in an air fryer basket.
6. Slide the basket into the air fryer oven. Cook at 390°F (199°C) for 8 minutes.
7. Flip the fish chunks halfway through the cooking time.
8. When cooking is complete, they should be no longer translucent in the center and golden brown. Remove the fish chunks from the air fryer oven to a plate. Serve warm.

Panko Crab Sticks with Mayo Sauce

Prep time: 5 minutes | Cook time: 12 minutes | Serves 4

Crab Sticks:
2 eggs
1 cup flour
⅓ cup panko bread crumbs
1 tablespoon old bay seasoning
1 pound (454 g) crab sticks
Cooking spray
Mayo Sauce:
½ cup mayonnaise
1 lime, juiced
2 garlic cloves, minced

1. In a bowl, beat the eggs. In a shallow bowl, place the flour. In another shallow bowl, thoroughly combine the panko bread crumbs and old bay seasoning.
2. Dredge the crab sticks in the flour, shaking off any excess, then in the beaten eggs, finally press them in the bread crumb mixture to coat well.
3. Arrange the crab sticks in an air fryer basket and spray with cooking spray.
4. Slide the basket into the air fryer oven. Cook at 390°F (199°C) for 12 minutes.
5. Flip the crab sticks halfway through the cooking time.
6. Meanwhile, make the sauce by whisking together the mayo, lime juice, and garlic in a small bowl.
7. When cooking is complete, remove from the air fryer oven. Serve the crab sticks with the mayo sauce on the side.

Homemade Fish Sticks

Prep time: 10 minutes | Cook time: 8 minutes | Makes 8 fish sticks

8 ounces (227 g) fish fillets (pollock or cod), cut into ½×3-inch strips
Salt, to taste (optional)
½ cup plain bread crumbs
Cooking spray

1. Season the fish strips with salt to taste, if desired.
2. Place the bread crumbs on a plate. Roll the fish strips in the bread crumbs to coat. Spritz the fish strips with cooking spray.
3. Arrange the fish strips in an air fryer basket.
4. Slide the basket into the air fryer oven. Cook at 390°F (199°C) for 8 minutes.
5. When cooking is complete, they should be golden brown. Remove from the air fryer oven and cool for 5 minutes before serving.

Paprika Shrimp

Prep time: 5 minutes | Cook time: 10 minutes | Serves 4

1 pound (454 g) tiger shrimp
2 tablespoons olive oil
½ tablespoon old bay seasoning
¼ tablespoon smoked paprika
¼ teaspoon cayenne pepper
A pinch of sea salt

1. Toss all the ingredients in a large bowl until the shrimp are evenly coated.
2. Arrange the shrimp in an air fryer basket.
3. Slide the basket into the air fryer oven. Cook at 380°F (193°C) for 10 minutes.
4. When cooking is complete, the shrimp should be pink and cooked through. Remove from the air fryer oven and serve hot.

Parmesan-Crusted Hake with Garlic Sauce

Prep time: 5 minutes | Cook time: 10 minutes | Serves 3

Fish:
6 tablespoons mayonnaise
1 tablespoon fresh lime juice
1 teaspoon Dijon mustard
1 cup grated Parmesan cheese
Salt, to taste
¼ teaspoon ground black pepper, or more to taste
3 hake fillets, patted dry
Nonstick cooking spray
Garlic Sauce:
¼ cup plain Greek yogurt
2 tablespoons olive oil
2 cloves garlic, minced
½ teaspoon minced tarragon leaves

1. Mix the mayo, lime juice, and mustard in a shallow bowl and whisk to combine. In another shallow bowl, stir together the grated Parmesan cheese, salt, and pepper.
2. Dredge each fillet in the mayo mixture, then roll them in the cheese mixture until they are evenly coated on both sides.
3. Spray an air fryer basket with nonstick cooking spray. Place the fillets in the basket.
4. Slide the basket into the air fryer oven. Cook at 395°F (202°C) for 10 minutes.
5. Flip the fillets halfway through the cooking time.
6. Meanwhile, in a small bowl, whisk all the ingredients for the sauce until well incorporated.
7. When cooking is complete, the fish should flake apart with a fork. Remove the fillets from the air fryer oven and serve warm alongside the sauce.

Parmesan Fish Fillets

Prep time: 8 minutes | Cook time: 17 minutes | Serves 4

⅓ cup grated Parmesan cheese
½ teaspoon fennel seed
½ teaspoon tarragon
⅓ teaspoon mixed peppercorns
2 eggs, beaten
4 (4-ounce / 113-g) fish fillets, halved
2 tablespoons dry white wine
1 teaspoon seasoned salt

1. Place the grated Parmesan cheese, fennel seed, tarragon, and mixed peppercorns in a food processor and pulse for about 20 seconds until well combined. Transfer the cheese mixture to a shallow dish.
2. Place the beaten eggs in another shallow dish.
3. Drizzle the dry white wine over the top of fish fillets. Dredge each fillet in the beaten eggs on both sides, shaking off any excess, then roll them in the cheese mixture until fully coated. Season with the salt.
4. Arrange the fillets in an air fryer basket.
5. Slide the basket into the air fryer oven. Cook at 345°F (174°C) for 17 minutes.
6. Flip the fillets once halfway through the cooking time.
7. When cooking is complete, the fish should be cooked through no longer translucent. Remove from the air fryer oven and cool for 5 minutes before serving.

Pecan-Crusted Catfish Fillets

Prep time: 5 minutes | Cook time: 12 minutes | Serves 4

½ cup pecan meal
1 teaspoon fine sea salt
¼ teaspoon ground black pepper
4 (4-ounce / 113-g) catfish fillets
Avocado oil spray
For Garnish (Optional):
Fresh oregano
Pecan halves

1. Spray an air fryer basket with avocado oil spray.
2. Combine the pecan meal, sea salt, and black pepper in a large bowl. Dredge each catfish fillet in the meal mixture, turning until well coated. Spritz the fillets with avocado oil spray, then transfer to the air fryer basket.
3. Slide the basket into the air fryer oven. Cook at 375°F (190°C) for 12 minutes.
4. Flip the fillets halfway through the cooking time.
5. When cooking is complete, the fish should be cooked through and no longer translucent. Remove from the air fryer oven and sprinkle the oregano sprigs and pecan halves on top for garnish, if desired. Serve immediately.

Parmesan-Crusted Halibut Fillets

Prep time: 5 minutes | Cook time: 10 minutes | Serves 4

2 medium-sized halibut fillets
Dash of tabasco sauce
1 teaspoon curry powder
½ teaspoon ground coriander
½ teaspoon hot paprika
Kosher salt and freshly cracked mixed peppercorns, to taste
2 eggs
1½ tablespoons olive oil
½ cup grated Parmesan cheese

1. On a clean work surface, drizzle the halibut fillets with the tabasco sauce. Sprinkle with the curry powder, coriander, hot paprika, salt, and cracked mixed peppercorns. Set aside.
2. In a shallow bowl, beat the eggs until frothy. In another shallow bowl, combine the olive oil and Parmesan cheese.
3. One at a time, dredge the halibut fillets in the beaten eggs, shaking off any excess, then roll them over the Parmesan cheese until evenly coated.
4. Arrange the halibut fillets in an air fryer basket.
5. Slide the basket into the air fryer oven. Cook at 365°F (185°C) for 10 minutes.
6. When cooking is complete, the fish should be golden brown and crisp. Cool for 5 minutes before serving.

Roasted Halibut Steaks with Parsley

Prep time: 5 minutes | Cook time: 10 minutes | Serves 4

1 pound (454 g) halibut steaks
¼ cup vegetable oil
2½ tablespoons Worcester sauce
2 tablespoons honey
2 tablespoons vermouth
1 tablespoon freshly squeezed lemon juice
1 tablespoon fresh parsley leaves, coarsely chopped
Salt and pepper, to taste
1 teaspoon dried basil

1. Put all the ingredients in a large mixing dish and gently stir until the fish is coated evenly. Transfer the fish to an air fryer basket.
2. Slide the basket into the air fryer oven. Cook at 390°F (199°C) for 10 minutes.
3. Flip the fish halfway through cooking time.
4. When cooking is complete, the fish should reach an internal temperature of at least 145°F (63°C) on a meat thermometer. Remove from the air fryer oven and let the fish cool for 5 minutes before serving.

Roasted Scallops with Snow Peas

Prep time: 10 minutes | Cook time: 8 minutes | Serves 4

1 pound (454 g) sea scallops
3 tablespoons hoisin sauce
½ cup toasted sesame seeds
6 ounces (170 g) snow peas, trimmed
3 teaspoons vegetable oil, divided
1 teaspoon soy sauce
1 teaspoon sesame oil
1 cup roasted mushrooms

1. Brush the scallops with the hoisin sauce. Put the sesame seeds in a shallow dish. Roll the scallops in the sesame seeds until evenly coated.
2. Combine the snow peas with 1 teaspoon of vegetable oil, the sesame oil, and soy sauce in a medium bowl and toss to coat.
3. Grease a sheet pan with the remaining 2 teaspoons of vegetable oil. Put the scallops in the middle of the pan and arrange the snow peas around the scallops in a single layer.
4. Slide the pan into the air fryer oven. Cook at 375°F (190°C) for 8 minutes.
5. After 5 minutes, remove the pan and flip the scallops. Fold in the mushrooms and stir well. Return to the air fryer oven and continue cooking.
6. When done, remove from the air fryer oven and cool for 5 minutes. Serve warm.

Piri-Piri King Prawns

Prep time: 10 minutes | Cook time: 8 minutes | Serves 2

12 king prawns, rinsed
1 tablespoon coconut oil
Salt and ground black pepper, to taste
1 teaspoon onion powder
1 teaspoon garlic paste
1 teaspoon curry powder
½ teaspoon piri piri powder
½ teaspoon cumin powder

1. Combine all the ingredients in a large bowl and toss until the prawns are completely coated. Place the prawns in an air fryer basket.
2. Slide the basket into the air fryer oven. Cook at 360°F (182°C) for 8 minutes.
3. Flip the prawns halfway through the cooking time.
4. When cooking is complete, the prawns will turn pink. Remove from the air fryer oven and serve hot.

Parmesan-Crusted Salmon Patties

Prep time: 10 minutes | Cook time: 13 minutes | Serves 4

1 pound (454 g) salmon, chopped into ½-inch pieces
2 tablespoons coconut flour
2 tablespoons grated Parmesan cheese
1½ tablespoons milk
½ white onion, peeled and finely chopped
½ teaspoon butter, at room temperature
½ teaspoon chipotle powder
½ teaspoon dried parsley flakes
⅓ teaspoon ground black pepper
⅓ teaspoon smoked cayenne pepper
1 teaspoon fine sea salt

1. Put all the ingredients for the salmon patties in a bowl and stir to combine well.
2. Scoop out 2 tablespoons of the salmon mixture and shape into a patty with your palm, about ½ inch thick. Repeat until all the mixture is used. Transfer to the refrigerator for about 2 hours until firm.
3. When ready, arrange the salmon patties in an air fryer basket.
4. Slide the basket into the air fryer oven. Cook at 395°F (202°C) for 13 minutes.
5. Flip the patties halfway through the cooking time.
6. When cooking is complete, the patties should be golden brown. Remove from the air fryer oven and cool for 5 minutes before serving.

Spiced Red Snapper

Prep time: 13 minutes | Cook time: 10 minutes | Serves 4

1 teaspoon olive oil
1½ teaspoons black pepper
¼ teaspoon garlic powder
¼ teaspoon thyme
⅛ teaspoon cayenne pepper
4 (4-ounce / 113-g) red snapper fillets, skin on
4 thin slices lemon
Nonstick cooking spray

1. Spritz an air fryer basket with nonstick cooking spray.
2. In a small bowl, stir together the olive oil, black pepper, garlic powder, thyme, and cayenne pepper. Rub the mixture all over the fillets until coated.
3. Lay the fillets, skin-side down, in an air fryer basket and top each fillet with a slice of lemon.
4. Slide the basket into the air fryer oven. Cook at 390°F (199°C) for 10 minutes.
5. Flip the fillets halfway through.
6. When cooking is complete, the fish should be cooked through. Let the fish cool for 5 minutes and serve.

Shrimp and Cherry Tomato Kebabs

Prep time: 15 minutes | Cook time: 5 minutes | Serves 4

1½ pounds (680 g) jumbo shrimp, cleaned, shelled and deveined
1 pound (454 g) cherry tomatoes
2 tablespoons butter, melted
1 tablespoons Sriracha sauce
Sea salt and ground black pepper, to taste
1 teaspoon dried parsley flakes
½ teaspoon dried basil
½ teaspoon dried oregano
½ teaspoon mustard seeds
½ teaspoon marjoram

Special Equipment:
4 to 6 wooden skewers, soaked in water for 30 minutes

1. Put all the ingredients in a large bowl and toss to coat well.
2. Make the kebabs: Thread, alternating jumbo shrimp and cherry tomatoes, onto the wooden skewers. Place the kebabs in an air fryer basket.
3. Slide the basket into the air fryer oven. Cook at 400°F (205°C) for 5 minutes.
4. When cooking is complete, the shrimp should be pink and the cherry tomatoes should be softened. Remove from the air fryer oven. Let the shrimp and cherry tomato kebabs cool for 5 minutes and serve hot.

Snapper with Tomatoes and Olives

Prep time: 9 minutes | Cook time: 18 minutes | Serves 4

2 tablespoons extra-virgin olive oil
2 large garlic cloves, minced
½ onion, finely chopped
1 (14.5-ounce / 411-g) can diced tomatoes, drained
¼ cup sliced green olives
3 tablespoons capers, divided
2 tablespoons chopped fresh parsley, divided
½ teaspoon dried oregano
4 (6-ounce / 170-g) snapper fillets
½ teaspoon kosher salt

1. Grease a sheet pan generously with olive oil, then Cook at 375°F (190°C) for 18 minutes.
2. Remove the pan and add the garlic and onion to the olive oil in the pan, stirring to coat. Return to the air fryer oven and continue cooking.
3. After 2 minutes, remove from the air fryer oven. Stir in the tomatoes, olives, 1½ tablespoons of capers, 1 tablespoon of parsley, and oregano. Return to the air fryer oven and continue cooking for 6 minutes until heated through.
4. Meanwhile, rub the fillets with the salt on both sides.
5. After another 6 minutes, remove the pan. Put the fillets in the center of the sheet pan and spoon some of the sauce over them. Return to the air fryer oven and continue cooking, or until the fish is flaky.
6. When cooked, remove from the air fryer oven. Scatter the remaining 1½ tablespoons of capers and 1 tablespoon of parsley on top of the fillets, then serve.

Sole and Cauliflower Fritters

Prep time: 5 minutes | Cook time: 24 minutes | Serves 2

½ pound (227 g) sole fillets
½ pound (227 g) mashed cauliflower
½ cup red onion, chopped
1 bell pepper, finely chopped
1 egg, beaten
2 garlic cloves, minced
2 tablespoons fresh parsley, chopped
1 tablespoon olive oil
1 tablespoon coconut aminos
½ teaspoon scotch bonnet pepper, minced
½ teaspoon paprika
Salt and white pepper, to taste
Cooking spray

1. Spray an air fryer basket with cooking spray. Place the sole fillets in the basket.
2. Slide the basket into the air fryer oven. Cook at 395°F (202°C) for 10 minutes.
3. Flip the fillets halfway through.
4. When cooking is complete, transfer the fish fillets to a large bowl. Mash the fillets into flakes. Add the remaining ingredients and stir to combine.
5. Make the fritters: Scoop out 2 tablespoons of the fish mixture and shape into a patty about ½ inch thick with your hands. Repeat with the remaining fish mixture. Place the patties in the air fryer basket.
6. Slide the basket into the air fryer oven. Cook at 380°F (193°C) for 14 minutes.
7. Flip the patties halfway through.
8. When cooking is complete, they should be golden brown and cooked through. Remove the basket from the air fryer oven and cool for 5 minutes before serving.

Fish and Seafood

Tuna Lettuce Wraps

Prep time: 10 minutes | Cook time: 4 to 7 minutes | Serves 4

1 pound (454 g) fresh tuna steak, cut into 1-inch cubes
2 garlic cloves, minced
1 tablespoon grated fresh ginger
½ teaspoon toasted sesame oil
4 low-sodium whole-wheat tortillas
2 cups shredded romaine lettuce
1 red bell pepper, thinly sliced
¼ cup low-fat mayonnaise

1. Combine the tuna cubes, garlic, ginger, and sesame oil in a medium bowl and toss until well coated. Allow to sit for 10 minutes.
2. When ready, place the tuna cubes in an air fryer basket.
3. Slide the basket into the air fryer oven. Cook at 390ºF (199ºC) for 6 minutes.
4. When cooking is complete, the tuna cubes should be cooked through and golden brown. Remove the tuna cubes from the air fryer oven to a plate.
5. Make the wraps: Place the tortillas on a flat work surface and top each tortilla evenly with the cooked tuna, lettuce, bell pepper, and finish with the mayonnaise. Roll them up and serve immediately.

Sticky Hoisin Tuna

Prep time: 15 minutes | Cook time: 5 minutes | Serves 4

½ cup hoisin sauce
2 tablespoons rice wine vinegar
2 teaspoons sesame oil
2 teaspoons dried lemongrass
1 teaspoon garlic powder
¼ teaspoon red pepper flakes
½ small onion, quartered and thinly sliced
8 ounces (227 g) fresh tuna, cut into 1-inch cubes
Cooking spray
3 cups cooked jasmine rice

1. In a small bowl, whisk together the hoisin sauce, vinegar, sesame oil, lemongrass, garlic powder, and red pepper flakes.
2. Add the sliced onion and tuna cubes and gently toss until the fish is evenly coated.
3. Arrange the coated tuna cubes in an air fryer basket.
4. Slide the basket into the air fryer oven. Cook at 390ºF (199ºC) for 5 minutes.
5. Flip the fish halfway through the cooking time.
6. When cooking is complete, the fish should be flaked. Continue cooking for 1 minute, if necessary. Remove from the air fryer oven and serve over hot jasmine rice.

Tex-Mex Salmon Bowl

Prep time: 115 minutes | Cook time: 12 minutes | Serves 4

12 ounces (340 g) salmon fillets, cut into 1½-inch cubes
1 red onion, chopped
1 jalapeño pepper, minced
1 red bell pepper, chopped
¼ cup low-sodium salsa
2 teaspoons peanut oil or safflower oil
2 tablespoons low-sodium tomato juice
1 teaspoon chili powder

1. Mix the salmon cubes, red onion, jalapeño, red bell pepper, salsa, peanut oil, tomato juice, chili powder in a medium metal bowl and stir until well incorporated.
2. Place the metal bowl into the air fryer oven. Cook at 370ºF (188ºC) for 12 minutes.
3. Stir the ingredients once halfway through the cooking time.
4. When cooking is complete, the salmon should be cooked through and the veggies should be fork-tender. Serve warm.

Tilapia Meunière with Vegetables

Prep time: 10 minutes | Cook time: 20 minutes | Serves 4

10 ounces (283 g) Yukon Gold potatoes, sliced ¼-inch thick
5 tablespoons unsalted butter, melted, divided
1 teaspoon kosher salt, divided
4 (8-ounce / 227-g) tilapia fillets
½ pound (227 g) green beans, trimmed
Juice of 1 lemon
2 tablespoons chopped fresh parsley, for garnish

1. In a large bowl, drizzle the potatoes with 2 tablespoons of melted butter and ¼ teaspoon of kosher salt. Transfer the potatoes to a sheet pan.
2. Slide the pan into the air fryer oven. Cook at 375ºF (190ºC) for 20 minutes.
3. Meanwhile, season both sides of the fillets with ½ teaspoon of kosher salt. Put the green beans in the medium bowl and sprinkle with the remaining ¼ teaspoon of kosher salt and 1 tablespoon of butter, tossing to coat.
4. After 10 minutes, remove the pan and push the potatoes to one side. Put the fillets in the middle of the pan and add the green beans on the other side. Drizzle the remaining 2 tablespoons of butter over the fillets. Return to the air fryer oven and continue cooking, or until the fish flakes easily with a fork and the green beans are crisp-tender.
5. When cooked, remove from the air fryer oven. Drizzle the lemon juice over the fillets and sprinkle the parsley on top for garnish. Serve hot.

Spicy Orange Shrimp

Prep time: 40 minutes | Cook time: 12 minutes | Serves 4

⅓ cup orange juice
3 teaspoons minced garlic
1 teaspoon Old Bay seasoning
¼ to ½ teaspoon cayenne pepper
1 pound (454 g) medium shrimp, thawed, deveined, peeled, with tails off, and patted dry
Cooking spray

1. Stir together the orange juice, garlic, Old Bay seasoning, and cayenne pepper in a medium bowl. Add the shrimp to the bowl and toss to coat well.
2. Cover the bowl with plastic wrap and marinate in the refrigerator for 30 minutes.
3. Spritz an air fryer basket with cooking spray. Place the shrimp in the basket and spray with cooking spray.
4. Slide the basket into the air fryer oven. Cook at 400°F (205°C) for 12 minutes.
5. Flip the shrimp halfway through the cooking time.
6. When cooked, the shrimp should be opaque and crisp. Remove from the air fryer oven and serve hot.

Meats

Apple-Glazed Pork

Prep time: 15 minutes | Cook time: 19 minutes | Serves 4

1 sliced apple
1 small onion, sliced
2 tablespoons apple cider vinegar, divided
½ teaspoon thyme
½ teaspoon rosemary
¼ teaspoon brown sugar
3 tablespoons olive oil, divided
¼ teaspoon smoked paprika
4 pork chops
Salt and ground black pepper, to taste

1. Combine the apple slices, onion, 1 tablespoon of vinegar, thyme, rosemary, brown sugar, and 2 tablespoons of olive oil in a baking pan. Stir to mix well.
2. Slide the pan into the air fryer oven. Cook at 350°F (180°C) for 4 minutes.
3. Stir the mixture halfway through.
4. Meanwhile, combine the remaining vinegar and olive oil, and paprika in a large bowl. Sprinkle with salt and ground black pepper. Stir to mix well. Dredge the pork in the mixture and toss to coat well.
5. Place the pork in the air fryer basket.
6. When cooking is complete, remove the baking pan from the air fryer oven and place in the air fryer basket.
7. Cook in the air fryer oven for 10 minutes. Flip the pork chops halfway through.
8. When cooking is complete, the pork should be lightly browned.
9. Remove the pork from the air fryer oven and baste with baked apple mixture on both sides. Put the pork back to the air fryer oven and air fry for an additional 5 minutes. Flip halfway through.
10. Serve immediately.

Air Fried Beef Satay with Peanut Dipping Sauce

Prep time: 30 minutes | Cook time: 5 minutes | Serves 4

8 ounces (227 g) London broil, sliced into 8 strips
2 teaspoons curry powder
½ teaspoon kosher salt
Cooking spray
Peanut Dipping sauce:
2 tablespoons creamy peanut butter
1 tablespoon reduced-sodium soy sauce
2 teaspoons rice vinegar
1 teaspoon honey
1 teaspoon grated ginger

Special Equipment:
4 bamboo skewers, cut into halves and soaked in water for 20 minutes to keep them from burning while cooking

1. Spritz an air fryer basket with cooking spray.
2. In a bowl, place the London broil strips and sprinkle with the curry powder and kosher salt to season. Thread the strips onto the soaked skewers.
3. Arrange the skewers in the prepared air fryer basket and spritz with cooking spray.
4. Slide the basket into the air fryer oven. Cook at 360°F (182°C) for 5 minutes.
5. Flip the beef halfway through the cooking time.
6. When cooking is complete, the beef should be well browned.
7. In the meantime, stir together the peanut butter, soy sauce, rice vinegar, honey, and ginger in a bowl to make the dipping sauce.
8. Transfer the beef to the serving dishes and let rest for 5 minutes. Serve with the peanut dipping sauce on the side.

Air Fried Crispy Venison

Prep time: 10 minutes | Cook time: 10 minutes | Serves 4

2 eggs
¼ cup milk
1 cup whole wheat flour
½ teaspoon salt
¼ teaspoon ground black pepper
1 pound (454 g) venison backstrap, sliced
Cooking spray

1. Spritz an air fryer basket with cooking spray.
2. Whisk the eggs with milk in a large bowl. Combine the flour with salt and ground black pepper in a shallow dish.
3. Dredge the venison in the flour first, then into the egg mixture. Shake the excess off and roll the venison back over the flour to coat well.
4. Arrange the venison in the basket and spritz with cooking spray.
5. Slide the basket into the air fryer oven. Cook at 360°F (182°C) for 10 minutes.
6. Flip the venison halfway through.
7. When cooking is complete, the internal temperature of the venison should reach at least 145°F (63°C) for medium rare.
8. Serve immediately.

Air Fried Golden Wasabi Spam

Prep time: 5 minutes | Cook time: 12 minutes | Serves 3

⅔ cup all-purpose flour
2 large eggs
1½ tablespoons wasabi paste
2 cups panko breadcrumbs
6 ½-inch-thick spam slices
Cooking spray

1. Spritz an air fryer basket with cooking spray.
2. Pour the flour in a shallow plate. Whisk the eggs with wasabi in a large bowl. Pour the panko in a separate shallow plate.
3. Dredge the spam slices in the flour first, then dunk in the egg mixture, and then roll the spam over the panko to coat well. Shake the excess off.
4. Arrange the spam slices in the basket and spritz with cooking spray.
5. Slide the basket into the air fryer oven. Cook at 400°F (205°C) for 12 minutes.
6. Flip the spam slices halfway through.
7. When cooking is complete, the spam slices should be golden and crispy.
8. Serve immediately.

Air Fried London Broil

Prep time: 8 hours 5 minutes | Cook time: 25 minutes | Serves 6

2 tablespoons Worcestershire sauce
2 tablespoons minced onion
¼ cup honey
⅔ cup ketchup
2 tablespoons apple cider vinegar
½ teaspoon paprika
¼ cup olive oil
1 teaspoon salt
1 teaspoon freshly ground black pepper
2 pounds (907 g) London broil, top round (about 1-inch thick)

1. Combine all the ingredients, except for the London broil, in a large bowl. Stir to mix well.
2. Pierce the meat with a fork generously on both sides, then dunk the meat in the mixture and press to coat well.
3. Wrap the bowl in plastic and refrigerate to marinate for at least 8 hours.
4. Discard the marinade and transfer the London broil to the air fryer basket.
5. Slide the basket into the air fryer oven. Cook at 400°F (205°C) for 25 minutes.
6. Flip the meat halfway through the cooking time.
7. When cooking is complete, the meat should be well browned.
8. Transfer the cooked London broil on a plate and allow to cool for 5 minutes before slicing to serve.

Apple and Pork Bake

Prep time: 10 minutes | Cook time: 45 minutes | Serves 4

2 apples, peeled, cored, and sliced
1 teaspoon ground cinnamon, divided
4 boneless pork chops (½-inch thick)
Salt and freshly ground black pepper, to taste
3 tablespoons brown sugar
¾ cup water
1 tablespoon olive oil

1. Layer apples in bottom of a baking pan. Sprinkle with ½ teaspoon of cinnamon.
2. Trim fat from pork chops. Lay on top of the apple slices. Sprinkle with salt and pepper.
3. In a small bowl, combine the brown sugar, water, and remaining cinnamon. Pour the mixture over the chops. Drizzle chops with 1 tablespoon of olive oil.
4. Slide the pan into the air fryer oven. Cook at 375°F (190°C) for 45 minutes.
5. When cooking is complete, an instant-read thermometer inserted in the pork should register 165°F (74°C).
6. Allow to rest for 3 minutes before serving.

Asparagus and Prosciutto Tart

Prep time: 10 minutes | Cook time: 25 minutes | Serves 4

All-purpose flour, for dusting
1 sheet (½ package) frozen puff pastry, thawed
½ cup grated Parmesan cheese
1 pound (454 g) (or more) asparagus, trimmed
8 ounces (227 g) thinly sliced prosciutto, sliced into ribbons about ½-inch wide
2 teaspoons aged balsamic vinegar

1. On a lightly floured cutting board, unwrap and unfold the puff pastry and roll it lightly with a rolling pin to press the folds together. Place it on a sheet pan.
2. Roll about ½ inch of the pastry edges up to form a ridge around the perimeter. Crimp the corners together to create a solid rim around the pastry. Using a fork, pierce the bottom of the pastry all over. Scatter the cheese over the bottom of the pastry.
3. Arrange the asparagus spears on top of the cheese in a single layer with 4 or 5 spears pointing one way, the next few pointing the opposite direction. You may need to trim them so they fit within the border of the pastry shell. Lay the prosciutto on top more or less evenly.
4. Slide the pan into the air fryer oven. Cook at 375°F (190°C) for 25 minutes.
5. After about 15 minutes, check the tart, rotating the pan if the crust is not browning evenly and continue cooking until the pastry is golden brown and the edges of the prosciutto pieces are browned.
6. Remove from the air fryer oven. Allow to cool for 5 minutes before slicing.
7. Drizzle with the balsamic vinegar just before serving.

Bacon-Wrapped Sausage with Tomato Relish

Prep time: 1 hour 15 minutes | Cook time: 32 minutes | Serves 4

8 pork sausages
8 bacon strips
Relish:
8 large tomatoes, chopped
1 small onion, peeled
1 clove garlic, peeled
1 tablespoon white wine vinegar
3 tablespoons chopped parsley
1 teaspoon smoked paprika
2 tablespoons sugar
Salt and ground black pepper, to taste

1. Purée the tomatoes, onion, and garlic in a food processor until well mixed and smooth.
2. Pour the purée in a saucepan and drizzle with white wine vinegar. Sprinkle with salt and ground black pepper. Simmer over medium heat for 10 minutes.
3. Add the parsley, paprika, and sugar to the saucepan and cook for 10 more minutes or until it has a thick consistency. Keep stirring during the cooking. Refrigerate for an hour to chill.
4. Wrap the sausage with bacon strips and secure with toothpicks, then place them in the air fryer basket.
5. Slide the basket into the air fryer oven. Cook at 350°F (180°C) for 12 minutes.
6. Flip the bacon-wrapped sausage halfway through.
7. When cooking is complete, the bacon should be crispy and browned.
8. Transfer the bacon-wrapped sausage on a plate and baste with the relish or just serve with the relish alongside.

Beef and Spinach Meatloaves

Prep time: 15 minutes | Cook time: 45 minutes | Serves 2

1 large egg, beaten
1 cup frozen spinach
⅓ cup almond meal
¼ cup chopped onion
¼ cup plain Greek milk
¼ teaspoon salt
¼ teaspoon dried sage
2 teaspoons olive oil, divided
Freshly ground black pepper, to taste
½ pound (227 g) extra-lean ground beef
¼ cup tomato paste
1 tablespoon granulated stevia
¼ teaspoon Worcestershire sauce
Cooking spray

1. Coat a shallow baking pan with cooking spray.
2. In a large bowl, combine the beaten egg, spinach, almond meal, onion, milk, salt, sage, 1 teaspoon of olive oil, and pepper.
3. Crumble the beef over the spinach mixture. Mix well to combine. Divide the meat mixture in half. Shape each half into a loaf. Place the loaves in the prepared pan.
4. In a small bowl, whisk together the tomato paste, stevia, Worcestershire sauce, and remaining 1 teaspoon of olive oil. Spoon half of the sauce over each meatloaf.
5. Cook at 350°F (180°C) for 40 minutes.
6. When cooking is complete, an instant-read thermometer inserted in the center of the meatloaves should read at least 165°F (74°C).
7. Serve immediately.

Beef and Tomato Sauce Meatloaf

Prep time: 15 minutes | Cook time: 25 minutes | Serves 4

1½ pounds (680 g) ground beef
1 cup tomato sauce
½ cup breadcrumbs
2 egg whites
½ cup grated Parmesan cheese
1 diced onion
2 tablespoons chopped parsley
2 tablespoons minced ginger
2 garlic cloves, minced
½ teaspoon dried basil
1 teaspoon cayenne pepper
Salt and ground black pepper, to taste
Cooking spray

1. Spritz a meatloaf pan with cooking spray.
2. Combine all the ingredients in a large bowl. Stir to mix well.
3. Pour the meat mixture in the prepared meatloaf pan and press with a spatula to make it firm.
4. Slide the pan into the air fryer oven. Cook at 360°F (182°C) for 25 minutes.
5. When cooking is complete, the beef should be well browned.
6. Serve immediately.

Beef Meatballs with Zesty Marinara Sauce

Prep time: 5 minutes | Cook time: 8 minutes | Serves 4

1 pound (454 g) lean ground sirloin beef
2 tablespoons seasoned breadcrumbs
¼ teaspoon kosher salt
1 large egg, beaten
1 cup marinara sauce, for serving
Cooking spray

1. Spritz an air fryer basket with cooking spray.
2. Mix all the ingredients, except for the marinara sauce, into a bowl until well blended. Shape the mixture into sixteen meatballs.
3. Arrange the meatballs in the prepared air fryer basket and mist with cooking spray.
4. Slide the basket into the air fryer oven. Cook at 360°F (182°C) for 8 minutes.
5. Flip the meatballs halfway through.
6. When cooking is complete, the meatballs should be well browned.
7. Divide the meatballs among four plates and serve warm with the marinara sauce.

Air Fried Beef and Mushroom Stroganoff

Prep time: 15 minutes | Cook time: 14 minutes | Serves 4

1 pound (454 g) beef steak, thinly sliced
8 ounces (227 g) mushrooms, sliced
1 whole onion, chopped
2 cups beef broth
1 cup sour cream
4 tablespoons butter, melted
2 cups cooked egg noodles

1. Combine the mushrooms, onion, beef broth, sour cream and butter in a bowl until well blended. Add the beef steak to another bowl.
2. Spread the mushroom mixture over the steak and let marinate for 10 minutes.
3. Pour the marinated steak in a baking pan.
4. Slide the pan into the air fryer oven. Cook at 400°F (205°C) for 14 minutes.
5. Flip the steak halfway through the cooking time.
6. When cooking is complete, the steak should be browned and the vegetables should be tender.
7. Serve hot with the cooked egg noodles.

Bacon-Wrapped Hot Dogs with Mayo-Ketchup Sauce

Prep time: 5 minutes | Cook time: 10 minutes | Serves 5

10 thin slices of bacon
5 pork hot dogs, halved
1 teaspoon cayenne pepper
Sauce:
¼ cup mayonnaise
4 tablespoons low-carb ketchup
1 teaspoon rice vinegar
1 teaspoon chili powder

1. Arrange the slices of bacon on a clean work surface. One by one, place the halved hot dog on one end of each slice, season with cayenne pepper and wrap the hot dog with the bacon slices and secure with toothpicks as needed.
2. Place wrapped hot dogs in the air fryer basket.
3. Slide the basket into the air fryer oven. Cook at 390°F (199°C) for 10 minutes.
4. Flip the bacon-wrapped hot dogs halfway through.
5. When cooking is complete, the bacon should be crispy and browned.
6. Make the sauce: Stir all the ingredients for the sauce in a small bowl. Wrap the bowl in plastic and set in the refrigerator until ready to serve.
7. Transfer the hot dogs to a platter and serve hot with the sauce.

Bo Luc Lac

Prep time: 50 minutes | Cook time: 4 minutes | Serves 4

For the Meat:
2 teaspoons soy sauce
4 garlic cloves, minced
1 teaspoon kosher salt
2 teaspoons sugar
¼ teaspoon ground black pepper
1 teaspoon toasted sesame oil
1½ pounds (680 g) top sirloin steak, cut into 1-inch cubes
Cooking spray
For the Salad:
1 head Bibb lettuce, leaves separated and torn into large pieces
¼ cup fresh mint leaves
½ cup halved grape tomatoes
½ red onion, halved and thinly sliced
2 tablespoons apple cider vinegar
1 garlic clove, minced
2 teaspoons sugar
¼ teaspoon kosher salt
¼ teaspoon ground black pepper
2 tablespoons vegetable oil
For Serving:
Lime wedges, for garnish
Coarse salt and freshly cracked black pepper, to taste

1. Combine the ingredients for the meat, except for the steak, in a large bowl. Stir to mix well.
2. Dunk the steak cubes in the bowl and press to coat. Wrap the bowl in plastic and marinate under room temperature for at least 30 minutes.
3. Spritz an air fryer basket with cooking spray.
4. Discard the marinade and transfer the steak cubes in the prepared air fryer basket.
5. Slide the basket into the air fryer oven. Cook at 450ºF (235ºC) for 4 minutes.
6. Flip the steak cubes halfway through.
7. When cooking is complete, the steak cubes should be lightly browned but still have a little pink.
8. Meanwhile, combine the ingredients for the salad in a separate large bowl. Toss to mix well.
9. Pour the salad in a large serving bowl and top with the steak cubes. Squeeze the lime wedges over and sprinkle with salt and black pepper before serving.

Calf's Liver Golden Strips

Prep time: 15 minutes | Cook time: 4 to 5 minutes | Serves 4

1 pound (454 g) sliced calf's liver, cut into about ½-inch-wide strips
Salt and ground black pepper, to taste
2 eggs
2 tablespoons milk
½ cup whole wheat flour
1½ cups panko bread crumbs
½ cup plain bread crumbs
½ teaspoon salt
¼ teaspoon ground black pepper
Cooking spray

1. Sprinkle the liver strips with salt and pepper.
2. Beat together the egg and milk in a bowl. Place wheat flour in a shallow dish. In a second shallow dish, mix panko, plain bread crumbs, ½ teaspoon salt, and ¼ teaspoon pepper.
3. Dip liver strips in flour, egg wash, and then bread crumbs, pressing in coating slightly to make crumbs stick.
4. Spritz an air fryer basket with cooking spray. Place strips in a single layer in the air fryer basket.
5. Cook at 400ºF (205ºC) for 4 minutes.
6. After 2 minutes, remove from the air fryer oven. Flip the strips with tongs. Return to the air fryer oven and continue cooking.
7. When cooking is complete, the liver strips should be crispy and golden.
8. Serve immediately.

Caraway Crusted Beef Steaks

Prep time: 5 minutes | Cook time: 10 minutes | Serves 4

4 beef steaks
2 teaspoons caraway seeds
2 teaspoons garlic powder
Sea salt and cayenne pepper, to taste
1 tablespoon melted butter
⅓ cup almond flour
2 eggs, beaten

1. Add the beef steaks to a large bowl and toss with the caraway seeds, garlic powder, salt and pepper until well coated.
2. Stir together the melted butter and almond flour in a bowl. Whisk the eggs in a different bowl.
3. Dredge the seasoned steaks in the eggs, then dip in the almond and butter mixture.
4. Arrange the coated steaks in the air fryer basket.
5. Slide the basket into the air fryer oven. Cook at 355ºF (179ºC) for 10 minutes.
6. Flip the steaks once halfway through to ensure even cooking.
7. When cooking is complete, the internal temperature of the beef steaks should reach at least 145ºF (63ºC) on a meat thermometer.
8. Transfer the steaks to plates. Let cool for 5 minutes and serve hot.

Carne Asada

Prep time: 5 minutes | Cook time: 15 minutes | Serves 4

3 chipotle peppers in adobo, chopped
⅓ cup chopped fresh oregano
⅓ cup chopped fresh parsley
4 cloves garlic, minced
Juice of 2 limes
1 teaspoon ground cumin seeds
⅓ cup olive oil
1 to 1½ pounds (454 g to 680 g) flank steak
Salt, to taste

1. Combine the chipotle, oregano, parsley, garlic, lime juice, cumin, and olive oil in a large bowl. Stir to mix well.
2. Dunk the flank steak in the mixture and press to coat well. Wrap the bowl in plastic and marinate under room temperature for at least 30 minutes.
3. Discard the marinade and place the steak in the air fryer basket. Sprinkle with salt.
4. Slide the basket into the air fryer oven. Cook at 390°F (199°C) for 15 minutes.
5. Flip the steak halfway through the cooking time.
6. When cooking is complete, the steak should be medium-rare or reach your desired doneness.
7. Remove the steak from the air fryer oven and slice to serve.

Easy Lamb Chops with Asparagus

Prep time: 10 minutes | Cook time: 15 minutes | Serves 4

4 asparagus spears, trimmed
2 tablespoons olive oil, divided
1 pound (454 g) lamb chops
1 garlic clove, minced
2 teaspoons chopped fresh thyme, for serving
Salt and ground black pepper, to taste

1. Spritz an air fryer basket with cooking spray.
2. On a large plate, brush the asparagus with 1 tablespoon olive oil, then sprinkle with salt. Set aside.
3. On a separate plate, brush the lamb chops with remaining olive oil and sprinkle with salt and ground black pepper.
4. Arrange the lamb chops in the basket.
5. Slide the basket into the air fryer oven. Cook at 400°F (205°C) for 15 minutes.
6. Flip the lamb chops and add the asparagus and garlic halfway through.
7. When cooking is complete, the lamb should be well browned and the asparagus should be tender.
8. Serve them on a plate with thyme on top.

Crispy Pork Tenderloin

Prep time: 5 minutes | Cook time: 10 minutes | Serves 6

2 large egg whites
1½ tablespoons Dijon mustard
2 cups crushed pretzel crumbs
1½ pounds (680 g) pork tenderloin, cut into ¼-pound (113-g) sections
Cooking spray

1. Spritz an air fryer basket with cooking spray.
2. Whisk the egg whites with Dijon mustard in a bowl until bubbly. Pour the pretzel crumbs in a separate bowl.
3. Dredge the pork tenderloin in the egg white mixture and press to coat. Shake the excess off and roll the tenderloin over the pretzel crumbs.
4. Arrange the well-coated pork tenderloin in the basket and spritz with cooking spray.
5. Slide the basket into the air fryer oven. Cook at 350°F (180°C) for 10 minutes.
6. After 5 minutes, remove from the air fryer oven. Flip the pork. Return to the air fryer oven and continue cooking.
7. When cooking is complete, the pork should be golden brown and crispy.
8. Serve immediately.

Dijon Pork Tenderloin

Prep time: 15 minutes | Cook time: 15 minutes | Serves 4

3 tablespoons Dijon mustard
3 tablespoons honey
1 teaspoon dried rosemary
1 tablespoon olive oil
1 pound (454 g) pork tenderloin, rinsed and drained
Salt and freshly ground black pepper, to taste

1. In a small bowl, combine the Dijon mustard, honey, and rosemary. Stir to combine.
2. Rub the pork tenderloin with salt and pepper on all sides on a clean work surface.
3. Heat the olive oil in an air fryer oven-safe skillet over high heat. Sear the pork loin on all sides in the skillet for 6 minutes or until golden brown. Flip the pork halfway through.
4. Remove from the heat and spread honey-mustard mixture evenly to coat the pork loin.
5. Slide the skillet into the air fryer oven. Cook at 425°F (220°C) for 15 minutes.
6. When cooking is complete, an instant-read thermometer inserted in the pork should register at least 145°F (63°C).
7. Remove from the air fryer oven and allow to rest for 3 minutes. Slice the pork into ½-inch slices and serve.

Cinnamon-Beef Kofta

Prep time: 10 minutes | Cook time: 13 minutes | Makes 12 koftas

1½ pounds (680 g) lean ground beef
1 teaspoon onion powder
¾ teaspoon ground cinnamon
¾ teaspoon ground dried turmeric
1 teaspoon ground cumin
¾ teaspoon salt
¼ teaspoon cayenne
12 (3½- to 4-inch-long) cinnamon sticks
Cooking spray

1. Spritz an air fryer basket with cooking spray.
2. Combine all the ingredients, except for the cinnamon sticks, in a large bowl. Toss to mix well.
3. Divide and shape the mixture into 12 balls, then wrap each ball around each cinnamon stick and leave a quarter of the length uncovered.
4. Arrange the beef-cinnamon sticks in the prepared basket and spritz with cooking spray.
5. Slide the basket into the air fryer oven. Cook at 375°F (190°C) for 13 minutes.
6. Flip the sticks halfway through the cooking.
7. When cooking is complete, the beef should be browned.
8. Serve immediately.

Chuck and Sausage Subs

Prep time: 15 minutes | Cook time: 24 minutes | Serves 4

1 large egg
¼ cup whole milk
24 saltines, crushed but not pulverized
1 pound (454 g) ground chuck
1 pound (454 g) Italian sausage, casings removed
4 tablespoons grated Parmesan cheese, divided
1 teaspoon kosher salt
4 sub rolls, split
1 cup Marinara sauce
¾ cup shredded Mozzarella cheese

1. In a large bowl, whisk the egg into the milk, then stir in the crackers. Let sit for 5 minutes to hydrate.
2. With your hands, break the ground chuck and sausage into the milk mixture, alternating beef and sausage. When you've added half of the meat, sprinkle 2 tablespoons of the grated Parmesan and the salt over it, then continue breaking up the meat until it's all in the bowl. Gently mix everything together. Try not to overwork the meat, but get it all combined.
3. Form the mixture into balls about the size of a golf ball. You should get about 24 meatballs. Flatten the balls slightly to prevent them from rolling, then place them on a baking pan, about 2 inches apart.
4. Slide the pan into the air fryer oven. Cook at 400°F (205°C) for 20 minutes.
5. After 10 minutes, remove from the air fryer oven and turn over the meatballs. Return to the air fryer oven and continue cooking.
6. When cooking is complete, remove from the air fryer oven. Place the meatballs on a rack. Wipe off the baking pan.
7. Open the rolls, cut-side up, on the baking pan. Place 3 to 4 meatballs on the base of each roll, and top each sandwich with ¼ cup of marinara sauce. Divide the Mozzarella among the top halves of the buns and sprinkle the remaining Parmesan cheese over the Mozzarella.
8. Slide the pan into the air fryer oven. Cook for 4 minutes.
9. Check the sandwiches after 2 minutes; the Mozzarella cheese should be melted and bubbling slightly.
10. When cooking is complete, remove from the air fryer oven. Close the sandwiches and serve.

Citrus Carnitas

Prep time: 1 hour 10 minutes | Cook time: 25 minutes | Serves 6

2½ pounds (1.1 kg) boneless country-style pork ribs, cut into 2-inch pieces
3 tablespoons olive brine
1 tablespoon minced fresh oregano leaves
⅓ cup orange juice
1 teaspoon ground cumin
1 tablespoon minced garlic
1 teaspoon salt
1 teaspoon ground black pepper
Cooking spray

1. Combine all the ingredients in a large bowl. Toss to coat the pork ribs well. Wrap the bowl in plastic and refrigerate for at least an hour to marinate.
2. Spritz an air fryer basket with cooking spray.
3. Arrange the marinated pork ribs in the basket and spritz with cooking spray.
4. Slide the basket into the air fryer oven. Cook at 400°F (205°C) for 25 minutes.
5. Flip the ribs halfway through.
6. When cooking is complete, the ribs should be well browned.
7. Serve immediately.

Char Siu

Prep time: 8 hours 10 minutes | Cook time: 15 minutes | Serves 4

¼ cup honey
1 teaspoon Chinese five-spice powder
1 tablespoon Shaoxing wine (rice cooking wine)
1 tablespoon hoisin sauce
2 teaspoons minced garlic
2 teaspoons minced fresh ginger
2 tablespoons soy sauce
1 tablespoon sugar
1 pound (454 g) fatty pork shoulder, cut into long, 1-inch-thick pieces
Cooking spray

1. Combine all the ingredients, except for the pork should, in a microwave-safe bowl. Stir to mix well. Microwave until the honey has dissolved. Stir periodically.
2. Pierce the pork pieces generously with a fork, then put the pork in a large bowl. Pour in half of the honey mixture. Set the remaining sauce aside until ready to serve.
3. Press the pork pieces into the mixture to coat and wrap the bowl in plastic and refrigerate to marinate for at least 8 hours.
4. Spritz an air fryer basket with cooking spray.
5. Discard the marinade and transfer the pork pieces in the air fryer basket.
6. Slide the basket into the air fryer oven. Cook at 400°F (205°C) for 15 minutes.
7. Flip the pork halfway through.
8. When cooking is complete, the pork should be well browned.
9. Meanwhile, microwave the remaining marinade on high for a minute or until it has a thick consistency. Stir periodically.
10. Remove the pork from the air fryer oven and allow to cool for 10 minutes before serving with the thickened marinade.

Classic Walliser Schnitzel

Prep time: 5 minutes | Cook time: 14 minutes | Serves 2

½ cup pork rinds
½ tablespoon fresh parsley
½ teaspoon fennel seed
½ teaspoon mustard
⅓ tablespoon cider vinegar
1 teaspoon garlic salt
⅓ teaspoon ground black pepper
2 eggs
2 pork schnitzel, halved
Cooking spray

1. Spritz an air fryer basket with cooking spray.
2. Put the pork rinds, parsley, fennel seeds, and mustard in a food processor. Pour in the vinegar and sprinkle with salt and ground black pepper. Pulse until well combined and smooth.
3. Pour the pork rind mixture in a large bowl. Whisk the eggs in a separate bowl.
4. Dunk the pork schnitzel in the whisked eggs, then dunk in the pork rind mixture to coat well. Shake the excess off.
5. Arrange the schnitzel in the basket and spritz with cooking spray.
6. Slide the basketinto the air fryer oven. Cook at 350°F (180°C) for 14 minutes.
7. After 7 minutes, remove from the air fryer oven. Flip the schnitzel. Return to the air fryer oven and continue cooking.
8. When cooking is complete, the schnitzel should be golden and crispy.
9. Serve immediately.

Gold Cutlets with Aloha Salsa

Prep time: 20 minutes | Cook time: 7 minutes | Serves 4

2 eggs
2 tablespoons milk
¼ cup all-purpose flour
¼ cup panko bread crumbs
4 teaspoons sesame seeds
1 pound (454 g) boneless, thin pork cutlets (½-inch thick)
¼ cup cornstarch
Salt and ground lemon pepper, to taste
Cooking spray
Aloha Salsa:
1 cup fresh pineapple, chopped in small pieces
¼ cup red bell pepper, chopped
½ teaspoon ground cinnamon
1 teaspoon soy sauce
¼ cup red onion, finely chopped
⅛ teaspoon crushed red pepper
⅛ teaspoon ground black pepper

1. In a medium bowl, stir together all ingredients for salsa. Cover and refrigerate while cooking the pork.
2. Beat together eggs and milk in a large bowl. In another bowl, mix the flour, panko, and sesame seeds. Pour the cornstarch in a shallow dish.
3. Sprinkle pork cutlets with lemon pepper and salt. Dip pork cutlets in cornstarch, egg mixture, and then panko coating. Spritz both sides with cooking spray.
4. Cook at 400°F (205°C) for 7 minutes.
5. After 3 minutes, remove from the air fryer oven. Flip the cutlets with tongs. Return to the air fryer oven and continue cooking.
6. When cooking is complete, the pork should be crispy and golden brown on both sides.
7. Serve the fried cutlets with the Aloha salsa on the side.

Golden Lamb Chops

Prep time: 5 minutes | Cook time: 25 minutes | Serves 4

1 cup all-purpose flour
2 teaspoons dried sage leaves
2 teaspoons garlic powder
1 tablespoon mild paprika
1 tablespoon salt
4 (6-ounce / 170-g) bone-in lamb shoulder chops, fat trimmed
Cooking spray

1. Spritz an air fryer basket with cooking spray.
2. Combine the flour, sage leaves, garlic powder, paprika, and salt in a large bowl. Stir to mix well. Dunk in the lamb chops and toss to coat well.
3. Arrange the lamb chops in the basket and spritz with cooking spray.
4. Slide the basket into the air fryer oven. Cook at 375°F (190°C) for 25 minutes.
5. Flip the chops halfway through.
6. When cooking is complete, the chops should be golden brown and reaches your desired doneness.
7. Serve immediately.

Hearty Mushroom and Sausage Calzones

Prep time: 10 minutes | Cook time: 24 minutes | Serves 4

2 links Italian sausages (about ½ pound / 227 g)
1 pound (454 g) pizza dough, thawed
3 tablespoons olive oil, divided
¼ cup Marinara sauce
½ cup roasted mushrooms
1 cup shredded Mozzarella cheese

1. Place the sausages in a baking pan.
2. Slide the pan into the air fryer oven. Cook at 375°F (190°C) for 12 minutes.
3. After 6 minutes, remove from the air fryer oven and turn over the sausages. Return to the air fryer oven and continue cooking.
4. While the sausages cook, divide the pizza dough into 4 equal pieces. One at a time, place a piece of dough onto a square of parchment paper 9 inches in diameter. Brush the dough on both sides with ¾ teaspoon of olive oil, then top the dough with another piece of parchment. Press the dough into a 7-inch circle. Remove the top piece of parchment and set aside. Repeat with the remaining pieces of dough.
5. When cooking is complete, remove from the air fryer oven. Place the sausages on a cutting board. Let them cool for several minutes, then slice into ¼-inch rounds and cut each round into 4 pieces.
6. One at a time, spread a tablespoon of marinara sauce over half of a dough circle, leaving a ½-inch border at the edges. Cover with a quarter of the sausage pieces and add a quarter of the mushrooms. Sprinkle with ¼ cup of cheese. Pull the other side of the dough over the filling and pinch the edges together to seal. Transfer from the parchment to the baking pan. Repeat with the other rounds of dough, sauce, sausage, mushrooms, and cheese.
7. Brush the tops of the calzones with 1 tablespoon of olive oil.
8. Slide the pan into the air fryer oven. Cook at 450°F (235°C) for 12 minutes.
9. After 6 minutes, remove from the air fryer oven. The calzones should be golden brown. Turn over the calzones and brush the tops with the remaining olive oil. Return to the air fryer oven and continue cooking.
10. When cooking is complete, the crust should be a deep golden brown on both sides. Remove from the air fryer oven. The center should be molten; let cool for several minutes before serving.

Lahmacun (Turkish Pizza)

Prep time: 20 minutes | Cook time: 10 minutes | Serves 4

4 (6-inch) flour tortillas
For the Meat Topping:
4 ounces (113 g) ground lamb or 85% lean ground beef
¼ cup finely chopped green bell pepper
¼ cup chopped fresh parsley
1 small plum tomato, deseeded and chopped
2 tablespoons chopped yellow onion
1 garlic clove, minced
2 teaspoons tomato paste
¼ teaspoon sweet paprika
¼ teaspoon ground cumin
⅛ to ¼ teaspoon red pepper flakes
⅛ teaspoon ground allspice
⅛ teaspoon kosher salt
⅛ teaspoon black pepper
For Serving:
¼ cup chopped fresh mint
1 teaspoon extra-virgin olive oil
1 lemon, cut into wedges

1. Combine all the ingredients for the meat topping in a medium bowl until well mixed.
2. Lay the tortillas on a clean work surface. Spoon the meat mixture on the tortillas and spread all over.
3. Place the tortillas in the air fryer basket.
4. Slide the basket into the air fryer oven. Cook at 400°F (205°C) for 10 minutes.
5. When cooking is complete, the edge of the tortilla should be golden and the meat should be lightly browned.
6. Transfer them to a serving dish. Top with chopped fresh mint and drizzle with olive oil. Squeeze the lemon wedges on top and serve.

Homemade Teriyaki Pork Ribs

Prep time: 5 minutes | Cook time: 30 minutes | Serves 4

¼ cup soy sauce
¼ cup honey
1 teaspoon garlic powder
1 teaspoon ground dried ginger
4 (8-ounce / 227-g) boneless country-style pork ribs
Cooking spray

1. Spritz an air fryer basket with cooking spray.
2. Make the teriyaki sauce: combine the soy sauce, honey, garlic powder, and ginger in a bowl. Stir to mix well.
3. Brush the ribs with half of the teriyaki sauce, then arrange the ribs in the basket. Spritz with cooking spray.
4. Slide the basket into the air fryer oven. Cook at 350°F (180°C) for 30 minutes.
5. After 15 minutes, remove from the air fryer oven. Flip the ribs and brush with remaining teriyaki sauce. Return to the air fryer oven and continue cooking.
6. When cooking is complete, the internal temperature of the ribs should reach at least 145°F (63°C).
7. Serve immediately.

Lamb Kofta

Prep time: 25 minutes | Cook time: 10 minutes | Serves 4

1 pound (454 g) ground lamb
1 tablespoon ras el hanout (North African spice)
½ teaspoon ground coriander
1 teaspoon onion powder
1 teaspoon garlic powder
1 teaspoon cumin
2 tablespoons mint, chopped
Salt and ground black pepper, to taste

Special Equipment:
4 bamboo skewers

1. Combine the ground lamb, ras el hanout, coriander, onion powder, garlic powder, cumin, mint, salt, and ground black pepper in a large bowl. Stir to mix well.
2. Transfer the mixture into sausage molds and sit the bamboo skewers in the mixture. Refrigerate for 15 minutes.
3. Spritz an air fryer basket with cooking spray. Place the lamb skewers in the basket and spritz with cooking spray.
4. Slide the basket into the air fryer oven. Cook at 380°F (193°C) for 10 minutes.
5. Flip the lamb skewers halfway through.
6. When cooking is complete, the lamb should be well browned.
7. Serve immediately.

Italian Sausages and Red Grapes

Prep time: 10 minutes | Cook time: 20 minutes | Serves 6

2 pounds (905 g) seedless red grapes
3 shallots, sliced
2 teaspoons fresh thyme
2 tablespoons olive oil
½ teaspoon kosher salt
Freshly ground black pepper, to taste
6 links (about 1½ pounds / 680 g) hot Italian sausage
3 tablespoons balsamic vinegar

1. Place the grapes in a large bowl. Add the shallots, thyme, olive oil, salt, and pepper. Gently toss. Place the grapes in a baking pan. Arrange the sausage links evenly in the pan.
2. Slide the pan into the air fryer oven. Cook at 375°F (190°C) for 20 minutes.
3. After 10 minutes, remove the pan. Turn over the sausages and sprinkle the vinegar over the sausages and grapes. Gently toss the grapes and move them to one side of the pan. Return to the air fryer oven and continue cooking.
4. When cooking is complete, the grapes should be very soft and the sausages browned. Serve immediately.

Kielbasa Sausage with Pineapple and Bell Peppers

Prep time: 15 minutes | Cook time: 10 minutes | Serves 2 to 4

¾ pound (340 g) kielbasa sausage, cut into ½-inch slices
1 (8-ounce / 227-g) can pineapple chunks in juice, drained
1 cup bell pepper chunks
1 tablespoon barbecue seasoning
1 tablespoon soy sauce
Cooking spray

1. Spritz an air fryer basket with cooking spray.
2. Combine all the ingredients in a large bowl. Toss to mix well.
3. Pour the sausage mixture in the air fryer basket.
4. Slide the basket into the air fryer oven. Cook at 390°F (199°C) for 10 minutes.
5. After 5 minutes, remove from the air fryer oven. Stir the sausage mixture. Return to the air fryer oven and continue cooking.
6. When cooking is complete, the sausage should be lightly browned and the bell pepper and pineapple should be soft.
7. Serve immediately.

Italian Steak and Spinach Rolls

Prep time: 50 minutes | Cook time: 9 minutes | Serves 4

2 teaspoons dried Italian seasoning
2 cloves garlic, minced
1 tablespoon vegetable oil
1 teaspoon kosher salt
1 teaspoon ground black pepper
1 pound (454 g) flank steak, ¼ to ½ inch thick
1 (10-ounce / 284-g) package frozen spinach, thawed and squeezed dry
½ cup diced jarred roasted red pepper
1 cup shredded Mozzarella cheese
Cooking spray

7. Combine the Italian seasoning, garlic, vegetable oil, salt, and ground black pepper in a large bowl. Stir to mix well.
8. Dunk the steak in the seasoning mixture and toss to coat well. Wrap the bowl in plastic and marinate under room temperature for at least 30 minutes.
9. Spritz an air fryer basket with cooking spray.
10. Remove the marinated steak from the bowl and unfold on a clean work surface, then spread the top of the steak with a layer of spinach, a layer of red pepper and a layer of cheese. Leave a ¼-inch edge uncovered.
11. Roll the steak up to wrap the filling, then secure with 3 toothpicks. Cut the roll in half and transfer the rolls in the prepared air fryer basket, seam side down.
12. Slide the basket into the air fryer oven. Cook at 400°F (205°C) for 9 minutes.
13. Flip the rolls halfway through the cooking.
14. When cooking is complete, the steak should be lightly browned and the internal temperature reaches at least 145°F (63°C).
15. Remove the rolls from the air fryer oven and slice to serve.

Lamb Loin Chops with Horseradish Cream Sauce

Prep time: 10 minutes | Cook time: 13 minutes | Serves 4

For the Lamb:
4 lamb loin chops
2 tablespoons vegetable oil
1 clove garlic, minced
½ teaspoon kosher salt
½ teaspoon black pepper
For the Horseradish Cream Sauce:
1 to 1½ tablespoons prepared horseradish
1 tablespoon Dijon mustard
½ cup mayonnaise
2 teaspoons sugar
Cooking spray

1. Spritz an air fryer basket with cooking spray.
2. Place the lamb chops on a plate. Rub with the oil and sprinkle with the garlic, salt and black pepper. Let sit to marinate for 30 minutes at room temperature.
3. Make the horseradish cream sauce: Mix the horseradish, mustard, mayonnaise, and sugar in a bowl until well combined. Set half of the sauce aside until ready to serve.
4. Arrange the marinated chops in the air fryer basket.
5. Slide the basket into the air fryer oven. Cook at 325°F (163°C) for 10 minutes.
6. Flip the lamb chops halfway through.
7. When cooking is complete, the lamb should be lightly browned.
8. Transfer the chops from the air fryer oven to the bowl of the horseradish sauce. Roll to coat well.
9. Put the coated chops back in the air fryer basket in the air fryer oven. Cook at 400°F (205°C) and the time to 3 minutes.
10. When cooking is complete, the internal temperature should reach 145°F (63°C) on a meat thermometer (for medium-rare). Flip the lamb halfway through.
11. Serve hot with the horseradish cream sauce.

Lamb Rack with Pistachio

Prep time: 10 minutes | Cook time: 20 minutes | Serves 2

½ cup finely chopped pistachios
1 teaspoon chopped fresh rosemary
3 tablespoons panko breadcrumbs
2 teaspoons chopped fresh oregano
1 tablespoon olive oil
Salt and freshly ground black pepper, to taste
1 lamb rack, bones fat trimmed and frenched
1 tablespoon Dijon mustard

1. Put the pistachios, rosemary, breadcrumbs, oregano, olive oil, salt, and black pepper in a food processor. Pulse to combine until smooth.
2. Rub the lamb rack with salt and black pepper on a clean work surface, then place it in the air fryer basket.
3. Slide the basket into the air fryer oven. Cook at 380°F (193°C) for 12 minutes.
4. Flip the lamb halfway through.
5. When cooking is complete, the lamb should be lightly browned.
6. Transfer the lamb on a plate and brush with Dijon mustard on the fat side, then sprinkle with the pistachios mixture over the lamb rack to coat well.
7. Put the lamb rack back to the air fryer oven and air fry for 8 more minutes or until the internal temperature of the rack reaches at least 145°F (63°C).
8. Remove the lamb rack from the air fryer oven with tongs and allow to cool for 5 minutes before slicing to serve.

Lechon Kawali

Prep time: 10 minutes | Cook time: 30 minutes | Serves 4

1 pound (454 g) pork belly, cut into three thick chunks
6 garlic cloves
2 bay leaves
2 tablespoons soy sauce
1 teaspoon kosher salt
1 teaspoon ground black pepper
3 cups water
Cooking spray

1. Put all the ingredients in a pressure cooker, then put the lid on and cook on high for 15 minutes.
2. Natural release the pressure and release any remaining pressure, transfer the tender pork belly on a clean work surface. Allow to cool under room temperature until you can handle.
3. Generously spritz an air fryer basket with cooking spray.
4. Cut each chunk into two slices, then put the pork slices in the basket.
5. Slide the basket into the air fryer oven. Cook at 400°F (205°C) for 15 minutes.
6. After 7 minutes, remove from the air fryer oven. Flip the pork. Return to the air fryer oven and continue cooking.
7. When cooking is complete, the pork fat should be crispy.
8. Serve immediately.

Lemony Pork Loin Chop Schnitzel

Prep time: 15 minutes | Cook time: 15 minutes | Serves 4

4 thin boneless pork loin chops
2 tablespoons lemon juice
½ cup flour
¼ teaspoon marjoram
1 teaspoon salt
1 cup panko breadcrumbs
2 eggs
Lemon wedges, for serving
Cooking spray

1. On a clean work surface, drizzle the pork chops with lemon juice on both sides.
2. Combine the flour with marjoram and salt on a shallow plate. Pour the breadcrumbs on a separate shallow dish. Beat the eggs in a large bowl.
3. Dredge the pork chops in the flour, then dunk in the beaten eggs to coat well. Shake the excess off and roll over the breadcrumbs. Arrange the pork chops in the air fryer basket and spritz with cooking spray.
4. Slide the basket into the air fryer oven. Cook at 400°F (205°C) for 15 minutes.
5. After 7 minutes, remove from the air fryer oven. Flip the pork. Return to the air fryer oven and continue cooking.
6. When cooking is complete, the pork should be crispy and golden.
7. Squeeze the lemon wedges over the fried chops and serve immediately.

Lush Salisbury Steak with Mushroom Gravy

Prep time: 20 minutes | Cook time: 33 minutes | Serves 2

For the Mushroom Gravy:
¾ cup sliced button mushrooms
¼ cup thinly sliced onions
¼ cup unsalted butter, melted
½ teaspoon fine sea salt
¼ cup beef broth
For the Steaks:
½ pound (227 g) ground beef (85% lean)
1 tablespoon dry mustard
2 tablespoons tomato paste
¼ teaspoon garlic powder
½ teaspoon onion powder
½ teaspoon fine sea salt
¼ teaspoon ground black pepper
Chopped fresh thyme leaves, for garnish

1. Toss the mushrooms and onions with butter in a baking pan to coat well, then sprinkle with salt.
2. Slide the pan into the air fryer oven. Cook at 390°F (199°C) for 8 minutes.
3. Stir the mixture halfway through the cooking.
4. When cooking is complete, the mushrooms should be tender.
5. Pour the broth in the baking pan for 10 more minutes to make the gravy.
6. Meanwhile, combine all the ingredients for the steaks, except for the thyme leaves, in a large bowl. Stir to mix well. Shape the mixture into two oval steaks.
7. Arrange the steaks over the gravy for 15 minutes. When cooking is complete, the patties should be browned. Flip the steaks halfway through.
8. Transfer the steaks onto a plate and pour the gravy over. Sprinkle with fresh thyme and serve immediately.

Macadamia Nuts Crusted Pork Rack

Prep time: 5 minutes | Cook time: 35 minutes | Serves 2

1 clove garlic, minced
2 tablespoons olive oil
1 pound (454 g) rack of pork
1 cup chopped macadamia nuts
1 tablespoon breadcrumbs
1 tablespoon rosemary, chopped
1 egg
Salt and ground black pepper, to taste

1. Combine the garlic and olive oil in a small bowl. Stir to mix well.
2. On a clean work surface, rub the pork rack with the garlic oil and sprinkle with salt and black pepper on both sides.
3. Combine the macadamia nuts, breadcrumbs, and rosemary in a shallow dish. Whisk the egg in a large bowl.
4. Dredge the pork in the egg, then roll the pork over the macadamia nut mixture to coat well. Shake the excess off.
5. Arrange the pork in the air fryer basket.
6. Slide the basket into the air fryer oven. Cook at 350°F (180°C) for 30 minutes.
7. After 30 minutes, remove from the air fryer oven. Flip the pork rack. Return to the air fryer oven and increase temperature to 390°F (199°C) for 5 minutes. Keep cooking.
8. When cooking is complete, the pork should be browned.
9. Serve immediately.

Meat and Rice Stuffed Bell Peppers

Prep time: 20 minutes | Cook time: 18 minutes | Serves 4

¾ pound (340 g) lean ground beef
4 ounces (113 g) lean ground pork
¼ cup onion, minced
1 (15-ounce / 425-g) can crushed tomatoes
1 teaspoon Worcestershire sauce
1 teaspoon barbecue seasoning
1 teaspoon honey
½ teaspoon dried basil
½ cup cooked brown rice
½ teaspoon garlic powder
½ teaspoon oregano
½ teaspoon salt
2 small bell peppers, cut in half, stems removed, deseeded
Cooking spray

1. Spritz a baking pan with cooking spray.
2. Arrange the beef, pork, and onion in the baking pan.
3. Slide the pan into the air fryer oven. Cook at 360°F (182°C) for 8 minutes.
4. Break the ground meat into chunks halfway through the cooking.
5. When cooking is complete, the ground meat should be lightly browned.
6. Meanwhile, combine the tomatoes, Worcestershire sauce, barbecue seasoning, honey, and basil in a saucepan. Stir to mix well.
7. Transfer the cooked meat mixture to a large bowl and add the cooked rice, garlic powder, oregano, salt, and ¼ cup of the tomato mixture. Stir to mix well.
8. Stuff the pepper halves with the mixture, then arrange the pepper halves in the air fryer basket.
9. Place the pan into the air fryer oven and cook for 10 more minutes.
10. When cooking is complete, the peppers should be lightly charred.
11. Serve the stuffed peppers with the remaining tomato sauce on top.

Mushroom in Bacon-Wrapped Filets Mignons

Prep time: 10 minutes | Cook time: 13 minutes | Serves 8

1 ounce (28 g) dried porcini mushrooms
½ teaspoon granulated white sugar
½ teaspoon salt
½ teaspoon ground white pepper
8 (4-ounce / 113-g) filets mignons or beef tenderloin steaks
8 thin-cut bacon strips

1. Put the mushrooms, sugar, salt, and white pepper in a spice grinder and grind to combine.
2. On a clean work surface, rub the filets mignons with the mushroom mixture, then wrap each filet with a bacon strip. Secure with toothpicks if necessary.
3. Arrange the bacon-wrapped filets mignons in the air fryer basket, seam side down.
4. Slide the basket into the air fryer oven. Cook at 400°F (205°C) for 13 minutes.
5. Flip the filets halfway through.
6. When cooking is complete, the filets should be medium rare.
7. Serve immediately.

New York Strip with Honey-Mustard Butter

Prep time: 5 minutes | Cook time: 14 minutes | Serves 4

2 pounds (907 g) New York Strip
1 teaspoon cayenne pepper
1 tablespoon honey
1 tablespoon Dijon mustard
½ stick butter, softened
Sea salt and freshly ground black pepper, to taste
Cooking spray

1. Spritz an air fryer basket with cooking spray.
2. Sprinkle the New York Strip with cayenne pepper, salt, and black pepper on a clean work surface.
3. Arrange the New York Strip in the prepared basket and spritz with cooking spray.
4. Slide the basket into the air fryer oven. Cook at 400°F (205°C) for 14 minutes.
5. Flip the New York Strip halfway through.
6. When cooking is complete, the strips should be browned.
7. Meanwhile, combine the honey, mustard, and butter in a small bowl. Stir to mix well.
8. Transfer the air fried New York Strip onto a plate and baste with the honey-mustard butter before serving.

Panko Crusted Calf's Liver Strips

Prep time: 15 minutes | Cook time: 5 minutes | Serves 4

1 pound (454 g) sliced calf's liver, cut into ½-inch wide strips
2 eggs
2 tablespoons milk
½ cup whole wheat flour
2 cups panko breadcrumbs
Salt and ground black pepper, to taste
Cooking spray

1. Spritz an air fryer basket with cooking spray.
2. Rub the calf's liver strips with salt and ground black pepper on a clean work surface.
3. Whisk the eggs with milk in a large bowl. Pour the flour in a shallow dish. Pour the panko on a separate shallow dish.
4. Dunk the liver strips in the flour, then in the egg mixture. Shake the excess off and roll the strips over the panko to coat well.
5. Arrange the liver strips in the basket and spritz with cooking spray.
6. Slide the basket into the air fryer oven. Cook at 390°F (199°C) for 5 minutes.
7. Flip the strips halfway through.
8. When cooking is complete, the strips should be browned.
9. Serve immediately.

Pork, Bell Pepper, and Pineapple Skewers

Prep time: 10 minutes | Cook time: 12 minutes | Serves 4

¼ teaspoon kosher salt or ⅛ teaspoon fine salt
1 medium pork tenderloin (about 1 pound / 454 g), cut into 1½-inch chunks
1 green bell pepper, seeded and cut into 1-inch pieces
1 red bell pepper, seeded and cut into 1-inch pieces
2 cups fresh pineapple chunks
¾ cup Teriyaki Sauce or store-bought variety, divided

Special Equipment:
12 (9- to 12-inch) wooden skewers, soaked in water for about 30 minutes

1. Sprinkle the pork cubes with the salt.
2. Thread the pork, bell peppers, and pineapple onto a skewer. Repeat until all skewers are complete. Brush the skewers generously with about half of the Teriyaki Sauce. Place them on a sheet pan.
3. Slide the pan into the air fryer oven. Cook at 375°F (190°C) for 10 minutes.
4. After about 5 minutes, remove from the air fryer oven. Turn over the skewers and brush with the remaining half of Teriyaki Sauce. Transfer the pan back to the air fryer oven and continue cooking until the vegetables are tender and browned in places and the pork is browned and cooked through.
5. Remove the pan from the air fryer oven and serve.

Ravioli with Beef-Marinara Sauce

Prep time: 10 minutes | Cook time: 10 minutes | Serves 4

1 (20-ounce / 567-g) package frozen cheese ravioli
1 teaspoon kosher salt
1¼ cups water
6 ounces (170 g) cooked ground beef
2½ cups Marinara sauce
¼ cup grated Parmesan cheese, for garnish

1. Place the ravioli in an even layer on a baking pan. Stir the salt into the water until dissolved and pour it over the ravioli.
2. Slide the pan into the air fryer oven. Cook at 450°F (235°C) for 10 minutes.
3. While the ravioli is cooking, mix the ground beef into the marinara sauce in a medium bowl.
4. After 6 minutes, remove from the air fryer oven. Blot off any remaining water, or drain the ravioli and return them to the pan. Pour the meat sauce over the ravioli. Return to the air fryer oven and continue cooking.
5. When cooking is complete, remove from the air fryer oven. The ravioli should be tender and sauce heated through. Gently stir the ingredients. Serve the ravioli with the Parmesan cheese, if desired.

Easy Pork Chop Roast

Prep time: 5 minutes | Cook time: 20 minutes | Serves 2

2 (10-ounce / 284-g) bone-in, center cut pork chops, 1-inch thick
2 teaspoons Worcestershire sauce
Salt and ground black pepper, to taste
Cooking spray

1. Rub the Worcestershire sauce on both sides of pork chops.
2. Season with salt and pepper to taste.
3. Spritz an air fryer basket with cooking spray and place the chops in the air fryer basket side by side.
4. Cook at 350°F (180°C) for 20 minutes.
5. After 10 minutes, remove from the air fryer oven. Flip the pork chops with tongs. Return to the air fryer oven and continue cooking.
6. When cooking is complete, the pork should be well browned on both sides.
7. Let rest for 5 minutes before serving.

Pork and Tricolor Vegetables Kebabs

Prep time: 1 hour 20 minutes | Cook time: 8 minutes | Serves 4

For the Pork:
1 pound (454 g) pork steak, cut in cubes
1 tablespoon white wine vinegar
3 tablespoons steak sauce
¼ cup soy sauce
1 teaspoon powdered chili
1 teaspoon red chili flakes
2 teaspoons smoked paprika
1 teaspoon garlic salt
For the Vegetable:
1 green squash, deseeded and cut in cubes
1 yellow squash, deseeded and cut in cubes
1 red pepper, cut in cubes
1 green pepper, cut in cubes
Salt and ground black pepper, to taste
Cooking spray

Special Equipment:
4 bamboo skewers, soaked in water for at least 30 minutes

1. Combine the ingredients for the pork in a large bowl. Press the pork to dunk in the marinade. Wrap the bowl in plastic and refrigerate for at least an hour.
2. Spritz an air fryer basket with cooking spray.
3. Remove the pork from the marinade and run the skewers through the pork and vegetables alternatively. Sprinkle with salt and pepper to taste.
4. Arrange the skewers in the basket and spritz with cooking spray.
5. Slide the basket into the air fryer oven. Cook at 380°F (193°C) for 8 minutes.
6. After 4 minutes, remove from the air fryer oven. Flip the skewers. Return to the air fryer oven and continue cooking.
7. When cooking is complete, the pork should be browned and the vegetables should be lightly charred and tender.
8. Serve immediately.

Pork Butt with Garlicky Coriander-Parsley Sauce

Prep time: 1 hour 15 minutes | Cook time: 30 minutes | Serves 4

1 teaspoon golden flaxseeds meal
1 egg white, well whisked
1 tablespoon soy sauce
1 teaspoon lemon juice, preferably freshly squeezed
1 tablespoon olive oil
1 pound (454 g) pork butt, cut into pieces 2-inches long
Salt and ground black pepper, to taste
Garlicky Coriander-Parsley Sauce:
3 garlic cloves, minced
⅓ cup fresh coriander leaves
⅓ cup fresh parsley leaves
1 teaspoon lemon juice
½ tablespoon salt
⅓ cup extra-virgin olive oil

1. Combine the flaxseeds meal, egg white, soy sauce, lemon juice, salt, black pepper, and olive oil in a large bowl. Dunk the pork strips in and press to submerge.
2. Wrap the bowl in plastic and refrigerate to marinate for at least an hour.
3. Arrange the marinated pork strips in the air fryer basket.
4. Slide the basket into the air fryer oven. Cook at 380°F (193°C) for 30 minutes.
5. After 15 minutes, remove from the air fryer oven. Flip the pork. Return to the air fryer oven and continue cooking.
6. When cooking is complete, the pork should be well browned.
7. Meanwhile, combine the ingredients for the sauce in a small bowl. Stir to mix well. Arrange the bowl in the refrigerator to chill until ready to serve.
8. Serve the air fried pork strips with the chilled sauce.

Pork Fried Rice with Scrambled Egg

Prep time: 10 minutes | Cook time: 12 minutes | Serves 4

3 scallions, diced (about ½ cup)
½ red bell pepper, diced (about ½ cup)
2 teaspoons sesame oil
½ pound (227 g) pork tenderloin, diced
½ cup frozen peas, thawed
½ cup roasted mushrooms
½ cup soy sauce
2 cups cooked rice
1 egg, beaten

1. Place the scallions and red pepper on a baking pan. Drizzle with the sesame oil and toss the vegetables to coat them in the oil.
2. Slide the pan into the air fryer oven. Cook at 375°F (190°C) for 12 minutes.
3. While the vegetables are cooking, place the pork in a large bowl. Add the peas, mushrooms, soy sauce, and rice and toss to coat the ingredients with the sauce.
4. After about 4 minutes, remove from the air fryer oven. Place the pork mixture on the pan and stir the scallions and peppers into the pork and rice. Return to the air fryer oven and continue cooking.
5. After another 6 minutes, remove from the air fryer oven. Move the rice mixture to the sides to create an empty circle in the middle of the pan. Pour the egg in the circle. Return to the air fryer oven and continue cooking.
6. When cooking is complete, remove from the air fryer oven and stir the egg to scramble it. Stir the egg into the fried rice mixture. Serve immediately.

Pork Leg Roast with Candy Onions

Prep time: 10 minutes | Cook time: 52 minutes | Serves 4

2 teaspoons sesame oil
1 teaspoon dried sage, crushed
1 teaspoon cayenne pepper
1 rosemary sprig, chopped
1 thyme sprig, chopped
Sea salt and ground black pepper, to taste
2 pounds (907 g) pork leg roast, scored
½ pound (227 g) candy onions, sliced
4 cloves garlic, finely chopped
2 chili peppers, minced

1. In a mixing bowl, combine the sesame oil, sage, cayenne pepper, rosemary, thyme, salt and black pepper until well mixed. In another bowl, place the pork leg and brush with the seasoning mixture.
2. Place the seasoned pork leg in a baking pan. Slide the pan into the air fryer oven. Cook at 400°F (205°C) for 40 minutes.
3. After 20 minutes, remove from the air fryer oven. Flip the pork leg. Return to the air fryer oven and continue cooking.
4. After another 20 minutes, add the candy onions, garlic, and chili peppers to the pan and air fry for another 12 minutes.
5. When cooking is complete, the pork leg should be browned.
6. Transfer the pork leg to a plate. Let cool for 5 minutes and slice. Spread the juices left in the pan over the pork and serve warm with the candy onions.

Sausage Ratatouille

Prep time: 10 minutes | Cook time: 25 minutes | Serves 4

4 pork sausages
Ratatouille:
2 zucchinis, sliced
1 eggplant, sliced
15 ounces (425 g) tomatoes, sliced
1 red bell pepper, sliced
1 medium red onion, sliced
1 cup canned butter beans, drained
1 tablespoon balsamic vinegar
2 garlic cloves, minced
1 red chili, chopped
2 tablespoons fresh thyme, chopped
2 tablespoons olive oil

1. Place the sausages in the air fryer basket.
2. Slide the basket into the air fryer oven. Cook at 390°F (199°C) for 10 minutes.
3. After 7 minutes, remove from the air fryer oven. Flip the sausages. Return to the air fryer oven and continue cooking.
4. When cooking is complete, the sausages should be lightly browned.
5. Meanwhile, make the ratatouille: arrange the vegetable slices on a baking pan alternatively, then add the remaining ingredients on top.
6. Transfer the air fried sausage to a plate, then arrange the baking pan in the air fryer oven.
7. Bake for 15 minutes until the vegetables are tender. Give the vegetables a stir halfway through the baking.
8. Serve the ratatouille with the sausage on top.

Thai Curry Beef Meatballs

Prep time: 5 minutes | Cook time: 15 minutes | Serves 4

1 pound (454 g) ground beef
1 tablespoon sesame oil
2 teaspoons chopped lemongrass
1 teaspoon red Thai curry paste
1 teaspoon Thai seasoning blend
Juice and zest of ½ lime
Cooking spray

1. Spritz an air fryer basket with cooking spray.
2. In a medium bowl, combine all the ingredients until well blended.
3. Shape the meat mixture into 24 meatballs and arrange them in the basket.
4. Slide the basket into the air fryer oven. Cook at 380°F (193°C) for 15 minutes.
5. Flip the meatballs halfway through.
6. When cooking is complete, the meatballs should be browned.
7. Transfer the meatballs to plates. Let cool for 5 minutes before serving.

Pork Schnitzels with Sour Cream and Dill Sauce

Prep time: 5 minutes | Cook time: 4 minutes | Serves 4 to 6

½ cup flour
1½ teaspoons salt
Freshly ground black pepper, to taste
2 eggs
½ cup milk
1½ cups toasted breadcrumbs
1 teaspoon paprika
6 boneless, center cut pork chops (about 1½ pounds / 680 g), fat trimmed, pound to ½-inch thick
2 tablespoons olive oil
3 tablespoons melted butter
Lemon wedges, for serving
Sour Cream and Dill Sauce:
1 cup chicken stock
1½ tablespoons cornstarch
⅓ cup sour cream
1½ tablespoons chopped fresh dill
Salt and ground black pepper, to taste

1. Combine the flour with salt and black pepper in a large bowl. Stir to mix well. Whisk the egg with milk in a second bowl. Stir the breadcrumbs and paprika in a third bowl.
2. Dredge the pork chops in the flour bowl, then in the egg milk, and then into the breadcrumbs bowl. Press to coat well. Shake the excess off.
3. Arrange the pork chop in the air fryer basket, then brush with olive oil and butter on all sides.
4. Slide the basket into the air fryer oven. Cook at 400°F (205°C) for 4 minutes.
5. After 2 minutes, remove from the air fryer oven. Flip the pork. Return to the air fryer oven and continue cooking.
6. When cooking is complete, the pork chop should be golden brown and crispy.
7. Meanwhile, combine the chicken stock and cornstarch in a small saucepan and bring to a boil over medium-high heat. Simmer for 2 more minutes.
8. Turn off the heat, then mix in the sour cream, fresh dill, salt, and black pepper.
9. Remove the schnitzels from the air fryer oven to a plate and baste with sour cream and dill sauce. Squeeze the lemon wedges over and slice to serve.

Pork with Butternut Squash and Apples

Prep time: 15 minutes | Cook time: 13 minutes | Serves 4

4 boneless pork loin chops, ¾- to 1-inch thick
1 teaspoon kosher salt, divided
2 tablespoons Dijon mustard
2 tablespoons brown sugar
1 pound (454 g) butternut squash, cut into 1-inch cubes
1 large apple, peeled and cut into 12 to 16 wedges
1 medium onion, thinly sliced
½ teaspoon dried thyme
¼ teaspoon freshly ground black pepper
1 tablespoon unsalted butter, melted
½ cup chicken stock

1. Sprinkle the pork chops on both sides with ½ teaspoon of kosher salt. In a small bowl, whisk together the mustard and brown sugar. Baste about half of the mixture on one side of the pork chops. Place the chops, basted-side up, on a baking pan.
2. Place the squash in a large bowl. Add the apple, onion, thyme, remaining kosher salt, pepper, and butter and toss to coat. Arrange the squash-fruit mixture around the chops on the pan. Pour the chicken stock over the mixture, avoiding the chops.
3. Slide the pan into the air fryer oven. Cook at 350°F (180°C) for 13 minutes.
4. After about 7 minutes, remove from the air fryer oven. Gently toss the squash mixture and turn over the chops. Baste the chops with the remaining mustard mixture. Return to the air fryer oven and continue cooking.
5. When cooking is complete, the pork chops should register at least 145°F (63°C) in the center on a meat thermometer, and the squash and apples should be tender. If necessary, continue cooking for up to 3 minutes more.
6. Remove from the air fryer oven. Spoon the squash and apples onto four plates, and place a pork chop on top. Serve immediately.

Pork Sausage with Cauliflower Mash

Prep time: 5 minutes | Cook time: 27 minutes | Serves 6

1 pound (454 g) cauliflower, chopped
6 pork sausages, chopped
½ onion, sliced
3 eggs, beaten
⅓ cup Colby cheese
1 teaspoon cumin powder
½ teaspoon tarragon
½ teaspoon sea salt
½ teaspoon ground black pepper
Cooking spray

1. Spritz a baking pan with cooking spray.
2. In a saucepan over medium heat, boil the cauliflower until tender. Place the boiled cauliflower in a food processor and pulse until puréed. Transfer to a large bowl and combine with remaining ingredients until well blended.
3. Pour the cauliflower and sausage mixture into the pan.
4. Slide the pan into the air fryer oven. Cook at 365°F (185°C) for 27 minutes.
5. When cooking is complete, the sausage should be lightly browned.
6. Divide the mixture among six serving dishes and serve warm.

Reuben Beef Rolls with Thousand Island Sauce

Prep time: 15 minutes | Cook time: 10 minutes | Makes 10 rolls

½ pound (227 g) cooked corned beef, chopped
½ cup drained and chopped sauerkraut
1 (8-ounce / 227-g) package cream cheese, softened
½ cup shredded Swiss cheese
20 slices prosciutto
Cooking spray
Thousand Island Sauce:
¼ cup chopped dill pickles
¼ cup tomato sauce
¾ cup mayonnaise
Fresh thyme leaves, for garnish
2 tablespoons sugar
⅛ teaspoon fine sea salt
Ground black pepper, to taste

1. Spritz an air fryer basket with cooking spray.
2. Combine the beef, sauerkraut, cream cheese, and Swiss cheese in a large bowl. Stir to mix well.
3. Unroll a slice of prosciutto on a clean work surface, then top with another slice of prosciutto crosswise. Scoop up 4 tablespoons of the beef mixture in the center.
4. Fold the top slice sides over the filling as the ends of the roll, then roll up the long sides of the bottom prosciutto and make it into a roll shape. Overlap the sides by about 1 inch. Repeat with remaining filling and prosciutto.
5. Arrange the rolls in the prepared basket, seam side down, and spritz with cooking spray.
6. Slide the basket into the air fryer oven. Cook at 400°F (205°C) for 10 minutes.
7. Flip the rolls halfway through.
8. When cooking is complete, the rolls should be golden and crispy.
9. Meanwhile, combine the ingredients for the sauce in a small bowl. Stir to mix well.
10. Serve the rolls with the dipping sauce.

Spicy Pork Chops with Carrots and Mushrooms

Prep time: 10 minutes | Cook time: 15 minutes | Serves 4

2 carrots, cut into sticks
1 cup mushrooms, sliced
2 garlic cloves, minced
2 tablespoons olive oil
1 pound (454 g) boneless pork chops
1 teaspoon dried oregano
1 teaspoon dried thyme
1 teaspoon cayenne pepper
Salt and ground black pepper, to taste
Cooking spray

1. In a mixing bowl, toss together the carrots, mushrooms, garlic, olive oil and salt until well combined.
2. Add the pork chops to a different bowl and season with oregano, thyme, cayenne pepper, salt and black pepper.
3. Lower the vegetable mixture in the greased air fryer basket. Place the seasoned pork chops on top.
4. Slide the basket into the air fryer oven. Cook at 360°F (182°C) for 15 minutes.
5. After 7 minutes, remove from the air fryer oven. Flip the pork and stir the vegetables. Return to the air fryer oven and continue cooking.
6. When cooking is complete, the pork chops should be browned and the vegetables should be tender.
7. Transfer the pork chops to the serving dishes and let cool for 5 minutes. Serve warm with vegetable on the side.

Sriracha Beef and Broccoli

Prep time: 10 minutes | Cook time: 15 minutes | Serves 4

12 ounces (340 g) broccoli, cut into florets (about 4 cups)
1 pound (454 g) flat iron steak, cut into thin strips
½ teaspoon kosher salt
¾ cup soy sauce
1 teaspoon Sriracha sauce
3 tablespoons freshly squeezed orange juice
1 teaspoon cornstarch
1 medium onion, thinly sliced

1. Line a baking pan with aluminum foil. Place the broccoli on top and sprinkle with 3 tablespoons of water. Seal the broccoli in the foil in a single layer.
2. Slide the pan into the air fryer oven. Cook at 375°F (190°C) for 6 minutes.
3. While the broccoli steams, sprinkle the steak with the salt. In a small bowl, whisk together the soy sauce, Sriracha, orange juice, and cornstarch. Place the onion and beef in a large bowl.
4. When cooking is complete, remove from the air fryer oven. Open the packet of broccoli and use tongs to transfer the broccoli to the bowl with the beef and onion, discarding the foil and remaining water. Pour the sauce over the beef and vegetables and toss to coat. Place the mixture in the baking pan.
5. Slide the pan into the air fryer oven. Cook at 375°F (190°C) for 9 minutes.
6. After about 4 minutes, remove from the air fryer oven and gently toss the ingredients. Return the pan to air fryer oven and continue cooking.
7. When cooking is complete, the sauce should be thickened, the vegetables tender, and the beef barely pink in the center. Serve warm.

Roasted Lamb Chops with Potatoes

Prep time: 10 minutes | Cook time: 20 minutes | Serves 4

8 (½-inch thick) lamb loin chops (about 2 pounds / 907 g)
2 teaspoons kosher salt or 1 teaspoon fine salt, divided
¾ cup plain whole milk yogurt
2 garlic cloves, minced or smashed
1 tablespoon freshly grated ginger (1- or 2-inch piece) or 1 teaspoon ground ginger
1 teaspoon curry powder
1 teaspoon smoked paprika
½ teaspoon cayenne pepper
12 ounces (340 g) small red potatoes, quartered
Cooking spray

1. Sprinkle the lamb chops on both sides with 1 teaspoon of kosher salt and set aside.
2. Meanwhile, make the marinade by stirring together the yogurt, garlic, ginger, curry powder, paprika, cayenne pepper, and remaining 1 teaspoon of kosher salt in a large bowl.
3. Transfer 2 tablespoons of the marinade to a resealable plastic bag, leaving those 2 tablespoons in the bowl. Place the lamb chops in the bag. Squeeze out as much air as possible and squish the bag around so that the chops are well coated with the marinade. Set aside.
4. Add the potatoes to the bowl and toss until well coated. Spritz a sheet pan with cooking spray. Arrange the potatoes in the pan.
5. Slide the pan into the air fryer oven. Cook at 375°F (190°C) for 10 minutes.
6. Once cooking is complete, remove the pan from the air fryer oven.
7. Remove the chops from the marinade, draining off all but a thin coat. Put them in the pan.
8. Slide the pan into the air fryer oven. Cook for 10 minutes.
9. After 5 minutes, remove from the air fryer oven and turn over the chops and potatoes. Slide the pan into the air fryer oven and continue cooking until the lamb read 145°F (63°C) on a meat thermometer. If you want it more well done, continue cooking for another few minutes.
10. Remove the pan from the air fryer oven and serve.

Salsa Beef Meatballs

Prep time: 10 minutes | Cook time: 10 minutes | Serves 4

1 pound (454 g) ground beef (85% lean)
½ cup salsa
¼ cup diced green or red bell peppers
1 large egg, beaten
¼ cup chopped onions
½ teaspoon chili powder
1 clove garlic, minced
½ teaspoon ground cumin
1 teaspoon fine sea salt
Lime wedges, for serving
Cooking spray

1. Spritz an air fryer basket with cooking spray.
2. Combine all the ingredients in a large bowl. Stir to mix well.
3. Divide and shape the mixture into 1-inch balls. Arrange the balls in the basket and spritz with cooking spray.
4. Slide the basket into the air fryer oven. Cook at 350°F (180°C) for 10 minutes.
5. Flip the balls with tongs halfway through.
6. When cooking is complete, the balls should be well browned.
7. Transfer the balls on a plate and squeeze the lime wedges over before serving.

Simple Pork Meatballs with Red Chili

Prep time: 5 minutes | Cook time: 15 minutes | Serves 4

1 pound (454 g) ground pork
2 cloves garlic, finely minced
1 cup scallions, finely chopped
1½ tablespoons Worcestershire sauce
½ teaspoon freshly grated ginger root
1 teaspoon turmeric powder
1 tablespoon oyster sauce
1 small sliced red chili, for garnish
Cooking spray

1. Spritz an air fryer basket with cooking spray.
2. Combine all the ingredients, except for the red chili in a large bowl. Toss to mix well.
3. Shape the mixture into equally sized balls, then arrange them in the air fryer basket and spritz with cooking spray.
4. Slide the basket into the air fryer oven. Cook at 350°F (180°C) for 15 minutes.
5. After 7 minutes, remove from the air fryer oven. Flip the balls. Return to the air fryer oven and continue cooking.
6. When cooking is complete, the balls should be lightly browned.
7. Serve the pork meatballs with red chili on top.

Sirloin Steak and Pepper Fajitas

Prep time: 10 minutes | Cook time: 15 minutes | Serves 4

8 (6-inch) flour tortillas
1 pound (454 g) top sirloin steak, sliced ¼-inch thick
1 red bell pepper, deseeded and sliced ½-inch thick
1 green bell pepper, deseeded and sliced ½-inch thick
1 jalapeño, deseeded and sliced thin
1 medium onion, sliced ½-inch thick
2 tablespoons vegetable oil
2 tablespoons Mexican seasoning
1 teaspoon kosher salt
2 tablespoons salsa
1 small avocado, sliced

1. Line a baking pan with aluminum foil. Place the tortillas on the foil in two stacks and wrap in the foil.
2. Slide the pan into the air fryer oven. Cook at 325°F (163°C) for 6 minutes.
3. After 3 minutes, remove from the air fryer oven and flip the packet of tortillas over. Return to the air fryer oven and continue cooking.
4. While the tortillas warm, place the steak, bell peppers, jalapeño, and onion in a large bowl and drizzle the oil over. Sprinkle with the Mexican seasoning and salt, and toss to coat.
5. When cooking is complete, remove from the air fryer oven and place the packet of tortillas on top of the air fryer oven to keep warm. Place the beef and peppers mixture on the baking pan, spreading out into a single layer as much as possible.
6. Slide the pan into the air fryer oven. Cook at 375°F (190°C) for 9 minutes.
7. After about 5 minutes, remove from the air fryer oven and stir the ingredients. Return to the air fryer oven and continue cooking.
8. When cooking is complete, the vegetables will be soft and browned in places, and the beef will be browned on the outside and barely pink inside. Remove from the air fryer oven. Unwrap the tortillas and spoon the fajita mixture into the tortillas. Serve with salsa and avocado slices.

Smoky Paprika Pork and Vegetable Kabobs

Prep time: 25 minutes | Cook time: 15 minutes | Serves 4

1 pound (454 g) pork tenderloin, cubed
1 teaspoon smoked paprika
Salt and ground black pepper, to taste
1 green bell pepper, cut into chunks
1 zucchini, cut into chunks
1 red onion, sliced
1 tablespoon oregano
Cooking spray

Special Equipment:
Small bamboo skewers, soaked in water for 20 minutes to keep them from burning while cooking

1. Spritz an air fryer basket with cooking spray.
2. Add the pork to a bowl and season with the smoked paprika, salt and black pepper. Thread the seasoned pork cubes and vegetables alternately onto the soaked skewers. Arrange the skewers in the basket.
3. Slide the basket into the air fryer oven. Cook at 350°F (180°C) for 15 minutes.
4. After 7 minutes, remove from the air fryer oven. Flip the pork skewers. Return to the air fryer oven and continue cooking.
5. When cooking is complete, the pork should be browned and vegetables are tender.
6. Transfer the skewers to the serving dishes and sprinkle with oregano. Serve hot.

Simple Ground Beef with Zucchini

Prep time: 5 minutes | Cook time: 12 minutes | Serves 4

1½ pounds (680 g) ground beef
1 pound (454 g) chopped zucchini
2 tablespoons extra-virgin olive oil
1 teaspoon dried oregano
1 teaspoon dried basil
1 teaspoon dried rosemary
2 tablespoons fresh chives, chopped

1. In a large bowl, combine all the ingredients, except for the chives, until well blended.
2. Place the beef and zucchini mixture in a baking pan.
3. Slide the pan into the air fryer oven. Cook at 400°F (205°C) for 12 minutes.
4. When cooking is complete, the beef should be browned and the zucchini should be tender.
5. Divide the beef and zucchini mixture among four serving dishes. Top with fresh chives and serve hot.

Spice-Coated Steaks with Cucumber and Snap Pea Salad

Prep time: 15 minutes | Cook time: 15 minutes | Serves 4

1 (1½-pound / 680-g) boneless top sirloin steak, trimmed and halved crosswise
1½ teaspoons chili powder
1½ teaspoons ground cumin
¾ teaspoon ground coriander
⅛ teaspoon cayenne pepper
⅛ teaspoon ground cinnamon
1¼ teaspoons plus ⅛ teaspoon salt, divided
½ teaspoon plus ⅛ teaspoon ground black pepper, divided
1 teaspoon plus 1½ tablespoons extra-virgin olive oil, divided
3 tablespoons mayonnaise
1½ tablespoons white wine vinegar
1 tablespoon minced fresh dill
1 small garlic clove, minced
8 ounces (227 g) sugar snap peas, strings removed and cut in half on bias
½ English cucumber, halved lengthwise and sliced thin
2 radishes, trimmed, halved and sliced thin
2 cups baby arugula

1. In a bowl, mix chili powder, cumin, coriander, cayenne pepper, cinnamon, 1¼ teaspoons salt and ½ teaspoon pepper until well combined.
2. Add the steaks to another bowl and pat dry with paper towels. Brush with 1 teaspoon oil and transfer to the bowl of spice mixture. Roll over to coat thoroughly.
3. Arrange the coated steaks in the air fryer basket, spaced evenly apart.
4. Slide the basket into the air fryer oven. Cook at 400°F (205°C) for 15 minutes.
5. Flip the steak halfway through to ensure even cooking.
6. When cooking is complete, an instant-read thermometer inserted in the thickest part of the meat should register at least 145°F (63°C).
7. Transfer the steaks to a clean work surface and wrap with aluminum foil. Let stand while preparing salad.
8. Make the salad: In a large bowl, stir together 1½ tablespoons olive oil, mayonnaise, vinegar, dill, garlic, ⅛ teaspoon salt, and ⅛ teaspoon pepper. Add snap peas, cucumber, radishes and arugula. Toss to blend well.
9. Slice the steaks and serve with the salad.

Spicy Pork Lettuce Wraps

Prep time: 10 minutes | Cook time: 12 minutes | Serves 4

1 (1-pound / 454-g) medium pork tenderloin, silver skin and external fat trimmed
⅔ cup soy sauce, divided
1 teaspoon cornstarch
1 medium jalapeño, deseeded and minced
1 can diced water chestnuts
½ large red bell pepper, deseeded and chopped
2 scallions, chopped, white and green parts separated
1 head butter lettuce
½ cup roasted, chopped almonds
¼ cup coarsely chopped cilantro

1. Cut the tenderloin into ¼-inch slices and place them on a baking pan. Baste with about 3 tablespoons of soy sauce. Stir the cornstarch into the remaining sauce and set aside.
2. Slide the pan into the air fryer oven. Cook at 375°F (190°C) for 12 minutes.
3. After 5 minutes, remove from the air fryer oven. Place the pork slices on a cutting board. Place the jalapeño, water chestnuts, red pepper, and the white parts of the scallions on the baking pan and pour the remaining sauce over. Stir to coat the vegetables with the sauce. Return to the air fryer oven and continue cooking.
4. While the vegetables cook, chop the pork into small pieces. Separate the lettuce leaves, discarding any tough outer leaves and setting aside the small inner leaves for another use. You'll want 12 to 18 leaves, depending on size and your appetites.
5. After 5 minutes, remove from the air fryer oven. Add the pork to the vegetables, stirring to combine. Return to the air fryer oven and continue cooking for the remaining 2 minutes until the pork is warmed back up and the sauce has reduced slightly.
6. When cooking is complete, remove from the air fryer oven. Place the pork and vegetables in a medium serving bowl and stir in half the green parts of the scallions. To serve, spoon some pork and vegetables into each of the lettuce leaves. Top with the remaining scallion greens and garnish with the nuts and cilantro.

Stuffed Beef Tenderloin with Feta Cheese

Prep time: 10 minutes | Cook time: 10 minutes | Serves 4

1½ pounds (680 g) beef tenderloin, pounded to ¼ inch thick
3 teaspoons sea salt
1 teaspoon ground black pepper
2 ounces (57 g) creamy goat cheese
½ cup crumbled feta cheese
¼ cup finely chopped onions
2 cloves garlic, minced
Cooking spray

1. Spritz an air fryer basket with cooking spray.
2. Unfold the beef tenderloin on a clean work surface. Rub the salt and pepper all over the beef tenderloin to season.
3. Make the filling for the stuffed beef tenderloins: Combine the goat cheese, feta, onions, and garlic in a medium bowl. Stir until well blended.
4. Spoon the mixture in the center of the tenderloin. Roll the tenderloin up tightly like rolling a burrito and use some kitchen twine to tie the tenderloin.
5. Arrange the tenderloin in the air fryer basket.
6. Slide the basket into the air fryer oven. Cook at 400°F (205°C) for 10 minutes.
7. Flip the tenderloin halfway through.
8. When cooking is complete, the instant-read thermometer inserted in the center of the tenderloin should register 135°F (57°C) for medium-rare.
9. Transfer to a platter and serve immediately.

Worcestershire Ribeye Steaks

Prep time: 35 minutes | Cook time: 10 to 12 minutes | Serves 2 to 4

2 (8-ounce / 227-g) boneless ribeye steaks
4 teaspoons Worcestershire sauce
½ teaspoon garlic powder
Salt and ground black pepper, to taste
4 teaspoons olive oil

1. Brush the steaks with Worcestershire sauce on both sides. Sprinkle with garlic powder and coarsely ground black pepper. Drizzle the steaks with olive oil. Allow steaks to marinate for 30 minutes.
2. Transfer the steaks in the air fryer basket.
3. Cook at 400°F (205°C) for 4 minutes.
4. After 2 minutes, remove from the air fryer oven. Flip the steaks. Return to the air fryer oven and continue cooking.
5. When cooking is complete, the steaks should be well browned.
6. Remove the steaks from the air fryer basket and let sit for 5 minutes. Salt and serve.

Sumptuous Beef and Pork Sausage Meatloaf

Prep time: 10 minutes | Cook time: 25 minutes | Serves 4

¾ pound (340 g) ground chuck
4 ounces (113 g) ground pork sausage
2 eggs, beaten
1 cup Parmesan cheese, grated
1 cup chopped shallot
3 tablespoons plain milk
1 tablespoon oyster sauce
1 tablespoon fresh parsley
1 teaspoon garlic paste
1 teaspoon chopped porcini mushrooms
½ teaspoon cumin powder
Seasoned salt and crushed red pepper flakes, to taste

1. In a large bowl, combine all the ingredients until well blended.
2. Place the meat mixture in a baking pan. Use a spatula to press the mixture to fill the pan.
3. Slide the pan into the air fryer oven. Cook at 360°F (182°C) for 25 minutes.
4. When cooking is complete, the meatloaf should be well browned.
5. Let the meatloaf rest for 5 minutes. Transfer to a serving dish and slice. Serve warm.

Tonkatsu

Prep time: 5 minutes | Cook time: 10 minutes | Serves 4

⅔ cup all-purpose flour
2 large egg whites
1 cup panko breadcrumbs
4 (4-ounce / 113-g) center-cut boneless pork loin chops (about ½ inch thick)
Cooking spray

1. Pour the flour in a bowl. Whisk the egg whites in a separate bowl. Spread the breadcrumbs on a large plate.
2. Dredge the pork loin chops in the flour first, press to coat well, then shake the excess off and dunk the chops in the eggs whites, and then roll the chops over the breadcrumbs. Shake the excess off.
3. Arrange the pork chops in the air fryer basket and spritz with cooking spray.
4. Slide the basket into the air fryer oven. Cook at 375°F (190°C) for 10 minutes.
5. After 5 minutes, remove from the air fryer oven. Flip the pork chops. Return to the air fryer oven and continue cooking.
6. When cooking is complete, the pork chops should be crunchy and lightly browned.
7. Serve immediately.

Teriyaki Rump Steak with Broccoli and Capsicum

Prep time: 5 minutes | Cook time: 13 minutes | Serves 4

½ pound (227 g) rump steak
⅓ cup teriyaki marinade
1½ teaspoons sesame oil
½ head broccoli, cut into florets
2 red capsicums, sliced
Fine sea salt and ground black pepper, to taste
Cooking spray

1. Toss the rump steak in a large bowl with teriyaki marinade. Wrap the bowl in plastic and refrigerate to marinate for at least an hour.
2. Spritz an air fryer basket with cooking spray.
3. Discard the marinade and transfer the steak in the basket. Spritz with cooking spray.
4. Slide the basket into the air fryer oven. Cook at 400°F (205°C) for 13 minutes.
5. Flip the steak halfway through.
6. When cooking is complete, the steak should be well browned.
7. Meanwhile, heat the sesame oil in a nonstick skillet over medium heat. Add the broccoli and capsicum. Sprinkle with salt and ground black pepper. Sauté for 5 minutes or until the broccoli is tender.
8. Transfer the air fried rump steak on a plate and top with the sautéed broccoli and capsicum. Serve hot.

Tuscan Air Fried Veal Loin

Prep time: 1 hour 10 minutes | Cook time: 12 minutes | Makes 3 veal chops

1½ teaspoons crushed fennel seeds
1 tablespoon minced fresh rosemary leaves
1 tablespoon minced garlic
1½ teaspoons lemon zest
1½ teaspoons salt
½ teaspoon red pepper flakes
2 tablespoons olive oil
3 (10-ounce / 284-g) bone-in veal loin, about ½ inch thick

1. Combine all the ingredients, except for the veal loin, in a large bowl. Stir to mix well.
2. Dunk the loin in the mixture and press to submerge. Wrap the bowl in plastic and refrigerate for at least an hour to marinate.
3. Arrange the veal loin in the air fryer basket.
4. Slide the basket into the air fryer oven. Cook at 400°F (205°C) for 12 minutes.
5. Flip the veal halfway through.
6. When cooking is complete, the internal temperature of the veal should reach at least 145°F (63°C) for medium rare.
7. Serve immediately.

Poultry

Apricot-Glazed Chicken Drumsticks

Prep time: 15 minutes | Cook time: 30 minutes | Makes 6 drumsticks

For the Glaze:
½ cup apricot preserves
½ teaspoon tamari
¼ teaspoon chili powder
2 teaspoons Dijon mustard
For the Chicken:
6 chicken drumsticks
½ teaspoon seasoning salt
1 teaspoon salt
½ teaspoon ground black pepper
Cooking spray

Make the glaze:
1. Combine the ingredients for the glaze in a saucepan, then heat over low heat for 10 minutes or until thickened.
2. Turn off the heat and sit until ready to use.

Make the Chicken:
1. Spritz an air fryer basket with cooking spray.
2. Combine the seasoning salt, salt, and pepper in a small bowl. Stir to mix well.
3. Place the chicken drumsticks in the air fryer basket. Spritz with cooking spray and sprinkle with the salt mixture on both sides.
4. Slide the basket into the air fryer oven. Cook at 370°F (188°C) for 20 minutes.
5. Flip the chicken halfway through.
6. When cooking is complete, the chicken should be well browned.
7. Baste the chicken with the glaze and air fry for 2 more minutes or until the chicken tenderloin is glossy.
8. Serve immediately.

Air Fried Chicken Potatoes with Sun-Dried Tomato

Prep time: 15 minutes | Cook time: 25 minutes | Serves 2

2 teaspoons minced fresh oregano, divided
2 teaspoons minced fresh thyme, divided
2 teaspoons extra-virgin olive oil, plus extra as needed
1 pound (454 g) fingerling potatoes, unpeeled
2 (12-ounce / 340-g) bone-in split chicken breasts, trimmed
1 garlic clove, minced
¼ cup oil-packed sun-dried tomatoes, patted dry and chopped
1½ tablespoons red wine vinegar
1 tablespoon capers, rinsed and minced
1 small shallot, minced
Salt and ground black pepper, to taste

1. Combine 1 teaspoon of oregano, 1 teaspoon of thyme, ¼ teaspoon of salt, ¼ teaspoon of ground black pepper, 1 teaspoons of olive oil in a large bowl. Add the potatoes and toss to coat well.
2. Combine the chicken with remaining thyme, oregano, and olive oil. Sprinkle with garlic, salt, and pepper. Toss to coat well.
3. Place the potatoes in the air fryer basket, then arrange the chicken on top of the potatoes.
4. Slide the basket into the air fryer oven. Cook at 350°F (180°C) for 25 minutes.
5. Flip the chicken and potatoes halfway through.
6. When cooking is complete, the internal temperature of the chicken should reach at least 165°F (74°C) and the potatoes should be wilted.
7. Meanwhile, combine the sun-dried tomatoes, vinegar, capers, and shallot in a separate large bowl. Sprinkle with salt and ground black pepper. Toss to mix well.
8. Remove the chicken and potatoes from the air fryer oven and allow to cool for 10 minutes. Serve with the sun-dried tomato mix.

Air Fried Chicken Wings with Buffalo Sauce

Prep time: 10 minutes | Cook time: 20 minutes | Serves 6

16 chicken drumettes (party wings)
Chicken seasoning or rub, to taste
1 teaspoon garlic powder
Ground black pepper, to taste
¼ cup buffalo wings sauce
Cooking spray

1. Spritz an air fryer basket with cooking spray.
2. Rub the chicken wings with chicken seasoning, garlic powder, and ground black pepper on a clean work surface.
3. Arrange the chicken wings in the air fryer basket. Spritz with cooking spray.
4. Slide the basket into the air fryer oven. Cook at 400°F (205°C) for 10 minutes.
5. Flip the chicken wings halfway through.
6. When cooking is complete, the chicken wings should be lightly browned.
7. Transfer the chicken wings in a large bowl, then pour in the buffalo wings sauce and toss to coat well.
8. Put the wings back to the air fryer oven for 7 minutes. Flip the wings halfway through.
9. When cooking is complete, the wings should be heated through. Serve immediately.

Bacon-Wrapped Chicken Breasts Rolls

Prep time: 10 minutes | Cook time: 15 minutes | Serves 4

¼ cup chopped fresh chives
2 tablespoons lemon juice
1 teaspoon dried sage
1 teaspoon fresh rosemary leaves
½ cup fresh parsley leaves
4 cloves garlic, peeled
1 teaspoon ground fennel
3 teaspoons sea salt
½ teaspoon red pepper flakes
4 (4-ounce / 113-g) boneless, skinless chicken breasts, pounded to ¼ inch thick
8 slices bacon
Sprigs of fresh rosemary, for garnish
Cooking spray

1. Spritz an air fryer basket with cooking spray.
2. Put the chives, lemon juice, sage, rosemary, parsley, garlic, fennel, salt, and red pepper flakes in a food processor, then pulse to purée until smooth.
3. Unfold the chicken breasts on a clean work surface, then brush the top side of the chicken breasts with the sauce.
4. Roll the chicken breasts up from the shorter side, then wrap each chicken rolls with 2 bacon slices to cover. Secure with toothpicks.
5. Arrange the rolls in the air fryer basket.
6. Slide the basket into the air fryer oven. Cook at 340°F (171°C) for 10 minutes.
7. Flip the rolls halfway through.
8. After 10 minutes, increase temperature to 390°F (199°C) for 5 minutes.
9. When cooking is complete, the bacon should be browned and crispy.
10. Transfer the rolls to a large plate. Discard the toothpicks and spread with rosemary sprigs before serving.

Bacon-Wrapped and Cheese-Stuffed Chicken

Prep time: 10 minutes | Cook time: 20 minutes | Serves 4

4 (5-ounce / 142-g) boneless, skinless chicken breasts, pounded to ¼ inch thick
1 cup cream cheese
2 tablespoons chopped fresh chives
8 slices thin-cut bacon
Sprig of fresh cilantro, for garnish
Cooking spray

1. Spritz an air fryer basket with cooking spray.
2. On a clean work surface, slice the chicken horizontally to make a 1-inch incision on top of each chicken breast with a knife, then cut into the chicken to make a pocket. Leave a ½-inch border along the sides and bottom.
3. Combine the cream cheese and chives in a bowl. Stir to mix well, then gently pour the mixture into the chicken pockets.
4. Wrap each stuffed chicken breast with 2 bacon slices, then secure the ends with toothpicks.
5. Arrange them in the air fryer basket.
6. Slide the basket into the air fryer oven. Cook at 400°F (205°C) for 20 minutes.
7. Flip the bacon-wrapped chicken halfway through the cooking time.
8. When cooking is complete, the bacon should be browned and crispy.
9. Transfer them on a large plate and serve with cilantro on top.

Bacon-Wrapped Turkey with Carrots

Prep time: 10 minutes | Cook time: 25 minutes | Serves 4

2 (12-ounce / 340-g) turkey tenderloins
1 teaspoon kosher salt, divided
6 slices bacon
3 tablespoons balsamic vinegar
2 tablespoons honey
1 tablespoon Dijon mustard
½ teaspoon dried thyme
6 large carrots, peeled and cut into ¼-inch rounds
1 tablespoon olive oil

1. Sprinkle the turkey with ¾ teaspoon of the salt. Wrap each tenderloin with 3 strips of bacon, securing the bacon with toothpicks. Place the turkey in a baking pan.
2. In a small bowl, mix the balsamic vinegar, honey, mustard, and thyme.
3. Place the carrots in a medium bowl and drizzle with the oil. Add 1 tablespoon of the balsamic mixture and ¼ teaspoon of kosher salt and toss to coat. Place these on the pan around the turkey tenderloins. Baste the tenderloins with about one-half of the remaining balsamic mixture.
4. Slide the pan into the air fryer oven. Cook at 375°F (190°C) for 25 minutes.
5. After 13 minutes, remove from the air fryer oven. Gently stir the carrots. Flip the tenderloins and baste with the remaining balsamic mixture. Return to the air fryer oven and continue cooking.
6. When cooking is complete, the carrots should tender and the center of the tenderloins should register 165°F (74°C) on a meat thermometer. Remove from the air fryer oven. Slice the turkey and serve with the carrots.

Barbecue Chicken and Coleslaw Tostadas

Prep time: 15 minutes | Cook time: 10 minutes | Makes 4 tostadas

Coleslaw:
¼ cup sour cream
¼ small green cabbage, finely chopped
½ tablespoon white vinegar
½ teaspoon garlic powder
½ teaspoon salt
¼ teaspoon ground black pepper
Tostadas:
2 cups pulled rotisserie chicken
½ cup barbecue sauce
4 corn tortillas
½ cup shredded Mozzarella cheese
Cooking spray

Make the Coleslaw:
1. Combine the ingredients for the coleslaw in a large bowl. Toss to mix well.
2. Refrigerate until ready to serve.

Make the Tostadas:
1. Spritz an air fryer basket with cooking spray.
2. Toss the chicken with barbecue sauce in a separate large bowl to combine well. Set aside.
3. Place one tortilla in the air fryer basket and spritz with cooking spray.
4. Slide the basket into the air fryer oven. Cook at 370°F (188°C) for 10 minutes.
5. Flip the tortilla and spread the barbecue chicken and cheese over halfway through.
6. When cooking is complete, the tortilla should be browned and the cheese should be melted.
7. Serve the tostadas with coleslaw on top.

Bell Pepper Stuffed Chicken Roll-Ups

Prep time: 10 minutes | Cook time: 12 minutes | Serves 4

2 (4-ounce / 113-g) boneless, skinless chicken breasts, slice in half horizontally
1 tablespoon olive oil
Juice of ½ lime
2 tablespoons taco seasoning
½ green bell pepper, cut into strips
½ red bell pepper, cut into strips
¼ onion, sliced

1. Unfold the chicken breast slices on a clean work surface. Rub with olive oil, then drizzle with lime juice and sprinkle with taco seasoning.
2. Top the chicken slices with equal amount of bell peppers and onion. Roll them up and secure with toothpicks.
3. Arrange the chicken roll-ups in the air fryer basket.
4. Slide the basket into the air fryer oven. Cook at 400°F (205°C) for 12 minutes.
5. Flip the chicken roll-ups halfway through.
6. When cooking is complete, the internal temperature of the chicken should reach at least 165°F (74°C).
7. Remove the chicken from the air fryer oven. Discard the toothpicks and serve immediately.

Braised Chicken with Hot Peppers

Prep time: 10 minutes | Cook time: 27 minutes | Serves 4

4 bone-in, skin-on chicken thighs (about 1½ pounds / 680 g)
1½ teaspoon kosher salt, divided
1 link sweet Italian sausage (about 4 ounces / 113 g), whole
8 ounces (227 g) miniature bell peppers, halved and deseeded
1 small onion, thinly sliced
2 garlic cloves, minced
1 tablespoon olive oil
4 hot pickled cherry peppers, deseeded and quartered, along with 2 tablespoons pickling liquid from the jar
¼ cup chicken stock
Cooking spray

1. Salt the chicken thighs on both sides with 1 teaspoon of kosher salt. Spritz a baking pan with cooking spray and place the thighs skin-side down on the pan. Add the sausage.
2. Slide the pan into the air fryer oven. Cook at 375°F (190°C) for 27 minutes.
3. While the chicken and sausage cook, place the bell peppers, onion, and garlic in a large bowl. Sprinkle with the remaining kosher salt and add the olive oil. Toss to coat.
4. After 10 minutes, remove from the air fryer oven and flip the chicken thighs and sausage. Add the pepper mixture to the pan. Return to the air fryer oven and continue cooking.
5. After another 10 minutes, remove from the air fryer oven and add the pickled peppers, pickling liquid, and stock. Stir the pickled peppers into the peppers and onion. Return to the air fryer oven and continue cooking.
6. When cooking is complete, the peppers and onion should be soft and the chicken should read 165°F (74°C) on a meat thermometer. Remove from the air fryer oven. Slice the sausage into thin pieces and stir it into the pepper mixture. Spoon the peppers over four plates. Top with a chicken thigh.

Bruschetta Chicken

Prep time: 10 minutes | Cook time: 10 minutes | Serves 4

Bruschetta Stuffing:
1 tomato, diced
3 tablespoons balsamic vinegar
1 teaspoon Italian seasoning
2 tablespoons chopped fresh basil
3 garlic cloves, minced
2 tablespoons extra-virgin olive oil
Chicken:
4 (4-ounce / 113-g) boneless, skinless chicken breasts, cut 4 slits each
1 teaspoon Italian seasoning
Chicken seasoning or rub, to taste
Cooking spray

1. Spritz an air fryer basket with cooking spray.
2. Combine the ingredients for the bruschetta stuffing in a bowl. Stir to mix well. Set aside.
3. Rub the chicken breasts with Italian seasoning and chicken seasoning on a clean work surface.
4. Arrange the chicken breasts, slits side up, in the air fryer basket and spritz with cooking spray.
5. Slide the basket into the air fryer oven. Cook at 370°F (188°C) for 10 minutes.
6. Flip the breast and fill the slits with the bruschetta stuffing halfway through.
7. When cooking is complete, the chicken should be well browned.
8. Serve immediately.

Cheese-Encrusted Chicken Tenderloins with Peanuts

Prep time: 10 minutes | Cook time: 12 minutes | Serves 4

½ cup grated Parmesan cheese
½ teaspoon garlic powder
1 teaspoon red pepper flakes
Sea salt and ground black pepper, to taste
2 tablespoons peanut oil
1½ pounds (680 g) chicken tenderloins
2 tablespoons peanuts, roasted and roughly chopped
Cooking spray

1. Spritz an air fryer basket with cooking spray.
2. Combine the Parmesan cheese, garlic powder, red pepper flakes, salt, black pepper, and peanut oil in a large bow. Stir to mix well.
3. Dip the chicken tenderloins in the cheese mixture, then press to coat well. Shake the excess off.
4. Transfer the chicken tenderloins in the air fryer basket.
5. Slide the basket into the air fryer oven. Cook at 360°F (182°C) for 12 minutes.
6. Flip the tenderloin halfway through.
7. When cooking is complete, the tenderloin should be well browned.
8. Transfer the chicken tenderloins on a large plate and top with roasted peanuts before serving.

Cheesy Marinara Chicken Breasts

Prep time: 30 minutes | Cook time: 1 hour | Serves 2

1 large egg
¼ cup almond meal
2 (6-ounce / 170-g) boneless, skinless chicken breast halves
1 (8-ounce / 227-g) jar marinara sauce, divided
4 tablespoons shredded Mozzarella cheese, divided
4 tablespoons grated Parmesan cheese, divided
4 tablespoons chopped fresh basil, divided
Salt and freshly ground black pepper, to taste
Cooking spray

1. Spritz an air fryer basket with cooking spray.
2. In a shallow bowl, beat the egg.
3. In a separate shallow bowl, place the almond meal.
4. Dip 1 chicken breast half into the egg, then into the almond meal to coat. Place the coated chicken in the air fryer basket. Repeat with the remaining 1 chicken breast half.
5. Slide the basket into the air fryer oven. Cook at 350°F (180°C) for 40 minutes.
6. After 20 minutes, remove from the air fryer oven and flip the chicken. Return the basket to air fryer oven and continue cooking.
7. When cooking is complete, the chicken should no longer pink and the juices run clear.
8. In a baking pan, pour half of marinara sauce.
9. Place the cooked chicken in the sauce. Cover with the remaining marinara.
10. Sprinkle 2 tablespoons of Mozzarella cheese and 2 tablespoons of soy Parmesan cheese on each chicken breast. Top each with 2 tablespoons of basil.
11. Place the baking pan back in the air fryer oven and set the baking time to 20 minutes. Flip the chicken halfway through the cooking time.
12. When cooking is complete, an instant-read thermometer inserted into the center of the chicken should read at least 165°F (74°C).
13. Remove the pan from air fryer oven and divide between 2 plates. Season with salt and pepper and serve.

Balsamic Chicken Breast Roast

Prep time: 35 minutes | Cook time: 40 minutes | Serves 2

¼ cup balsamic vinegar
2 teaspoons dried oregano
2 garlic cloves, minced
1 tablespoon olive oil
⅛ teaspoon salt
½ teaspoon freshly ground black pepper
2 (4-ounce / 113-g) boneless, skinless, chicken-breast halves
Cooking spray

1. In a small bowl, add the vinegar, oregano, garlic, olive oil, salt, and pepper. Mix to combine.
2. Put the chicken in a resealable plastic bag. Pour the vinegar mixture in the bag with the chicken, seal the bag, and shake to coat the chicken. Refrigerate for 30 minutes to marinate.
3. Spritz a baking pan with cooking spray. Put the chicken in the prepared baking pan and pour the marinade over the chicken.
4. Slide the pan into the air fryer oven. Cook at 400°F (205°C) for 40 minutes.
5. After 20 minutes, remove from the air fryer oven. Flip the chicken. Return to the air fryer oven and continue cooking.
6. When cooking is complete, the internal temperature of the chicken should registers at least 165°F (74°C).
7. Let sit for 5 minutes, then serve.

Cheesy Pepperoni and Chicken Pizza

Prep time: 15 minutes | Cook time: 15 minutes | Serves 6

2 cups cooked chicken, cubed
1 cup pizza sauce
20 slices pepperoni
¼ cup grated Parmesan cheese
1 cup shredded Mozzarella cheese
Cooking spray

1. Spritz a baking pan with cooking spray.
2. Arrange the chicken cubes in the prepared baking pan, then top the cubes with pizza sauce and pepperoni. Stir to coat the cubes and pepperoni with sauce. Scatter the cheeses on top.
3. Slide the pan into the air fryer oven. Cook at 375°F (190°C) for 15 minutes.
4. When cooking is complete, the pizza should be frothy and the cheeses should be melted.
5. Serve immediately.

Cheesy Turkey Burgers

Prep time: 10 minutes | Cook time: 25 minutes | Serves 4

2 medium yellow onions
1 tablespoon olive oil
1½ teaspoons kosher salt, divided
1¼ pound (567 g) ground turkey
⅓ cup mayonnaise
1 tablespoon Dijon mustard
2 teaspoons Worcestershire sauce
4 slices sharp Cheddar cheese (about 4 ounces / 113 g in total)
4 hamburger buns, sliced

1. Trim the onions and cut them in half through the root. Cut one of the halves in half. Grate one quarter. Place the grated onion in a large bowl. Thinly slice the remaining onions and place in a medium bowl with the oil and ½ teaspoon of kosher salt. Toss to coat. Place the onions in a single layer on a baking pan.
2. Slide the pan into the air fryer oven. Cook at 350°F (180°C) for 10 minutes.
3. While the onions are cooking, add the turkey to the grated onion. Add the remaining kosher salt, mayonnaise, mustard, and Worcestershire sauce. Mix just until combined, being careful not to overwork the turkey. Divide the mixture into 4 patties, each about ¾-inch thick.
4. When cooking is complete, remove from the air fryer oven. Move the onions to one side of the pan and place the burgers on the pan. Poke your finger into the center of each burger to make a deep indentation.
5. Slide the pan into the air fryer oven. Cook for 12 minutes.
6. After 6 minutes, remove the pan. Turn the burgers and stir the onions. Return to the air fryer oven and continue cooking. After about 4 minutes, remove the pan and place the cheese slices on the burgers. Return to the air fryer oven and continue cooking for about 1 minute, or until the cheese is melted and the center of the burgers has reached at least 165°F (74°C) on a meat thermometer.
7. When cooking is complete, remove from the air fryer oven. Loosely cover the burgers with foil.
8. Lay out the buns, cut-side up, on the air fryer basket. Cook for 3 minutes. Check the buns after 2 minutes; they should be lightly browned.
9. Remove the buns from the air fryer oven. Assemble the burgers and serve.

Chicken and Ham Meatballs with Dijon Sauce

Prep time: 10 minutes | Cook time: 15 minutes | Serves 4

Meatballs:
½ pound (227 g) ham, diced
½ pound (227 g) ground chicken
½ cup grated Swiss cheese
1 large egg, beaten
3 cloves garlic, minced
¼ cup chopped onions
1½ teaspoons sea salt
1 teaspoon ground black pepper
Cooking spray
Dijon Sauce:
3 tablespoons Dijon mustard
2 tablespoons lemon juice
¼ cup chicken broth, warmed
¾ teaspoon sea salt
¼ teaspoon ground black pepper
Chopped fresh thyme leaves, for garnish

1. Spritz an air fryer basket with cooking spray.
2. Combine the ingredients for the meatballs in a large bowl. Stir to mix well, then shape the mixture in twelve 1½-inch meatballs.
3. Arrange the meatballs in the air fryer basket.
4. Slide the basket into the air fryer oven. Cook at 390°F (199°C) for 15 minutes.
5. Flip the balls halfway through.
6. When cooking is complete, the balls should be lightly browned.
7. Meanwhile, combine the ingredients, except for the thyme leaves, for the sauce in a small bowl. Stir to mix well.
8. Transfer the cooked meatballs on a large plate, then baste the sauce over. Garnish with thyme leaves and serve.

Chicken and Sweet Potato Curry

Prep time: 10 minutes | Cook time: 20 minutes | Serves 4

1 pound (454 g) boneless, skinless chicken thighs
1 teaspoon kosher salt, divided
¼ cup unsalted butter, melted
1 tablespoon curry powder
2 medium sweet potatoes, peeled and cut in 1-inch cubes
12 ounces (340 g) Brussels sprouts, halved

1. Sprinkle the chicken thighs with ½ teaspoon of kosher salt. Place them in the single layer on a baking pan.
2. In a small bowl, stir together the butter and curry powder.
3. Place the sweet potatoes and Brussels sprouts in a large bowl. Drizzle half the curry butter over the vegetables and add the remaining kosher salt. Toss to coat. Transfer the vegetables to the baking pan and place in a single layer around the chicken. Brush half of the remaining curry butter over the chicken.
4. Slide the pan into the air fryer oven. Cook at 400°F (205°C) for 20 minutes.
5. After 10 minutes, remove from the air fryer oven and turn over the chicken thighs. Baste them with the remaining curry butter. Return to the air fryer oven and continue cooking.
6. Cooking is complete when the sweet potatoes are tender and the chicken is cooked through and reads 165°F (74°C) on a meat thermometer.

Duck Breasts with Marmalade Balsamic Glaze

Prep time: 5 minutes | Cook time: 13 minutes | Serves 4

4 (6-ounce / 170-g) skin-on duck breasts
1 teaspoon salt
¼ cup orange marmalade
1 tablespoon white balsamic vinegar
¾ teaspoon ground black pepper

1. Cut 10 slits into the skin of the duck breasts, then sprinkle with salt on both sides.
2. Place the breasts in an air fryer basket, skin side up.
3. Slide the basket into the air fryer oven. Cook at 400°F (205°C) for 10 minutes.
4. Meanwhile, combine the remaining ingredients in a small bowl. Stir to mix well.
5. When cooking is complete, brush the duck skin with the marmalade mixture. Flip the breast and air fry for 3 more minutes or until the skin is crispy and the breast is well browned.
6. Serve immediately.

Chicken Ciabatta Sandwiches

Prep time: 12 minutes | Cook time: 13 minutes | Serves 4

2 (8-ounce / 227-g) boneless, skinless chicken breasts
1 teaspoon kosher salt, divided
1 cup all-purpose flour
1 teaspoon Italian seasoning
2 large eggs
2 tablespoons plain yogurt
2 cups panko bread crumbs
1⅓ cups grated Parmesan cheese, divided
2 tablespoons olive oil
4 ciabatta rolls, split in half
½ cup marinara sauce
½ cup shredded Mozzarella cheese

1. Lay the chicken breasts on a cutting board and cut each one in half parallel to the board so you have 4 fairly even, flat fillets. Place a piece of plastic wrap over the chicken pieces and use a rolling pin to gently pound them to an even thickness, about ½-inch thick. Season the chicken on both sides with ½ teaspoon of kosher salt.
2. Place the flour on a plate and add the remaining kosher salt and the Italian seasoning. Mix with a fork to distribute evenly. In a wide bowl, whisk together the eggs with the yogurt. In a small bowl combine the panko, 1 cup of Parmesan cheese, and olive oil. Place this in a shallow bowl.
3. Lightly dredge both sides of the chicken pieces in the seasoned flour, and then dip them in the egg wash to coat completely, letting the excess drip off. Finally, dredge the chicken in the bread crumbs. Carefully place the breaded chicken pieces in the air fryer basket.
4. Slide the basket into the air fryer oven. Cook at 375°F (190°C) for 10 minutes.
5. After 5 minutes, remove the air fryer basket from the air fryer oven. Carefully turn the chicken over. Return the air fryer basket to the air fryer oven and continue cooking. When cooking is complete, remove the air fryer basket from the air fryer oven.
6. Unfold the rolls on the air fryer basket and spread each half with 1 tablespoon of marinara sauce. Place a chicken breast piece on the bottoms of the buns and sprinkle the remaining Parmesan cheese over the chicken pieces. Divide the Mozzarella among the top halves of the buns.
7. Slide the basket into the air fryer oven. Cook for 3 minutes.
8. Check the sandwiches halfway through. When cooking is complete, the Mozzarella cheese should be melted and bubbly.
9. Remove the air fryer basket from the air fryer oven. Close the sandwiches and serve.

Chicken Rochambeau with Mushroom Sauce

Prep time: 25 minutes | Cook time: 30 minutes | Serves 4

1 tablespoon melted butter
¼ cup all-purpose flour
4 chicken tenders, cut in half crosswise
4 slices ham, ¼-inch thick, large enough to cover an English muffin
2 English muffins, split in halves
Salt and ground black pepper, to taste
Cooking spray
Mushroom Sauce:
2 tablespoons butter
½ cup chopped mushrooms
½ cup chopped green onions
2 tablespoons flour
1 cup chicken broth
1½ teaspoons Worcestershire sauce
¼ teaspoon garlic powder

1. Put the butter in a baking pan. Combine the flour, salt, and ground black pepper in a shallow dish. Roll the chicken tenders over to coat well.
2. Arrange the chicken in the baking pan and flip to coat with the melted butter.
3. Slide the pan into the air fryer oven. Cook at 390°F (199°C) for 10 minutes.
4. Flip the tenders halfway through.
5. When cooking is complete, the juices of chicken tenders should run clear.
6. Meanwhile, make the mushroom sauce: melt 2 tablespoons of butter in a saucepan over medium-high heat.
7. Add the mushrooms and onions to the saucepan and sauté for 3 minutes or until the onions are translucent.
8. Gently mix in the flour, broth, Worcestershire sauce, and garlic powder until smooth.
9. Reduce the heat to low and simmer for 5 minutes or until it has a thick consistency. Set the sauce aside until ready to serve.
10. When broiling is complete, remove the baking pan from the air fryer oven and set the ham slices into the air fryer basket.
11. Cook for 5 minutes. Flip the ham slices halfway through.
12. When cooking is complete, the ham slices should be heated through.
13. Remove the ham slices from the air fryer oven and set in the English muffin halves and warm for 1 minute.
14. Arrange each ham slice on top of each muffin half, then place each chicken tender over the ham slice.
15. Transfer to the air fryer oven for 2 minutes.
16. Serve with the sauce on top.

Chicken Schnitzel

Prep time: 15 minutes | Cook time: 5 minutes | Serves 4

½ cup all-purpose flour
1 teaspoon marjoram
½ teaspoon thyme
1 teaspoon dried parsley flakes
½ teaspoon salt
1 egg
1 teaspoon lemon juice
1 teaspoon water
1 cup breadcrumbs
4 chicken tenders, pounded thin, cut in half lengthwise
Cooking spray

1. Spritz an air fryer basket with cooking spray.
2. Combine the flour, marjoram, thyme, parsley, and salt in a shallow dish. Stir to mix well.
3. Whisk the egg with lemon juice and water in a large bowl. Pour the breadcrumbs in a separate shallow dish.
4. Roll the chicken halves in the flour mixture first, then in the egg mixture, and then roll over the breadcrumbs to coat well. Shake the excess off.
5. Arrange the chicken halves in the air fryer basket and spritz with cooking spray on both sides.
6. Slide the basket into the air fryer oven. Cook at 390°F (199°C) for 5 minutes.
7. Flip the halves halfway through.
8. When cooking is complete, the chicken halves should be golden brown and crispy.
9. Serve immediately.

Deep Fried Duck Leg Quarters

Prep time: 5 minutes | Cook time: 45 minutes | Serves 4

4 (½-pound / 227-g) skin-on duck leg quarters
2 medium garlic cloves, minced
½ teaspoon salt
½ teaspoon ground black pepper

1. Spritz an air fryer basket with cooking spray.
2. On a clean work surface, rub the duck leg quarters with garlic, salt, and black pepper.
3. Arrange the leg quarters in the air fryer basket and spritz with cooking spray.
4. Slide the basket into the air fryer oven. Cook at 300°F (150°C) for 30 minutes.
5. After 30 minutes, remove from the air fryer oven. Flip the leg quarters. Increase temperature to 375°F (190°C) for 15 minutes. Return to the air fryer oven and continue cooking.
6. When cooking is complete, the leg quarters should be well browned and crispy.
7. Remove the duck leg quarters from the air fryer oven and allow to cool for 10 minutes before serving.

Chicken Shawarma

Prep time: 10 minutes | Cook time: 18 minutes | Serves 4

1½ pounds (680 g) boneless, skinless chicken thighs
1¼ teaspoon kosher salt, divided
2 tablespoons plus 1 teaspoon olive oil, divided
⅔ cup plus 2 tablespoons plain Greek yogurt, divided
2 tablespoons freshly squeezed lemon juice (about 1 medium lemon)
4 garlic cloves, minced, divided
1 tablespoon Shawarma Seasoning
4 pita breads, cut in half
2 cups cherry tomatoes
½ small cucumber, peeled, deseeded, and chopped
1 tablespoon chopped fresh parsley

1. Sprinkle the chicken thighs on both sides with 1 teaspoon of kosher salt. Place in a resealable plastic bag and set aside while you make the marinade.
2. In a small bowl, mix 2 tablespoons of olive oil, 2 tablespoons of yogurt, the lemon juice, 3 garlic cloves, and Shawarma Seasoning until thoroughly combined. Pour the marinade over the chicken. Seal the bag, squeezing out as much air as possible. And massage the chicken to coat it with the sauce. Set aside.
3. Wrap 2 pita breads each in two pieces of aluminum foil and place on a baking pan.
4. Slide the pan into the air fryer oven. Cook at 300°F (150°C) for 6 minutes.
5. After 3 minutes, remove from the air fryer oven and turn over the foil packets. Return to the air fryer oven and continue cooking. When cooking is complete, remove from the air fryer oven and place the foil-wrapped pitas on the top of the air fryer oven to keep warm.
6. Remove the chicken from the marinade, letting the excess drip off into the bag. Place them on the baking pan. Arrange the tomatoes around the sides of the chicken. Discard the marinade.
7. Slide the pan into the air fryer oven. Cook for 12 minutes.
8. After 6 minutes, remove from the air fryer oven and turn over the chicken. Return to the air fryer oven and continue cooking.
9. Wrap the cucumber in a paper towel to remove as much moisture as possible. Place them in a small bowl. Add the remaining yogurt, kosher salt, olive oil, garlic clove, and parsley. Whisk until combined.
10. When cooking is complete, the chicken should be browned, crisp along its edges, and sizzling. Remove the pan from the air fryer oven and place the chicken on a cutting board. Cut each thigh into several pieces. Unwrap the pitas. Spread a tablespoon of sauce into a pita half. Add some chicken and add 2 roasted tomatoes. Serve.

Chicken Thighs in Waffles

Prep time: 1 hour 20 minutes | Cook time: 20 minutes | Serves 4

For the chicken:
4 chicken thighs, skin on
1 cup low-fat buttermilk
½ cup all-purpose flour
½ teaspoon garlic powder
½ teaspoon mustard powder
1 teaspoon kosher salt
½ teaspoon freshly ground black pepper
¼ cup honey, for serving
Cooking spray
For the waffles:
½ cup all-purpose flour
½ cup whole wheat pastry flour
1 large egg, beaten
1 cup low-fat buttermilk
1 teaspoon baking powder
2 tablespoons canola oil
½ teaspoon kosher salt
1 tablespoon granulated sugar

1. Combine the chicken thighs with buttermilk in a large bowl. Wrap the bowl in plastic and refrigerate to marinate for at least an hour.
2. Spritz an air fryer basket with cooking spray.
3. Combine the flour, mustard powder, garlic powder, salt, and black pepper in a shallow dish. Stir to mix well.
4. Remove the thighs from the buttermilk and pat dry with paper towels. Sit the bowl of buttermilk aside.
5. Dip the thighs in the flour mixture first, then into the buttermilk, and then into the flour mixture. Shake the excess off.
6. Arrange the thighs in the air fryer basket and spritz with cooking spray.
7. Slide the basket into the air fryer oven. Cook at 360°F (182°C) for 20 minutes.
8. Flip the thighs halfway through.
9. When cooking is complete, an instant-read thermometer inserted in the thickest part of the chicken thighs should register at least 165°F (74°C).
10. Meanwhile, make the waffles: combine the ingredients for the waffles in a large bowl. Stir to mix well, then arrange the mixture in a waffle iron and cook until a golden and fragrant waffle forms.
11. Remove the waffles from the waffle iron and slice into 4 pieces. Remove the chicken thighs from the air fryer oven and allow to cool for 5 minutes.
12. Arrange each chicken thigh on each waffle piece and drizzle with 1 tablespoon of honey. Serve warm.

Easy Cajun Chicken Drumsticks

Prep time: 5 minutes | Cook time: 18 minutes | Serves 5

1 tablespoon olive oil
10 chicken drumsticks
1½ tablespoons Cajun seasoning
Salt and ground black pepper, to taste

1. Grease the air fryer basket with olive oil.
2. On a clean work surface, rub the chicken drumsticks with Cajun seasoning, salt, and ground black pepper.
3. Arrange the seasoned chicken drumsticks in the air fryer basket.
4. Slide the basket into the air fryer oven. Cook at 390°F (199°C) for 18 minutes.
5. Flip the drumsticks halfway through.
6. When cooking is complete, the drumsticks should be lightly browned.
7. Remove the chicken drumsticks from the air fryer oven. Serve immediately.

Chicken Skewers with Corn Salad

Prep time: 17 minutes | Cook time: 10 minutes | Serves 4

1 pound (454 g) boneless, skinless chicken breast, cut into 1½-inch chunks
1 green bell pepper, deseeded and cut into 1-inch pieces
1 red bell pepper, deseeded and cut into 1-inch pieces
1 large onion, cut into large chunks
2 tablespoons fajita seasoning
3 tablespoons vegetable oil, divided
2 teaspoons kosher salt, divided
2 cups corn, drained
¼ teaspoon granulated garlic
1 teaspoon freshly squeezed lime juice
1 tablespoon mayonnaise
3 tablespoons grated Parmesan cheese

Special Equipment:
12 wooden skewers, soaked in water for at least 30 minutes

1. Place the chicken, bell peppers, and onion in a large bowl. Add the fajita seasoning, 2 tablespoons of vegetable oil, and 1½ teaspoons of kosher salt. Toss to coat evenly.
2. Alternate the chicken and vegetables on the skewers, making about 12 skewers.
3. Place the corn in a medium bowl and add the remaining vegetable oil. Add the remaining kosher salt and the garlic, and toss to coat. Place the corn in an even layer on a baking pan and place the skewers on top.
4. Slide the pan into the air fryer oven. Cook at 375°F (190°C) for 10 minutes.
5. After about 5 minutes, remove from the air fryer oven and turn the skewers. Return to the air fryer oven and continue cooking.
6. When cooking is complete, remove from the air fryer oven. Place the skewers on a platter. Put the corn back to the bowl and combine with the lime juice, mayonnaise, and Parmesan cheese. Stir to mix well. Serve the skewers with the corn.

Chicken Thighs with Radish Slaw

Prep time: 10 minutes | Cook time: 27 minutes | Serves 4

4 bone-in, skin-on chicken thighs
1½ teaspoon kosher salt, divided
1 tablespoon smoked paprika
½ teaspoon granulated garlic
½ teaspoon dried oregano
¼ teaspoon freshly ground black pepper
3 cups shredded cabbage
½ small red onion, thinly sliced
4 large radishes, julienned
3 tablespoons red wine vinegar
2 tablespoons olive oil
Cooking spray

1. Salt the chicken thighs on both sides with 1 teaspoon of kosher salt. In a small bowl, combine the paprika, garlic, oregano, and black pepper. Sprinkle half this mixture over the skin sides of the thighs. Spritz a baking pan with cooking spray and place the thighs skin-side down on the pan. Sprinkle the remaining spice mixture over the other sides of the chicken pieces.
2. Slide the pan into the air fryer oven. Cook at 375°F (190°C) for 27 minutes.
3. After 10 minutes, remove from the air fryer oven and turn over the chicken thighs. Return to the air fryer oven and continue cooking.
4. While the chicken cooks, place the cabbage, onion, and radishes in a large bowl. Sprinkle with the remaining kosher salt, vinegar, and olive oil. Toss to coat.
5. After another 9 to 10 minutes, remove from the air fryer oven and place the chicken thighs on a cutting board. Place the cabbage mixture in the pan and toss with the chicken fat and spices.
6. Spread the cabbage in an even layer on the pan and place the chicken on it, skin-side up. Return to the air fryer oven and continue cooking. Roast for another 7 to 8 minutes.
7. When cooking is complete, the cabbage is just becoming tender. Remove from the air fryer oven. Taste and adjust the seasoning if necessary. Serve.

Crispy Chicken Skin

Prep time: 5 minutes | Cook time: 6 minutes | Serves 4

1 pound (454 g) chicken skin, cut into slices
1 teaspoon melted butter
½ teaspoon crushed chili flakes
1 teaspoon dried dill
Salt and ground black pepper, to taste

1. Combine all the ingredients in a large bowl. Toss to coat the chicken skin well.
2. Transfer the skin in the air fryer basket.
3. Slide the basket into the air fryer oven. Cook at 360°F (182°C) for 6 minutes.
4. Stir the skin halfway through.
5. When cooking is complete, the skin should be crispy.
6. Serve immediately.

Chicken with Asparagus, Beans, and Arugula

Prep time: 20 minutes | Cook time: 25 minutes | Serves 2

1 cup canned cannellini beans, rinsed
1½ tablespoons red wine vinegar
1 garlic clove, minced
2 tablespoons extra-virgin olive oil, divided
Salt and ground black pepper, to taste
½ red onion, sliced thinly
8 ounces (227 g) asparagus, trimmed and cut into 1-inch lengths
2 (8-ounce / 227-g) boneless, skinless chicken breasts, trimmed
¼ teaspoon paprika
½ teaspoon ground coriander
2 ounces (57 g) baby arugula, rinsed and drained

1. Warm the beans in microwave for 1 minutes and combine with red wine vinegar, garlic, 1 tablespoon of olive oil, ¼ teaspoon of salt, and ¼ teaspoon of ground black pepper in a bowl. Stir to mix well.
2. Combine the onion with ⅛ teaspoon of salt, ⅛ teaspoon of ground black pepper, and 2 teaspoons of olive oil in a separate bowl. Toss to coat well.
3. Place the onion in an air fryer basket.
4. Slide the basket into the air fryer oven. Cook at 400°F (205°C) for 2 minutes.
5. After 2 minutes, add the asparagus for 8 minutes. Stir the vegetable halfway through.
6. When cooking is complete, the asparagus should be tender.
7. Transfer the onion and asparagus to the bowl with beans. Set aside.
8. Toss the chicken breasts with remaining ingredients, except for the baby arugula, in a large bowl.
9. Put the chicken breasts in the air fryer basket. Slide the basket into the air fryer oven. Cook for 14 minutes. Flip the breasts halfway through.
10. When cooking is complete, the internal temperature of the chicken reaches at least 165°F (74°C).
11. Remove the chicken from the air fryer oven and serve on an aluminum foil with asparagus, beans, onion, and arugula. Sprinkle with salt and ground black pepper. Toss to serve.

Chicken with Potatoes and Corn

Prep time: 10 minutes | Cook time: 25 minutes | Serves 4

4 bone-in, skin-on chicken thighs
2 teaspoons kosher salt, divided
1 cup Bisquick baking mix
½ cup butter, melted, divided
1 pound (454 g) small red potatoes, quartered
3 ears corn, shucked and cut into rounds 1- to 1½-inches thick
⅓ cup heavy whipping cream
½ teaspoon freshly ground black pepper

1. Sprinkle the chicken on all sides with 1 teaspoon of kosher salt. Place the baking mix in a shallow dish. Brush the thighs on all sides with ¼ cup of butter, then dredge them in the baking mix, coating them all on sides. Place the chicken in the center of a baking pan.
2. Place the potatoes in a large bowl with 2 tablespoons of butter and toss to coat. Place them on one side of the chicken on the pan.
3. Place the corn in a medium bowl and drizzle with the remaining butter. Sprinkle with ¼ teaspoon of kosher salt and toss to coat. Place on the pan on the other side of the chicken.
4. Slide the pan into the air fryer oven. Cook at 375°F (190°C) for 25 minutes.
5. After 20 minutes, remove from the air fryer oven and transfer the potatoes back to the bowl. Return the pan to air fryer oven and continue cooking.
6. As the chicken continues cooking, add the cream, black pepper, and remaining kosher salt to the potatoes. Lightly mash the potatoes with a potato masher.
7. When cooking is complete, the corn should be tender and the chicken cooked through, reading 165°F (74°C) on a meat thermometer. Remove the pan from the air fryer oven and serve the chicken with the smashed potatoes and corn on the side.

China Spicy Turkey Thighs

Prep time: 10 minutes | Cook time: 25 minutes | Serves 6

2 pounds (907 g) turkey thighs
1 teaspoon Chinese five-spice powder
¼ teaspoon Sichuan pepper
1 teaspoon pink Himalayan salt
1 tablespoon Chinese rice vinegar
1 tablespoon mustard
1 tablespoon chili sauce
2 tablespoons soy sauce
Cooking spray

1. Spritz an air fryer basket with cooking spray.
2. Rub the turkey thighs with five-spice powder, Sichuan pepper, and salt on a clean work surface.
3. Put the turkey thighs in the air fryer basket and spritz with cooking spray.
4. Slide the basket into the air fryer oven. Cook at 360°F (182°C) for 22 minutes.
5. Flip the thighs at least three times during the cooking.
6. When cooking is complete, the thighs should be well browned.
7. Meanwhile, heat the remaining ingredients in a saucepan over medium-high heat. Cook for 3 minutes or until the sauce is thickened and reduces to two thirds.
8. Transfer the thighs onto a plate and baste with sauce before serving.

Creole Hens

Prep time: 10 minutes | Cook time: 40 minutes | Serves 4

½ tablespoon Creole seasoning
½ tablespoon garlic powder
½ tablespoon onion powder
½ tablespoon freshly ground black pepper
½ tablespoon paprika
2 tablespoons olive oil
2 Cornish hens
Cooking spray

1. Spritz an air fryer basket with cooking spray.
2. In a small bowl, mix the Creole seasoning, garlic powder, onion powder, pepper, and paprika.
3. Pat the Cornish hens dry and brush each hen all over with the olive oil. Rub each hen with the seasoning mixture. Place the Cornish hens in the air fryer basket.
4. Cook at 375°F (190°C) for 30 minutes.
5. After 15 minutes, remove from the air fryer oven. Flip the hens over and baste it with any drippings collected in the bottom drawer of the air fryer oven. Return to the air fryer oven and continue cooking.
6. When cooking is complete, a thermometer inserted into the thickest part of the hens should reach at least 165°F (74°C).
7. Let the hens rest for 10 minutes before carving.

Drumsticks with Barbecue-Honey Sauce

Prep time: 5 minutes | Cook time: 18 minutes | Serves 5

1 tablespoon olive oil
10 chicken drumsticks
Chicken seasoning or rub, to taste
Salt and ground black pepper, to taste
1 cup barbecue sauce
¼ cup honey

1. Grease the air fryer basket with olive oil.
2. Rub the chicken drumsticks with chicken seasoning or rub, salt and ground black pepper on a clean work surface.
3. Arrange the chicken drumsticks in the air fryer basket.
4. Slide the basket into the air fryer oven. Cook at 390°F (199°C) for 18 minutes.
5. Flip the drumsticks halfway through.
6. When cooking is complete, the drumsticks should be lightly browned.
7. Meanwhile, combine the barbecue sauce and honey in a small bowl. Stir to mix well.
8. Remove the drumsticks from the air fryer oven and baste with the sauce mixture to serve.

Easy Chicken Fingers

Prep time: 20 minutes | Cook time: 10 minutes | Makes 12 chicken fingers

½ cup all-purpose flour
2 cups panko breadcrumbs
2 tablespoons canola oil
1 large egg
3 boneless and skinless chicken breasts, each cut into 4 strips
Kosher salt and freshly ground black pepper, to taste
Cooking spray

1. Spritz an air fryer basket with cooking spray.
2. Pour the flour in a large bowl. Combine the panko and canola oil on a shallow dish. Whisk the egg in a separate bowl.
3. Rub the chicken strips with salt and ground black pepper on a clean work surface, then dip the chicken in the bowl of flour. Shake the excess off and dunk the chicken strips in the bowl of whisked egg, then roll the strips over the panko to coat well.
4. Arrange the strips in the air fryer basket.
5. Slide the basket into the air fryer oven. Cook at 360°F (182°C) for 10 minutes.
6. Flip the strips halfway through.
7. When cooking is complete, the strips should be crunchy and lightly browned.
8. Serve immediately.

Golden Chicken Cutlets

Prep time: 15 minutes | Cook time: 15 minutes | Serves 4

2 tablespoons panko breadcrumbs
¼ cup grated Parmesan cheese
⅛ tablespoon paprika
½ tablespoon garlic powder
2 large eggs
4 chicken cutlets
1 tablespoon parsley
Salt and ground black pepper, to taste
Cooking spray

1. Spritz an air fryer basket with cooking spray.
2. Combine the breadcrumbs, Parmesan, paprika, garlic powder, salt, and ground black pepper in a large bowl. Stir to mix well. Beat the eggs in a separate bowl.
3. Dredge the chicken cutlets in the beaten eggs, then roll over the breadcrumbs mixture to coat well. Shake the excess off.
4. Transfer the chicken cutlets in the air fryer basket and spritz with cooking spray.
5. Slide the basket into the air fryer oven. Cook at 400°F (205°C) for 15 minutes.
6. Flip the cutlets halfway through.
7. When cooking is complete, the cutlets should be crispy and golden brown.
8. Serve with parsley on top.

Glazed Duck with Cherry Sauce

Prep time: 20 minutes | Cook time: 32 minutes | Serves 12

1 whole duck (about 5 pounds / 2.3 kg in total), split in half, back and rib bones removed, fat trimmed
1 teaspoon olive oil
Salt and freshly ground black pepper, to taste
Cherry Sauce:
1 tablespoon butter
1 shallot, minced
½ cup sherry
1 cup chicken stock
1 teaspoon white wine vinegar
¾ cup cherry preserves
1 teaspoon fresh thyme leaves
Salt and freshly ground black pepper, to taste

1. On a clean work surface, rub the duck with olive oil, then sprinkle with salt and ground black pepper to season.
2. Place the duck in an air fryer basket, breast side up.
3. Slide the basket into the air fryer oven. Cook at 400°F (205°C) for 25 minutes.
4. Flip the ducks halfway through the cooking time.
5. Meanwhile, make the cherry sauce: Heat the butter in a skillet over medium-high heat or until melted.
6. Add the shallot and sauté for 5 minutes or until lightly browned.
7. Add the sherry and simmer for 6 minutes or until it reduces in half.
8. Add the chicken stick, white wine vinegar, and cherry preserves. Stir to combine well. Simmer for 6 more minutes or until thickened.
9. Fold in the thyme leaves and sprinkle with salt and ground black pepper. Stir to mix well.
10. When the cooking of the duck is complete, glaze the duck with a quarter of the cherry sauce, then air fry for another 4 minutes.
11. Flip the duck and glaze with another quarter of the cherry sauce. Air fry for an additional 3 minutes.
12. Transfer the duck on a large plate and serve with remaining cherry sauce.

Gnocchi with Chicken and Spinach

Prep time: 10 minutes | Cook time: 13 minutes | Serves 4

1 (1-pound / 454-g) package shelf-stable gnocchi
1¼ cups chicken stock
½ teaspoon kosher salt
1 pound (454 g) chicken breast, cut into 1-inch chunks
1 cup heavy whipping cream
2 tablespoons sun-dried tomato purée
1 garlic clove, minced
1 cup frozen spinach, thawed and drained
1 cup grated Parmesan cheese

1. Place the gnocchi in an even layer on a baking pan. Pour the chicken stock over the gnocchi.
2. Slide the pan into the air fryer oven. Cook at 450°F (235°C) for 7 minutes.
3. While the gnocchi are cooking, sprinkle the salt over the chicken pieces. In a small bowl, mix the cream, tomato purée, and garlic.
4. When cooking is complete, blot off any remaining stock, or drain the gnocchi and return it to the pan. Top the gnocchi with the spinach and chicken. Pour the cream mixture over the ingredients in the pan.
5. Slide the pan into the air fryer oven. Cook at 400°F (205°C) for 6 minutes.
6. After 4 minutes, remove from the air fryer oven and gently stir the ingredients. Return to the air fryer oven and continue cooking.
7. When cooking is complete, the gnocchi should be tender and the chicken should be cooked through. Remove from the air fryer oven. Stir in the Parmesan cheese until it's melted and serve.

Golden Chicken Fries

Prep time: 20 minutes | Cook time: 6 minutes | Serves 4 to 6

1 pound (454 g) chicken tenders, cut into about ½-inch-wide strips
Salt, to taste
¼ cup all-purpose flour
2 eggs
¾ cup panko bread crumbs
¾ cup crushed organic nacho cheese tortilla chips
Cooking spray
Seasonings:
½ teaspoon garlic powder
1 tablespoon chili powder
½ teaspoon onion powder
1 teaspoon ground cumin

1. Stir together all seasonings in a small bowl and set aside.
2. Sprinkle the chicken with salt. Place strips in a large bowl and sprinkle with 1 tablespoon of the seasoning mix. Stir well to distribute seasonings.
3. Add flour to chicken and stir well to coat all sides.
4. Beat eggs in a separate bowl.
5. In a shallow dish, combine the panko, crushed chips, and the remaining 2 teaspoons of seasoning mix.
6. Dip chicken strips in eggs, then roll in crumbs. Mist with oil or cooking spray. Arrange the chicken strips in a single layer in the air fryer basket.
7. Cook at 400°F (205°C) for 6 minutes.
8. After 4 minutes, remove from the air fryer oven. Flip the strips with tongs. Return to the air fryer oven and continue cooking.
9. When cooking is complete, the chicken should be crispy and its juices should be run clear.
10. Allow to cool under room temperature before serving.

Hawaiian Chicken Bites

Prep time: 1 hour 15 minutes | Cook time: 15 minutes | Serves 4

½ cup pineapple juice
2 tablespoons apple cider vinegar
½ tablespoon minced ginger
½ cup ketchup
2 garlic cloves, minced
½ cup brown sugar
2 tablespoons sherry
½ cup soy sauce
4 chicken breasts, cubed
Cooking spray

1. Combine the pineapple juice, cider vinegar, ginger, ketchup, garlic, and sugar in a saucepan. Stir to mix well. Heat over low heat for 5 minutes or until thickened. Fold in the sherry and soy sauce.
2. Dunk the chicken cubes in the mixture. Press to submerge. Wrap the bowl in plastic and refrigerate to marinate for at least an hour.
3. Spritz an air fryer basket with cooking spray.
4. Remove the chicken cubes from the marinade. Shake the excess off and put in the air fryer basket. Spritz with cooking spray.
5. Slide the basket into the air fryer oven. Cook at 360°F (182°C) for 15 minutes.
6. Flip the chicken cubes at least three times during the air frying.
7. When cooking is complete, the chicken cubes should be glazed and well browned.
8. Serve immediately.

Herbed Turkey Breast with Simple Dijon Sauce

Prep time: 5 minutes | Cook time: 30 minutes | Serves 4

1 teaspoon chopped fresh sage
1 teaspoon chopped fresh tarragon
1 teaspoon chopped fresh thyme leaves
1 teaspoon chopped fresh rosemary leaves
1½ teaspoons sea salt
1 teaspoon ground black pepper
1 (2-pound / 907-g) turkey breast
3 tablespoons Dijon mustard
3 tablespoons butter, melted
Cooking spray

1. Spritz an air fryer basket with cooking spray.
2. Combine the herbs, salt, and black pepper in a small bowl. Stir to mix well. Set aside.
3. Combine the Dijon mustard and butter in a separate bowl. Stir to mix well.
4. Rub the turkey with the herb mixture on a clean work surface, then brush the turkey with Dijon mixture.
5. Arrange the turkey in the air fryer basket.
6. Slide the basket into the air fryer oven. Cook at 390°F (199°C) for 30 minutes.
7. Flip the turkey breast halfway through.
8. When cooking is complete, an instant-read thermometer inserted in the thickest part of the turkey breast should reach at least 165°F (74°C).
9. Transfer the cooked turkey breast on a large plate and slice to serve.

Honey Glazed Chicken Breasts

Prep time: 5 minutes | Cook time: 10 minutes | Serves 4

4 (4-ounce / 113-g) boneless, skinless chicken breasts
Chicken seasoning or rub, to taste
Salt and ground black pepper, to taste
¼ cup honey
2 tablespoons soy sauce
2 teaspoons grated fresh ginger
2 garlic cloves, minced
Cooking spray

1. Spritz an air fryer basket with cooking spray.
2. Rub the chicken breasts with chicken seasoning, salt, and black pepper on a clean work surface.
3. Arrange the chicken breasts in the air fryer basket and spritz with cooking spray.
4. Slide the basket into the air fryer oven. Cook at 400°F (205°C) for 10 minutes.
5. Flip the chicken breasts halfway through.
6. When cooking is complete, the internal temperature of the thickest part of the chicken should reach at least 165°F (74°C).
7. Meanwhile, combine the honey, soy sauce, ginger, and garlic in a saucepan and heat over medium-high heat for 3 minutes or until thickened. Stir constantly.
8. Remove the chicken from the air fryer oven and serve with the honey glaze.

Italian Chicken Breasts with Tomatoes

Prep time: 10 minutes | Cook time: 35 minutes | Serves 8

3 pounds (1.4 kg) chicken breasts, bone-in
1 teaspoon minced fresh basil
1 teaspoon minced fresh rosemary
2 tablespoons minced fresh parsley
1 teaspoon cayenne pepper
½ teaspoon salt
½ teaspoon freshly ground black pepper
4 medium Roma tomatoes, halved
Cooking spray

1. Spritz an air fryer basket with cooking spray.
2. Combine all the ingredients, except for the chicken breasts and tomatoes, in a large bowl. Stir to mix well.
3. Dunk the chicken breasts in the mixture and press to coat well.
4. Transfer the chicken breasts in the air fryer basket.
5. Slide the basket into the air fryer oven. Cook at 370°F (188°C) for 20 minutes.
6. Flip the breasts halfway through the cooking time.
7. When cooking is complete, the internal temperature of the thickest part of the breasts should reach at least 165°F (74°C).
8. Remove the cooked chicken breasts from the air fryer oven and adjust the temperature to 350°F (180°C).
9. Place the tomatoes in the air fryer basket and spritz with cooking spray. Sprinkle with a touch of salt.
10. Set time to 10 minutes. Stir the tomatoes halfway through the cooking time.
11. When cooking is complete, the tomatoes should be tender.
12. Serve the tomatoes with chicken breasts on a large serving plate.

Korean Flavor Glazed Chicken Wings

Prep time: 10 minutes | Cook time: 25 minutes | Serves 4

Wings:
2 pounds (907 g) chicken wings
1 teaspoon salt
1 teaspoon ground black pepper
Sauce:
2 tablespoons gochujang
1 tablespoon mayonnaise
1 tablespoon minced ginger
1 tablespoon minced garlic
1 teaspoon agave nectar
2 packets Splenda
1 tablespoon sesame oil
For Garnish:
2 teaspoons sesame seeds
¼ cup chopped green onions

1. Line a baking pan with aluminum foil, then arrange the rack on the pan.
2. On a clean work surface, rub the chicken wings with salt and ground black pepper, then arrange the seasoned wings on the rack.
3. Slide the pan into the air fryer oven. Cook at 400°F (205°C) for 20 minutes.
4. Flip the wings halfway through.
5. When cooking is complete, the wings should be well browned.
6. Meanwhile, combine the ingredients for the sauce in a small bowl. Stir to mix well. Reserve half of the sauce in a separate bowl until ready to serve.
7. Remove the air fried chicken wings from the air fryer oven and toss with remaining half of the sauce to coat well.
8. Place the wings back to the air fryer oven. Set time to 5 minutes.
9. When cooking is complete, the internal temperature of the wings should reach at least 165°F (74°C).
10. Remove the wings from the air fryer oven and place on a large plate. Sprinkle with sesame seeds and green onions. Serve with reserved sauce.

Lettuce Chicken Tacos with Peanut Sauce

Prep time: 10 minutes | Cook time: 6 minutes | Serves 4

1 pound (454 g) ground chicken
2 cloves garlic, minced
¼ cup diced onions
¼ teaspoon sea salt
Cooking spray
Peanut Sauce:
¼ cup creamy peanut butter, at room temperature
2 tablespoons tamari
1½ teaspoons hot sauce
2 tablespoons lime juice
2 tablespoons grated fresh ginger
2 tablespoons chicken broth
2 teaspoons sugar
For Serving:
2 small heads butter lettuce, leaves separated
Lime slices (optional)

1. Spritz a baking pan with cooking spray.
2. Combine the ground chicken, garlic, and onions in the baking pan, then sprinkle with salt. Use a fork to break the ground chicken and combine them well.
3. Slide the pan into the air fryer oven. Cook at 350ºF (180ºC) for 5 minutes.
4. Stir them halfway through the cooking time.
5. When cooking is complete, the chicken should be lightly browned.
6. Meanwhile, combine the ingredients for the sauce in a small bowl. Stir to mix well.
7. Pour the sauce in the pan of chicken, then bake for 1 more minute or until heated through.
8. Unfold the lettuce leaves on a large serving plate, then divide the chicken mixture on the lettuce leaves. Drizzle with lime juice and serve immediately.

Lettuce-Wrapped Turkey and Mushroom Meatballs

Prep time: 10 minutes | Cook time: 15 minutes | Serves 6

Sauce:
2 tablespoons tamari
2 tablespoons tomato sauce
1 tablespoon lime juice
¼ teaspoon peeled and grated fresh ginger
1 clove garlic, smashed to a paste
½ cup chicken broth
⅓ cup sugar
2 tablespoons toasted sesame oil
Cooking spray
Meatballs:
2 pounds (907 g) ground turkey
¾ cup finely chopped button mushrooms
2 large eggs, beaten
1½ teaspoons tamari
¼ cup finely chopped green onions, plus more for garnish
2 teaspoons peeled and grated fresh ginger
1 clove garlic, smashed
2 teaspoons toasted sesame oil
2 tablespoons sugar
For Serving:
Lettuce leaves, for serving
Sliced red chiles, for garnish (optional)
Toasted sesame seeds, for garnish (optional)

1. Spritz an air fryer basket with cooking spray.
2. Combine the ingredients for the sauce in a small bowl. Stir to mix well. Set aside.
3. Combine the ingredients for the meatballs in a large bowl. Stir to mix well, then shape the mixture in twelve 1½-inch meatballs.
4. Arrange the meatballs in the air fryer basket, then baste with the sauce.
5. Slide the basket into the air fryer oven. Cook at 350ºF (180ºC) for 15 minutes.
6. Flip the balls halfway through.
7. When cooking is complete, the meatballs should be golden brown.
8. Unfold the lettuce leaves on a large serving plate, then transfer the cooked meatballs on the leaves. Spread the red chiles and sesame seeds over the balls, then serve.

Wings

Prep time: 10 minutes | Cook time: 15 minutes | Serves 4

1 tablespoon olive oil
8 whole chicken wings
Chicken seasoning or rub, to taste
1 teaspoon garlic powder
Freshly ground black pepper, to taste

1. Grease the air fryer basket with olive oil.
2. On a clean work surface, rub the chicken wings with chicken seasoning and rub, garlic powder, and ground black pepper.
3. Arrange the well-coated chicken wings in the air fryer basket.
4. Slide the basket into the air fryer oven. Cook at 400ºF (205ºC) for 15 minutes.
5. Flip the chicken wings halfway through.
6. When cooking is complete, the internal temperature of the chicken wings should reach at least 165ºF (74ºC).
7. Remove the chicken wings from the air fryer oven. Serve immediately.

Gold Livers

Prep time: 10 minutes | Cook time: 10 minutes | Serves 4

2 eggs
2 tablespoons water
¾ cup flour
2 cups panko breadcrumbs
1 teaspoon salt
½ teaspoon ground black pepper
20 ounces (567 g) chicken livers
Cooking spray

1. Spritz an air fryer basket with cooking spray.
2. Whisk the eggs with water in a large bowl. Pour the flour in a separate bowl. Pour the panko on a shallow dish and sprinkle with salt and pepper.
3. Dredge the chicken livers in the flour. Shake the excess off, then dunk the livers in the whisked eggs, and then roll the livers over the panko to coat well.
4. Arrange the livers in the air fryer basket and spritz with cooking spray.
5. Slide the basket into the air fryer oven. Cook at 390°F (199°C) for 10 minutes.
6. Flip the livers halfway through.
7. When cooking is complete, the livers should be golden and crispy.
8. Serve immediately.

Lime Chicken with Cilantro

Prep time: 35 minutes | Cook time: 10 minutes | Serves 4

4 (4-ounce / 113-g) boneless, skinless chicken breasts
½ cup chopped fresh cilantro
Juice of 1 lime
Chicken seasoning or rub, to taste
Salt and ground black pepper, to taste
Cooking spray

1. Put the chicken breasts in the large bowl, then add the cilantro, lime juice, chicken seasoning, salt, and black pepper. Toss to coat well.
2. Wrap the bowl in plastic and refrigerate to marinate for at least 30 minutes.
3. Spritz an air fryer basket with cooking spray.
4. Remove the marinated chicken breasts from the bowl and place in the air fryer basket. Spritz with cooking spray.
5. Slide the basket into the air fryer oven. Cook at 400°F (205°C) for 10 minutes.
6. Flip the breasts halfway through.
7. When cooking is complete, the internal temperature of the chicken should reach at least 165°F (74°C).
8. Serve immediately.

Nice Goulash

Prep time: 5 minutes | Cook time: 17 minutes | Serves 2

2 red bell peppers, chopped
1 pound (454 g) ground chicken
2 medium tomatoes, diced
½ cup chicken broth
Salt and ground black pepper, to taste
Cooking spray

1. Spritz a baking pan with cooking spray.
2. Set the bell pepper in the baking pan.
3. Slide the pan into the air fryer oven. Cook at 365°F (185°C) for 5 minutes.
4. Stir the bell pepper halfway through.
5. When broiling is complete, the bell pepper should be tender.
6. Add the ground chicken and diced tomatoes in the baking pan and stir to mix well.
7. Set the time of air fryer oven to 12 minutes. Press Start. Stir the mixture and mix in the chicken broth, salt and ground black pepper halfway through.
8. When cooking is complete, the chicken should be well browned.
9. Serve immediately.

Peach and Cherry Chicken

Prep time: 8 minutes | Cook time: 15 minutes | Serves 4

⅓ cup peach preserves
1 teaspoon ground rosemary
½ teaspoon black pepper
½ teaspoon salt
½ teaspoon marjoram
1 teaspoon light olive oil
1 pound (454 g) boneless chicken breasts, cut in 1½-inch chunks
1 (10-ounce / 284-g) package frozen dark cherries, thawed and drained
Cooking spray

2. In a medium bowl, mix peach preserves, rosemary, pepper, salt, marjoram, and olive oil.
3. Stir in chicken chunks and toss to coat well with the preserve mixture.
4. Spritz an air fryer basket with cooking spray and lay chicken chunks in the air fryer basket.
5. Cook at 400°F (205°C) for 15 minutes.
6. After 7 minutes, remove from the air fryer oven. Flip the chicken chunks. Return to the air fryer oven and continue cooking.
7. When cooking is complete, the chicken should no longer pink and the juices should run clear.
8. Scatter the cherries over and cook for an additional minute to heat cherries.
9. Serve immediately.

Pineapple Chicken

Prep time: 10 minutes | Cook time: 10 minutes | Serves 6

1½ pounds (680 g) boneless, skinless chicken breasts, cut into 1-inch chunks
¾ cup soy sauce
2 tablespoons ketchup
2 tablespoons brown sugar
2 tablespoons rice vinegar
1 red bell pepper, cut into 1-inch chunks
1 green bell pepper, cut into 1-inch chunks
6 scallions, cut into 1-inch pieces
1 cup (¾-inch chunks) fresh pineapple, rinsed and drained
Cooking spray

1. Place the chicken in a large bowl. Add the soy sauce, ketchup, brown sugar, vinegar, red and green peppers, and scallions. Toss to coat.
2. Spritz a baking pan with cooking spray and place the chicken and vegetables on the pan.
3. Slide the pan into the air fryer oven. Cook at 375°F (190°C) for 10 minutes.
4. After 6 minutes, remove from the air fryer oven. Add the pineapple chunks to the pan and stir. Return to the air fryer oven and continue cooking.
5. When cooking is complete, remove from the air fryer oven. Serve with steamed rice, if desired.

Pomegranate Chicken with Couscous Salad

Prep time: 25 minutes | Cook time: 20 minutes | Serves 4

3 tablespoons plus 2 teaspoons pomegranate molasses
½ teaspoon ground cinnamon
1 teaspoon minced fresh thyme
Salt and ground black pepper, to taste
2 (12-ounce / 340-g) bone-in split chicken breasts, trimmed
¼ cup chicken broth
¼ cup water
½ cup couscous
1 tablespoon minced fresh parsley
2 ounces (57 g) cherry tomatoes, quartered
1 scallion, white part minced, green part sliced thin on bias
1 tablespoon extra-virgin olive oil
1 ounce (28 g) feta cheese, crumbled
Cooking spray

1. Spritz an air fryer basket with cooking spray.
2. Combine 3 tablespoons of pomegranate molasses, cinnamon, thyme, and ⅛ teaspoon of salt in a small bowl. Stir to mix well. Set aside.
3. Place the chicken breasts in the air fryer basket, skin side down, and spritz with cooking spray. Sprinkle with salt and ground black pepper.
4. Slide the basket into the air fryer oven. Cook at 350°F (180°C) for 20 minutes.
5. Flip the chicken and brush with pomegranate molasses mixture halfway through.
6. Meanwhile, pour the broth and water in a pot and bring to a boil over medium-high heat. Add the couscous and sprinkle with salt. Cover and simmer for 7 minutes or until the liquid is almost absorbed.
7. Combine the remaining ingredients, except for the cheese, with cooked couscous in a large bowl. Toss to mix well. Scatter with the feta cheese.
8. When cooking is complete, remove the chicken from the air fryer oven and allow to cool for 10 minutes. Serve with vegetable and couscous salad.

Ritzy Chicken Roast

Prep time: 15 minutes | Cook time: 1 hour | Serves 6

1 teaspoon Italian seasoning
½ teaspoon garlic powder
½ teaspoon paprika
1 teaspoon salt
½ teaspoon freshly ground black pepper
½ teaspoon onion powder
2 tablespoons olive oil
1 (3-pound / 1.4-kg) whole chicken, giblets removed, pat dry
Cooking spray

1. Spritz an air fryer basket with cooking spray.
2. In a small bowl, mix the Italian seasoning, garlic powder, paprika, salt, pepper, and onion powder.
3. Brush the chicken with the olive oil and rub it with the seasoning mixture.
4. Tie the chicken legs with butcher's twine. Place the chicken in the air fryer basket, breast side down.
5. Slide the basket in the air fryer oven. Cook at 350°F (180°C) for an hour.
6. After 30 minutes, remove from the air fryer oven. Flip the chicken over and baste it with any drippings collected in the bottom drawer of the air fryer oven. Return to the air fryer oven and continue cooking.
7. When cooking is complete, a thermometer inserted into the thickest part of the thigh should reach at least 165°F (74°C).
8. Let the chicken rest for 10 minutes before carving and serving.

Rosemary Turkey Breast

Prep time: 2 hours 20 minutes | Cook time: 30 minutes | Serves 6

½ teaspoon dried rosemary
2 minced garlic cloves
2 teaspoons salt
1 teaspoon ground black pepper
¼ cup olive oil
2½ pounds (1.1 kg) turkey breast
¼ cup pure maple syrup
1 tablespoon stone-ground brown mustard
1 tablespoon melted vegan butter

1. Combine the rosemary, garlic, salt, ground black pepper, and olive oil in a large bowl. Stir to mix well.
2. Dunk the turkey breast in the mixture and wrap the bowl in plastic. Refrigerate for 2 hours to marinate.
3. Remove the bowl from the refrigerator and let sit for half an hour before cooking.
4. Spritz an air fryer basket with cooking spray.
5. Remove the turkey from the marinade and place in the air fryer basket.
6. Slide the basket into the air fryer oven. Cook at 400°F (205°C) for 20 minutes.
7. Flip the breast halfway through.
8. When cooking is complete, the breast should be well browned.
9. Meanwhile, combine the remaining ingredients in a small bowl. Stir to mix well.
10. Pour half of the butter mixture over the turkey breast in the air fryer oven and air fry for 10 more minutes. Flip the breast and pour the remaining half of butter mixture over halfway through.
11. Transfer the turkey on a plate and slice to serve.

Rosemary Turkey Scotch Eggs

Prep time: 15 minutes | Cook time: 12 minutes | Serves 4

1 egg
1 cup panko breadcrumbs
½ teaspoon rosemary
1 pound (454 g) ground turkey
4 hard-boiled eggs, peeled
Salt and ground black pepper, to taste
Cooking spray

1. Spritz an air fryer basket with cooking spray.
2. Whisk the egg with salt in a bowl. Combine the breadcrumbs with rosemary in a shallow dish.
3. Stir the ground turkey with salt and ground black pepper in a separate large bowl, then divide the ground turkey into four portions.
4. Wrap each hard-boiled egg with a portion of ground turkey. Dredge in the whisked egg, then roll over the breadcrumb mixture.
5. Place the wrapped eggs in the air fryer basket and spritz with cooking spray.
6. Slide the basket into the air fryer oven. Cook at 400°F (205°C) for 12 minutes.
7. Flip the eggs halfway through.
8. When cooking is complete, the scotch eggs should be golden brown and crunchy.
9. Serve immediately.

Spicy Chicken Skewers with Satay Sauce

Prep time: 5 minutes | Cook time: 10 minutes | Serves 4

4 (6-ounce / 170-g) boneless, skinless chicken breasts, sliced into strips
1 teaspoon sea salt
1 teaspoon paprika
Cooking spray
Satay Sauce:
¼ cup creamy almond butter
½ teaspoon hot sauce
1½ tablespoons coconut vinegar
2 tablespoons chicken broth
1 teaspoon peeled and minced fresh ginger
1 clove garlic, minced
1 teaspoon sugar
For Serving:
¼ cup chopped cilantro leaves
Red pepper flakes, to taste
Thinly sliced red, orange, or / and yellow bell peppers

Special Equipment:
16 wooden or bamboo skewers, soaked in water for 15 minutes

1. Spritz an air fryer basket with cooking spray.
2. Run the bamboo skewers through the chicken strips, then arrange the chicken skewers in the air fryer basket and sprinkle with salt and paprika.
3. Slide the basket into the air fryer oven. Cook at 400°F (205°C) for 10 minutes.
4. Flip the chicken skewers halfway during the cooking.
5. When cooking is complete, the chicken should be lightly browned.
6. Meanwhile, combine the ingredients for the sauce in a small bowl. Stir to mix well.
7. Transfer the cooked chicken skewers on a large plate, then top with cilantro, sliced bell peppers, red pepper flakes. Serve with the sauce or just baste the sauce over before serving.

Simple Air Fried Chicken Simple Chicken Nuggets

Prep time: 10 minutes | Cook time: 8 minutes | Serves 4

1 pound (454 g) boneless, skinless chicken breasts, cut into 1-inch pieces
2 tablespoons panko breadcrumbs
6 tablespoons breadcrumbs
Chicken seasoning or rub, to taste
Salt and ground black pepper, to taste
2 eggs
Cooking spray

1. Spritz an air fryer basket with cooking spray.
2. Combine the breadcrumbs, chicken seasoning, salt, and black pepper in a large bowl. Stir to mix well. Whisk the eggs in a separate bowl.
3. Dunk the chicken pieces in the egg mixture, then in the breadcrumb mixture. Shake the excess off.
4. Arrange the well-coated chicken pieces in the air fryer basket. Spritz with cooking spray.
5. Slide the basket into the air fryer oven. Cook at 400°F (205°C) for 8 minutes.
6. Flip the chicken halfway through.
7. When cooking is complete, the chicken should be crispy and golden brown.
8. Serve immediately.

Thai Drumsticks with Green Beans

Prep time: 5 minutes | Cook time: 25 minutes | Serves 4

8 skin-on chicken drumsticks
1 teaspoon kosher salt, divided
1 pound (454 g) green beans, trimmed
2 garlic cloves, minced
2 tablespoons vegetable oil
⅓ cup Thai sweet chili sauce

1. Salt the drumsticks on all sides with ½ teaspoon of kosher salt. Let sit for a few minutes, then blot dry with a paper towel. Place on a baking pan.
2. Slide the pan into the air fryer oven. Cook at 375°F (190°C) for 25 minutes.
3. While the chicken cooks, place the green beans in a large bowl. Add the remaining kosher salt, the garlic, and oil. Toss to coat.
4. After 15 minutes, remove from the air fryer oven. Brush the drumsticks with the sweet chili sauce. Place the green beans in the pan. Return to the air fryer oven and continue cooking.
5. When cooking is complete, the green beans should be sizzling and browned in spots and the chicken cooked through, reading 165°F (74°C) on a meat thermometer. Serve the chicken with the green beans on the side.

Simple Herbed Hens

Prep time: 2 hours 15 minutes | Cook time: 30 minutes | Serves 8

4 (1¼-pound / 567-g) Cornish hens, giblets removed, split lengthwise
2 cups white wine, divided
2 garlic cloves, minced
1 small onion, minced
½ teaspoon celery seeds
½ teaspoon poultry seasoning
½ teaspoon paprika
½ teaspoon dried oregano
¼ teaspoon freshly ground black pepper

1. Place the hens, cavity side up, on a rack in a baking pan. Pour 1½ cups of the wine over the hens; set aside.
2. In a shallow bowl, combine the garlic, onion, celery seeds, poultry seasoning, paprika, oregano, and pepper. Sprinkle half of the combined seasonings over the cavity of each split half. Cover and refrigerate. Allow the hens to marinate for 2 hours.
3. Transfer the hens in the air fryer basket. Slide the basket into the air fryer oven. Cook at 350°F (180°C) for 90 minutes.
4. Remove the basket from the air fryer oven halfway through the baking, turn breast side up, and remove the skin. Pour the remaining ½ cup of wine over the top, and sprinkle with the remaining seasonings.
5. When cooking is complete, the inner temperature of the hens should be at least 165°F (74°C). Transfer the hens to a serving platter and serve hot.

Simple Whole Chicken Bake

Prep time: 10 minutes | Cook time: 1 hour | Serves 2 to 4

½ cup melted butter
3 tablespoons garlic, minced
Salt, to taste
1 teaspoon ground black pepper
1 (1-pound / 454-g) whole chicken

1. Combine the butter with garlic, salt, and ground black pepper in a small bowl.
2. Brush the butter mixture over the whole chicken, then place the chicken in an air fryer basket, skin side down.
3. Slide the basket into the air fryer oven. Cook at 350°F (180°C) for 60 minutes.
4. Flip the chicken halfway through.
5. When cooking is complete, an instant-read thermometer inserted in the thickest part of the chicken should register at least 165°F (74°C).
6. Remove the chicken from the air fryer oven and allow to cool for 15 minutes before serving.

Spicy Tandoori Chicken Drumsticks

Prep time: 70 minutes | Cook time: 14 minutes | Serves 4

8 (4- to 5-ounce / 113- to 142-g) skinless bone-in chicken drumsticks
½ cup plain full-fat or low-fat yogurt
¼ cup buttermilk
2 teaspoons minced garlic
2 teaspoons minced fresh ginger
2 teaspoons ground cinnamon
2 teaspoons ground coriander
2 teaspoons mild paprika
1 teaspoon salt
1 teaspoon Tabasco hot red pepper sauce

1. In a large bowl, stir together all the ingredients except for chicken drumsticks until well combined. Add the chicken drumsticks to the bowl and toss until well coated. Cover in plastic and set in the refrigerator to marinate for 1 hour, tossing once.
2. Arrange the marinated drumsticks in an air fryer basket, leaving enough space between them.
3. Slide the basket into the air fryer oven. Cook at 375°F (190°C) for 14 minutes.
4. Flip the drumsticks once halfway through to ensure even cooking.
5. When cooking is complete, the internal temperature of the chicken drumsticks should reach 160°F (71°C) on a meat thermometer.
6. Transfer the drumsticks to plates. Rest for 5 minutes before serving.

Strawberry-Glazed Turkey

Prep time: 15 minutes | Cook time: 37 minutes | Serves 2

2 pounds (907 g) turkey breast
1 tablespoon olive oil
Salt and ground black pepper, to taste
1 cup fresh strawberries

1. Rub the turkey bread with olive oil on a clean work surface, then sprinkle with salt and ground black pepper.
2. Transfer the turkey in an air fryer basket and spritz with cooking spray.
3. Slide the basket into the air fryer oven. Cook at 375°F (190°C) for 30 minutes.
4. Flip the turkey breast halfway through.
5. Meanwhile, put the strawberries in a food processor and pulse until smooth.
6. When cooking is complete, spread the puréed strawberries over the turkey and fry for 7 more minutes.
7. Serve immediately.

Turkey and Carrot Meatloaves

Prep time: 6 minutes | Cook time: 24 minutes | Serves 4

¼ cup grated carrot
2 garlic cloves, minced
2 tablespoons ground almonds
⅓ cup minced onion
2 teaspoons olive oil
1 teaspoon dried marjoram
1 egg white
¾ pound (340 g) ground turkey breast

1. In a medium bowl, stir together the carrot, garlic, almonds, onion, olive oil, marjoram, and egg white.
2. Add the ground turkey. Mix until combined.
3. Double 16 foil muffin cup liners to make 8 cups. Divide the turkey mixture evenly among the liners. Place the muffin cups on the air fryer basket.
4. Slide the basket into the air fryer oven. Cook at 400°F (205°C) for 24 minutes.
5. When cooking is complete, the meatloaves should reach an internal temperature of 165°F (74°C) on a meat thermometer.
6. Serve immediately.

Sweet-and-Sour Chicken Nuggets

Prep time: 15 minutes | Cook time: 15 minutes | Serves 4

1 cup cornstarch
Chicken seasoning or rub, to taste
Salt and ground black pepper, to taste
2 eggs
2 (4-ounce/ 113-g) boneless, skinless chicken breasts, cut into 1-inch pieces
1½ cups sweet-and-sour sauce
Cooking spray

1. Spritz an air fryer basket with cooking spray.
2. Combine the cornstarch, chicken seasoning, salt, and pepper in a large bowl. Stir to mix well. Whisk the eggs in a separate bowl.
3. Dredge the chicken pieces in the bowl of cornstarch mixture first, then in the bowl of whisked eggs, and then in the cornstarch mixture again.
4. Arrange the well-coated chicken pieces in the air fryer basket. Spritz with cooking spray.
5. Slide the basket into the air fryer oven. Cook at 360°F (182°C) for 15 minutes.
6. Flip the chicken halfway through.
7. When cooking is complete, the chicken should be golden brown and crispy.
8. Transfer the chicken pieces on a large serving plate, then baste with sweet-and-sour sauce before serving.

Spanish Chicken and Pepper Baguette

Prep time: 10 minutes | Cook time: 20 minutes | Serves 2

1¼ pounds (567 g) assorted small chicken parts, breasts cut into halves
¼ teaspoon salt
¼ teaspoon ground black pepper
2 teaspoons olive oil
½ pound (227 g) mini sweet peppers
¼ cup light mayonnaise
¼ teaspoon smoked paprika
½ clove garlic, crushed
Baguette, for serving
Cooking spray

1. Spritz an air fryer basket with cooking spray.
2. Toss the chicken with salt, ground black pepper, and olive oil in a large bowl.
3. Arrange the sweet peppers and chicken in the air fryer basket.
4. Slide the basket into the air fryer oven. Cook at 375°F (190°C) for 20 minutes.
5. Flip the chicken and transfer the peppers on a plate halfway through.
6. When cooking is complete, the chicken should be well browned.
7. Meanwhile, combine the mayo, paprika, and garlic in a small bowl. Stir to mix well.
8. Assemble the baguette with chicken and sweet pepper, then spread with mayo mixture and serve.

Teriyaki Chicken Thighs with Lemony Snow Peas

Prep time: 30 minutes | Cook time: 34 minutes | Serves 4

¼ cup chicken broth
½ teaspoon grated fresh ginger
⅛ teaspoon red pepper flakes
1½ tablespoons soy sauce
4 (5-ounce / 142-g) bone-in chicken thighs, trimmed
1 tablespoon mirin
½ teaspoon cornstarch
1 tablespoon sugar
6 ounces (170 g) snow peas, strings removed
⅛ teaspoon lemon zest
1 garlic clove, minced
¼ teaspoon salt
Ground black pepper, to taste
½ teaspoon lemon juice

1. Combine the broth, ginger, pepper flakes, and soy sauce in a large bowl. Stir to mix well.
2. Pierce 10 to 15 holes into the chicken skin. Put the chicken in the broth mixture and toss to coat well. Let sit for 10 minutes to marinate.
3. Transfer the marinated chicken on a plate and pat dry with paper towels.
4. Scoop 2 tablespoons of marinade in a microwave-safe bowl and combine with mirin, cornstarch and sugar. Stir to mix well. Microwave for 1 minute or until frothy and has a thick consistency. Set aside.
5. Arrange the chicken in an air fryer basket, skin side up.
6. Slide the basket into the air fryer oven. Cook at 400°F (205°C) for 25 minutes.
7. Flip the chicken halfway through.
8. When cooking is complete, brush the chicken skin with marinade mixture. Air fry the chicken for 5 more minutes or until glazed.
9. Remove the chicken from the air fryer oven. Allow the chicken to cool for 10 minutes.
10. Meanwhile, combine the snow peas, lemon zest, garlic, salt, and ground black pepper in a small bowl. Toss to coat well.
11. Transfer the snow peas in the air fryer basket.
12. Cook at 400°F (205°C) for 3 minutes.
13. When cooking is complete, the peas should be soft.
14. Remove the peas from the air fryer oven and toss with lemon juice.
15. Serve the chicken with lemony snow peas.

Yakitori

Prep time: 10 minutes | Cook time: 15 minutes | Serves 4

½ cup mirin
¼ cup dry white wine
½ cup soy sauce
1 tablespoon light brown sugar
1½ pounds (680 g) boneless, skinless chicken thighs, cut into 1½-inch pieces, fat trimmed
4 medium scallions, trimmed, cut into 1½-inch pieces
Cooking spray

Special Equipment:
4 (4-inch) bamboo skewers, soaked in water for at least 30 minutes

1. Combine the mirin, dry white wine, soy sauce, and brown sugar in a saucepan. Bring to a boil over medium heat. Keep stirring.
2. Boil for another 2 minutes or until it has a thick consistency. Turn off the heat.
3. Spritz an air fryer basket with cooking spray.
4. Run the bamboo skewers through the chicken pieces and scallions alternatively.
5. Arrange the skewers in the air fryer basket, then brush with mirin mixture on both sides. Spritz with cooking spray.
6. Slide the basket into the air fryer oven. Cook at 400°F (205°C) for 10 minutes.
7. Flip the skewers halfway through.
8. When cooking is complete, the chicken and scallions should be glossy.
9. Serve immediately.

Super Lemon Chicken

Prep time: 5 minutes | Cook time: 35 minutes | Serves 6

3 (8-ounce / 227-g) boneless, skinless chicken breasts, halved, rinsed
1 cup dried bread crumbs
¼ cup olive oil
¼ cup chicken broth
Zest of 1 lemon
3 medium garlic cloves, minced
½ cup fresh lemon juice
½ cup water
¼ cup minced fresh oregano
1 medium lemon, cut into wedges
¼ cup minced fresh parsley, divided
Cooking spray

1. Pour the bread crumbs in a shadow dish, then roll the chicken breasts in the bread crumbs to coat.
2. Spritz a skillet with cooking spray, and brown the coated chicken breasts over medium heat about 3 minutes on each side. Transfer the browned chicken to a baking pan.
3. In a small bowl, combine the remaining ingredients, except the lemon and parsley. Pour the sauce over the chicken.
4. Slide the baking pan in the air fryer oven. Cook at 325°F (163°C) for 30 minutes.
5. After 15 minutes, remove from the air fryer oven. Flip the breasts. Return to the air fryer oven and continue cooking.
6. When cooking is complete, the chicken should no longer pink.
7. Transfer to a serving platter, and spoon the sauce over the chicken. Garnish with the lemon and parsley.

Turkey and Bean Stuffed Peppers

Prep time: 20 minutes | Cook time: 15 minutes | Serves 4

½ pound (227 g) lean ground turkey
4 medium bell peppers
1 (15-ounce / 425-g) can black beans, drained and rinsed
1 cup shredded Cheddar cheese
1 cup cooked long-grain brown rice
1 cup mild salsa
1¼ teaspoons chili powder
1 teaspoon salt
½ teaspoon ground cumin
½ teaspoon freshly ground black pepper
Chopped fresh cilantro, for garnish
Cooking spray

1. In a large skillet over medium-high heat, cook the turkey, breaking it up with a spoon, until browned, about 5 minutes. Drain off any excess fat.
2. Cut about ½ inch off the tops of the peppers and then cut in half lengthwise. Remove and discard the seeds and set the peppers aside.
3. In a large bowl, combine the browned turkey, black beans, Cheddar cheese, rice, salsa, chili powder, salt, cumin, and black pepper. Spoon the mixture into the bell peppers.
4. Lightly spray the air fryer basket with cooking spray. Arrange the bell peppers in the basket.
5. Slide the basket in the air fryer oven. Cook at 350°F (180°C) for 15 minutes.
6. When cooking is complete, the stuffed peppers should be lightly charred and wilted.
7. Allow to cool for a few minutes and garnish with cilantro before serving.

Turkey and Cauliflower Meatloaf

Prep time: 15 minutes | Cook time: 50 minutes | Serves 6

2 pounds (907 g) lean ground turkey
1⅓ cups riced cauliflower
2 large eggs, lightly beaten
¼ cup almond flour
⅔ cup chopped yellow or white onion
1 teaspoon ground dried turmeric
1 teaspoon ground cumin
1 teaspoon ground coriander
1 tablespoon minced garlic
1 teaspoon salt
1 teaspoon ground black pepper
Cooking spray

1. Spritz a loaf pan with cooking spray.
2. Combine all the ingredients in a large bowl. Stir to mix well. Pour half of the mixture in the prepared loaf pan and press with a spatula to coat the bottom evenly. Spritz the mixture with cooking spray.
3. Slide the pan into the air fryer oven. Cook at 350°F (180°C) for 25 minutes.
4. When cooking is complete, the meat should be well browned and the internal temperature should reach at least 165°F (74°C).
5. Remove the loaf pan from the air fryer oven and serve immediately.

Thai Game Hens with Cucumber and Chile Salad

Prep time: 25 minutes | Cook time: 25 minutes | Serves 6

2 (1¼-pound / 567-g) Cornish game hens, giblets discarded
1 tablespoon fish sauce
6 tablespoons chopped fresh cilantro
2 teaspoons lime zest
1 teaspoon ground coriander
2 garlic cloves, minced
2 tablespoons packed light brown sugar
2 teaspoons vegetable oil
Salt and ground black pepper, to taste
1 English cucumber, halved lengthwise and sliced thin
1 Thai chile, stemmed, deseeded, and minced
2 tablespoons chopped dry-roasted peanuts
1 small shallot, sliced thinly
1 tablespoon lime juice
Lime wedges, for serving
Cooking spray

1. Arrange a game hen on a clean work surface, remove the backbone with kitchen shears, then pound the hen breast to flat. Cut the breast in half. Repeat with the remaining game hen.
2. Loose the breast and thigh skin with your fingers, then pat the game hens dry and pierce about 10 holes into the fat deposits of the hens. Tuck the wings under the hens.
3. Combine 2 teaspoons of fish sauce, ¼ cup of cilantro, lime zest, coriander, garlic, 4 teaspoons of sugar, 1 teaspoon of vegetable oil, ½ teaspoon of salt, and ⅛ teaspoon of ground black pepper in a small bowl. Stir to mix well.
4. Rub the fish sauce mixture under the breast and thigh skin of the game hens, then let sit for 10 minutes to marinate.
5. Spritz an air fryer basket with cooking spray.
6. Arrange the marinated game hens in the basket, skin side down.
7. Slide the basket into the air fryer oven. Cook at 400°F (205°C) for 25 minutes.
8. Flip the game hens halfway through the cooking time.
9. When cooking is complete, the hen skin should be golden brown and the internal temperature of the hens should read at least 165°F (74°C).
10. Meanwhile, combine all the remaining ingredients, except for the lime wedges, in a large bowl and sprinkle with salt and black pepper. Toss to mix well.
11. Transfer the fried hens on a large plate, then sit the salad aside and squeeze the lime wedges over before serving.

Rotisserie Recipes

Whole Rotisserie Chicken

Prep time: 10 minutes | Cook time: 45 minutes | Serves 4

3 pounds (1.4 kg) tied whole chicken
3 cloves garlic, halved
1 whole lemon, quartered
2 sprigs fresh rosemary whole
2 tablespoons olive oil
Chicken Rub:
½ teaspoon fresh ground pepper
½ teaspoon salt
1 teaspoon garlic powder
1 teaspoon dried oregano
1 teaspoon paprika
1 sprig rosemary (leaves only)

1. Mix together the rub ingredients in a small bowl. Set aside.
2. Place the chicken on a clean cutting board. Ensure the cavity of the chicken is clean. Stuff the chicken cavity with the garlic, lemon, and rosemary.
3. Tie your chicken with twine if needed. Pat the chicken dry.
4. Drizzle the olive oil all over and coat the entire chicken with a brush.
5. Shake the rub on the chicken and rub in until the chicken is covered.
6. Using the rotisserie spit, push through the chicken and attach the rotisserie forks.
7. If desired, place aluminum foil onto the drip tray.
11. Place the prepared chicken with rotisserie fork in the air fryer oven. Cook at 375°F (190°C) for 40 minutes. Check the temperature in 5 minute increments after the 40 minutes.
8. At 40 minutes, check the temperature every 5 minutes until the chicken reaches 165°F (74°C) in the breast, or 165°F (85°C) in the thigh.
9. Once cooking is complete, remove the chicken using the fetch rack and, using gloves, carefully remove the chicken from the spit.
10. Let the chicken sit, covered, for 5 to 10 minutes.
11. Slice and serve.

Air Fried Beef Roast

Prep time: 5 minutes | Cook time: 38 minutes | Serves 6

2.5 pound (1.1 kg) beef roast
1 tablespoon olive oil
1 tablespoon Poultry seasoning

1. Tie the beef roast and rub the olive oil all over the roast. Sprinkle with the seasoning.
2. Using the rotisserie spit, push through the beef roast and attach the rotisserie forks.
3. If desired, place aluminum foil onto the drip tray.
4. Place the prepared beef with rotisserie fork in the air fryer oven. Cook at 360°F (182°C), Rotate for 38 minutes for medium rare beef.
5. When cooking is complete, remove the beef roast using the fetch rack and, using gloves, carefully remove the beef roast from the spit.
6. Let cool for 5 minutes before serving.

Marinated Medium Rare Rotisserie Beef

Prep time: 15 minutes | Cook time: 1 hour 40 minutes | Serves 6 to 8

5 pounds (2.3 kg) eye round beef roast
2 onions, sliced
3 cups white wine
3 cloves garlic, minced
1 teaspoon chopped fresh rosemary
1 teaspoon celery seeds
1 teaspoon fresh thyme leaves
¾ cup olive oil
1 tablespoon coarse sea salt
1 tablespoon ground black pepper
1 teaspoon dried sage
2 tablespoons unsalted butter

1. Place beef roast and onions in a large resealable bag.
2. In a small bowl, combine the wine, garlic, rosemary, celery seeds, thyme leaves, oil, salt, pepper, and sage.
3. Pour the marinade mixture over the beef roast and seal the bag. Refrigerate the roast for up to one day.
4. Remove the beef roast from the marinade. Using the rotisserie spit, push through the beef roast and attach the rotisserie forks.
5. If desired, place aluminum foil onto the drip tray.
6. Place the rotisserie fork in the air fryer oven. Cook at 400°F (205°C), Rotate for 1 hour 40 minutes.
7. Baste the beef roast with marinade for every 30 minutes.
8. When cooking is complete, remove the beef using the fetch rack and, using gloves, carefully remove the beef from the spit.
9. Remove the roast to a platter and allow the roast to rest for 10 minutes.
10. Slice thin and serve.

Easy Rotisserie Chicken

Prep time: 10 minutes | Cook time: 50 minutes | Serves 4

2 cups buttermilk
¼ cup olive oil
1 teaspoon garlic powder
1 tablespoon sea salt
1 whole chicken
Salt and pepper, to taste

1. In a large bag, place the buttermilk, oil, garlic powder, and sea salt and mix to combine.
2. Add the whole chicken and let marinate for 24 hours up to two days.
3. Remove the chicken and sprinkle with the salt and pepper.
4. Truss the chicken, removing the wings and ensuring the legs are tied closely together and the thighs are held in place.
5. Using the rotisserie spit, push through the chicken and attach the rotisserie forks.
6. If desired, place aluminum foil onto the drip tray.
7. Place the prepared chicken with rotisserie fork in the air fryer oven. Cook at 380°F (193°C), Rotate for 50 minutes.
8. When cooking is complete, the chicken should be dark brown and internal temperature should measure 165°F (74°C) (measure at the meatiest part of the thigh).
9. Remove the chicken using the fetch rack and, using gloves, carefully remove the chicken from the spit.
10. Let sit for 10 minutes before slicing and serving.

Sriracha Honey Pork Tenderloin

Prep time: 20 minutes | Cook time: 25 minutes | Serves 2 to 3

1 pound (454 g) pork tenderloin
2 tablespoons Sriracha hot sauce
2 tablespoons honey
1½ teaspoons kosher salt

1. Stir together the Sriracha hot sauce, honey and salt in a bowl. Rub the sauce all over the pork tenderloin.
2. Using the rotisserie spit, push through the pork tenderloin and attach the rotisserie forks.
3. If desired, place aluminum foil onto the drip tray.
4. Place the prepared pork tenderloin with rotisserie fork in the air fryer oven. Cook at 350°F (180°C), Rotate for 20 minutes.
5. When cooking is complete, remove the pork tenderloin using the fetch rack and, using gloves, carefully remove the pork from the spit.
6. Let rest for 5 minutes and serve.

Bourbon Rotisserie Pork Shoulder

Prep time: 30 minutes | Cook time: 4 hours 30 minutes | Serves 6 to 8

1 (5-pound / 2.3-kg) boneless pork shoulder
1 tablespoon kosher salt
For the Rub:
2 teaspoons ground black peppercorns
2 teaspoons ground mustard seed
2 tablespoons light brown sugar
1 teaspoon onion powder
1 teaspoon garlic powder
1 teaspoon paprika
For the Mop:
1 cup bourbon
1 small onion, granulated
¼ cup corn syrup
¼ cup ketchup
2 tablespoons brown mustard
½ cup light brown sugar

1. Combine the ingredients for the rub in a small bowl. Stir to mix well.
2. Season pork shoulder all over with rub, wrap in plastic, and place in refrigerator for 12 to 15 hours.
3. Remove roast from the fridge and let meat stand at room temperature for 30 to 45 minutes. Season with kosher salt.
4. Whisk ingredients for mop in a medium bowl. Set aside until ready to use.
5. Using the rotisserie spit, push through the pork shoulder and attach the rotisserie forks.
6. If desired, place aluminum foil onto the drip tray.
7. Place the rotisserie fork in the air fryer oven. Cook at 450ºF (235ºC), Rotate for 30 minutes.
8. After 30 minutes, reduce the temperature to 250ºF (121ºC) and roast for 4 more hours or until an meat thermometer inserted in the center of the pork reads at least 145ºF (63ºC).
9. After the first hour of cooking, apply mop over the pork for every 20 minutes.
10. When cooking is complete, remove the pork using the fetch rack and, using gloves, carefully remove the pork tenderloin from the spit.
11. Let stand for 10 minutes before slicing and serving.

Greek Rotisserie Lamb Leg

Prep time: 25 minutes | Cook time: 1 hour 30 minutes | Serves 4 to 6

3 pounds (1.4 kg) leg of lamb, boned in
For the Marinade:
1 tablespoon lemon zest (about 1 lemon)
3 tablespoons lemon juice (about 1½ lemons)
3 cloves garlic, minced
1 teaspoon onion powder
1 teaspoon fresh thyme
¼ cup fresh oregano
¼ cup olive oil
1 teaspoon ground black pepper
For the Herb Dressing:
1 tablespoon lemon juice (about ½ lemon)
¼ cup chopped fresh oregano
1 teaspoon fresh thyme
1 tablespoon olive oil
1 teaspoon sea salt
Ground black pepper, to taste

1. Place lamb leg into a large resealable plastic bag. Combine the ingredients for the marinade in a small bowl. Stir to mix well.
2. Pour the marinade over the lamb, making sure the meat is completely coated. Seal the bag and place in the refrigerator. Marinate for 4 to 6 hours before grilling.
3. Remove the lamb leg from the marinade. Using the rotisserie spit, push through the lamb leg and attach the rotisserie forks.
4. If desired, place aluminum foil onto the drip tray.
5. Place the rotisserie fork in the air fryer oven. Cook at 350ºF (180ºC), Rotate for 1 hour 30 minutes.
6. Baste the lamb leg with marinade for every 30 minutes.
7. Meanwhile, combine the ingredients for the herb dressing in a bowl. Stir to mix well.
8. When cooking is complete, remove the lamb leg using the fetch rack and, using gloves, carefully remove the lamb leg from the spit.
9. Cover lightly with aluminum foil for 8 to 10 minutes.
10. Carve the leg and arrange on a platter,. Drizzle with herb dressing. Serve immediately.

Honey Glazed Rotisserie Ham

Prep time: 20 minutes | Cook time: 3 hours | Serves 6

1 (5-pound/2.3-kg) cooked boneless ham, pat dry
For the Glaze:
½ cup honey
2 teaspoons lemon juice
1 teaspoon ground cloves
1 teaspoon cinnamon
½ cup brown sugar

1. Using the rotisserie spit, push through the ham and attach the rotisserie forks.
2. If desired, place aluminum foil onto the drip tray.
3. Place the prepared ham with rotisserie fork in the air fryer oven. Cook at 250ºF (121ºC), Rotate for 3 hours.
4. place the prepared ham with rotisserie spit into the air fryer oven.
5. Meanwhile, combine the ingredients for the glaze in a small bowl. Stir to mix well.
6. When the ham has reached 145ºF (63ºC), brush the glaze mixture over all surfaces of the ham.
7. When cooking is complete, remove the ham using the fetch rack and, using gloves, carefully remove the ham from the spit.
8. Let it rest for 10 minutes covered loosely with foil and then carve and serve.

Apple and Carrot Stuffed Rotisserie Turkey

Prep time: 30 minutes | Cook time: 3 hours | Serves 12 to 14

1 (12-pound/5.4-kg) turkey, giblet removed, rinsed and pat dry
For the Seasoning:
¼ cup lemon pepper
2 tablespoons chopped fresh parsley
1 tablespoon celery salt
2 cloves garlic, minced
2 teaspoons ground black pepper
1 teaspoon sage
For the Stuffing:
1 medium onion, cut into 8 equal parts
1 carrot, sliced
1 apple, cored and cut into 8 thick slices

1. Mix together the seasoning in a small bowl. Rub over the surface and inside of the turkey.
2. Stuff the turkey with the onions, carrots, and apples. Using the rotisserie spit, push through the turkey and attach the rotisserie forks.
3. If desired, place aluminum foil onto the drip tray.
4. Place the prepared turkey with rotisserie fork in the air fryer oven. Cook at 350°F (180°C), Rotate for 3 hours.
5. When cooking is complete, the internal temperature should read at least 180°F (82°C). Remove the turkey using the fetch rack and, using gloves, carefully remove the turkey from the spit.
6. Server hot.

Red Wine Rotisserie Lamb Leg

Prep time: 25 minutes | Cook time: 1 hour 30 hours | Serves 6 to 8

1 (5-pound / 2.3-kg) leg of lamb, bone-in, fat trimmed, rinsed and drained
For the Marinade:
¼ cup dry red wine
1 large shallot, roughly chopped
4 garlic cloves, peeled and roughly chopped
5 large sage leaves
Juice of 1 lemon
2 teaspoons Worcestershire sauce
½ teaspoon allspice
¾ cup fresh mint leaves
3 tablespoons fresh rosemary
⅓ cup beef stock
½ teaspoon coriander powder
2 teaspoons brown sugar
½ teaspoon cayenne pepper
½ cup olive oil
2 teaspoons salt
1 teaspoon black pepper
For the Baste:
1 cup beef stock
¼ cup marinade mixture
Garnish: salt and black pepper

1. Combine the marinade ingredients in a large bowl. Stir to mix well. Remove ¼ cup of the marinade and set aside.
2. Apply remaining marinade onto lamb leg. Place the lamb leg into a baking dish, cover and refrigerate for 1 to 2 hours.
3. Combine the ingredients for the baste in a small bowl. Stir to mix well. Set aside until ready to use.
4. Using the rotisserie spit, push through the lamb leg and attach the rotisserie forks.
5. If desired, place aluminum foil onto the drip tray.
6. Place the rotisserie fork in the air fryer oven. Cook at 350°F (180°C), Rotate for 1 hour 30 minutes.
7. After the first 30 minutes of cooking, apply the baste over the lamb leg for every 20 minutes.
8. When cooking is complete, remove the lamb leg using the fetch rack and, using gloves, carefully remove the lamb leg from the spit.
9. Carve and serve.

Rotisserie Chicken with Lemon

Prep time: 10 minutes | Cook time: 40 minutes | Serves 6

1 (4 pounds / 1.8 kg) whole chicken
2 teaspoons paprika
1½ teaspoons thyme
1 teaspoon onion powder
1 teaspoon garlic powder
Salt and pepper, to taste
¼ cup butter, melted
2 tablespoons olive oil
1 lemon, sliced
2 sprigs rosemary

1. Remove the giblets from the chicken cavity and carefully loosen the skin starting at the neck.
2. In a bowl, mix together the paprika, thyme, onion powder, garlic powder, salt, and pepper. Set aside.
3. Rub the melted butter under the skin and pat the skin back into place.
4. Truss the chicken, ensuring the wings and legs are tied closely together and the cavity is closed up.
5. Drizzle the olive oil all over the chicken and rub it into the chicken.
6. Rub the spice mixture onto the chicken's skin.
7. Place the lemon slices and sprigs of rosemary into the cavity.
8. Using the rotisserie spit, push through the chicken and attach the rotisserie forks.
9. If desired, place aluminum foil onto the drip tray.
10. Place the prepared chicken with rotisserie fork in the air fryer oven. Cook at 380°F (193°C), Rotate for 40 minutes.
11. When cooking is complete, remove the chicken using the fetch rack and, using gloves, carefully remove the chicken from the spit.
12. Let sit for 10 minutes before slicing and serving.

Staples

Air Fryer Oven Grits

Prep time: 3 minutes | Cook time: 1 hour 5 minutes | Makes about 4 cups

1 cup grits or polenta (not instant or quick cook)
2 cups chicken or vegetable stock
2 cups milk
2 tablespoons unsalted butter, cut into 4 pieces
1 teaspoon kosher salt or ½ teaspoon fine salt

1. Add the grits to a baking pan. Stir in the stock, milk, butter, and salt.
2. Cook at 325°F (163°C) for 1 hour and 5 minutes.
3. After 15 minutes, remove from the air fryer oven and stir the polenta. Return to the air fryer oven and continue cooking.
4. After 30 minutes, remove the pan again and stir the polenta again. Return to the air fryer oven and continue cooking for 15 to 20 minutes, or until the polenta is soft and creamy and the liquid is absorbed.
5. When done, remove from the air fryer oven.
6. Serve immediately.

Roasted Mushrooms

Prep time: 8 minutes | Cook time: 30 minutes | Makes about 1½ cups

1 pound (454 g) button or cremini mushrooms, washed, stems trimmed, and cut into quarters or thick slices
¼ cup water
1 teaspoon kosher salt or ½ teaspoon fine salt
3 tablespoons unsalted butter, cut into pieces, or extra-virgin olive oil

1. Place a large piece of aluminum foil on a sheet pan. Place the mushroom pieces in the middle of the foil. Spread them out into an even layer. Pour the water over them, season with the salt, and add the butter. Wrap the mushrooms in the foil.
2. Cook at 325°F (163°C) for 15 minutes.
3. After 15 minutes, remove from the air fryer oven. Transfer the foil packet to a cutting board and carefully unwrap it. Pour the mushrooms and cooking liquid from the foil onto the sheet pan.
4. Return the pan to the air fryer oven. Cook at 350°F (180°C) for 15 minutes.
5. After about 10 minutes, remove from the air fryer oven and stir the mushrooms. Return to the air fryer oven and continue cooking for anywhere from 5 to 15 more minutes, or until the liquid is mostly gone and the mushrooms start to brown.
6. Serve immediately.

Asian Dipping Sauce

Prep time: 15 minutes | Cook time: 0 minutes | Makes about 1 cup

¼ cup rice vinegar
¼ cup hoisin sauce
¼ cup low-sodium chicken or vegetable stock
3 tablespoons soy sauce
1 tablespoon minced or grated ginger
1 tablespoon minced or pressed garlic
1 teaspoon chili-garlic sauce or sriracha (or more to taste)

1. Stir together all the ingredients in a small bowl, or place in a jar with a tight-fitting lid and shake until well mixed.
2. Use immediately.

Classic Marinara Sauce

Prep time: 15 minutes | Cook time: 30 minutes | Makes about 3 cups

¼ cup extra-virgin olive oil
3 garlic cloves, minced
1 small onion, chopped (about ½ cup)
2 tablespoons minced or puréed sun-dried tomatoes (optional)
1 (28-ounce / 794-g) can crushed tomatoes
½ teaspoon dried basil
½ teaspoon dried oregano
¼ teaspoon red pepper flakes
1 teaspoon kosher salt or ½ teaspoon fine salt, plus more as needed

1. Heat the oil in a medium saucepan over medium heat.
2. Add the garlic and onion and sauté for 2 to 3 minutes, or until the onion is softened. Add the sun-dried tomatoes (if desired) and cook for 1 minute until fragrant. Stir in the crushed tomatoes, scraping any brown bits from the bottom of the pot. Fold in the basil, oregano, red pepper flakes, and salt. Stir well.
3. Bring to a simmer. Cook covered for about 30 minutes, stirring occasionally.
4. Turn off the heat and allow the sauce to cool for about 10 minutes.
5. Taste and adjust the seasoning, adding more salt if needed.
6. Use immediately.

Caesar Salad Dressing

Prep time: 5 minutes | Cook time: 0 minutes | Makes about ⅔ cup

½ cup extra-virgin olive oil
2 tablespoons freshly squeezed lemon juice
1 teaspoon anchovy paste
¼ teaspoon kosher salt or ⅛ teaspoon fine salt
¼ teaspoon minced or pressed garlic
1 egg, beaten

1. Add all the ingredients to a tall, narrow container.
2. Purée the mixture with an immersion blender until smooth.
3. Use immediately.

Enchilada Sauce

Prep time: 15 minutes | Cook time: 0 minutes | Makes 2 cups

3 large ancho chiles, stems and seeds removed, torn into pieces
1½ cups very hot water
2 garlic cloves, peeled and lightly smashed
2 tablespoons wine vinegar
1½ teaspoons sugar
½ teaspoon dried oregano
½ teaspoon ground cumin
2 teaspoons kosher salt or 1 teaspoon fine salt

1. Mix together the chile pieces and hot water in a bowl and let stand for 10 to 15 minutes.
2. Pour the chiles and water into a blender jar. Fold in the garlic, vinegar, sugar, oregano, cumin, and salt and blend until smooth.
3. Use immediately.

Shawarma Spice Mix

Prep time: 5 minutes | Cook time: 0 minutes | Makes about 1 tablespoon

1 teaspoon smoked paprika
1 teaspoon cumin
¼ teaspoon turmeric
¼ teaspoon kosher salt or ⅛ teaspoon fine salt
¼ teaspoon cinnamon
¼ teaspoon allspice
¼ teaspoon red pepper flakes
¼ teaspoon freshly ground black pepper

1. Stir together all the ingredients in a small bowl.
2. Use immediately or place in an airtight container in the pantry.

Simple Teriyaki Sauce

Prep time: 5 minutes | Cook time: 0 minutes | Makes ¾ cup

½ cup soy sauce
3 tablespoons honey
1 tablespoon rice wine or dry sherry
1 tablespoon rice vinegar
2 teaspoons minced fresh ginger
2 garlic cloves, smashed

1. Beat together all the ingredients in a small bowl.
2. Use immediately.

Southwest Seasoning

Prep time: 5 minutes | Cook time: 0 minutes | Makes about ¾ cups

3 tablespoons ancho chile powder
3 tablespoons paprika
2 tablespoons dried oregano
2 tablespoons freshly ground black pepper
2 teaspoons cayenne
2 teaspoons cumin
1 tablespoon granulated onion
1 tablespoon granulated garlic

1. Stir together all the ingredients in a small bowl.
2. Use immediately or place in an airtight container in the pantry.

Air Fryer Oven Baked Rice

Prep time: 3 minutes | Cook time: 35 minutes | Makes about 4 cups

1 cup long-grain white rice, rinsed and drained
1 tablespoon unsalted butter, melted, or 1 tablespoon extra-virgin olive oil
2 cups water
1 teaspoon kosher salt or ½ teaspoon fine salt

1. Add the butter and rice to a baking pan and stir to coat. Pour in the water and sprinkle with the salt. Stir until the salt is dissolved.
2. Cook at 325°F (163°C) for 35 minutes.
3. After 20 minutes, remove from the air fryer oven. Stir the rice. Transfer the pan back to the air fryer oven and continue cooking for 10 to 15 minutes, or until the rice is mostly cooked through and the water is absorbed.
4. When done, remove from the air fryer oven and cover with aluminum foil. Let stand for 10 minutes. Using a fork, gently fluff the rice.
5. Serve immediately.

Vegan and Vegetarian

Asian-Inspired Broccoli

Prep time: 5 minutes | Cook time: 10 minutes | Serves 2

12 ounces (340 g) broccoli florets
2 tablespoons Asian hot chili oil
1 teaspoon ground Sichuan peppercorns (or black pepper)
2 garlic cloves, finely chopped
1 (2-inch) piece fresh ginger, peeled and finely chopped
Kosher salt and freshly ground black pepper

1. Toss the broccoli florets with the chili oil, Sichuan peppercorns, garlic, ginger, salt, and pepper in a mixing bowl until thoroughly coated.
2. Transfer the broccoli florets to an air fryer basket.
3. Slide the basket into the air fryer oven. Cook at 375°F (190°C) for 10 minutes.
4. Stir the broccoli florets halfway through the cooking time.
5. When cooking is complete, the broccoli florets should be lightly browned and tender. Remove the broccoli from the air fryer oven and serve on a plate.

Caramelized Eggplant with Yogurt Sauce

Prep time: 5 minutes | Cook time: 15 minutes | Serves 2

1 medium eggplant, quartered and cut crosswise into ½-inch-thick slices
2 tablespoons vegetable oil
Kosher salt and freshly ground black pepper, to taste
½ cup plain yogurt (not Greek)
2 tablespoons harissa paste
1 garlic clove, grated
2 teaspoons honey

1. Toss the eggplant slices with the vegetable oil, salt, and pepper in a large bowl until well coated.
2. Lay the eggplant slices in an air fryer basket.
3. Slide the basket into the air fryer oven. Cook at 400°F (205°C) for 15 minutes.
4. Stir the slices two to three times during cooking.
5. Meanwhile, make the yogurt sauce by whisking together the yogurt, harissa paste, and garlic in a small bowl.
6. When cooking is complete, the eggplant slices should be golden brown. Spread the yogurt sauce on a platter, and pile the eggplant slices over the top. Serve drizzled with the honey.

Air Fried Winter Vegetables

Prep time: 5 minutes | Cook time: 16 minutes | Serves 2

1 parsnip, sliced
1 cup sliced butternut squash
1 small red onion, cut into wedges
½ chopped celery stalk
1 tablespoon chopped fresh thyme
2 teaspoons olive oil
Salt and black pepper, to taste

1. Toss all the ingredients in a large bowl until the vegetables are well coated.
2. Transfer the vegetables to an air fryer basket.
3. Slide the basket into the air fryer oven. Cook at 380°F (193°C) for 16 minutes.
4. Stir the vegetables halfway through the cooking time.
5. When cooking is complete, the vegetables should be golden brown and tender. Remove from the air fryer oven and serve warm.

Bean, Salsa, and Cheese Tacos

Prep time: 12 minutes | Cook time: 7 minutes | Serves 4

1 (15-ounce / 425-g) can black beans, drained and rinsed
½ cup prepared salsa
1½ teaspoons chili powder
4 ounces (113 g) grated Monterey Jack cheese
2 tablespoons minced onion
8 (6-inch) flour tortillas
2 tablespoons vegetable or extra-virgin olive oil
Shredded lettuce, for serving

1. In a medium bowl, add the beans, salsa and chili powder. Coarsely mash them with a potato masher. Fold in the cheese and onion and stir until combined.
2. Arrange the flour tortillas on a cutting board and spoon 2 to 3 tablespoons of the filling into each tortilla. Fold the tortillas over, pressing lightly to even out the filling. Brush the tacos on one side with half the olive oil and put them, oiled side down, on a sheet pan. Brush the top side with the remaining olive oil.
3. Slide the pan into the air fryer oven. Cook at 400°F (205°C) for 7 minutes.
4. Flip the tacos halfway through the cooking time.
5. Remove the pan from the air fryer oven and allow to cool for 5 minutes. Serve with the shredded lettuce on the side.

Balsamic Asparagus

Prep time: 15 minutes | Cook time: 10 minutes | Serves 4

4 tablespoons olive oil, plus more for greasing
4 tablespoons balsamic vinegar
1½ pounds (680 g) asparagus spears, trimmed
Salt and freshly ground black pepper, to taste

13. Grease an air fryer basket with olive oil.
14. In a shallow bowl, stir together the 4 tablespoons of olive oil and balsamic vinegar to make a marinade.
15. Put the asparagus spears in the bowl so they are thoroughly covered by the marinade and allow to marinate for 5 minutes.
16. Put the asparagus in the greased air fryer basket in a single layer and season with salt and pepper.
17. Slide the basket into the air fryer oven. Cook at 350°F (180°C) for 10 minutes.
18. Flip the asparagus halfway through the cooking time.
19. When done, the asparagus should be tender and lightly browned. Cool for 5 minutes before serving.

Crispy Eggplant Slices with Parsley

Prep time: 5 minutes | Cook time: 12 minutes | Serves 4

1 cup flour
4 eggs
Salt, to taste
2 cups bread crumbs
1 teaspoon Italian seasoning
2 eggplants, sliced
2 garlic cloves, sliced
2 tablespoons chopped parsley
Cooking spray

1. Spritz an air fryer basket with cooking spray. Set aside.
2. On a plate, place the flour. In a shallow bowl, whisk the eggs with salt. In another shallow bowl, combine the bread crumbs and Italian seasoning.
3. Dredge the eggplant slices, one at a time, in the flour, then in the whisked eggs, finally in the bread crumb mixture to coat well.
4. Lay the coated eggplant slices in the air fryer basket.
5. Slide the basket into the air fryer oven. Cook at 390°F (199°C) for 12 minutes.
6. Flip the eggplant slices halfway through the cooking time.
7. When cooking is complete, the eggplant slices should be golden brown and crispy. Transfer the eggplant slices to a plate and sprinkle the garlic and parsley on top before serving.

Cinnamon Celery Roots

Prep time: 10 minutes | Cook time: 20 minutes | Serves 4

2 celery roots, peeled and diced
1 teaspoon extra-virgin olive oil
1 teaspoon butter, melted
½ teaspoon ground cinnamon
Sea salt and freshly ground black pepper, to taste

1. Line a baking sheet with aluminum foil.
2. Toss the celery roots with the olive oil in a large bowl until well coated. Transfer them to the prepared baking sheet.
3. Slide the baking sheet into the air fryer oven. Cook at 350°F (180°C) for 20 minutes.
4. When done, the celery roots should be very tender. Remove from the air fryer oven to a serving bowl. Stir in the butter and cinnamon and mash them with a potato masher until fluffy.
5. Season with salt and pepper to taste. Serve immediately.

Cashew Cauliflower with Yogurt Sauce

Prep time: 5 minutes | Cook time: 12 minutes | Serves 2

4 cups cauliflower florets (about half a large head)
1 tablespoon olive oil
1 teaspoon curry powder
Salt, to taste
½ cup toasted, chopped cashews, for garnish
Yogurt Sauce:
¼ cup plain yogurt
2 tablespoons sour cream
1 teaspoon honey
1 teaspoon lemon juice
Pinch cayenne pepper
Salt, to taste
1 tablespoon chopped fresh cilantro, plus leaves for garnish

1. In a large mixing bowl, toss the cauliflower florets with the olive oil, curry powder, and salt.
2. Place the cauliflower florets in an air fryer basket.
3. Slide the basket into the air fryer oven. Cook at 400°F (205°C) for 12 minutes.
4. Stir the cauliflower florets twice during cooking.
5. When cooking is complete, the cauliflower should be golden brown.
6. Meanwhile, mix all the ingredients for the yogurt sauce in a small bowl and whisk to combine.
7. Remove the cauliflower from the air fryer oven and drizzle with the yogurt sauce. Scatter the toasted cashews and cilantro on top and serve immediately.

Baked Turnip and Zucchini

Prep time: 5 minutes | Cook time: 18 minutes | Serves 4

3 turnips, sliced
1 large zucchini, sliced
1 large red onion, cut into rings
2 cloves garlic, crushed
1 tablespoon olive oil
Salt and black pepper, to taste

1. Put the turnips, zucchini, red onion, and garlic in a baking pan. Drizzle the olive oil over the top and sprinkle with the salt and pepper.
2. Slide the pan into the air fryer oven. Cook at 330°F (166°C) for 18 minutes.
3. When cooking is complete, the vegetables should be tender. Remove from the air fryer oven and serve on a plate.

Cheesy Asparagus and Potato Platter

Prep time: 5 minutes | Cook time: 26 minutes | Serves 5

4 medium potatoes, cut into wedges
Cooking spray
1 bunch asparagus, trimmed
2 tablespoons olive oil
Salt and pepper, to taste
Cheese Sauce:
¼ cup crumbled cottage cheese
¼ cup buttermilk
1 tablespoon whole-grain mustard
Salt and black pepper, to taste

1. Spritz an air fryer basket with cooking spray.
2. Put the potatoes in an air fryer basket.
3. Slide the basket into the air fryer oven. Cook at 400°F (205°C) for 20 minutes.
4. Stir the potatoes halfway through.
5. When cooking is complete, the potatoes should be golden brown.
6. Remove the potatoes from the air fryer oven to a platter. Cover the potatoes with foil to keep warm. Set aside.
7. Place the asparagus in the air fryer basket and drizzle with the olive oil. Sprinkle with salt and pepper.
8. Cook at 400°F (205°C) for 6 minutes. Stir the asparagus halfway through.
9. When cooking is complete, the asparagus should be crispy.
10. Meanwhile, make the cheese sauce by stirring together the cottage cheese, buttermilk, and mustard in a small bowl. Season as needed with salt and pepper.
11. Transfer the asparagus to the platter of potatoes and drizzle with the cheese sauce. Serve immediately.

Cheesy Broccoli Tots

Prep time: 20 minutes | Cook time: 15 minutes | Serves 4

12 ounces (340 g) frozen broccoli, thawed, drained, and patted dry
1 large egg, lightly beaten
½ cup seasoned whole-wheat bread crumbs
¼ cup shredded reduced-fat sharp Cheddar cheese
¼ cup grated Parmesan cheese
1½ teaspoons minced garlic
Salt and freshly ground black pepper, to taste
Cooking spray

1. Spritz an air fryer basket lightly with cooking spray.
2. Place the remaining ingredients into a food processor and process until the mixture resembles a coarse meal. Transfer the mixture to a bowl.
3. Using a tablespoon, scoop out the broccoli mixture and form into 24 oval "tater tot" shapes with your hands.
4. Put the tots in the prepared air fryer basket, spacing them 1 inch apart. Mist the tots lightly with cooking spray.
5. Slide the basket into the air fryer oven. Cook at 375°F (190°C) for 15 minutes.
6. Flip the tots halfway through the cooking time.
7. When done, the tots will be lightly browned and crispy. Remove from the air fryer oven and serve on a plate.

Crispy Fried Okra with Chili

Prep time: 5 minutes | Cook time: 10 minutes | Serves 4

3 tablespoons sour cream
2 tablespoons flour
2 tablespoons semolina
½ teaspoon red chili powder
Salt and black pepper, to taste
1 pound (454 g) okra, halved
Cooking spray

1. Spray an air fryer basket with cooking spray. Set aside.
2. In a shallow bowl, place the sour cream. In another shallow bowl, thoroughly combine the flour, semolina, red chili powder, salt, and pepper.
3. Dredge the okra in the sour cream, then roll in the flour mixture until evenly coated. Transfer the okra to an air fryer basket.
4. Slide the basket into the air fryer oven. Cook at 400°F (205°C) for 10 minutes.
5. Flip the okra halfway through the cooking time.
6. When cooking is complete, the okra should be golden brown and crispy. Remove from the air fryer oven. Cool for 5 minutes before serving.

Crispy Tofu Sticks

Prep time: 5 minutes | Cook time: 14 minutes | Serves 4

2 tablespoons olive oil, divided
½ cup flour
½ cup crushed cornflakes
Salt and black pepper, to taste
14 ounces (397 g) firm tofu, cut into ½-inch-thick strips

1. Grease an air fryer basket with 1 tablespoon of olive oil.
2. Combine the flour, cornflakes, salt, and pepper on a plate.
3. Dredge the tofu strips in the flour mixture until they are completely coated. Transfer the tofu strips to the greased air fryer basket.
4. Drizzle the remaining 1 tablespoon of olive oil over the top of tofu strips.
5. Slide the basket into the air fryer oven. Cook at 360°F (182°C) for 14 minutes.
6. Flip the tofu strips halfway through the cooking time.
7. When cooking is complete, the tofu strips should be crispy. Remove from the air fryer oven and serve warm.

Cheesy Rice and Olives Stuffed Peppers

Prep time: 5 minutes | Cook time: 16 to 17 minutes | Serves 4

4 red bell peppers, tops sliced off
2 cups cooked rice
1 cup crumbled feta cheese
1 onion, chopped
¼ cup sliced kalamata olives
¾ cup tomato sauce
1 tablespoon Greek seasoning
Salt and black pepper, to taste
2 tablespoons chopped fresh dill, for serving

1. Microwave the red bell peppers for 1 to 2 minutes until tender.
2. When ready, transfer the red bell peppers to a plate to cool.
3. Mix the cooked rice, feta cheese, onion, kalamata olives, tomato sauce, Greek seasoning, salt, and pepper in a medium bowl and stir until well combined.
4. Divide the rice mixture among the red bell peppers and transfer to a greased baking dish.
5. Slide the baking dish into the air fryer oven. Cook at 360°F (182°C) for 15 minutes.
6. When cooking is complete, the rice should be heated through and the vegetables should be soft.
7. Remove from the air fryer oven and serve with the dill sprinkled on top.

Cream Cheese Stuffed Bell Peppers

Prep time: 5 minutes | Cook time: 15 minutes | Serves 2

2 bell peppers, tops and seeds removed
Salt and pepper, to taste
⅔ cup cream cheese
2 tablespoons mayonnaise
1 tablespoon chopped fresh celery stalks
Cooking spray

1. Spritz an air fryer basket with cooking spray.
2. Place the peppers in an air fryer basket.
3. Slide the basket into the air fryer oven. Cook at 400°F (205°C) for 10 minutes.
4. Flip the peppers halfway through.
5. When cooking is complete, the peppers should be crisp-tender.
6. Remove from the air fryer oven to a plate and season with salt and pepper.
7. Mix the cream cheese, mayo, and celery in a small bowl and stir to incorporate. Evenly stuff the roasted peppers with the cream cheese mixture with a spoon. Serve immediately.

Fried Root Vegetable Medley with Thyme

Prep time: 10 minutes | Cook time: 22 minutes | Serves 4

2 carrots, sliced
2 potatoes, cut into chunks
1 rutabaga, cut into chunks
1 turnip, cut into chunks
1 beet, cut into chunks
8 shallots, halved
2 tablespoons olive oil
Salt and black pepper, to taste
2 tablespoons tomato pesto
2 tablespoons water
2 tablespoons chopped fresh thyme

1. Toss the carrots, potatoes, rutabaga, turnip, beet, shallots, olive oil, salt, and pepper in a large mixing bowl until the root vegetables are evenly coated.
2. Place the root vegetables in an air fryer basket.
3. Slide the basket into the air fryer oven. Cook at 400°F (205°C) for 22 minutes.
4. Stir the vegetables twice during cooking.
5. When cooking is complete, the vegetables should be tender.
6. Meanwhile, in a small bowl, whisk together the tomato pesto and water until smooth.
7. When ready, remove the root vegetables from the air fryer oven to a platter. Drizzle with the tomato pesto mixture and sprinkle with the thyme. Serve immediately.

Cayenne Tahini Kale

Prep time: 5 minutes | Cook time: 15 minutes | Serves 2 to 4

Dressing:
¼ cup tahini
¼ cup fresh lemon juice
2 tablespoons olive oil
1 teaspoon sesame seeds
½ teaspoon garlic powder
¼ teaspoon cayenne pepper
Kale:
4 cups packed torn kale leaves (stems and ribs removed and leaves torn into palm-size pieces)
Kosher salt and freshly ground black pepper, to taste

1. Make the dressing: Whisk together the tahini, lemon juice, olive oil, sesame seeds, garlic powder, and cayenne pepper in a large bowl until well mixed.
2. Add the kale and massage the dressing thoroughly all over the leaves. Sprinkle the salt and pepper to season.
3. Place the kale in an air fryer basket.
4. Slide the basket into the air fryer oven. Cook at 350°F (180°C) for 15 minutes.
5. When cooking is complete, the leaves should be slightly wilted and crispy. Remove from the air fryer oven and serve on a plate.

Cheese-Walnut Stuffed Mushrooms

Prep time: 5 minutes | Cook time: 10 minutes | Serves 4

4 large portobello mushrooms
1 tablespoon canola oil
½ cup shredded Mozzarella cheese
⅓ cup minced walnuts
2 tablespoons chopped fresh parsley
Cooking spray

1. Spritz an air fryer basket with cooking spray.
2. On a clean work surface, remove the mushroom stems. Scoop out the gills with a spoon and discard. Coat the mushrooms with canola oil. Top each mushroom evenly with the shredded Mozzarella cheese, followed by the minced walnuts.
3. Arrange the mushrooms in the air fryer basket.
4. Slide the basket into the air fryer oven. Cook at 350°F (180°C) for 10 minutes.
5. When cooking is complete, the mushroom should be golden brown.
6. Transfer the mushrooms to a plate and sprinkle the parsley on top for garnish before serving.

Hearty Roasted Veggie Salad

Prep time: 5 minutes | Cook time: 20 minutes | Serves 2

1 potato, chopped
1 carrot, sliced diagonally
1 cup cherry tomatoes
½ small beetroot, sliced
¼ onion, sliced
½ teaspoon turmeric
½ teaspoon cumin
¼ teaspoon sea salt
2 tablespoons olive oil, divided
A handful of arugula
A handful of baby spinach
Juice of 1 lemon
3 tablespoons canned chickpeas, for serving
Parmesan shavings, for serving

1. Combine the potato, carrot, cherry tomatoes, beetroot, onion, turmeric, cumin, salt, and 1 tablespoon of olive oil in a large bowl and toss until well coated.
2. Arrange the veggies in an air fryer basket.
3. Slide the basket into the air fryer oven. Cook at 370°F (188°C) for 20 minutes.
4. Stir the vegetables halfway through.
5. When cooking is complete, the potatoes should be golden brown.
6. Let the veggies cool for 5 to 10 minutes in the air fryer oven.
7. Put the arugula, baby spinach, lemon juice, and remaining 1 tablespoon of olive oil in a salad bowl and stir to combine. Mix in the roasted veggies and toss well.
8. Scatter the chickpeas and Parmesan shavings on top and serve immediately.

Lemony Wax Beans

Prep time: 5 minutes | Cook time: 12 minutes | Serves 4

2 pounds (907 g) wax beans
2 tablespoons extra-virgin olive oil
Salt and freshly ground black pepper, to taste
Juice of ½ lemon, for serving

1. Line a baking sheet with aluminum foil.
2. Toss the wax beans with the olive oil in a large bowl. Lightly season with salt and pepper.
3. Spread out the wax beans on the baking sheet.
4. Place the baking sheet into the air fryer oven. Cook at 400°F (205°C) for 12 minutes.
5. When done, the beans will be caramelized and tender. Remove from the air fryer oven to a plate and serve sprinkled with the lemon juice.

Easy Cheesy Vegetable Quesadilla

Prep time: 5 minutes | Cook time: 10 minutes | Serves 1

1 teaspoon olive oil
2 flour tortillas
¼ zucchini, sliced
¼ yellow bell pepper, sliced
¼ cup shredded gouda cheese
1 tablespoon chopped cilantro
½ green onion, sliced

1. Coat an air fryer basket with 1 teaspoon of olive oil.
2. Arrange a flour tortilla in the air fryer basket and scatter the top with zucchini, bell pepper, gouda cheese, cilantro, and green onion. Place the other flour tortilla on top.
3. Slide the basket into the air fryer oven. Cook at 390ºF (199ºC) for 10 minutes.
4. When cooking is complete, the tortillas should be lightly browned and the vegetables should be tender. Remove from the air fryer oven and cool for 5 minutes before slicing into wedges.

Rosemary Beets with Balsamic Glaze

Prep time: 5 minutes | Cook time: 10 minutes | Serves 2

Beet:
2 beets, cubed
2 tablespoons olive oil
2 springs rosemary, chopped
Salt and black pepper, to taste
Balsamic Glaze:
⅓ cup balsamic vinegar
1 tablespoon honey

1. Combine the beets, olive oil, rosemary, salt, and pepper in a mixing bowl and toss until the beets are completely coated.
2. Place the beets in an air fryer basket.
3. Slide the basket into the air fryer oven. Cook at 400ºF (205ºC) for 10 minutes.
4. Stir the vegetables halfway through.
5. When cooking is complete, the beets should be crisp and browned at the edges.
6. Meanwhile, make the balsamic glaze: Place the balsamic vinegar and honey in a small saucepan and bring to a boil over medium heat. When the sauce boils, reduce the heat to medium-low heat and simmer until the liquid is reduced by half.
7. When ready, remove the beets from the air fryer oven to a platter. Pour the balsamic glaze over the top and serve immediately.

Cheesy Cabbage Wedges

Prep time: 5 minutes | Cook time: 20 minutes | Serves 4

4 tablespoons melted butter
1 head cabbage, cut into wedges
1 cup shredded Parmesan cheese
Salt and black pepper, to taste
½ cup shredded Mozzarella cheese

1. Brush the melted butter over the cut sides of cabbage wedges and sprinkle both sides with the Parmesan cheese. Season with salt and pepper to taste.
2. Place the cabbage wedges in an air fryer basket.
3. Slide the basket into the air fryer oven. Cook at 380ºF (193ºC) for 20 minutes.
4. Flip the cabbage halfway through the cooking time.
5. When cooking is complete, the cabbage wedges should be lightly browned. Transfer the cabbage wedges to a plate and serve with the Mozzarella cheese sprinkled on top.

Spicy Thai-Style Vegetables

Prep time: 10 minutes | Cook time: 8 minutes | Serves 4

1 small head Napa cabbage, shredded, divided
1 medium carrot, cut into thin coins
8 ounces (227 g) snow peas
1 red or green bell pepper, sliced into thin strips
1 tablespoon vegetable oil
2 tablespoons soy sauce
1 tablespoon sesame oil
2 tablespoons brown sugar
2 tablespoons freshly squeezed lime juice
2 teaspoons red or green Thai curry paste
1 serrano chile, deseeded and minced
1 cup frozen mango slices, thawed
½ cup chopped roasted peanuts or cashews

1. Put half the Napa cabbage in a large bowl, along with the carrot, snow peas, and bell pepper. Drizzle with the vegetable oil and toss to coat. Spread them evenly on a sheet pan.
2. Slide the pan into the air fryer oven. Cook at 375ºF (190ºC) for 8 minutes.
3. Meanwhile, whisk together the soy sauce, sesame oil, brown sugar, lime juice, and curry paste in a small bowl.
4. When done, the vegetables should be tender and crisp. Remove the pan and put the vegetables back into the bowl. Add the chile, mango slices, and the remaining cabbage. Pour over the dressing and toss to coat. Top with the roasted nuts and serve.

Crispy Veggies with Halloumi

Prep time: 5 minutes | Cook time: 14 minutes | Serves 2

2 zucchinis, cut into even chunks
1 large eggplant, peeled, cut into chunks
1 large carrot, cut into chunks
6 ounces (170 g) halloumi cheese, cubed
2 teaspoons olive oil
Salt and black pepper, to taste
1 teaspoon dried mixed herbs

1. Combine the zucchinis, eggplant, carrot, cheese, olive oil, salt, and pepper in a large bowl and toss to coat well.
2. Spread the mixture evenly in an air fryer basket.
3. Slide the basket into the air fryer oven. Cook at 340°F (171°C) for 14 minutes.
4. Stir the mixture once during cooking.
5. When cooking is complete, they should be crispy and golden. Remove from the air fryer oven and serve topped with mixed herbs.

Sweet and Spicy Broccoli

Prep time: 10 minutes | Cook time: 15 to 20 minutes | Serves 4

½ teaspoon olive oil, plus more for greasing
1 pound (454 g) fresh broccoli, cut into florets
½ tablespoon minced garlic
Salt, to taste
Sauce:
1½ tablespoons soy sauce
2 teaspoons hot sauce or sriracha
1½ teaspoons honey
1 teaspoon white vinegar
Freshly ground black pepper, to taste

1. Grease an air fryer basket with olive oil.
2. Add the broccoli florets, ½ teaspoon of olive oil, and garlic to a large bowl and toss well. Season with salt to taste.
3. Put the broccoli in the air fryer basket.
4. Slide the basket into the air fryer oven. Cook at 400°F (205°C) for 15 minutes.
5. Stir the broccoli florets three times during cooking.
6. Meanwhile, whisk together all the ingredients for the sauce in a small bowl until well incorporated. If the honey doesn't incorporate well, microwave the sauce for 10 to 20 seconds until the honey is melted.
7. When cooking is complete, the broccoli should be lightly browned and crispy. Continue cooking for 5 minutes, if desired. Remove from the air fryer oven to a serving bowl. Pour over the sauce and toss to combine. Add more salt and pepper, if needed. Serve warm.

Herbed Broccoli with Cheese

Prep time: 5 minutes | Cook time: 18 minutes | Serves 4

1 large-sized head broccoli, stemmed and cut into small florets
2½ tablespoons canola oil
2 teaspoons dried basil
2 teaspoons dried rosemary
Salt and ground black pepper, to taste
⅓ cup grated yellow cheese

1. Bring a pot of lightly salted water to a boil. Add the broccoli florets to the boiling water and let boil for about 3 minutes.
2. Drain the broccoli florets well and transfer to a large bowl. Add the canola oil, basil, rosemary, salt, and black pepper to the bowl and toss until the broccoli is fully coated. Place the broccoli in an air fryer basket.
3. Slide the basket into the air fryer oven. Cook at 390°F (199°C) for 15 minutes.
4. Stir the broccoli halfway through the cooking time.
5. When cooking is complete, the broccoli should be crisp. Remove from the air fryer oven. Serve the broccoli warm with grated cheese sprinkled on top.

Sesame-Thyme Whole Maitake Mushrooms

Prep time: 5 minutes | Cook time: 15 minutes | Serves 2

1 tablespoon soy sauce
2 teaspoons toasted sesame oil
3 teaspoons vegetable oil, divided
1 garlic clove, minced
7 ounces (198 g) maitake (hen of the woods) mushrooms
½ teaspoon flaky sea salt
½ teaspoon sesame seeds
½ teaspoon finely chopped fresh thyme leaves

1. Whisk together the soy sauce, sesame oil, 1 teaspoon of vegetable oil, and garlic in a small bowl.
2. Arrange the mushrooms in an air fryer basket. Drizzle the soy sauce mixture over the mushrooms.
3. Slide the basket into the air fryer oven. Cook at 300°F (150°C) for 15 minutes.
4. After 10 minutes, remove from the air fryer oven. Flip the mushrooms and sprinkle the sea salt, sesame seeds, and thyme leaves on top. Drizzle the remaining 2 teaspoons of vegetable oil all over. Return to the air fryer oven and continue roasting for an additional 5 minutes.
5. When cooking is complete, remove the mushrooms from the air fryer oven to a plate and serve hot.

Garlicky Sesame Carrots

Prep time: 5 minutes | Cook time: 16 minutes | Serves 4 to 6

1 pound (454 g) baby carrots
1 tablespoon sesame oil
½ teaspoon dried dill
Pinch salt
Freshly ground black pepper, to taste
6 cloves garlic, peeled
3 tablespoons sesame seeds

1. In a medium bowl, drizzle the baby carrots with the sesame oil. Sprinkle with the dill, salt, and pepper and toss to coat well.
2. Place the baby carrots in an air fryer basket.
3. Slide the basket into the air fryer oven. Cook at 380°F (193°C) for 16 minutes.
4. After 8 minutes, remove from the air fryer oven and stir in the garlic. Return to the air fryer oven and continue roasting for 8 minutes more.
5. When cooking is complete, the carrots should be lightly browned. Remove the basket from the air fryer oven and serve sprinkled with the sesame seeds.

Honey-Glazed Roasted Veggies

Prep time: 15 minutes | Cook time: 20 minutes | Makes 3 cups

Glaze:
2 tablespoons raw honey
2 teaspoons minced garlic
¼ teaspoon dried marjoram
¼ teaspoon dried basil
¼ teaspoon dried oregano
⅛ teaspoon dried sage
⅛ teaspoon dried rosemary
⅛ teaspoon dried thyme
½ teaspoon salt
¼ teaspoon ground black pepper
Veggies:
3 to 4 medium red potatoes, cut into 1- to 2-inch pieces
1 small zucchini, cut into 1- to 2-inch pieces
1 small carrot, sliced into ¼-inch rounds
1 (10.5-ounce / 298-g) package cherry tomatoes, halved
1 cup sliced mushrooms
3 tablespoons olive oil

1. Combine the honey, garlic, marjoram, basil, oregano, sage, rosemary, thyme, salt, and pepper in a small bowl and stir to mix well. Set aside.
2. Place the red potatoes, zucchini, carrot, cherry tomatoes, and mushroom in a large bowl. Drizzle with the olive oil and toss to coat.
3. Pour the veggies into an air fryer basket.
4. Slide the basket into the air fryer oven. Cook at 380°F (193°C) for 15 minutes.
5. Stir the veggies halfway through.
6. When cooking is complete, the vegetables should be tender.
7. When ready, transfer the roasted veggies to the large bowl. Pour the honey mixture over the veggies, tossing to coat.
8. Spread out the veggies in a baking pan and place in the air fryer oven.
9. Increase the temperature to 390°F (199°C) for 5 minutes on Roast.
10. When cooking is complete, the veggies should be tender and glazed. Serve warm.

Roasted Bell Peppers with Garlic

Prep time: 10 minutes | Cook time: 22 minutes | Serves 4

1 green bell pepper, sliced into 1-inch strips
1 red bell pepper, sliced into 1-inch strips
1 orange bell pepper, sliced into 1-inch strips
1 yellow bell pepper, sliced into 1-inch strips
2 tablespoons olive oil, divided
½ teaspoon dried marjoram
Pinch salt
Freshly ground black pepper, to taste
1 head garlic

1. Toss the bell peppers with 1 tablespoon of olive oil in a large bowl until well coated. Season with the marjoram, salt, and pepper. Toss again and set aside.
2. Cut off the top of a head of garlic. Place the garlic cloves on a large square of aluminum foil. Drizzle the top with the remaining 1 tablespoon of olive oil and wrap the garlic cloves in foil.
3. Transfer the garlic to an air fryer basket.
4. Slide the basket into the air fryer oven. Cook at 330°F (166°C) for 15 minutes.
5. After 15 minutes, remove the air fryer basket from the air fryer oven and add the bell peppers. Return to the air fryer oven for 7 minutes.
6. When cooking is complete or until the garlic is soft and the bell peppers are tender.
7. Transfer the cooked bell peppers to a plate. Remove the garlic and unwrap the foil. Let the garlic rest for a few minutes. Once cooled, squeeze the roasted garlic cloves out of their skins and add them to the plate of bell peppers. Stir well and serve immediately.

Vegan and Vegetarian

Italian Baked Tofu

Prep time: 5 minutes | Cook time: 10 minutes | Serves 2

1 tablespoon soy sauce
1 tablespoon water
⅓ teaspoon garlic powder
⅓ teaspoon onion powder
⅓ teaspoon dried oregano
⅓ teaspoon dried basil
Black pepper, to taste
6 ounces (170 g) extra firm tofu, pressed and cubed

1. In a large mixing bowl, whisk together the soy sauce, water, garlic powder, onion powder, oregano, basil, and black pepper. Add the tofu cubes, stirring to coat, and let them marinate for 10 minutes.
2. Arrange the tofu in an air fryer basket.
3. Slide the basket into the air fryer oven. Cook at 390°F (199°C) for 10 minutes.
4. Flip the tofu halfway through the cooking time.
5. When cooking is complete, the tofu should be crisp.
6. Remove from the air fryer oven to a plate and serve.

Vegetable and Cheese Stuffed Tomatoes

Prep time: 10 minutes | Cook time: 18 minutes | Serves 4

4 medium beefsteak tomatoes, rinsed
½ cup grated carrot
1 medium onion, chopped
1 garlic clove, minced
2 teaspoons olive oil
2 cups fresh baby spinach
¼ cup crumbled low-sodium feta cheese
½ teaspoon dried basil

1. On your cutting board, cut a thin slice off the top of each tomato. Scoop out a ¼- to ½-inch-thick tomato pulp and place the tomatoes upside down on paper towels to drain. Set aside.
2. Stir together the carrot, onion, garlic, and olive oil in a baking pan.
3. Slide the pan into the air fryer oven. Cook at 350°F (180°C) for 5 minutes.
4. Stir the vegetables halfway through.
5. When cooking is complete, the carrot should be crisp-tender.
6. Remove the pan from the air fryer oven and stir in the spinach, feta cheese, and basil.
7. Spoon ¼ of the vegetable mixture into each tomato and transfer the stuffed tomatoes to the air fryer oven. Set time to 13 minutes.
8. When cooking is complete, the filling should be hot and the tomatoes should be lightly caramelized.
9. Let the tomatoes cool for 5 minutes and serve.

Honey-Glazed Baby Carrots

Prep time: 5 minutes | Cook time: 12 minutes | Serves 4

1 pound (454 g) baby carrots
2 tablespoons olive oil
1 tablespoon honey
1 teaspoon dried dill
Salt and black pepper, to taste

1. Place the carrots in a large bowl. Add the olive oil, honey, dill, salt, and pepper and toss to coat well.
2. Transfer the carrots to an air fryer basket.
3. Slide the basket into the air fryer oven. Cook at 350°F (180°C) for 12 minutes.
4. Stir the carrots once during cooking.
5. When cooking is complete, the carrots should be crisp-tender. Remove from the air fryer oven and serve warm.

Roasted Asparagus with Eggs and Tomatoes

Prep time: 10 minutes | Cook time: 12 minutes | Serves 4

2 pounds (907 g) asparagus, trimmed
3 tablespoons extra-virgin olive oil, divided
1 teaspoon kosher salt, divided
1 pint cherry tomatoes
4 large eggs
¼ teaspoon freshly ground black pepper

1. Put the asparagus on a sheet pan and drizzle with 2 tablespoons of olive oil, tossing to coat. Season with ½ teaspoon of kosher salt.
2. Slide the pan into the air fryer oven. Cook at 375°F (190°C) for 12 minutes.
3. Meanwhile, toss the cherry tomatoes with the remaining 1 tablespoon of olive oil in a medium bowl until well coated.
4. After 6 minutes, remove the pan and toss the asparagus. Evenly spread the asparagus in the middle of the sheet pan. Add the tomatoes around the perimeter of the pan. Return to the air fryer oven and continue cooking.
5. After 2 minutes, remove from the air fryer oven.
6. Carefully crack the eggs, one at a time, over the asparagus, spacing them out. Season with the remaining ½ teaspoon of kosher salt and the pepper. Return to the air fryer oven and continue cooking. Cook for an additional 3 to 7 minutes, or until the eggs are cooked to your desired doneness.
7. When done, divide the asparagus and eggs among four plates. Top each plate evenly with the tomatoes and serve.

Garlic Stuffed Mushrooms

Prep time: 5 minutes | Cook time: 12 minutes | Serves 2

18 medium-sized white mushrooms
1 small onion, peeled and chopped
4 garlic cloves, peeled and minced
2 tablespoons olive oil
2 teaspoons cumin powder
A pinch ground allspice
Fine sea salt and freshly ground black pepper, to taste

1. On a clean work surface, remove the mushroom stems. Using a spoon, scoop out the mushroom gills and discard.
2. Thoroughly combine the onion, garlic, olive oil, cumin powder, allspice, salt, and pepper in a mixing bowl. Stuff the mushrooms evenly with the mixture.
3. Place the stuffed mushrooms in an air fryer basket.
4. Slide the basket into the air fryer oven. Cook at 345°F (174°C) for 12 minutes.
5. When cooking is complete, the mushroom should be browned.
6. Cool for 5 minutes before serving.

Ratatouille

Prep time: 10 minutes | Cook time: 12 minutes | Serves 6

1 medium zucchini, sliced ½-inch thick
1 small eggplant, peeled and sliced ½-inch thick
2 teaspoons kosher salt, divided
4 tablespoons extra-virgin olive oil, divided
3 garlic cloves, minced
1 small onion, chopped
1 small red bell pepper, cut into ½-inch chunks
1 small green bell pepper, cut into ½-inch chunks
½ teaspoon dried oregano
¼ teaspoon freshly ground black pepper
1 pint cherry tomatoes
2 tablespoons minced fresh basil
1 cup panko bread crumbs
½ cup grated Parmesan cheese (optional)

1. Season one side of the zucchini and eggplant slices with ¾ teaspoon of salt. Put the slices, salted side down, on a rack set over a baking sheet. Sprinkle the other sides with ¾ teaspoon of salt. Allow to sit for 10 minutes, or until the slices begin to exude water. When ready, rinse and dry them. Cut the zucchini slices into quarters and the eggplant slices into eighths.
2. Pour the zucchini and eggplant into a large bowl, along with 2 tablespoons of olive oil, garlic, onion, bell peppers, oregano, and black pepper. Toss to coat well. Arrange the vegetables on a sheet pan.
3. Slide the pan into the air fryer oven. Cook at 375°F (190°C) for 12 minutes.
4. Meanwhile, add the tomatoes and basil to the large bowl. Sprinkle with the remaining ½ teaspoon of salt and 1 tablespoon of olive oil. Toss well and set aside.
5. Stir together the remaining 1 tablespoon of olive oil, panko, and Parmesan cheese (if desired) in a small bowl.
6. After 6 minutes, remove the pan and add the tomato mixture to the sheet pan and stir to mix well. Scatter the panko mixture on top. Return to the air fryer oven and continue cooking for 6 minutes, or until the vegetables are softened and the topping is golden brown.
7. Cool for 5 minutes before serving.

Stuffed Squash with Tomatoes and Poblano

Prep time: 5 minutes | Cook time: 30 minutes | Serves 4

1 pound (454 g) butternut squash, ends trimmed
2 teaspoons olive oil, divided
6 grape tomatoes, halved
1 poblano pepper, cut into strips
Salt and black pepper, to taste
¼ cup grated Mozzarella cheese

1. Using a large knife, cut the squash in half lengthwise on a flat work surface. This recipe just needs half of the squash. Scoop out the flesh to make room for the stuffing. Coat the squash half with 1 teaspoon of olive oil.
2. Put the squash half in an air fryer basket.
3. Slide the basket into the air fryer oven. Cook at 350°F (180°C) for 15 minutes.
4. Flip the squash halfway through.
5. When cooking is complete, the squash should be tender.
6. Meanwhile, thoroughly combine the tomatoes, poblano pepper, remaining 1 teaspoon of olive oil, salt, and pepper in a bowl.
7. Remove the basket from the air fryer oven and spoon the tomato mixture into the squash. Return to the air fryer oven. Cook for 15 more minutes.
8. After 12 minutes, remove from the air fryer oven. Scatter the Mozzarella cheese on top. Return to the air fryer oven and continue cooking.
9. When cooking is complete, the tomatoes should be soft and the cheese should be melted.
10. Cool for 5 minutes before serving.

Lemony Brussels Sprouts and Tomatoes

Prep time: 15 minutes | Cook time: 20 minutes | Serves 4

1 pound (454 g) Brussels sprouts, trimmed and halved
1 tablespoon extra-virgin olive oil
Sea Salt and freshly ground black pepper, to taste
½ cup sun-dried tomatoes, chopped
2 tablespoons freshly squeezed lemon juice
1 teaspoon lemon zest

1. Line a large baking sheet with aluminum foil.
2. Toss the Brussels sprouts with the olive oil in a large bowl. Sprinkle with salt and black pepper.
3. Spread the Brussels sprouts in a single layer on the baking sheet.
4. Slide the baking sheet into the air fryer oven. Cook at 400°F (205°C) for 20 minutes.
5. When done, the Brussels sprouts should be caramelized. Remove from the air fryer oven to a serving bowl, along with the tomatoes, lemon juice, and lemon zest. Toss to combine. Serve immediately.

Tofu, Carrot and Cauliflower Rice

Prep time: 10 minutes | Cook time: 22 minutes | Serves 4

½ block tofu, crumbled
1 cup diced carrot
½ cup diced onions
2 tablespoons soy sauce
1 teaspoon turmeric
Cauliflower:
3 cups cauliflower rice
½ cup chopped broccoli
½ cup frozen peas
2 tablespoons soy sauce
1 tablespoon minced ginger
2 garlic cloves, minced
1 tablespoon rice vinegar
1½ teaspoons toasted sesame oil

1. Mix the tofu, carrot, onions, soy sauce, and turmeric in a baking dish and stir until well incorporated.
2. Slide the baking dish into the air fryer oven. Cook at 370°F (188°C) for 10 minutes.
3. Flip the tofu and carrot halfway through the cooking time.
4. When cooking is complete, the tofu should be crisp.
5. Meanwhile, in a large bowl, combine all the ingredients for the cauliflower and toss well.
6. Remove the dish from the air fryer oven and add the cauliflower mixture to the tofu and stir to combine.
7. Return the baking dish to the air fryer oven for 12 minutes on Roast.
8. When cooking is complete, the vegetables should be tender.
9. Cool for 5 minutes before serving.

Maple and Pecan Granola

Prep time: 5 minutes | Cook time: 20 minutes | Serves 4

1½ cups rolled oats
¼ cup maple syrup
¼ cup pecan pieces
1 teaspoon vanilla extract
½ teaspoon ground cinnamon

1. Line a baking sheet with parchment paper.
2. Mix together the oats, maple syrup, pecan pieces, vanilla, and cinnamon in a large bowl and stir until the oats and pecan pieces are completely coated. Spread the mixture evenly on the baking sheet.
3. Slide the baking sheet into the air fryer oven. Cook at 300°F (150°C) for 20 minutes.
4. Stir once halfway through the cooking time.
5. When done, remove from the air fryer oven and cool for 30 minutes before serving. The granola may still be a bit soft right after removing, but it will gradually firm up as it cools.

Mediterranean Baked Eggs with Spinach

Prep time: 10 minutes | Cook time: 10 minutes | Serves 2

2 tablespoons olive oil
4 eggs, whisked
5 ounces (142 g) fresh spinach, chopped
1 medium-sized tomato, chopped
1 teaspoon fresh lemon juice
½ teaspoon ground black pepper
½ teaspoon coarse salt
½ cup roughly chopped fresh basil leaves, for garnish

1. Generously grease a baking pan with olive oil.
2. Stir together the remaining ingredients except the basil leaves in the greased baking pan until well incorporated.
3. Slide the baking pan in the air fryer oven. Cook at 280°F (137°C) for 10 minutes.
4. When cooking is complete, the eggs should be completely set and the vegetables should be tender. Remove from the air fryer oven and serve garnished with the fresh basil leaves.

Paprika Cauliflower

Prep time: 10 minutes | Cook time: 20 minutes | Serves 4

1 large head cauliflower, broken into small florets
2 teaspoons smoked paprika
1 teaspoon garlic powder
Salt and freshly ground black pepper, to taste
Cooking spray

1. Spray an air fryer basket with cooking spray.
2. In a medium bowl, toss the cauliflower florets with the smoked paprika and garlic powder until evenly coated. Sprinkle with salt and pepper.
3. Place the cauliflower florets in the air fryer basket and lightly mist with cooking spray.
4. Slide the basket into the air fryer oven. Cook at 400°F (205°C) for 20 minutes.
5. Stir the cauliflower four times during cooking.
6. Remove the cauliflower from the air fryer oven and serve hot.

Stuffed Portobellos with Peppers and Cheese

Prep time: 15 minutes | Cook time: 15 minutes | Serves 4

4 tablespoons sherry vinegar or white wine vinegar
6 garlic cloves, minced, divided
1 tablespoon fresh thyme leaves
1 teaspoon Dijon mustard
1 teaspoon kosher salt, divided
¼ cup plus 3¼ teaspoons extra-virgin olive oil, divided
8 portobello mushroom caps, each about 3 inches across, patted dry
1 small red or yellow bell pepper, thinly sliced
1 small green bell pepper, thinly sliced
1 small onion, thinly sliced
¼ teaspoon red pepper flakes
Freshly ground black pepper, to taste
4 ounces (113 g) shredded Fontina cheese

4. Stir together the vinegar, 4 minced garlic cloves, thyme, mustard, and ½ teaspoon of kosher salt in a small bowl. Slowly pour in ¼ cup of olive oil, whisking constantly, or until an emulsion is formed. Reserve 2 tablespoons of the marinade and set aside.
5. Put the mushrooms in a resealable plastic bag and pour in the marinade. Seal and shake the bag, coating the mushrooms in the marinade. Transfer the mushrooms to a sheet pan, gill-side down.
6. Put the remaining 2 minced garlic cloves, bell peppers, onion, red pepper flakes, remaining ½ teaspoon of salt, and black pepper in a medium bowl. Drizzle with the remaining 3¼ teaspoons of olive oil and toss well. Transfer the bell pepper mixture to the sheet pan.
7. Slide the pan into the air fryer oven. Cook at 375°F (190°C) for 12 minutes.
8. After 7 minutes, remove the pan and stir the peppers and flip the mushrooms. Return to the air fryer oven and continue cooking for 5 minutes.
9. Remove the pan from the air fryer oven and place the pepper mixture onto a cutting board and coarsely chop.
10. Brush both sides of the mushrooms with the reserved 2 tablespoons marinade. Stuff the caps evenly with the pepper mixture. Scatter the cheese on top.
11. Slide the pan into the air fryer oven. Cook for 3 minutes.
12. When done, the mushrooms should be tender and the cheese should be melted.
13. Serve warm.

Stuffed Peppers with Beans and Rice

Prep time: 10 minutes | Cook time: 18 minutes | Serves 4

4 medium red, green, or yellow bell peppers, halved and deseeded
4 tablespoons extra-virgin olive oil, divided
½ teaspoon kosher salt, divided
1 (15-ounce / 425-g) can chickpeas
1½ cups cooked white rice
½ cup diced roasted red peppers
¼ cup chopped parsley
½ small onion, finely chopped
3 garlic cloves, minced
½ teaspoon cumin
¼ teaspoon freshly ground black pepper
¾ cup panko bread crumbs

1. Brush the peppers inside and out with 1 tablespoon of olive oil. Season the insides with ¼ teaspoon of kosher salt. Arrange the peppers on a sheet pan, cut side up.
2. Place the chickpeas with their liquid into a large bowl. Lightly mash the beans with a potato masher. Sprinkle with the remaining ¼ teaspoon of kosher salt and 1 tablespoon of olive oil. Add the rice, red peppers, parsley, onion, garlic, cumin, and black pepper to the bowl and stir to incorporate.
3. Divide the mixture among the bell pepper halves.
4. Stir together the remaining 2 tablespoons of olive oil and panko in a small bowl. Top the pepper halves with the panko mixture.
5. Slide the pan into the air fryer oven. Cook at 375°F (190°C) for 18 minutes.
6. When done, the peppers should be slightly wrinkled, and the panko should be golden brown.
7. Remove from the air fryer oven and serve on a plate.

Panko Green Beans

Prep time: 5 minutes | Cook time: 15 minutes | Serves 4

½ cup flour
2 eggs
1 cup panko bread crumbs
½ cup grated Parmesan cheese
1 teaspoon cayenne pepper
Salt and black pepper, to taste
1½ pounds (680 g) green beans

1. In a bowl, place the flour. In a separate bowl, lightly beat the eggs. In a separate shallow bowl, thoroughly combine the bread crumbs, cheese, cayenne pepper, salt, and pepper.
2. Dip the green beans in the flour, then in the beaten eggs, finally in the bread crumb mixture to coat well. Transfer the green beans to an air fryer basket.
3. Slide the basket into the air fryer oven. Cook at 400ºF (205ºC) for 15 minutes.
4. Stir the green beans halfway through the cooking time.
5. When cooking is complete, remove from the air fryer oven to a bowl and serve.

Parmesan Zucchini Chips

Prep time: 5 minutes | Cook time: 14 minutes | Serves 4

2 egg whites
Salt and black pepper, to taste
½ cup seasoned bread crumbs
2 tablespoons grated Parmesan cheese
¼ teaspoon garlic powder
2 medium zucchini, sliced
Cooking spray

1. Spritz an air fryer basket with cooking spray.
2. In a bowl, beat the egg whites with salt and pepper. In a separate bowl, thoroughly combine the bread crumbs, Parmesan cheese, and garlic powder.
3. Dredge the zucchini slices in the egg white, then coat in the bread crumb mixture.
4. Arrange the zucchini slices in the air fryer basket.
5. Slide the basket into the air fryer oven. Cook at 400ºF (205ºC) for 14 minutes.
6. Flip the zucchini halfway through.
7. When cooking is complete, the zucchini should be tender.
8. Remove from the air fryer oven to a plate and serve.

Roasted Vegetables with Basil

Prep time: 15 minutes | Cook time: 20 minutes | Serves 2

1 small eggplant, halved and sliced
1 yellow bell pepper, cut into thick strips
1 red bell pepper, cut into thick strips
2 garlic cloves, quartered
1 red onion, sliced
1 tablespoon extra-virgin olive oil
Salt and freshly ground black pepper, to taste
½ cup chopped fresh basil, for garnish
Cooking spray

1. Grease a nonstick baking dish with cooking spray.
2. Place the eggplant, bell peppers, garlic, and red onion in the greased baking dish. Drizzle with the olive oil and toss to coat well. Spritz any uncoated surfaces with cooking spray.
3. Slide the baking dish into the air fryer oven. Cook at 350ºF (180ºC) for 20 minutes.
4. Flip the vegetables halfway through the cooking time.
5. When done, remove from the air fryer oven and sprinkle with salt and pepper.
6. Sprinkle the basil on top for garnish and serve.

Roasted Vegetable Mélange with Herbs

Prep time: 10 minutes | Cook time: 16 minutes | Serves 4

1 (8-ounce / 227-g) package sliced mushrooms
1 yellow summer squash, sliced
1 red bell pepper, sliced
3 cloves garlic, sliced
1 tablespoon olive oil
½ teaspoon dried basil
½ teaspoon dried thyme
½ teaspoon dried tarragon

1. Toss the mushrooms, squash, and bell pepper with the garlic and olive oil in a large bowl until well coated. Mix in the basil, thyme, and tarragon and toss again.
2. Spread the vegetables evenly in an air fryer basket.
3. Slide the basket into the air fryer oven. Cook at 350ºF (180ºC) for 16 minutes.
4. When cooking is complete, the vegetables should be fork-tender. Remove from the air fryer oven. Cool for 5 minutes before serving.

Roasted Vegetables with Rice

Prep time: 5 minutes | Cook time: 12 minutes | Serves 4

2 teaspoons melted butter
1 cup chopped mushrooms
1 cup cooked rice
1 cup peas
1 carrot, chopped
1 red onion, chopped
1 garlic clove, minced
Salt and black pepper, to taste
2 hard-boiled eggs, grated
1 tablespoon soy sauce

1. Coat a baking dish with melted butter.
2. Stir together the mushrooms, cooked rice, peas, carrot, onion, garlic, salt, and pepper in a large bowl until well mixed. Pour the mixture into the prepared baking dish.
3. Slide the baking dish into the air fryer oven. Cook at 380°F (193°C) for 12 minutes.
4. When cooking is complete, remove from the air fryer oven. Divide the mixture among four plates. Serve warm with a sprinkle of grated eggs and a drizzle of soy sauce.

Stuffed Portobello Mushrooms with Vegetables

Prep time: 5 minutes | Cook time: 8 minutes | Serves 4

4 portobello mushrooms, stem removed
1 tablespoon olive oil
1 tomato, diced
½ green bell pepper, diced
½ small red onion, diced
½ teaspoon garlic powder
Salt and black pepper, to taste
½ cup grated Mozzarella cheese

1. Using a spoon to scoop out the gills of the mushrooms and discard them. Brush the mushrooms with the olive oil.
2. In a mixing bowl, stir together the remaining ingredients except the Mozzarella cheese. Using a spoon to stuff each mushroom with the filling and scatter the Mozzarella cheese on top.
3. Arrange the mushrooms in an air fryer basket.
4. Slide the basket into the air fryer oven. Cook at 330°F (166°C) for 8 minutes.
5. When cooking is complete, the cheese should be melted.
6. Serve warm.

Rosemary Roasted Squash with Cheese

Prep time: 5 minutes | Cook time: 20 minutes | Serves 2

1 pound (454 g) butternut squash, cut into wedges
2 tablespoons olive oil
1 tablespoon dried rosemary
Salt, to salt
1 cup crumbled goat cheese
1 tablespoon maple syrup

1. Toss the squash wedges with the olive oil, rosemary, and salt in a large bowl until well coated.
2. Transfer the squash wedges to an air fryer basket, spreading them out in as even a layer as possible.
3. Slide the basket into the air fryer oven. Cook at 350°F (180°C) for 20 minutes.
4. After 10 minutes, remove from the air fryer oven and flip the squash. Return to the air fryer oven and continue cooking for 10 minutes.
5. When cooking is complete, the squash should be golden brown. Remove from the air fryer oven. Sprinkle the goat cheese on top and serve drizzled with the maple syrup.

Roasted Brussels Sprouts with Parmesan

Prep time: 10 minutes | Cook time: 20 minutes | Serves 4

1 pound (454 g) fresh Brussels sprouts, trimmed
1 tablespoon olive oil
½ teaspoon salt
⅛ teaspoon pepper
¼ cup grated Parmesan cheese

1. In a large bowl, combine the Brussels sprouts with olive oil, salt, and pepper and toss until evenly coated.
2. Spread the Brussels sprouts evenly in an air fryer basket.
3. Slide the basket into the air fryer oven. Cook at 330°F (166°C) for 20 minutes.
4. Stir the Brussels sprouts twice during cooking.
5. When cooking is complete, the Brussels sprouts should be golden brown and crisp. Remove from the air fryer oven. Sprinkle the grated Parmesan cheese on top and serve warm.

Vegan and Vegetarian

Spicy Kung Pao Tofu

Prep time: 10 minutes | Cook time: 10 minutes | Serves 4

⅓ cup Asian-Style sauce
1 teaspoon cornstarch
½ teaspoon red pepper flakes, or more to taste
1 pound (454 g) firm or extra-firm tofu, cut into 1-inch cubes
1 small carrot, peeled and cut into ¼-inch-thick coins
1 small green bell pepper, cut into bite-size pieces
3 scallions, sliced, whites and green parts separated
3 tablespoons roasted unsalted peanuts

1. In a large bowl, whisk together the sauce, cornstarch, and red pepper flakes. Fold in the tofu, carrot, pepper, and the white parts of the scallions and toss to coat. Spread the mixture evenly on a sheet pan.
2. Slide the pan into the air fryer basket. Cook at 375°F (190°C) for 10 minutes.
3. Stir the ingredients once halfway through the cooking time.
4. When done, remove from the air fryer oven. Serve sprinkled with the peanuts and scallion greens.

Sweet-and-Sour Brussels Sprouts

Prep time: 5 minutes | Cook time: 20 minutes | Serves 2

¼ cup Thai sweet chili sauce
2 tablespoons black vinegar or balsamic vinegar
½ teaspoon hot sauce
2 small shallots, cut into ¼-inch-thick slices
8 ounces (227 g) Brussels sprouts, trimmed (large sprouts halved)
Kosher salt and freshly ground black pepper, to taste
2 teaspoons lightly packed fresh cilantro leaves, for garnish

1. Place the chili sauce, vinegar, and hot sauce in a large bowl and whisk to combine.
2. Add the shallots and Brussels sprouts and toss to coat. Sprinkle with the salt and pepper. Transfer the Brussels sprouts and sauce to a baking pan.
3. Slide the pan into the air fryer oven. Cook at 390°F (199°C) for 20 minutes.
4. Stir the Brussels sprouts twice during cooking.
5. When cooking is complete, the Brussels sprouts should be crisp-tender. Remove from the air fryer oven. Sprinkle the cilantro on top for garnish and serve warm.

Simple Ratatouille

Prep time: 15 minutes | Cook time: 16 minutes | Serves 2

2 Roma tomatoes, thinly sliced
1 zucchini, thinly sliced
2 yellow bell peppers, sliced
2 garlic cloves, minced
2 tablespoons olive oil
2 tablespoons herbes de Prair fryer ovence
1 tablespoon vinegar
Salt and black pepper, to taste

1. Place the tomatoes, zucchini, bell peppers, garlic, olive oil, herbes de Prair fryer ovence, and vinegar in a large bowl and toss until the vegetables are evenly coated. Sprinkle with salt and pepper and toss again. Pour the vegetable mixture into a baking dish.
2. Slide the baking dish into the air fryer oven. Cook at 390°F (199°C) for 16 minutes.
3. Stir the vegetables halfway through.
4. When cooking is complete, the vegetables should be tender.
5. Let the vegetable mixture stand for 5 minutes in the air fryer oven before removing and serving.

Teriyaki Cauliflower

Prep time: 5 minutes | Cook time: 14 minutes | Serves 4

½ cup soy sauce
⅓ cup water
1 tablespoon brown sugar
1 teaspoon sesame oil
1 teaspoon cornstarch
2 cloves garlic, chopped
½ teaspoon chili powder
1 big cauliflower head, cut into florets

1. Make the teriyaki sauce: In a small bowl, whisk together the soy sauce, water, brown sugar, sesame oil, cornstarch, garlic, and chili powder until well combined.
2. Place the cauliflower florets in a large bowl and drizzle the top with the prepared teriyaki sauce and toss to coat well.
3. Put the cauliflower florets in an air fryer basket.
4. Slide the basket into the air fryer oven. Cook at 340°F (171°C) for 14 minutes.
5. Stir the cauliflower halfway through.
6. When cooking is complete, the cauliflower should be crisp-tender.
7. Let the cauliflower cool for 5 minutes before serving.

Tortellini with Veggies and Parmesan

Prep time: 10 minutes | Cook time: 16 minutes | Serves 4

8 ounces (227 g) sugar snap peas, trimmed
½ pound (227 g) asparagus, trimmed and cut into 1-inch pieces
2 teaspoons kosher salt or 1 teaspoon fine salt, divided
1 tablespoon extra-virgin olive oil
1½ cups water
1 (20-ounce / 340-g) package frozen cheese tortellini
2 garlic cloves, minced
1 cup heavy (whipping) cream
1 cup cherry tomatoes, halved
½ cup grated Parmesan cheese
¼ cup chopped fresh parsley or basil

1. Add the peas and asparagus to a large bowl. Add ½ teaspoon of kosher salt and the olive oil and toss until well coated. Place the veggies in a sheet pan.
2. Slide the pan into the air fryer oven. Cook at 450°F (235°C) for 4 minutes.
3. Meanwhile, dissolve 1 teaspoon of kosher salt in the water.
4. Once cooking is complete, remove from the air fryer oven and arrange the tortellini on the pan. Pour the salted water over the tortellini. Transfer the pan back to the air fryer oven.
5. Cook at 450°F (235°C) for 7 minutes.
6. Meantime, stir together the garlic, heavy cream, and remaining ½ teaspoon of kosher salt in a small bowl.
7. Once cooking is complete, remove from the air fryer oven. Blot off any remaining water with a paper towel. Gently stir the ingredients. Drizzle the cream over and top with the tomatoes.
8. Slide the pan into the air fryer oven. Cook at 375°F (190°C) for 5 minutes.
9. After 4 minutes, remove from the air fryer oven.
10. Add the Parmesan cheese and stir until the cheese is melted
11. Serve topped with the parsley.

Vegetarian Meatballs

Prep time: 15 minutes | Cook time: 18 minutes | Serves 3

½ cup grated carrots
½ cup sweet onions
2 tablespoons olive oil
1 cup rolled oats
½ cup roasted cashews
2 cups cooked chickpeas
Juice of 1 lemon
2 tablespoons soy sauce
1 tablespoon flax meal
1 teaspoon garlic powder
1 teaspoon cumin
½ teaspoon turmeric

1. Mix the carrots, onions, and olive oil in a baking dish and stir to combine.
2. Slide the baking dish into the air fryer oven. Cook at 350°F (180°C) for 6 minutes.
3. Stir the vegetables halfway through.
4. When cooking is complete, the vegetables should be tender.
5. Meanwhile, put the oats and cashews in a food processor or blender and pulse until coarsely ground. Transfer the mixture to a large bowl. Add the chickpeas, lemon juice, and soy sauce to the food processor and pulse until smooth. Transfer the chickpea mixture to the bowl of oat and cashew mixture.
6. Remove the carrots and onions from the air fryer oven to the bowl of chickpea mixture. Add the flax meal, garlic powder, cumin, and turmeric and stir to incorporate.
7. Scoop tablespoon-sized portions of the veggie mixture and roll them into balls with your hands. Transfer the balls to an air fryer basket.
8. Increase the temperature to 370°F (188°C) for 12 minutes on Bake. Flip the balls halfway through the cooking time.
9. When cooking is complete, the balls should be golden brown.
10. Serve warm.

Vegetable Sides

Blistered Shishito Peppers with Lime Juice

Prep time: 5 minutes | Cook time: 9 minutes | Serves 3

½ pound (227 g) shishito peppers, rinsed
Cooking spray
Sauce:
1 tablespoon tamari or shoyu
2 teaspoons fresh lime juice
2 large garlic cloves, minced

1. Spritz an air fryer basket with cooking spray.
2. Place the shishito peppers in the air fryer basket and spritz them with cooking spray.
3. Slide the basket into the air fryer oven. Cook at 392°F (200°C) for 9 minutes.
4. Meanwhile, whisk together all the ingredients for the sauce in a large bowl. Set aside.
5. After 3 minutes, remove from the air fryer oven. Flip the peppers and spritz them with cooking spray. Return to the air fryer oven and continue cooking.
6. After another 3 minutes, remove from the air fryer oven. Flip the peppers and spray with cooking spray. Return to the air fryer oven and continue roasting for 3 minutes more, or until the peppers are blistered and nicely browned.
7. When cooking is complete, remove the peppers from the air fryer oven to the bowl of sauce. Toss to coat well and serve immediately.

Scalloped Potatoes

Prep time: 5 minutes | Cook time: 15 to 20 minutes | Serves 4

2 cup sliced frozen potatoes, thawed
3 cloves garlic, minced
Pinch salt
Freshly ground black pepper, to taste
¾ cup heavy cream

1. Toss the potatoes with the garlic, salt, and black pepper in a baking pan until evenly coated. Pour the heavy cream over the top.
2. Slide the pan into the air fryer oven. Cook at 380°F (193°C) for 15 minutes.
3. When cooking is complete, the potatoes should be tender and the top golden brown. Check for doneness and bake for another 5 minutes if needed. Remove from the air fryer oven and serve hot.

Baked Potatoes with Yogurt and Chives

Prep time: 5 minutes | Cook time: 35 minutes | Serves 4

4 (7-ounce / 198-g) russet potatoes, rinsed
Olive oil spray
½ teaspoon kosher salt, divided
½ cup 2% plain Greek yogurt
¼ cup minced fresh chives
Freshly ground black pepper, to taste

1. Pat the potatoes dry and pierce them all over with a fork. Spritz the potatoes with olive oil spray. Sprinkle with ¼ teaspoon of the salt.
2. Transfer the potatoes to an air fryer basket.
3. Slide the basket into the air fryer oven. Cook at 400°F (205°C) for 35 minutes.
4. When cooking is complete, the potatoes should be fork-tender. Remove from the air fryer oven and split open the potatoes. Top with the yogurt, chives, the remaining ¼ teaspoon of salt, and finish with the black pepper. Serve immediately.

Butternut Squash Croquettes

Prep time: 5 minutes | Cook time: 17 minutes | Serves 4

⅓ butternut squash, peeled and grated
⅓ cup all-purpose flour
2 eggs, whisked
4 cloves garlic, minced
1½ tablespoons olive oil
1 teaspoon fine sea salt
⅓ teaspoon freshly ground black pepper, or more to taste
⅓ teaspoon dried sage
A pinch of ground allspice

1. Line an air fryer basket with parchment paper. Set aside.
2. In a mixing bowl, stir together all the ingredients until well combined.
3. Make the squash croquettes: Use a small cookie scoop to drop tablespoonfuls of the squash mixture onto a lightly floured surface and shape into balls with your hands. Transfer them to the air fryer basket.
4. Slide the basket into the air fryer oven. Cook at 345°F (174°C) for 17 minutes.
5. When cooking is complete, the squash croquettes should be golden brown. Remove from the air fryer oven to a plate and serve warm.

Balsamic-Glazed Carrots

Prep time: 5 minutes | Cook time: 18 minutes | Serves 3

3 medium-size carrots, cut into 2-inch × ½-inch sticks
1 tablespoon orange juice
2 teaspoons balsamic vinegar
1 teaspoon maple syrup
1 teaspoon avocado oil
½ teaspoon dried rosemary
¼ teaspoon sea salt
¼ teaspoon lemon zest

1. Put the carrots in a baking pan and sprinkle with the orange juice, balsamic vinegar, maple syrup, avocado oil, rosemary, sea salt, finished by the lemon zest. Toss well.
2. Slide the pan into the air fryer oven. Cook at 392°F (200°C) for 18 minutes.
3. Stir the carrots several times during the cooking process.
4. When cooking is complete, the carrots should be nicely glazed and tender. Remove from the air fryer oven and serve hot.

Chili Corn on the Cob

Prep time: 10 minutes | Cook time: 15 minutes | Serves 4

2 tablespoon olive oil, divided
2 tablespoons grated Parmesan cheese
1 teaspoon garlic powder
1 teaspoon chili powder
1 teaspoon ground cumin
1 teaspoon paprika
1 teaspoon salt
¼ teaspoon cayenne pepper (optional)
4 ears fresh corn, shucked

1. Grease an air fryer basket with 1 tablespoon of olive oil. Set aside.
2. Combine the Parmesan cheese, garlic powder, chili powder, cumin, paprika, salt, and cayenne pepper (if desired) in a small bowl and stir to mix well.
3. Lightly coat the ears of corn with the remaining 1 tablespoon of olive oil. Rub the cheese mixture all over the ears of corn until completely coated.
4. Arrange the ears of corn in the greased air fryer basket.
5. Slide the basket into the air fryer oven. Cook at 400°F (205°C) for 15 minutes.
6. Flip the ears of corn halfway through the cooking time.
7. When cooking is complete, they should be lightly browned. Remove from the air fryer oven and let them cool for 5 minutes before serving.

Buttered Broccoli with Parmesan

Prep time: 5 minutes | Cook time: 4 minutes | Serves 4

1 pound (454 g) broccoli florets
1 medium shallot, minced
2 tablespoons olive oil
2 tablespoons unsalted butter, melted
2 teaspoons minced garlic
¼ cup grated Parmesan cheese

1. Combine the broccoli florets with the shallot, olive oil, butter, garlic, and Parmesan cheese in a medium bowl and toss until the broccoli florets are thoroughly coated.
2. Place the broccoli florets in an air fryer basket.
3. Slide the basket into the air fryer oven. Cook at 360°F (182°C) for 4 minutes.
4. When cooking is complete, the broccoli florets should be crisp-tender. Remove from the air fryer oven and serve warm.

Sweet Brussels Sprouts

Prep time: 10 minutes | Cook time: 11 minutes | Serves 4

2½ cups trimmed Brussels sprouts
Sauce:
1½ teaspoons mellow white miso
1½ tablespoons maple syrup
1 teaspoon toasted sesame oil
1 teaspoons tamari or shoyu
1 teaspoon grated fresh ginger
2 large garlic cloves, finely minced
¼ to ½ teaspoon red chili flakes
Cooking spray

1. Spritz an air fryer basket with cooking spray.
2. Arrange the Brussels sprouts in the air fryer basket and spray them with cooking spray.
3. Slide the basket into the air fryer oven. Cook at 392°F (200°C) for 11 minutes.
4. After 6 minutes, remove from the air fryer oven. Flip the Brussels sprouts and spritz with cooking spray again. Return to the air fryer oven and continue cooking for 5 minutes more.
5. Meanwhile, make the sauce: Stir together the miso and maple syrup in a medium bowl. Add the sesame oil, tamari, ginger, garlic, and red chili flakes and whisk to combine.
6. When cooking is complete, the Brussels sprouts should be crisp-tender. Transfer the Brussels sprouts to the bowl of sauce, tossing to coat well. If you prefer a saltier taste, you can add additional ½ teaspoon tamari to the sauce. Serve immediately.

Creamy Corn Casserole

Prep time: 5 minutes | Cook time: 15 minutes | Serves 4

2 cups frozen yellow corn
1 egg, beaten
3 tablespoons flour
½ cup grated Swiss or Havarti cheese
½ cup light cream
¼ cup milk
Pinch salt
Freshly ground black pepper, to taste
2 tablespoons butter, cut into cubes
Nonstick cooking spray

1. Spritz a baking pan with nonstick cooking spray.
2. Stir together the remaining ingredients except the butter in a medium bowl until well incorporated. Transfer the mixture to the prepared baking pan and scatter with the butter cubes.
3. Slide the pan into the air fryer oven. Cook at 320°F (160°C) for 15 minutes.
4. When cooking is complete, the top should be golden brown and a toothpick inserted in the center should come out clean. Remove from the air fryer oven. Let the casserole cool for 5 minutes before slicing into wedges and serving.

Crispy Zucchini Sticks

Prep time: 5 minutes | Cook time: 14 minutes | Serves 4

2 small zucchini, cut into 2-inch × ½-inch sticks
3 tablespoons chickpea flour
2 teaspoons arrowroot (or cornstarch)
½ teaspoon garlic granules
¼ teaspoon sea salt
⅛ teaspoon freshly ground black pepper
1 tablespoon water
Cooking spray

1. Combine the zucchini sticks with the chickpea flour, arrowroot, garlic granules, salt, and pepper in a medium bowl and toss to coat. Add the water and stir to mix well.
2. Spritz an air fryer basket with cooking spray and spread out the zucchini sticks in the basket. Mist the zucchini sticks with cooking spray.
3. Slide the basket into the air fryer oven. Cook at 392°F (200°C) for 14 minutes.
4. Stir the sticks halfway through the cooking time.
5. When cooking is complete, the zucchini sticks should be crispy and nicely browned. Remove from the air fryer oven and serve warm.

Charred Green Beans with Sesame Seeds

Prep time: 5 minutes | Cook time: 8 minutes | Serves 4

1 tablespoon reduced-sodium soy sauce or tamari
½ tablespoon Sriracha sauce
4 teaspoons toasted sesame oil, divided
12 ounces (340 g) trimmed green beans
½ tablespoon toasted sesame seeds

1. Whisk together the soy sauce, Sriracha sauce, and 1 teaspoon of sesame oil in a small bowl until smooth. Set aside.
2. Toss the green beans with the remaining sesame oil in a large bowl until evenly coated.
3. Place the green beans in an air fryer basket.
4. Slide the basket into the air fryer oven. Cook at 375°F (190°C) for 8 minutes.
5. Stir the green beans halfway through the cooking time.
6. When cooking is complete, the green beans should be lightly charred and tender. Remove from the air fryer oven to a platter. Pour the prepared sauce over the top of green beans and toss well. Serve sprinkled with the toasted sesame seeds.

Crusted Brussels Sprouts with Sage

Prep time: 5 minutes | Cook time: 15 minutes | Serves 4

1 pound (454 g) Brussels sprouts, halved
1 cup bread crumbs
2 tablespoons grated Grana Padano cheese
1 tablespoon paprika
2 tablespoons canola oil
1 tablespoon chopped sage

1. Line an air fryer basket with parchment paper. Set aside.
2. In a small bowl, thoroughly mix the bread crumbs, cheese, and paprika. In a large bowl, place the Brussels sprouts and drizzle the canola oil over the top. Sprinkle with the bread crumb mixture and toss to coat.
3. Transfer the Brussels sprouts to the prepared air fryer basket.
4. Slide the basket into the air fryer oven. Cook at 400°F (205°C) for 15 minutes.
5. Stir the Brussels a few times during cooking.
6. When cooking is complete, the Brussels sprouts should be lightly browned and crisp. Transfer the Brussels sprouts to a plate and sprinkle the sage on top before serving.

Cheesy Broccoli Gratin

Prep time: 5 minutes | Cook time: 14 minutes | Serves 2

⅓ cup fat-free milk
1 tablespoon all-purpose or gluten-free flour
½ tablespoon olive oil
½ teaspoon ground sage
¼ teaspoon kosher salt
⅛ teaspoon freshly ground black pepper
2 cups roughly chopped broccoli florets
6 tablespoons shredded Cheddar cheese
2 tablespoons panko bread crumbs
1 tablespoon grated Parmesan cheese
Olive oil spray

1. Spritz a baking dish with olive oil spray.
2. Mix the milk, flour, olive oil, sage, salt, and pepper in a medium bowl and whisk to combine. Stir in the broccoli florets, Cheddar cheese, bread crumbs, and Parmesan cheese and toss to coat.
3. Pour the broccoli mixture into the prepared baking dish.
4. Slide the baking dish into the air fryer oven. Cook at 330°F (166°C) for 14 minutes.
5. When cooking is complete, the top should be golden brown and the broccoli should be tender. Remove from the air fryer oven and serve immediately.

Parmesan Asparagus Fries

Prep time: 15 minutes | Cook time: 6 minutes | Serves 4

2 egg whites
¼ cup water
¼ cup plus 2 tablespoons grated Parmesan cheese, divided
¾ cup panko bread crumbs
¼ teaspoon salt
12 ounces (340 g) fresh asparagus spears, woody ends trimmed
Cooking spray

1. In a shallow dish, whisk together the egg whites and water until slightly foamy. In a separate shallow dish, thoroughly combine ¼ cup of Parmesan cheese, bread crumbs, and salt.
2. Dip the asparagus in the egg white, then roll in the cheese mixture to coat well.
3. Place the asparagus in an air fryer basket, leaving space between each spear. Spritz the asparagus with cooking spray.
4. Slide the basket into the air fryer oven. Cook at 390°F (199°C) for 6 minutes.
5. When cooking is complete, the asparagus should be golden brown and crisp. Remove from the air fryer oven. Sprinkle with the remaining 2 tablespoons of cheese and serve hot.

Rosemary Roasted Potatoes

Prep time: 5 minutes | Cook time: 20 minutes | Serves 4

1½ pounds (680 g) small red potatoes, cut into 1-inch cubes
2 tablespoons olive oil
2 tablespoons minced fresh rosemary
1 tablespoon minced garlic
1 teaspoon salt, plus additional as needed
½ teaspoon freshly ground black pepper, plus additional as needed

1. Toss the potato cubes with the olive oil, rosemary, garlic, salt, and pepper in a large bowl until thoroughly coated.
2. Arrange the potato cubes in an air fryer basket.
3. Slide the basket into the air fryer oven. Cook at 400°F (205°C) for 20 minutes.
4. Stir the potatoes a few times during cooking for even cooking.
5. When cooking is complete, the potatoes should be tender. Remove from the air fryer oven to a plate. Taste and add additional salt and pepper as needed.

Spicy Broccoli with Hot Sauce

Prep time: 5 minutes | Cook time: 14 minutes | Serves 6

Broccoli:
1 medium-sized head broccoli, cut into florets
1½ tablespoons olive oil
1 teaspoon shallot powder
1 teaspoon porcini powder
½ teaspoon freshly grated lemon zest
½ teaspoon hot paprika
½ teaspoon granulated garlic
⅓ teaspoon fine sea salt
⅓ teaspoon celery seeds
Hot Sauce:
½ cup tomato sauce
1 tablespoon balsamic vinegar
½ teaspoon ground allspice

1. In a mixing bowl, combine all the ingredients for the broccoli and toss to coat. Transfer the broccoli to an air fryer basket.
2. Slide the basket into the air fryer oven. Cook at 360°F (182°C) for 14 minutes.
3. Meanwhile, make the hot sauce by whisking together the tomato sauce, balsamic vinegar, and allspice in a small bowl.
4. When cooking is complete, remove the broccoli from the air fryer oven and serve with the hot sauce.

Spicy Cabbage

Prep time: 5 minutes | Cook time: 7 minutes | Serves 4

1 head cabbage, sliced into 1-inch-thick ribbons
1 tablespoon olive oil
1 teaspoon garlic powder
1 teaspoon red pepper flakes
1 teaspoon salt
1 teaspoon freshly ground black pepper

1. Toss the cabbage with the olive oil, garlic powder, red pepper flakes, salt, and pepper in a large mixing bowl until well coated.
2. Transfer the cabbage to an air fryer basket.
3. Slide the basket into the air fryer oven. Cook at 350°F (180°C) for 7 minutes.
4. Flip the cabbage with tongs halfway through the cooking time.
5. When cooking is complete, the cabbage should be crisp. Remove from the air fryer oven to a plate and serve warm.

Cinnamon-Spiced Acorn Squash

Prep time: 5 minutes | Cook time: 15 minutes | Serves 2

1 medium acorn squash, halved crosswise and deseeded
1 teaspoon coconut oil
1 teaspoon light brown sugar
Few dashes of ground cinnamon
Few dashes of ground nutmeg

1. On a clean work surface, rub the cut sides of the acorn squash with coconut oil. Scatter with the brown sugar, cinnamon, and nutmeg.
2. Put the squash halves in an air fryer basket, cut-side up.
3. Slide the basket into the air fryer oven. Cook at 325°F (163°C) for 15 minutes.
4. When cooking is complete, the squash halves should be just tender when pierced in the center with a paring knife. Remove from the air fryer oven. Rest for 5 to 10 minutes and serve warm.

Garlic Roasted Asparagus

Prep time: 5 minutes | Cook time: 10 minutes | Serves 4

1 pound (454 g) asparagus, woody ends trimmed
2 tablespoons olive oil
1 tablespoon balsamic vinegar
2 teaspoons minced garlic
Salt and freshly ground black pepper, to taste

1. In a large shallow bowl, toss the asparagus with the olive oil, balsamic vinegar, garlic, salt, and pepper until thoroughly coated. Put the asparagus in an air fryer basket.
2. Slide the basket into the air fryer oven. Cook at 400°F (205°C) for 10 minutes.
3. Flip the asparagus with tongs halfway through the cooking time.
4. When cooking is complete, the asparagus should be crispy. Remove the basket from the air fryer oven and serve warm.

Simple Zucchini Crisps

Prep time: 5 minutes | Cook time: 14 minutes | Serves 4

2 zucchini, sliced into ¼- to ½-inch-thick rounds (about 2 cups)
¼ teaspoon garlic granules
⅛ teaspoon sea salt
Freshly ground black pepper, to taste (optional)
Cooking spray

1. Spritz an air fryer basket with cooking spray.
2. Put the zucchini rounds in the air fryer basket, spreading them out as much as possible. Top with a sprinkle of garlic granules, sea salt, and black pepper (if desired). Spritz the zucchini rounds with cooking spray.
3. Slide the basket into the air fryer oven. Cook at 392°F (200°C) for 14 minutes.
4. Flip the zucchini rounds halfway through.
5. When cooking is complete, the zucchini rounds should be crisp-tender. Remove from the air fryer oven. Let them rest for 5 minutes and serve.

Tamarind Sweet Potatoes

Prep time: 5 minutes | Cook time: 22 minutes | Serves 4

5 garnet sweet potatoes, peeled and diced
1½ tablespoons fresh lime juice
1 tablespoon butter, melted
2 teaspoons tamarind paste
1½ teaspoon ground allspice
⅓ teaspoon white pepper
½ teaspoon turmeric powder
A few drops liquid stevia

1. In a large mixing bowl, combine all the ingredients and toss until the sweet potatoes are evenly coated. Place the sweet potatoes in an air fryer basket.
2. Slide the basket into the air fryer oven. Cook at 400°F (205°C) for 22 minutes.
3. Stir the potatoes twice during cooking.
4. When cooking is complete, the potatoes should be crispy on the outside and soft on the inside. Let the potatoes cool for 5 minutes before serving.

Wraps and Sandwiches

Air Fried Cream Cheese Wontons

Prep time: 5 minutes | Cook time: 6 minutes | Serves 4

2 ounces (57 g) cream cheese, softened
1 tablespoon sugar
16 square wonton wrappers
Cooking spray

1. Spritz an air fryer basket with cooking spray.
2. In a mixing bowl, stir together the cream cheese and sugar until well mixed. Prepare a small bowl of water alongside.
3. On a clean work surface, lay the wonton wrappers. Scoop ¼ teaspoon of cream cheese in the center of each wonton wrapper. Dab the water over the wrapper edges. Fold each wonton wrapper diagonally in half over the filling to form a triangle.
4. Arrange the wontons in the basket. Spritz the wontons with cooking spray.
5. Slide the basket into the air fryer oven. Cook at 350°F (180°C) for 6 minutes.
6. Flip the wontons halfway through the cooking time.
7. When cooking is complete, the wontons will be golden brown and crispy.
8. Divide the wontons among four plates. Let rest for 5 minutes before serving.

Air Fried Crispy Spring Rolls

Prep time: 10 minutes | Cook time: 18 minutes | Serves 4

4 spring roll wrappers
½ cup cooked vermicelli noodles
1 teaspoon sesame oil
1 tablespoon freshly minced ginger
1 tablespoon soy sauce
1 clove garlic, minced
½ red bell pepper, deseeded and chopped
½ cup chopped carrot
½ cup chopped mushrooms
¼ cup chopped scallions
Cooking spray

1. Spritz an air fryer basket with cooking spray and set aside.
2. Heat the sesame oil in a saucepan on medium heat. Sauté the ginger and garlic in the sesame oil for 1 minute, or until fragrant. Add soy sauce, red bell pepper, carrot, mushrooms and scallions. Sauté for 5 minutes or until the vegetables become tender. Mix in vermicelli noodles. Turn off the heat and remove them from the saucepan. Allow to cool for 10 minutes.
3. Lay out one spring roll wrapper with a corner pointed toward you. Scoop the noodle mixture on spring roll wrapper and fold corner up over the mixture. Fold left and right corners toward the center and continue to roll to make firmly sealed rolls.
4. Arrange the spring rolls in the basket and spritz with cooking spray.
5. Slide the basket into the air fryer oven. Cook at 340°F (171°C) for 12 minutes.
6. Flip the spring rolls halfway through the cooking time.
7. When done, the spring rolls will be golden brown and crispy.
8. Serve warm.

Beef and Bell Pepper Fajitas

Prep time: 15 minutes | Cook time: 10 minutes | Serves 4

1 pound (454 g) beef sirloin steak, cut into strips
2 shallots, sliced
1 orange bell pepper, sliced
1 red bell pepper, sliced
2 garlic cloves, minced
2 tablespoons Cajun seasoning
1 tablespoon paprika
Salt and ground black pepper, to taste
4 corn tortillas
½ cup shredded Cheddar cheese
Cooking spray

1. Spritz an air fryer basket with cooking spray.
2. Combine all the ingredients, except for the tortillas and cheese, in a large bowl. Toss to coat well.
3. Pour the beef and vegetables in the basket and spritz with cooking spray.
4. Slide the basket into the air fryer oven. Cook at 360°F (182°C) for 10 minutes.
5. Stir the beef and vegetables halfway through the cooking time.
6. When cooking is complete, the meat will be browned and the vegetables will be soft and lightly wilted.
7. Unfold the tortillas on a clean work surface and spread the cooked beef and vegetables on top. Scatter with cheese and fold to serve.

Air Fried Philly Cheesesteaks

Prep time: 20 minutes | Cook time: 20 minutes | Serves 2

12 ounces (340 g) boneless rib-eye steak, sliced thinly
½ teaspoon Worcestershire sauce
½ teaspoon soy sauce
Kosher salt and ground black pepper, to taste
½ green bell pepper, stemmed, deseeded, and thinly sliced
½ small onion, halved and thinly sliced
1 tablespoon vegetable oil
2 soft hoagie rolls, split three-fourths of the way through
1 tablespoon butter, softened
2 slices provolone cheese, halved

1. Combine the steak, Worcestershire sauce, soy sauce, salt, and ground black pepper in a large bowl. Toss to coat well. Set aside.
2. Combine the bell pepper, onion, salt, ground black pepper, and vegetable oil in a separate bowl. Toss to coat the vegetables well.
3. Pour the steak and vegetables in an air fryer basket.
4. Slide the basket into the air fryer oven. Cook at 400°F (205°C) for 15 minutes.
5. When cooked, the steak will be browned and vegetables will be tender. Transfer them on a plate. Set aside.
6. Brush the hoagie rolls with butter and place in the basket.
7. Slide the basket in the air fryer oven and toast for 3 minutes. When done, the rolls should be lightly browned.
8. Transfer the rolls to a clean work surface and divide the steak and vegetable mix in between the rolls. Spread with cheese. Place the stuffed rolls back in the basket.
9. Cook for 2 minutes. Return the basket back to the air fryer oven. When done, the cheese should be melted.
10. Serve immediately.

Avocado and Slaw Tacos

Prep time: 15 minutes | Cook time: 6 minutes | Serves 4

¼ cup all-purpose flour
¼ teaspoon salt, plus more as needed
¼ teaspoon ground black pepper
2 large egg whites
1¼ cups panko bread crumbs
2 tablespoons olive oil
2 avocados, peeled and halved, cut into ½-inch-thick slices
½ small red cabbage, thinly sliced
1 deseeded jalapeño, thinly sliced
2 green onions, thinly sliced
½ cup cilantro leaves
¼ cup mayonnaise
Juice and zest of 1 lime
4 corn tortillas, warmed
½ cup sour cream
Cooking spray

1. Spritz an air fryer basket with cooking spray.
2. Pour the flour in a large bowl and sprinkle with salt and black pepper, then stir to mix well.
3. Whisk the egg whites in a separate bowl. Combine the panko with olive oil on a shallow dish.
4. Dredge the avocado slices in the bowl of flour, then into the egg to coat. Shake the excess off, then roll the slices over the panko.
5. Arrange the avocado slices in a single layer in the basket and spritz the cooking spray.
6. Slide the basket into the air fryer oven. Cook at 400°F (205°C) for 6 minutes.
7. Flip the slices halfway through with tongs.
8. When cooking is complete, the avocado slices should be tender and lightly browned.
9. Combine the cabbage, jalapeño, onions, cilantro leaves, mayo, lime juice and zest, and a touch of salt in a separate large bowl. Toss to mix well.
10. Unfold the tortillas on a clean work surface, then spread with cabbage slaw and air fried avocados. Top with sour cream and serve.

Avocado and Tomato Egg Rolls

Prep time: 10 minutes | Cook time: 5 minutes | Serves 5

10 egg roll wrappers
3 avocados, peeled and pitted
1 tomato, diced
Salt and ground black pepper, to taste
Cooking spray

1. Spritz an air fryer basket with cooking spray.
2. Put the tomato and avocados in a food processor. Sprinkle with salt and ground black pepper. Pulse to mix and coarsely mash until smooth.
3. Unfold the wrappers on a clean work surface, then divide the mixture in the center of each wrapper. Roll the wrapper up and press to seal.
4. Transfer the rolls to the basket and spritz with cooking spray.
5. Slide the basket into the air fryer oven. Cook at 350°F (180°C) for 5 minutes.
6. Flip the rolls halfway through the cooking time.
7. When cooked, the rolls should be golden brown.
8. Serve immediately.

Baja Fish Tacos

Prep time: 15 minutes | Cook time: 17 minutes | Makes 6 tacos

1 egg
5 ounces (142 g) Mexican beer
¾ cup all-purpose flour
¾ cup cornstarch
¼ teaspoon chili powder
½ teaspoon ground cumin
½ pound (227 g) cod, cut into large pieces
6 corn tortillas
Cooking spray
Salsa:
1 mango, peeled and diced
¼ red bell pepper, diced
½ small jalapeño, diced
¼ red onion, minced
Juice of half a lime
Pinch chopped fresh cilantro
¼ teaspoon salt
¼ teaspoon ground black pepper

1. Spritz an air fryer basket with cooking spray.
2. Whisk the egg with beer in a bowl. Combine the flour, cornstarch, chili powder, and cumin in a separate bowl.
3. Dredge the cod in the egg mixture first, then in the flour mixture to coat well. Shake the excess off.
4. Arrange the cod in the air fryer basket and spritz with cooking spray.
5. Slide the basket into the air fryer oven. Cook at 380°F (193°C) for 17 minutes.
6. Flip the cod halfway through the cooking time.
7. When cooked, the cod should be golden brown and crunchy.
8. Meanwhile, combine the ingredients for the salsa in a small bowl. Stir to mix well.
9. Unfold the tortillas on a clean work surface, then divide the fish on the tortillas and spread the salsa on top. Fold to serve.

Bulgogi Burgers

Prep time: 15 minutes | Cook time: 10 minutes | Serves 4

Burgers:
1 pound (454 g) 85% lean ground beef
2 tablespoons gochujang
¼ cup chopped scallions
2 teaspoons minced garlic
2 teaspoons minced fresh ginger
1 tablespoon soy sauce
1 tablespoon toasted sesame oil
2 teaspoons sugar
½ teaspoon kosher salt
4 hamburger buns
Cooking spray
Korean Mayo:
1 tablespoon gochujang
¼ cup mayonnaise
2 teaspoons sesame seeds
¼ cup chopped scallions
1 tablespoon toasted sesame oil

1. Combine the ingredients for the burgers, except for the buns, in a large bowl. Stir to mix well, then wrap the bowl in plastic and refrigerate to marinate for at least an hour.
2. Spritz an air fryer basket with cooking spray.
3. Divide the meat mixture into four portions and form into four balls. Bash the balls into patties.
4. Arrange the patties in the basket and spritz with cooking spray.
5. Slide the basket into the air fryer oven. Cook at 350°F (180°C) for 10 minutes.
6. Flip the patties halfway through the cooking time.
7. Meanwhile, combine the ingredients for the Korean mayo in a small bowl. Stir to mix well.
8. When cooking is complete, the patties should be golden brown.
9. Remove the patties from the air fryer oven and assemble with the buns, then spread the Korean mayo over the patties to make the burgers. Serve immediately.

Turkey, Leek, and Pepper Hamburger

Prep time: 10 minutes | Cook time: 20 minutes | Serves 4

1 cup leftover turkey, cut into bite-sized chunks
1 leek, sliced
1 Serrano pepper, deveined and chopped
2 bell peppers, deveined and chopped
2 tablespoons Tabasco sauce
½ cup sour cream
1 heaping tablespoon fresh cilantro, chopped
1 teaspoon hot paprika
¾ teaspoon kosher salt
½ teaspoon ground black pepper
4 hamburger buns
Cooking spray

1. Spritz a baking pan with cooking spray.
2. Mix all the ingredients, except for the buns, in a large bowl. Toss to combine well.
3. Pour the mixture in the baking pan.
4. Slide the pan into the air fryer oven. Cook at 385°F (196°C) for 20 minutes.
5. When done, the turkey will be well browned and the leek will be tender.
6. Assemble the hamburger buns with the turkey mixture and serve immediately.

Cheesy Bacon and Egg Wraps

Prep time: 15 minutes | Cook time: 10 minutes | Serves 3

3 corn tortillas
3 slices bacon, cut into strips
2 scrambled eggs
3 tablespoons salsa
1 cup grated Pepper Jack cheese
3 tablespoons cream cheese, divided
Cooking spray

1. Spritz an air fryer basket with cooking spray.
2. Unfold the tortillas on a clean work surface, divide the bacon and eggs in the middle of the tortillas, then spread with salsa and scatter with cheeses. Fold the tortillas over.
3. Arrange the tortillas in the basket.
4. Slide the basket into the air fryer oven. Cook at 390°F (199°C) for 10 minutes.
5. Flip the tortillas halfway through the cooking time.
6. When cooking is complete, the cheeses will be melted and the tortillas will be lightly browned.
7. Serve immediately.

Cheesy Spring Chicken Wraps

Prep time: 30 minutes | Cook time: 5 minutes | Serves 12

2 large-sized chicken breasts, cooked and shredded
2 spring onions, chopped
10 ounces (284 g) Ricotta cheese
1 tablespoon rice vinegar
1 tablespoon molasses
1 teaspoon grated fresh ginger
¼ cup soy sauce
⅓ teaspoon sea salt
¼ teaspoon ground black pepper, or more to taste
48 wonton wrappers
Cooking spray

1. Spritz an air fryer basket with cooking spray.
2. Combine all the ingredients, except for the wrappers in a large bowl. Toss to mix well.
3. Unfold the wrappers on a clean work surface, then divide and spoon the mixture in the middle of the wrappers.
4. Dab a little water on the edges of the wrappers, then fold the edge close to you over the filling. Tuck the edge under the filling and roll up to seal.
5. Arrange the wraps in the basket.
6. Slide the basket into the air fryer oven. Cook at 375°F (190°C) for 5 minutes.
7. Flip the wraps halfway through the cooking time.
8. When cooking is complete, the wraps should be lightly browned.
9. Serve immediately.

Cabbage and Mushroom Spring Rolls

Prep time: 20 minutes | Cook time: 14 minutes | Makes 14 spring rolls

2 tablespoons vegetable oil
4 cups sliced Napa cabbage
5 ounces (142 g) shiitake mushrooms, diced
3 carrots, cut into thin matchsticks
1 tablespoon minced fresh ginger
1 tablespoon minced garlic
1 bunch scallions, white and light green parts only, sliced
2 tablespoons soy sauce
1 (4-ounce / 113-g) package cellophane noodles
¼ teaspoon cornstarch
1 (12-ounce / 340-g) package frozen spring roll wrappers, thawed
Cooking spray

1. Heat the olive oil in a nonstick skillet over medium-high heat until shimmering.
2. Add the cabbage, mushrooms, and carrots and sauté for 3 minutes or until tender.
3. Add the ginger, garlic, and scallions and sauté for 1 minutes or until fragrant.
4. Mix in the soy sauce and turn off the heat. Discard any liquid remains in the skillet and allow to cool for a few minutes.
5. Bring a pot of water to a boil, then turn off the heat and pour in the noodles. Let sit for 10 minutes or until the noodles are al dente. Transfer 1 cup of the noodles in the skillet and toss with the cooked vegetables. Reserve the remaining noodles for other use.
6. Dissolve the cornstarch in a small dish of water, then place the wrappers on a clean work surface. Dab the edges of the wrappers with cornstarch.
7. Scoop up 3 tablespoons of filling in the center of each wrapper, then fold the corner in front of you over the filling. Tuck the wrapper under the filling, then fold the corners on both sides into the center. Keep rolling to seal the wrapper. Repeat with remaining wrappers.
8. Spritz an air fryer basket with cooking spray. Arrange the wrappers in the basket and spritz with cooking spray.
9. Slide the basket into the air fryer oven. Cook at 400°F (205°C) for 10 minutes.
10. Flip the wrappers halfway through the cooking time.
11. When cooking is complete, the wrappers will be golden brown.
12. Serve immediately.

Cabbage and Pork Gyoza

Prep time: 10 minutes | Cook time: 10 minutes | Makes 48 gyozas

1 pound (454 g) ground pork
1 head Napa cabbage (about 1 pound / 454 g), sliced thinly and minced
½ cup minced scallions
1 teaspoon minced fresh chives
1 teaspoon soy sauce
1 teaspoon minced fresh ginger
1 tablespoon minced garlic
1 teaspoon granulated sugar
2 teaspoons kosher salt
48 to 50 wonton or dumpling wrappers
Cooking spray

1. Spritz an air fryer basket with cooking spray. Set aside.
2. Make the filling: Combine all the ingredients, except for the wrappers in a large bowl. Stir to mix well.
3. Unfold a wrapper on a clean work surface, then dab the edges with a little water. Scoop up 2 teaspoons of the filling mixture in the center.
4. Make the gyoza: Fold the wrapper over to filling and press the edges to seal. Pleat the edges if desired. Repeat with remaining wrappers and fillings.
5. Arrange the gyozas in the basket and spritz with cooking spray.
6. Slide the basket into the air fryer oven. Cook at 360°F (182°C) for 10 minutes.
7. Flip the gyozas halfway through the cooking time.
8. When cooked, the gyozas will be golden brown.
9. Serve immediately.

Cheesy Potato Taquitos

Prep time: 5 minutes | Cook time: 6 minutes | Makes 12 taquitos

2 cups mashed potatoes
½ cup shredded Mexican cheese
12 corn tortillas
Cooking spray

1. Line a baking pan with parchment paper.
2. In a bowl, combine the potatoes and cheese until well mixed. Microwave the tortillas on high heat for 30 seconds, or until softened. Add some water to another bowl and set alongside.
3. On a clean work surface, lay the tortillas. Scoop 3 tablespoons of the potato mixture in the center of each tortilla. Roll up tightly and secure with toothpicks if necessary.
4. Arrange the filled tortillas, seam side down, in the prepared baking pan. Spritz the tortillas with cooking spray.
5. Slide the pan into the air fryer oven. Cook at 400°F (205°C) for 6 minutes.
6. Flip the tortillas halfway through the cooking time.
7. When cooked, the tortillas should be crispy and golden brown.
8. Serve hot.

Mexican Flavor Chicken Burgers

Prep time: 15 minutes | Cook time: 20 minutes | Serves 6 to 8

4 skinless and boneless chicken breasts
1 small head of cauliflower, sliced into florets
1 jalapeño pepper
3 tablespoons smoked paprika
1 tablespoon thyme
1 tablespoon oregano
1 tablespoon mustard powder
1 teaspoon cayenne pepper
1 egg
Salt and ground black pepper, to taste
2 tomatoes, sliced
2 lettuce leaves, chopped
6 to 8 brioche buns, sliced lengthwise
¾ cup taco sauce
Cooking spray

1. Spritz an air fryer basket with cooking spray. Set aside.
2. In a blender, add the cauliflower florets, jalapeño pepper, paprika, thyme, oregano, mustard powder and cayenne pepper and blend until the mixture has a texture similar to bread crumbs.
3. Transfer ¾ of the cauliflower mixture to a medium bowl and set aside. Beat the egg in a different bowl and set aside.
4. Add the chicken breasts to the blender with remaining cauliflower mixture. Sprinkle with salt and pepper. Blend until finely chopped and well mixed.
5. Remove the mixture from the blender and form into 6 to 8 patties. One by one, dredge each patty in the reserved cauliflower mixture, then into the egg. Dip them in the cauliflower mixture again for additional coating.
6. Place the coated patties into the basket and spritz with cooking spray.
7. Slide the basket into the air fryer oven. Cook at 350°F (180°C) for 20 minutes.
8. Flip the patties halfway through the cooking time.
9. When cooking is complete, the patties should be golden and crispy.
10. Transfer the patties to a clean work surface and assemble with the buns, tomato slices, chopped lettuce leaves and taco sauce to make burgers. Serve and enjoy.

Cheesy Veggie Wraps

Prep time: 15 minutes | Cook time: 9 minutes | Serves 4

8 ounces (227 g) green beans
2 portobello mushroom caps, sliced
1 large red pepper, sliced
2 tablespoons olive oil, divided
¼ teaspoon salt
1 (15-ounce / 425-g) can chickpeas, drained
3 tablespoons lemon juice
¼ teaspoon ground black pepper
4 (6-inch) whole-grain wraps
4 ounces (113 g) fresh herb or garlic goat cheese, crumbled
1 lemon, cut into wedges

1. Add the green beans, mushrooms, red pepper to a large bowl. Drizzle with 1 tablespoon olive oil and season with salt. Toss until well coated.
2. Transfer the vegetable mixture to a baking pan.
3. Slide the pan into the air fryer oven. Cook at 400°F (205°C) for 9 minutes.
4. Stir the vegetable mixture three times during cooking.
5. When cooked, the vegetables should be tender.
6. Meanwhile, mash the chickpeas with lemon juice, pepper and the remaining 1 tablespoon oil until well blended
7. Unfold the wraps on a clean work surface. Spoon the chickpea mash on the wraps and spread all over.
8. Divide the cooked veggies among wraps. Sprinkle 1 ounce crumbled goat cheese on top of each wrap. Fold to wrap. Squeeze the lemon wedges on top and serve.

Chicken and Yogurt Taquitos

Prep time: 15 minutes | Cook time: 12 minutes | Serves 4

1 cup cooked chicken, shredded
¼ cup Greek yogurt
¼ cup salsa
1 cup shredded Mozzarella cheese
Salt and ground black pepper, to taste
4 flour tortillas
Cooking spray

1. Spritz an air fryer basket with cooking spray.
2. Combine all the ingredients, except for the tortillas, in a large bowl. Stir to mix well.
3. Make the taquitos: Unfold the tortillas on a clean work surface, then scoop up 2 tablespoons of the chicken mixture in the middle of each tortilla. Roll the tortillas up to wrap the filling.
4. Arrange the taquitos in the basket and spritz with cooking spray.
5. Slide the basket into the air fryer oven. Cook at 380°F (193°C) for 12 minutes.
6. Flip the taquitos halfway through the cooking time.
7. When cooked, the taquitos should be golden brown and the cheese should be melted.
8. Serve immediately.

Prawn and Cabbage Egg Rolls Wraps

Prep time: 20 minutes | Cook time: 18 minutes | Serves 4

2 tablespoons olive oil
1 carrot, cut into strips
1-inch piece fresh ginger, grated
1 tablespoon minced garlic
2 tablespoons soy sauce
¼ cup chicken broth
1 tablespoon sugar
1 cup shredded Napa cabbage
1 tablespoon sesame oil
8 cooked prawns, minced
8 egg roll wrappers
1 egg, beaten
Cooking spray

1. Spritz an air fryer basket with cooking spray. Set aside.
2. Heat the olive oil in a nonstick skillet over medium heat until shimmering.
3. Add the carrot, ginger, and garlic and sauté for 2 minutes or until fragrant.
4. Pour in the soy sauce, broth, and sugar. Bring to a boil. Keep stirring.
5. Add the cabbage and simmer for 4 minutes or until the cabbage is tender.
6. Turn off the heat and mix in the sesame oil. Let sit for 15 minutes.
7. Use a strainer to remove the vegetables from the liquid, then combine with the minced prawns.
8. Unfold the egg roll wrappers on a clean work surface, then divide the prawn mixture in the center of wrappers.
9. Dab the edges of a wrapper with the beaten egg, then fold a corner over the filling and tuck the corner under the filling. Fold the left and right corner into the center. Roll the wrapper up and press to seal. Repeat with remaining wrappers.
10. Arrange the wrappers in the basket and spritz with cooking spray.
11. Slide the basket into the air fryer oven. Cook at 370°F (188°C) for 12 minutes.
12. Flip the wrappers halfway through the cooking time.
13. When cooking is complete, the wrappers should be golden.
14. Serve immediately.

Crispy Chicken Egg Rolls

Prep time: 10 minutes | Cook time: 23 to 24 minutes | Serves 4

1 pound (454 g) ground chicken
2 teaspoons olive oil
2 garlic cloves, minced
1 teaspoon grated fresh ginger
2 cups white cabbage, shredded
1 onion, chopped
¼ cup soy sauce
8 egg roll wrappers
1 egg, beaten
Cooking spray

1. Spritz an air fryer basket with cooking spray.
2. Heat olive oil in a saucepan over medium heat. Sauté the garlic and ginger in the olive oil for 1 minute, or until fragrant. Add the ground chicken to the saucepan. Sauté for 5 minutes, or until the chicken is cooked through. Add the cabbage, onion and soy sauce and sauté for 5 to 6 minutes, or until the vegetables become soft. Remove the saucepan from the heat.
3. Unfold the egg roll wrappers on a clean work surface. Divide the chicken mixture among the wrappers and brush the edges of the wrappers with the beaten egg. Tightly roll up the egg rolls, enclosing the filling. Arrange the rolls in the basket.
4. Slide the basket into the air fryer oven. Cook at 370°F (188°C) for 12 minutes.
5. Flip the rolls halfway through the cooking time.
6. When cooked, the rolls will be crispy and golden brown.
7. Transfer to a platter and let cool for 5 minutes before serving.

Crispy Crab and Cream Cheese Wontons

Prep time: 10 minutes | Cook time: 10 minutes | Serves 6 to 8

24 wonton wrappers, thawed if frozen
Cooking spray
Filling:
5 ounces (142 g) lump crabmeat, drained and patted dry
4 ounces (113 g) cream cheese, at room temperature
2 scallions, sliced
1½ teaspoons toasted sesame oil
1 teaspoon Worcestershire sauce
Kosher salt and ground black pepper, to taste

1. Spritz an air fryer basket with cooking spray.
2. In a medium-size bowl, place all the ingredients for the filling and stir until well mixed. Prepare a small bowl of water alongside.
3. On a clean work surface, lay the wonton wrappers. Scoop 1 teaspoon of the filling in the center of each wrapper. Wet the edges with a touch of water. Fold each wonton wrapper diagonally in half over the filling to form a triangle.
4. Arrange the wontons in the basket. Spritz the wontons with cooking spray.
5. Slide the basket into the air fryer oven. Cook at 350°F (180°C) for 10 minutes.
6. Flip the wontons halfway through the cooking time.
7. When cooking is complete, the wontons will be crispy and golden brown.
8. Serve immediately.

Crispy Tilapia Tacos

Prep time: 20 minutes | Cook time: 5 minutes | Serves 4

2 tablespoons milk
⅓ cup mayonnaise
¼ teaspoon garlic powder
1 teaspoon chili powder
1½ cups panko bread crumbs
½ teaspoon salt
4 teaspoons canola oil
1 pound (454 g) skinless tilapia fillets, cut into 3-inch-long and 1-inch-wide strips
4 small flour tortillas
Lemon wedges, for topping
Cooking spray

1. Spritz an air fryer basket with cooking spray.
2. Combine the milk, mayo, garlic powder, and chili powder in a bowl. Stir to mix well. Combine the panko with salt and canola oil in a separate bowl. Stir to mix well.
3. Dredge the tilapia strips in the milk mixture first, then dunk the strips in the panko mixture to coat well. Shake the excess off.
4. Arrange the tilapia strips in the basket.
5. Slide the basket into the air fryer oven. Cook at 400°F (205°C) for 5 minutes.
6. Flip the strips halfway through the cooking time.
7. When cooking is complete, the strips will be opaque on all sides and the panko will be golden brown.
8. Unfold the tortillas on a large plate, then divide the tilapia strips over the tortillas. Squeeze the lemon wedges on top before serving.

Eggplant Hoagies

Prep time: 15 minutes | Cook time: 12 minutes | Makes 3 hoagies

6 peeled eggplant slices (about ½ inch thick and 3 inches in diameter)
¼ cup jarred pizza sauce
6 tablespoons grated Parmesan cheese
3 Italian sub rolls, split open lengthwise, warmed
Cooking spray

1. Spritz an air fryer basket with cooking spray.
2. Arrange the eggplant slices in the basket and spritz with cooking spray.
3. Slide the basket into the air fryer oven. Cook at 350°F (180°C) for 10 minutes.
4. Flip the slices halfway through the cooking time.
5. When cooked, the eggplant slices should be lightly wilted and tender.
6. Divide and spread the pizza sauce and cheese on top of the eggplant slice
7. Slide the basket into the air fryer oven. Cook at 375°F (190°C) for 2 minutes. When cooked, the cheese will be melted.
8. Assemble each sub roll with two slices of eggplant and serve immediately.

Golden Cod Tacos with Salsa

Prep time: 5 minutes | Cook time: 15 minutes | Serves 4

2 eggs
1¼ cups Mexican beer
1½ cups coconut flour
1½ cups almond flour
½ tablespoon chili powder
1 tablespoon cumin
Salt, to taste
1 pound (454 g) cod fillet, slice into large pieces
4 toasted corn tortillas
4 large lettuce leaves, chopped
¼ cup salsa
Cooking spray

1. Spritz an air fryer basket with cooking spray.
2. Break the eggs in a bowl, then pour in the beer. Whisk to combine well.
3. Combine the coconut flour, almond flour, chili powder, cumin, and salt in a separate bowl. Stir to mix well.
4. Dunk the cod pieces in the egg mixture, then shake the excess off and dredge into the flour mixture to coat well. Arrange the cod in the basket.
5. Slide the basket into the air fryer oven. Cook at 375°F (190°C) for 15 minutes.
6. Flip the cod halfway through the cooking time.
7. When cooking is complete, the cod should be golden brown.
8. Unwrap the toasted tortillas on a large plate, then divide the cod and lettuce leaves on top. Baste with salsa and wrap to serve.

Empanadas

Prep time: 25 minutes | Cook time: 12 minutes | Makes 12 empanadas

1 cup boneless, skinless rotisserie chicken breast meat, chopped finely
¼ cup salsa verde
⅔ cup shredded Cheddar cheese
1 teaspoon ground cumin
1 teaspoon ground black pepper
2 purchased refrigerated pie crusts, from a minimum 14.1-ounce (400 g) box
1 large egg
2 tablespoons water
Cooking spray

1. Spritz an air fryer basket with cooking spray. Set aside.
2. Combine the chicken meat, salsa verde, Cheddar, cumin, and black pepper in a large bowl. Stir to mix well. Set aside.
3. Unfold the pie crusts on a clean work surface, then use a large cookie cutter to cut out 3½-inch circles as much as possible.
4. Roll the remaining crusts to a ball and flatten into a circle which has the same thickness of the original crust. Cut out more 3½-inch circles until you have 12 circles in total.
5. Make the empanadas: Divide the chicken mixture in the middle of each circle, about 1½ tablespoons each. Dab the edges of the circle with water. Fold the circle in half over the filling to shape like a half-moon and press to seal, or you can press with a fork.
6. Whisk the egg with water in a small bowl.
7. Arrange the empanadas in the basket and spritz with cooking spray. Brush with whisked egg.
8. Slide the basket into the air fryer oven. Cook at 350°F (180°C) for 12 minutes.
9. Flip the empanadas halfway through the cooking time.
10. When cooking is complete, the empanadas will be golden and crispy.
11. Serve immediately.

Wraps and Sandwiches

Korean Flavor Beef and Onion Tacos

Prep time: 1 hour 15 minutes | Cook time: 12 minutes | Serves 6

2 tablespoons gochujang
1 tablespoon soy sauce
2 tablespoons sesame seeds
2 teaspoons minced fresh ginger
2 cloves garlic, minced
2 tablespoons toasted sesame oil
2 teaspoons sugar
½ teaspoon kosher salt
1½ pounds (680 g) thinly sliced beef chuck
1 medium red onion, sliced
6 corn tortillas, warmed
¼ cup chopped fresh cilantro
½ cup kimchi
½ cup chopped green onions

1. Combine the gochujang, soy sauce, sesame seeds, ginger, garlic, sesame oil, sugar, and salt in a large bowl. Stir to mix well.
2. Dunk the beef chunk in the large bowl. Press to submerge, then wrap the bowl in plastic and refrigerate to marinate for at least 1 hour.
3. Remove the beef chunk from the marinade and transfer to an air fryer basket. Add the onion to the basket.
4. Slide the basket into the air fryer oven. Cook at 400°F (205°C) for 12 minutes.
5. Stir the mixture halfway through the cooking time.
6. When cooked, the beef will be well browned.
7. Unfold the tortillas on a clean work surface, then divide the fried beef and onion on the tortillas. Spread the cilantro, kimchi, and green onions on top.
8. Serve immediately.

Lamb and Feta Hamburgers

Prep time: 15 minutes | Cook time: 16 minutes | Makes 4 burgers

1½ pounds (680 g) ground lamb
¼ cup crumbled feta
1½ teaspoons tomato paste
1½ teaspoons minced garlic
1 teaspoon ground dried ginger
1 teaspoon ground coriander
¼ teaspoon salt
¼ teaspoon cayenne pepper
4 kaiser rolls or hamburger buns, split open lengthwise, warmed
Cooking spray

1. Spritz an air fryer basket with cooking spray.
2. Combine all the ingredients, except for the buns, in a large bowl. Coarsely stir to mix well.
3. Shape the mixture into four balls, then pound the balls into four 5-inch diameter patties.
4. Arrange the patties in the basket and spritz with cooking spray.
5. Slide the basket into the air fryer oven. Cook at 375°F (190°C) for 16 minutes.
6. Flip the patties halfway through the cooking time.
7. When cooking is complete, the patties should be well browned.
8. Assemble the buns with patties to make the burgers and serve immediately.

Montreal Steak and Seeds Burgers

Prep time: 15 minutes | Cook time: 10 minutes | Serves 4

1 teaspoon cumin seeds
1 teaspoon mustard seeds
1 teaspoon coriander seeds
1 teaspoon dried minced garlic
1 teaspoon dried red pepper flakes
1 teaspoon kosher salt
2 teaspoons ground black pepper
1 pound (454 g) 85% lean ground beef
2 tablespoons Worcestershire sauce
4 hamburger buns
Mayonnaise, for serving
Cooking spray

1. Spritz an air fryer basket with cooking spray.
2. Put the seeds, garlic, red pepper flakes, salt, and ground black pepper in a food processor. Pulse to coarsely ground the mixture.
3. Put the ground beef in a large bowl. Pour in the seed mixture and drizzle with Worcestershire sauce. Stir to mix well.
4. Divide the mixture into four parts and shape each part into a ball, then bash each ball into a patty. Arrange the patties in the basket.
5. Slide the basket into the air fryer oven. Cook at 350°F (180°C) for 10 minutes.
6. Flip the patties with tongs halfway through the cooking time.
7. When cooked, the patties will be well browned.
8. Assemble the buns with the patties, then drizzle the mayo over the patties to make the burgers. Serve immediately.

Pea and Potato Samosas with Chutney

Prep time: 30 minutes | Cook time: 22 minutes | Makes 16 samosas

Dough:
4 cups all-purpose flour, plus more for flouring the work surface
¼ cup plain yogurt
½ cup cold unsalted butter, cut into cubes
2 teaspoons kosher salt
1 cup ice water
Filling:
2 tablespoons vegetable oil
1 onion, diced
1½ teaspoons coriander
1½ teaspoons cumin
1 clove garlic, minced
1 teaspoon turmeric
1 teaspoon kosher salt
½ cup peas, thawed if frozen
2 cups mashed potatoes
2 tablespoons yogurt
Cooking spray
Chutney:
1 cup mint leaves, lightly packed
2 cups cilantro leaves, lightly packed
1 green chile pepper, deseeded and minced
½ cup minced onion
Juice of 1 lime
1 teaspoon granulated sugar
1 teaspoon kosher salt
2 tablespoons vegetable oil

1. Put the flour, yogurt, butter, and salt in a food processor. Pulse to combine until grainy. Pour in the water and pulse until a smooth and firm dough forms.
2. Transfer the dough on a clean and lightly floured working surface. Knead the dough and shape it into a ball. Cut in half and flatten the halves into 2 discs. Wrap them in plastic and let sit in refrigerator until ready to use.
3. Meanwhile, make the filling: Heat the vegetable oil in a saucepan over medium heat.
4. Add the onion and sauté for 5 minutes or until lightly browned.
5. Add the coriander, cumin, garlic, turmeric, and salt and sauté for 2 minutes or until fragrant.
6. Add the peas, potatoes, and yogurt and stir to combine well. Turn off the heat and allow to cool.
7. Meanwhile, combine the ingredients for the chutney in a food processor. Pulse to mix well until glossy. Pour the chutney in a bowl and refrigerate until ready to use.
8. Make the samosas: Remove the dough discs from the refrigerator and cut each disc into 8 parts. Shape each part into a ball, then roll the ball into a 6-inch circle. Cut the circle in half and roll each half into a cone.
9. Scoop up 2 tablespoons of the filling into the cone, press the edges of the cone to seal and form into a triangle. Repeat with remaining dough and filling.
10. Spritz an air fryer basket with cooking spray. Arrange the samosas in the basket and spritz with cooking spray.
11. Slide the basket into the air fryer oven. Cook at 360°F (182°C) for 15 minutes.
12. Flip the samosas halfway through the cooking time.
13. When cooked, the samosas will be golden brown and crispy.
14. Serve the samosas with the chutney.

Salsa Verde Golden Chicken Shrimp and Zucchini Curry Potstickers

Prep time: 35 minutes | Cook time: 5 minutes | Serves 10

½ pound (227 g) peeled and deveined shrimp, finely chopped
1 medium zucchini, coarsely grated
1 tablespoon fish sauce
1 tablespoon green curry paste
2 scallions, thinly sliced
¼ cup basil, chopped
30 round dumpling wrappers
Cooking spray

1. Combine the chopped shrimp, zucchini, fish sauce, curry paste, scallions, and basil in a large bowl. Stir to mix well.
2. Unfold the dumpling wrappers on a clean work surface, dab a little water around the edges of each wrapper, then scoop up 1 teaspoon of filling in the middle of each wrapper.
3. Make the potstickers: Fold the wrappers in half and press the edges to seal.
4. Spritz an air fryer basket with cooking spray.
5. Transfer the potstickers to the basket and spritz with cooking spray.
6. Slide the basket into the air fryer oven. Cook at 350°F (180°C) for 5 minutes.
7. Flip the potstickers halfway through the cooking time.
8. When cooking is complete, the potstickers should be crunchy and lightly browned.
9. Serve immediately.

Pork Momos

Prep time: 20 minutes | Cook time: 20 minutes | Serves 4

2 tablespoons olive oil
1 pound (454 g) ground pork
1 shredded carrot
1 onion, chopped
1 teaspoon soy sauce
16 wonton wrappers
Salt and ground black pepper, to taste
Cooking spray

1. Heat the olive oil in a nonstick skillet over medium heat until shimmering.
2. Add the ground pork, carrot, onion, soy sauce, salt, and ground black pepper and sauté for 10 minutes or until the pork is well browned and carrots are tender.
3. Unfold the wrappers on a clean work surface, then divide the cooked pork and vegetables on the wrappers. Fold the edges around the filling to form momos. Nip the top to seal the momos.
4. Arrange the momos in an air fryer basket and spritz with cooking spray.
5. Slide the basket into the air fryer oven. Cook at 320°F (160°C) for 10 minutes.
6. When cooking is complete, the wrappers will be lightly browned.
7. Serve immediately.

Spinach and Ricotta Pockets

Prep time: 20 minutes | Cook time: 10 minutes | Makes 8 pockets

2 large eggs, divided
1 tablespoon water
1 cup baby spinach, roughly chopped
¼ cup sun-dried tomatoes, finely chopped
1 cup ricotta cheese
1 cup basil, chopped
¼ teaspoon red pepper flakes
¼ teaspoon kosher salt
2 refrigerated rolled pie crusts
2 tablespoons sesame seeds

1. Spritz an air fryer basket with cooking spray.
2. Whisk an egg with water in a small bowl.
3. Combine the spinach, tomatoes, the other egg, ricotta cheese, basil, red pepper flakes, and salt in a large bowl. Whisk to mix well.
4. Unfold the pie crusts on a clean work surface and slice each crust into 4 wedges. Scoop up 3 tablespoons of the spinach mixture on each crust and leave ½ inch space from edges.
5. Fold the crust wedges in half to wrap the filling and press the edges with a fork to seal.
6. Arrange the wraps in the basket and spritz with cooking spray. Sprinkle with sesame seeds.
7. Slide the basket into the air fryer oven. Cook at 380°F (193°C) for 10 minutes.
8. Flip the wraps halfway through the cooking time.
9. When cooked, the wraps will be crispy and golden.
10. Serve immediately.

Sweet Potato and Black Bean Burritos

Prep time: 15 minutes | Cook time: 30 minutes | Makes 6 burritos

2 sweet potatoes, peeled and cut into a small dice
1 tablespoon vegetable oil
Kosher salt and ground black pepper, to taste
6 large flour tortillas
1 (16-ounce / 454-g) can refried black beans, divided
1½ cups baby spinach, divided
6 eggs, scrambled
¾ cup grated Cheddar cheese, divided
¼ cup salsa
¼ cup sour cream
Cooking spray

1. Put the sweet potatoes in a large bowl, then drizzle with vegetable oil and sprinkle with salt and black pepper. Toss to coat well.
2. Place the potatoes in an air fryer basket.
3. Slide the basket into the air fryer oven. Cook at 400°F (205°C) for 10 minutes.
4. Flip the potatoes halfway through the cooking time.
5. When done, the potatoes should be lightly browned. Remove the potatoes from the air fryer oven.
6. Unfold the tortillas on a clean work surface. Divide the black beans, spinach, air fried sweet potatoes, scrambled eggs, and cheese on top of the tortillas.
7. Fold the long side of the tortillas over the filling, then fold in the shorter side to wrap the filling to make the burritos.
8. Wrap the burritos in the aluminum foil and put in the basket.
9. Slide the basket into the air fryer oven. Cook at 350°F (180°C) for 20 minutes. Flip the burritos halfway through the cooking time.
10. Remove the burritos from the air fryer oven and spread with sour cream and salsa. Serve immediately.

Wraps and Sandwiches   161

Turkey Sliders with Chive Mayo

Prep time: 10 minutes | Cook time: 15 minutes | Serves 6

12 burger buns
Cooking spray
Turkey Sliders:
¾ pound (340 g) turkey, minced
1 tablespoon oyster sauce
¼ cup pickled jalapeno, chopped
2 tablespoons chopped scallions
1 tablespoon chopped fresh cilantro
1 to 2 cloves garlic, minced
Sea salt and ground black pepper, to taste
Chive Mayo:
1 tablespoon chives
1 cup mayonnaise
Zest of 1 lime
1 teaspoon salt

1. Spritz an air fryer basket with cooking spray.
2. Combine the ingredients for the turkey sliders in a large bowl. Stir to mix well. Shape the mixture into 6 balls, then bash the balls into patties.
3. Arrange the patties in the basket and spritz with cooking spray.
4. Slide the basket into the air fryer oven. Cook at 365°F (185°C) for 15 minutes.
5. Flip the patties halfway through the cooking time.
6. Meanwhile, combine the ingredients for the chive mayo in a small bowl. Stir to mix well.
7. When cooked, the patties will be well browned.
8. Smear the patties with chive mayo, then assemble the patties between two buns to make the sliders. Serve immediately.

Thai Pork Sliders

Prep time: 10 minutes | Cook time: 14 minutes | Makes 6 sliders

1 pound (454 g) ground pork
1 tablespoon Thai curry paste
1½ tablespoons fish sauce
¼ cup thinly sliced scallions, white and green parts
2 tablespoons minced peeled fresh ginger
1 tablespoon light brown sugar
1 teaspoon ground black pepper
6 slider buns, split open lengthwise, warmed
Cooking spray

1. Spritz an air fryer basket with cooking spray.
2. Combine all the ingredients, except for the buns in a large bowl. Stir to mix well.
3. Divide and shape the mixture into six balls, then bash the balls into six 3-inch-diameter patties.
4. Arrange the patties in the basket and spritz with cooking spray.
5. Slide the basket into the air fryer oven. Cook at 375°F (190°C) for 14 minutes.
6. Flip the patties halfway through the cooking time.
7. When cooked, the patties should be well browned.
8. Assemble the buns with patties to make the sliders and serve immediately.

Holiday Specials

Chocolate Buttermilk Cake

Prep time: 20 minutes | Cook time: 20 minutes | Serves 8

1 cup all-purpose flour
⅔ cup granulated white sugar
¼ cup unsweetened cocoa powder
¾ teaspoon baking soda
¼ teaspoon salt
⅔ cup buttermilk
2 tablespoons plus 2 teaspoons vegetable oil
1 teaspoon vanilla extract
Cooking spray

1. Spritz a baking pan with cooking spray.
2. Combine the flour, cocoa powder, baking soda, sugar, and salt in a large bowl. Stir to mix well.
3. Mix in the buttermilk, vanilla, and vegetable oil. Keep stirring until it forms a grainy and thick dough.
4. Scrape the chocolate batter from the bowl and transfer to the pan, level the batter in an even layer with a spatula.
5. Slide the pan into the air fryer oven. Cook at 325°F (163°C) for 20 minutes.
6. After 15 minutes, remove from the air fryer oven. Check the doneness. Return to the air fryer oven and continue cooking.
7. When done, a toothpick inserted in the center should come out clean.
8. Invert the cake on a cooling rack and allow to cool for 15 minutes before slicing to serve.

Air Fried Blistered Tomatoes

Prep time: 5 minutes | Cook time: 10 minutes | Serves 4 to 6

2 pounds (907 g) cherry tomatoes
2 tablespoons olive oil
2 teaspoons balsamic vinegar
½ teaspoon salt
½ teaspoon ground black pepper

1. Toss the cherry tomatoes with olive oil in a large bowl to coat well. Pour the tomatoes in a baking pan.
2. Slide the pan into the air fryer oven. Cook at 400°F (205°C) for 10 minutes.
3. Stir the tomatoes halfway through the cooking time.
4. When cooking is complete, the tomatoes will be blistered and lightly wilted.
5. Transfer the blistered tomatoes to a large bowl and toss with balsamic vinegar, salt, and black pepper before serving.

Arancini

Prep time: 5 minutes | Cook time: 30 minutes | Makes 10 arancini

⅔ cup raw white Arborio rice
2 teaspoons butter
½ teaspoon salt
1⅓ cups water
2 large eggs, well beaten
1¼ cups seasoned Italian-style dried bread crumbs
10 ¾-inch semi-firm Mozzarella cubes
Cooking spray

1. Pour the rice, butter, salt, and water in a pot. Stir to mix well and bring a boil over medium-high heat. Keep stirring.
2. Reduce the heat to low and cover the pot. Simmer for 20 minutes or until the rice is tender.
3. Turn off the heat and let sit, covered, for 10 minutes, then open the lid and fluffy the rice with a fork. Allow to cool for 10 more minutes.
4. Pour the beaten eggs in a bowl, then pour the bread crumbs in a separate bowl.
5. Scoop 2 tablespoons of the cooked rice up and form it into a ball, then press the Mozzarella into the ball and wrap.
6. Dredge the ball in the eggs first, then shake the excess off the dunk the ball in the bread crumbs. Roll to coat evenly. Repeat to make 10 balls in total with remaining rice.
7. Transfer the balls in an air fryer basket and spritz with cooking spray.
8. Slide the basket into the air fryer oven. Cook at 375°F (190°C) for 10 minutes.
9. When cooking is complete, the balls should be lightly browned and crispy.
10. Remove the balls from the air fryer oven and allow to cool before serving.

Kale Salad Sushi Rolls with Sriracha Mayonnaise

Prep time: 10 minutes | Cook time: 10 minutes | Serves 12

Kale Salad:
1½ cups chopped kale
1 tablespoon sesame seeds
¾ teaspoon soy sauce
¾ teaspoon toasted sesame oil
½ teaspoon rice vinegar
¼ teaspoon ginger
⅛ teaspoon garlic powder
Sushi Rolls:
3 sheets sushi nori
1 batch cauliflower rice
½ avocado, sliced
Sriracha Mayonnaise:
¼ cup Sriracha sauce
¼ cup vegan mayonnaise
Coating:
½ cup panko bread crumbs

1. In a medium bowl, toss all the ingredients for the salad together until well coated and set aside.
2. Place a sheet of nori on a clean work surface and spread the cauliflower rice in an even layer on the nori. Scoop 2 to 3 tablespoon of kale salad on the rice and spread over. Place 1 or 2 avocado slices on top. Roll up the sushi, pressing gently to get a nice, tight roll. Repeat to make the remaining 2 rolls.
3. In a bowl, stir together the Sriracha sauce and mayonnaise until smooth. Add bread crumbs to a separate bowl.
4. Dredge the sushi rolls in Sriracha Mayonnaise, then roll in bread crumbs till well coated.
5. Place the coated sushi rolls in an air fryer basket.
6. Slide the basket into the air fryer oven. Cook at 390°F (199°C) for 10 minutes.
7. Flip the sushi rolls halfway through the cooking time.
8. When cooking is complete, the sushi rolls will be golden brown and crispy.
9. Transfer to a platter and rest for 5 minutes before slicing each roll into 8 pieces. Serve warm.

Banana Cake

Prep time: 25 minutes | Cook time: 20 minutes | Serves 8

1 cup plus 1 tablespoon all-purpose flour
¼ teaspoon baking soda
¾ teaspoon baking powder
¼ teaspoon salt
9½ tablespoons granulated white sugar
5 tablespoons butter, at room temperature
2½ small ripe bananas, peeled
2 large eggs
5 tablespoons buttermilk
1 teaspoon vanilla extract
Cooking spray

1. Spritz a baking pan with cooking spray.
2. Combine the flour, baking soda, baking powder, and salt in a large bowl. Stir to mix well.
3. Beat the sugar and butter in a separate bowl with a hand mixer on medium speed for 3 minutes.
4. Beat in the bananas, eggs, buttermilk, and vanilla extract into the sugar and butter mix with a hand mixer.
5. Pour in the flour mixture and whip with hand mixer until sanity and smooth.
6. Scrape the batter into the pan and level the batter with a spatula.
7. Slide the pan into the air fryer oven. Cook at 325°F (163°C) for 20 minutes.
8. After 15 minutes, remove from the air fryer oven. Check the doneness. Return to the air fryer oven and continue cooking.
9. When done, a toothpick inserted in the center should come out clean.
10. Invert the cake on a cooling rack and allow to cool for 15 minutes before slicing to serve.

Chinese Pork and Mushroom Egg Rolls

Prep time: 40 minutes | Cook time: 33 minutes | Makes 25 egg rolls

Egg Rolls:
1 tablespoon mirin
3 tablespoons soy sauce, divided
1 pound (454 g) ground pork
3 tablespoons vegetable oil, plus more for brushing
5 ounces (142 g) shiitake mushrooms, minced
4 cups shredded Napa cabbage
¼ cup sliced scallions
1 teaspoon grated fresh ginger
1 clove garlic, minced
¼ teaspoon cornstarch
1 (1-pound / 454-g) package frozen egg roll wrappers, thawed
Dipping Sauce:
1 scallion, white and light green parts only, sliced
¼ cup rice vinegar
¼ cup soy sauce
Pinch sesame seeds
Pinch red pepper flakes
1 teaspoon granulated sugar

1. Line an air fryer basket with parchment paper. Set aside.
2. Combine the mirin and 1 tablespoon of soy sauce in a large bowl. Stir to mix well.
3. Dunk the ground pork in the mixture and stir to mix well. Wrap the bowl in plastic and marinate in the refrigerator for at least 10 minutes.
4. Heat the vegetable oil in a nonstick skillet over medium-high heat until shimmering. Add the mushrooms, cabbage, and scallions and sauté for 5 minutes or until tender.
5. Add the marinated meat, ginger, garlic, and remaining 2 tablespoons of soy sauce. Sauté for 3 minutes or until the pork is lightly browned. Turn off the heat and allow to cool until ready to use.
6. Put the cornstarch in a small bowl and pour in enough water to dissolve the cornstarch. Put the bowl alongside a clean work surface.
7. Put the egg roll wrappers in the air fryer basket.
8. Slide the basket into the air fryer oven. Cook at 400°F (205°C) for 15 minutes.
9. Flip the wrappers halfway through the cooking time.
10. When cooked, the wrappers will be golden brown. Remove the egg roll wrappers from the air fryer oven and allow to cool for 10 minutes or until you can handle them with your hands.
11. Lay out one egg roll wrapper on the work surface with a corner pointed toward you. Place 2 tablespoons of the pork mixture on the egg roll wrapper and fold corner up over the mixture. Fold left and right corners toward the center and continue to roll. Brush a bit of the dissolved cornstarch on the last corner to help seal the egg wrapper. Repeat with remaining wrappers to make 25 egg rolls in total.
12. Arrange the rolls in the basket and brush the rolls with more vegetable oil.
13. Cook for 10 minutes. Place the basket back to the air fryer oven. When done, the rolls should be well browned and crispy.
14. Meanwhile, combine the ingredients for the dipping sauce in a small bowl. Stir to mix well.
15. Serve the rolls with the dipping sauce immediately.

Chocolate and Coconut Macaroons

Prep time: 10 minutes | Cook time: 8 minutes | Makes 24 macaroons

3 large egg whites, at room temperature
¼ teaspoon salt
¾ cup granulated white sugar
4½ tablespoons unsweetened cocoa powder
2¼ cups unsweetened shredded coconut

1. Line an air fryer basket with parchment paper.
2. Whisk the egg whites with salt in a large bowl with a hand mixer on high speed until stiff peaks form.
3. Whisk in the sugar with the hand mixer on high speed until the mixture is thick. Mix in the cocoa powder and coconut.
4. Scoop 2 tablespoons of the mixture and shape the mixture in a ball. Repeat with remaining mixture to make 24 balls in total.
5. Arrange the balls in a single layer in the air fryer basket and leave a little space between each two balls.
6. Slide the basket into the air fryer oven. Cook at 375°F (190°C) for 8 minutes.
7. When cooking is complete, the balls should be golden brown.
8. Serve immediately.

Cinnamon Rolls with Cream Glaze

Prep time: 2 hours 15 minutes | Cook time: 5 minutes | Serves 8

1 pound (454 g) frozen bread dough, thawed
2 tablespoons melted butter
1½ tablespoons cinnamon
¾ cup brown sugar
Cooking spray
Cream Glaze:
4 ounces (113 g) softened cream cheese
½ teaspoon vanilla extract
2 tablespoons melted butter
1¼ cups powdered erythritol

1. Place the bread dough on a clean work surface, then roll the dough out into a rectangle with a rolling pin.
2. Brush the top of the dough with melted butter and leave 1-inch edges uncovered.
3. Combine the cinnamon and sugar in a small bowl, then sprinkle the dough with the cinnamon mixture.
4. Roll the dough over tightly, then cut the dough log into 8 portions. Wrap the portions in plastic, better separately, and let sit to rise for 1 or 2 hours.
5. Meanwhile, combine the ingredients for the glaze in a separate small bowl. Stir to mix well.
6. Spritz an air fryer basket with cooking spray. Transfer the risen rolls to the air fryer basket.
7. Slide the basket into the air fryer oven. Cook at 350°F (180°C) for 5 minutes.
8. Flip the rolls halfway through the cooking time.
9. When cooking is complete, the rolls will be golden brown.
10. Serve the rolls with the glaze.

Classic Churros

Prep time: 35 minutes | Cook time: 10 minutes | Makes 12 churros

4 tablespoons butter
¼ teaspoon salt
½ cup water
½ cup all-purpose flour
2 large eggs
2 teaspoons ground cinnamon
¼ cup granulated white sugar
Cooking spray

1. Put the butter, salt, and water in a saucepan. Bring to a boil until the butter is melted on high heat. Keep stirring.
2. Reduce the heat to medium and fold in the flour to form a dough. Keep cooking and stirring until the dough is dried out and coat the pan with a crust.
3. Turn off the heat and scrape the dough in a large bowl. Allow to cool for 15 minutes.
4. Break and whisk the eggs into the dough with a hand mixer until the dough is sanity and firm enough to shape.
5. Scoop up 1 tablespoon of the dough and roll it into a ½-inch-diameter and 2-inch-long cylinder. Repeat with remaining dough to make 12 cylinders in total.
6. Combine the cinnamon and sugar in a large bowl and dunk the cylinders into the cinnamon mix to coat.
7. Arrange the cylinders on a plate and refrigerate for 20 minutes.
8. Spritz an air fryer basket with cooking spray. Place the cylinders in the air fryer basket and spritz with cooking spray.
9. Slide the basket into the air fryer oven. Cook at 375°F (190°C) for 10 minutes.
10. Flip the cylinders halfway through the cooking time.
11. When cooked, the cylinders should be golden brown and fluffy.
12. Serve immediately.

Custard Donut Holes with Chocolate Glaze

Prep time: 1 hour 50 minutes | Cook time: 4 minutes | Makes 24 donut holes

Dough:
1½ cups bread flour
2 egg yolks
1 teaspoon active dry yeast
½ cup warm milk
½ teaspoon pure vanilla extract
2 tablespoons butter, melted
1 tablespoon sugar
¼ teaspoon salt
Cooking spray
Custard Filling:
1 (3.4-ounce / 96-g) box French vanilla instant pudding mix
¼ cup heavy cream
¾ cup whole milk
Chocolate Glaze:
⅓ cup heavy cream
1 cup chocolate chips

Special Equipment:
A pastry bag with a long tip

1. Combine the ingredients for the dough in a food processor, then pulse until a satiny dough ball forms.
2. Transfer the dough on a lightly floured work surface, then knead for 2 minutes by hand and shape the dough back to a ball.
3. Spritz a large bowl with cooking spray, then transfer the dough ball into the bowl. Wrap the bowl in plastic and let it rise for 1½ hours or until it doubled in size.
4. Transfer the risen dough on a floured work surface, then shape it into a 24-inch long log. Cut the log into 24 parts and shape each part into a ball.
5. Transfer the balls on two baking sheets and let sit to rise for 30 more minutes.
6. Spritz the balls with cooking spray.
7. Slide the baking sheets into the air fryer oven. Cook at 400°F (205°C) for 4 minutes.
8. Flip the balls halfway through the cooking time.
9. When cooked, the balls should be golden brown.
10. Meanwhile, combine the ingredients for the filling in a large bowl and whisk for 2 minutes with a hand mixer until well combined.
11. Pour the heavy cream in a saucepan, then bring to a boil. Put the chocolate chips in a small bowl and pour in the boiled heavy cream immediately. Mix until the chocolate chips are melted and the mixture is smooth.
12. Transfer the baked donut holes to a large plate, then pierce a hole into each donut hole and lightly hollow them.
13. Pour the filling in a pastry bag with a long tip and gently squeeze the filling into the donut holes. Then top the donut holes with chocolate glaze.
14. Allow to sit for 10 minutes, then serve.

Fried Dill Pickles with Buttermilk Dressing

Prep time: 45 minutes | Cook time: 8 minutes | Serves 6 to 8

Buttermilk Dressing:
¼ cup buttermilk
¼ cup chopped scallions
¾ cup mayonnaise
½ cup sour cream
½ teaspoon cayenne pepper
½ teaspoon onion powder
½ teaspoon garlic powder
1 tablespoon chopped chives
2 tablespoons chopped fresh dill
Kosher salt and ground black pepper, to taste
Fried Dill Pickles:
¾ cup all-purpose flour
1 (2-pound / 907-g) jar kosher dill pickles, cut into 4 spears, drained
2½ cups panko bread crumbs
2 eggs, beaten with 2 tablespoons water
Kosher salt and ground black pepper, to taste
Cooking spray

1. Combine the ingredients for the dressing in a bowl. Stir to mix well.
2. Wrap the bowl in plastic and refrigerate for 30 minutes or until ready to serve.
3. Pour the flour in a bowl and sprinkle with salt and ground black pepper. Stir to mix well. Put the bread crumbs in a separate bowl. Pour the beaten eggs in a third bowl.
4. Dredge the pickle spears in the flour, then into the eggs, and then into the panko to coat well. Shake the excess off.
5. Arrange the pickle spears in a single layer in an air fryer basket and spritz with cooking spray.
6. Slide the basket into the air fryer oven. Cook at 400°F (205°C) for 8 minutes.
7. Flip the pickle spears halfway through the cooking time.
8. When cooking is complete, remove from the air fryer oven.
9. Serve the pickle spears with buttermilk dressing.

Garlicky Olive Stromboli

Prep time: 25 minutes | Cook time: 25 minutes | Serves 8

4 large cloves garlic, unpeeled
3 tablespoons grated Parmesan cheese
½ cup packed fresh basil leaves
½ cup marinated, pitted green and black olives
¼ teaspoon crushed red pepper
½ pound (227 g) pizza dough, at room temperature
4 ounces (113 g) sliced provolone cheese (about 8 slices)
Cooking spray

1. Spritz an air fryer basket with cooking spray. Put the unpeeled garlic in the air fryer basket.
2. Slide the basket into the air fryer oven. Cook at 370°F (188°C) for 10 minutes.
3. When cooked, the garlic will be softened completely. Remove from the air fryer oven and allow to cool until you can handle.
4. Peel the garlic and place into a food processor with 2 tablespoons of Parmesan, basil, olives, and crushed red pepper. Pulse to mix well. Set aside.
5. Arrange the pizza dough on a clean work surface, then roll it out with a rolling pin into a rectangle. Cut the rectangle in half.
6. Sprinkle half of the garlic mixture over each rectangle half, and leave ½-inch edges uncover. Top them with the provolone cheese.
7. Brush one long side of each rectangle half with water, then roll them up. Spritz an air fryer basket with cooking spray. Transfer the rolls to the air fryer basket. Spritz with cooking spray and scatter with remaining Parmesan.
8. Cook for 15 minutes. Slide the basket into the air fryer oven. Flip the rolls halfway through the cooking time. When done, the rolls should be golden brown.
9. Remove the rolls from the air fryer oven and allow to cool for a few minutes before serving.

Golden Nuggets

Prep time: 15 minutes | Cook time: 4 minutes | Makes 20 nuggets

1 cup all-purpose flour, plus more for dusting
1 teaspoon baking powder
½ teaspoon butter, at room temperature, plus more for brushing
¼ teaspoon salt
¼ cup water
⅛ teaspoon onion powder
¼ teaspoon garlic powder
⅛ teaspoon seasoning salt
Cooking spray

1. Line an air fryer basket with parchment paper.
2. Mix the flour, baking powder, butter, and salt in a large bowl. Stir to mix well. Gradually whisk in the water until a sanity dough forms.
3. Put the dough on a lightly floured work surface, then roll it out into a ½-inch thick rectangle with a rolling pin.
4. Cut the dough into about twenty 1- or 2-inch squares, then arrange the squares in a single layer in the air fryer basket. Spritz with cooking spray.
5. Combine onion powder, garlic powder, and seasoning salt in a small bowl. Stir to mix well, then sprinkle the squares with the powder mixture.
6. Slide the basket into the air fryer oven. Cook at 370°F (188°C) for 4 minutes.
7. Flip the squares halfway through the cooking time.
8. When cooked, the dough squares should be golden brown.
9. Remove the golden nuggets from the air fryer oven and brush with more butter immediately. Serve warm.

Jewish Blintzes

Prep time: 5 minutes | Cook time: 10 minutes | Makes 8 blintzes

2 (7½-ounce / 213-g) packages farmer cheese, mashed
¼ cup cream cheese
¼ teaspoon vanilla extract
¼ cup granulated white sugar
8 egg roll wrappers
4 tablespoons butter, melted

1. Combine the farmer cheese, cream cheese, vanilla extract, and sugar in a bowl. Stir to mix well.
2. Unfold the egg roll wrappers on a clean work surface, spread ¼ cup of the filling at the edge of each wrapper and leave a ½-inch edge uncovering.
3. Wet the edges of the wrappers with water and fold the uncovered edge over the filling. Fold the left and right sides in the center, then tuck the edge under the filling and fold to wrap the filling.
4. Brush the wrappers with melted butter, then arrange the wrappers in a single layer in an air fryer basket, seam side down. Leave a little space between each two wrappers.
5. Slide the basket into the air fryer oven. Cook at 375°F (190°C) for 10 minutes.
6. When cooking is complete, the wrappers will be golden brown.
7. Serve immediately.

Holiday Specials 167

Milky Pecan Tart

Prep time: 2 hours 25 minutes | Cook time: 26 minutes | Serves 8

Tart Crust:
¼ cup firmly packed brown sugar
⅓ cup butter, softened
1 cup all-purpose flour
¼ teaspoon kosher salt
Filling:
¼ cup whole milk
4 tablespoons butter, diced
½ cup packed brown sugar
¼ cup pure maple syrup
1½ cups finely chopped pecans
¼ teaspoon pure vanilla extract
¼ teaspoon sea salt

1. Line a baking pan with aluminum foil, then spritz the pan with cooking spray.
2. Stir the brown sugar and butter in a bowl with a hand mixer until puffed, then add the flour and salt and stir until crumbled.
3. Pour the mixture in the prepared baking pan and tilt the pan to coat the bottom evenly.
4. Slide the pan into the air fryer oven. Cook at 350°F (180°C) for 13 minutes.
5. When done, the crust will be golden brown.
6. Meanwhile, pour the milk, butter, sugar, and maple syrup in a saucepan. Stir to mix well. Bring to a simmer, then cook for 1 more minute. Stir constantly.
7. Turn off the heat and mix the pecans and vanilla into the filling mixture.
8. Pour the filling mixture over the golden crust and spread with a spatula to coat the crust evenly.
9. Slide the basket into the air fryer oven. Bake for 12 minutes. When cooked, the filling mixture should be set and frothy.
10. Remove the baking pan from the air fryer oven and sprinkle with salt. Allow to sit for 10 minutes or until cooled.
11. Transfer the pan to the refrigerator to chill for at least 2 hours, then remove the aluminum foil and slice to serve.

Pão de Queijo

Prep time: 37 minutes | Cook time: 12 minutes | Makes 12 balls

2 tablespoons butter, plus more for greasing
½ cup milk
1½ cups tapioca flour
½ teaspoon salt
1 large egg
⅔ cup finely grated aged Asiago cheese

1. Put the butter in a saucepan and pour in the milk, heat over medium heat until the liquid boils. Keep stirring.
2. Turn off the heat and mix in the tapioca flour and salt to form a soft dough. Transfer the dough in a large bowl, then wrap the bowl in plastic and let sit for 15 minutes.
3. Break the egg in the bowl of dough and whisk with a hand mixer for 2 minutes or until a sanity dough forms. Fold the cheese in the dough. Cover the bowl in plastic again and let sit for 10 more minutes.
4. Grease a baking pan with butter.
5. Scoop 2 tablespoons of the dough into the baking pan. Repeat with the remaining dough to make dough 12 balls. Keep a little distance between each two balls.
6. Slide the pan into the air fryer oven. Cook at 375°F (190°C) for 12 minutes.
7. Flip the balls halfway through the cooking time.
8. When cooking is complete, the balls should be golden brown and fluffy.
9. Remove the balls from the air fryer oven and allow to cool for 5 minutes before serving.

Shrimp with Sriracha and Worcestershire Sauce

Prep time: 15 minutes | Cook time: 10 minutes | Serves 4

1 tablespoon Sriracha sauce
1 teaspoon Worcestershire sauce
2 tablespoons sweet chili sauce
¾ cup mayonnaise
1 egg, beaten
1 cup panko bread crumbs
1 pound (454 g) raw shrimp, shelled and deveined, rinsed and drained
Lime wedges, for serving
Cooking spray

1. Spritz an air fryer basket with cooking spray.
2. Combine the Sriracha sauce, Worcestershire sauce, chili sauce, and mayo in a bowl. Stir to mix well. Reserve ⅓ cup of the mixture as the dipping sauce.
3. Combine the remaining sauce mixture with the beaten egg. Stir to mix well. Put the panko in a separate bowl.
4. Dredge the shrimp in the sauce mixture first, then into the panko. Roll the shrimp to coat well. Shake the excess off.
5. Place the shrimp in the air fryer basket, then spritz with cooking spray.
6. Slide the basket into the air fryer oven. Cook at 360°F (182°C) for 10 minutes.
7. Flip the shrimp halfway through the cooking time.
8. When cooking is complete, the shrimp should be opaque.
9. Remove the shrimp from the air fryer oven and serve with reserve sauce mixture and squeeze the lime wedges over.

Simple Butter Cake

Prep time: 25 minutes | Cook time: 20 minutes | Serves 8

1 cup all-purpose flour
1¼ teaspoons baking powder
¼ teaspoon salt
½ cup plus 1½ tablespoons granulated white sugar
9½ tablespoons butter, at room temperature
2 large eggs
1 large egg yolk
2½ tablespoons milk
1 teaspoon vanilla extract
Cooking spray

1. Spritz a baking pan with cooking spray.
2. Combine the flour, baking powder, and salt in a large bowl. Stir to mix well.
3. Whip the sugar and butter in a separate bowl with a hand mixer on medium speed for 3 minutes.
4. Whip the eggs, egg yolk, milk, and vanilla extract into the sugar and butter mix with a hand mixer.
5. Pour in the flour mixture and whip with hand mixer until sanity and smooth.
6. Scrape the batter into the baking pan and level the batter with a spatula.
7. Slide the pan into the air fryer oven. Cook at 325°F (163°C) for 20 minutes.
8. After 15 minutes, remove from the air fryer oven. Check the doneness. Return to the air fryer oven and continue cooking.
9. When done, a toothpick inserted in the center should come out clean.
10. Invert the cake on a cooling rack and allow to cool for 15 minutes before slicing to serve.

Supplì al Telefono (Risotto Croquettes)

Prep time: 1 hour 40 minutes | Cook time: 54 minutes | Serves 6

Risotto Croquettes:
4 tablespoons unsalted butter
1 small yellow onion, minced
1 cup Arborio rice
3½ cups chicken stock
½ cup dry white wine
3 eggs
Zest of 1 lemon
½ cup grated Parmesan cheese
2 ounces (57 g) fresh Mozzarella cheese
¼ cup peas
2 tablespoons water
½ cup all-purpose flour
1½ cups panko bread crumbs
Kosher salt and ground black pepper, to taste
Cooking spray
Tomato Sauce:
2 tablespoons extra-virgin olive oil
4 cloves garlic, minced
¼ teaspoon red pepper flakes
1 (28-ounce / 794-g) can crushed tomatoes
2 teaspoons granulated sugar
Kosher salt and ground black pepper, to taste

1. Melt the butter in a pot over medium heat, then add the onion and salt to taste. Sauté for 5 minutes or until the onion in translucent.
2. Add the rice and stir to coat well. Cook for 3 minutes or until the rice is lightly browned. Pour in the chicken stock and wine.
3. Bring to a boil. Then cook for 20 minutes or until the rice is tender and liquid is almost absorbed.
4. Make the risotto: When the rice is cooked, break the egg into the pot. Add the lemon zest and Parmesan cheese. Sprinkle with salt and ground black pepper. Stir to mix well.
5. Pour the risotto in a baking sheet, then level with a spatula to spread the risotto evenly. Wrap the baking sheet in plastic and refrigerate for 1 hour.
6. Meanwhile, heat the olive oil in a saucepan over medium heat until shimmering.
7. Add the garlic and sprinkle with red pepper flakes. Sauté for a minute or until fragrant.
8. Add the crushed tomatoes and sprinkle with sugar. Stir to mix well. Bring to a boil. Reduce the heat to low and simmer for 15 minutes or until lightly thickened. Sprinkle with salt and pepper to taste. Set aside until ready to serve.
9. Remove the risotto from the refrigerator. Scoop the risotto into twelve 2-inch balls, then flatten the balls with your hands.
10. Arrange a about ½-inch piece of Mozzarella and 5 peas in the center of each flattened ball, then wrap them back into balls.
11. Transfer the balls to a baking sheet lined with parchment paper, then refrigerate for 15 minutes or until firm.
12. Whisk the remaining 2 eggs with 2 tablespoons of water in a bowl. Pour the flour in a second bowl and pour the panko in a third bowl.
13. Dredge the risotto balls in the bowl of flour first, then into the eggs, and then into the panko. Shake the excess off.
14. Transfer the balls to an air fryer basket and spritz with cooking spray.
15. Slide the basket into the air fryer oven. Cook at 400°F (205°C) for 10 minutes.
16. Flip the balls halfway through the cooking time.
17. When cooking is complete, the balls should be until golden brown.
18. Serve the risotto balls with the tomato sauce.

Holiday Specials

Teriyaki Shrimp Skewers

Prep time: 10 minutes | Cook time: 6 minutes | Makes 12 skewered shrimp

1½ tablespoons mirin
1½ teaspoons ginger juice
1½ tablespoons soy sauce
12 large shrimp (about 20 shrimps per pound), peeled and deveined
1 large egg
¾ cup panko bread crumbs
Cooking spray

1. Combine the mirin, ginger juice, and soy sauce in a large bowl. Stir to mix well.
2. Dunk the shrimp in the bowl of mirin mixture, then wrap the bowl in plastic and refrigerate for 1 hour to marinate.
3. Spritz an air fryer basket with cooking spray.
4. Run twelve 4-inch skewers through each shrimp.
5. Whisk the egg in the bowl of marinade to combine well. Pour the bread crumbs on a plate.
6. Dredge the shrimp skewers in the egg mixture, then shake the excess off and roll over the bread crumbs to coat well.
7. Arrange the shrimp skewers in the air fryer basket and spritz with cooking spray.
8. Slide the basket into the air fryer oven. Cook at 400°F (205°C) for 6 minutes.
9. Flip the shrimp skewers halfway through the cooking time.
10. When done, the shrimp will be opaque and firm.
11. Serve immediately.

Pigs in a Blanket

Prep time: 10 minutes | Cook time: 8 minutes | Makes 16 rolls

1 can refrigerated crescent roll dough
1 small package mini smoked sausages, patted dry
2 tablespoons melted butter
2 teaspoons sesame seeds
1 teaspoon onion powder

1. Place the crescent roll dough on a clean work surface and separate into 8 pieces. Cut each piece in half and you will have 16 triangles.
2. Make the pigs in the blanket: Arrange each sausage on each dough triangle, then roll the sausages up.
3. Brush the pigs with melted butter and place of the pigs in the blanket in an air fryer basket. Sprinkle with sesame seeds and onion powder.
4. Slide the basket into the air fryer oven. Cook at 330°F (166°C) for 8 minutes.
5. Flip the pigs halfway through the cooking time.
6. When cooking is complete, the pigs should be fluffy and golden brown.
7. Serve immediately.

Printed in Great Britain
by Amazon